THE
Later Diaries
OF
Ned Rorem
1961–1972

DA CAPO PRESS

Grateful acknowledgment is made to Howard Moss and Atheneum Publishers for
permission to reprint from "King Midas" from *Selected Poems* by Howard Moss, ©
1961; and to George Braziller, Inc., for permission to reprint in somewhat altered
form "Twenty Years After" and some additional paragraphs from *Critical Affairs*, for
many scattered paragraphs first published as "Random Notes from a Diary," in
Music from Inside Out, for several entries from *Music and People*. © 1970, 1967,1968 by
Ned Rorem.

A CIP catalog record for this book is available from the Library of Congress.
ISBN 0-306-80964-8

First Da Capo Press Edition 2000

Published by Da Capo Press
A Member of the Perseus Books Group
http://www.dacapopress.com

1 2 3 4 5 6 7 8 9 10——04 03 02 01 00

Contents

8 pages of photographs follow page 216

1961

Great art works, being unique, are final: they do not open doors, they close them.

—NR

Sitting in one denuded room whose center contains a mountain of packing cases to be removed tomorrow by Robert Phelps. Without paying last month's rent I fly Friday for London, meanwhile have already left, can only sit, wondering, for five days more.

Wondering about those three things (and there are only three) we all desire: success in love, success in society, success in work. Any two of these may be achieved and possessed simultaneously, but not all three—there isn't time. If you think you have the three, beware! You're teetering on the abyss. You can't have a lover *and* friends *and* career. And even just career and love are, in the long run, mutually exclusive.

Ten days in London robbed the bloom off this Paris I've missed so long. Has it been only three weeks since I abandoned the 13th Street apartment, dopey with flu, flew to London and collapsed? Yesterday, Julius and Arlette Katchen in a new Fiat met me at Orly, their prosy chatter distracting from the enjoyment of return. Yet aren't they precisely what I'm returning to? Thrill of coming back's aborted by too quick contact with humans. The first need's the nose's: smells of home, of baking bread, smokestacks reeking, are more immediately overwhelming than renewal of human love.

Virgil's *garçonnière* here in the Cour d'Ingres awaited primly, swept and stocked. But no sooner did I arrive that the Katchens (teaching me the principle of the *nouveau franc*), and the Graffmans (Naomi unchanged since the first postwar summer in Tanglewood where she posed on the lawns with exotic Tally Brown), took me out on the town. Less a French than a Jewish welcome. Always it's the Jews of any environment who first reach out to make me feel at home.

Late in the evening we strolled toward the Odéon via the busy street of the Ancienne Comédie where at a corner, stretched on her back with legs waving, a very old *clocharde* zealously masturbated. Knowing that passersby would offer no alternative, she was, for her practical purposes, alone. But her indifference to us rendered her more nasty than pitiable. (What a nice ugly resonant noun, *clocharde*, like a bell clanging between a set of withered kidney stones.)

9 May

Paris is different from what I'd expected, because similar to what I'd remembered. Yes, there are police around now with machine guns (no one pays attention), and a new breed of gigolo like scabies (everyone pays attention). If in Manhattan you can go out to buy a nail file and find the corner drugstore reduced to rubble which next week becomes a skyscraper-tenement that houses a race of intellect you never dreamed existed, here the same Proustian heads, after decades, reassuringly spout the same chilled wit. I alone have changed, for those heads no longer turn when I pass the Flore.

Virgil's sublet is a boon and I'm even working a little. Writing what? Letters mostly.

Dream: Enveloped by music—not by its sound but by the tools. Staves entwine us with their five endless tentacles while treble clefs unwind and re-stiffen into unstable towers which crash upon the sand, sand crushed from a trillion yellow neumes.

12 May

Although I no longer live in her house, Marie Laure is a daily companion. Arriving on the 63 bus each noon to Place d'Iéna, I lunch with whomever's around, then spend the afternoon working upstairs. But now that I've rented a piano which arrives tomorrow, the routine may change.

French table conversation, at least at the start of a meal, is, of course, about the menu at hand. The Business Lunch does not exist here. If their creamy *mousses* and heavy *Bordeaux* destroy their liver (*foie* is a euphemism for large intestine), their uncontaminated tobacco and leisurely siesta save them from lung cancer. They allow table talk to grow, are not literal-minded, leave room for expectorating voices though not at the expense of forgoing what enters the mouth. But I watch my table manners more with the working classes than with my peers, because the working classes are better bred.

21 May

In this cold spring of France nothing seems altered, except myself as the prince who awakens Sleeping Beauty. She won't get up. The fault's mine, cavorting as though past were present, while no one reacts. Four years since I made love well, four weeks since I made it at all. "Particularities" form my nest. Is time being wasted, or what's time for? Joy's not my strong point, boredom is; charity isn't, envy is. Decay of self-preservation.

Now that Oscar Dominguez is dead Marie Laure appears more *détendue*. Perhaps that's just time passing, time now spent on others. Yet for her, Oscar was the vital nuisance we all require; without him she's benign, although still chain-smoking those eternal *Gauloises de famille* kept in a gold case drawn forth from her skirts every ten minutes. (True, Jean Lafont exists to the point of occupying the room that for six years was mine. But he is a pacifier, not a surreal inflammation.)

Her reaction now to me seems too casual. I've been gone four years, and she took up the conversation as though we'd left off that morning. The childlike assumption that we're all a part of her life rather than that she's a part of ours is what makes us exasperatedly love Marie Laure.

27 May

The *femme de ménage* shows up every two days and I'm able for once to receive rather than to pay visits. Gave a party Wednesday early evening with the sun ablaze in the Cour d'Ingres below. A plump buffet skeletonized by friends and foes in unlikely couplings, Claude with Charlotte Aillaud, John Ashbery with a full open car entering the courtyard, Benjamin Lees with Ninette Lyon, Aaron Copland (not invited but welcome), Marie Laure de Noailles and Richard Négroux, Violette de Azevedo and Lise Deharme, Denise, José, all drinking scotch provided by Doda Conrad at PX prices.

Action seems forever governed by thoughts of sobriety. The past lies ahead. The future is happily The Thing No One Knows. Trapped by the future. Homemade atom bombs, now *à la portée de tout le monde*, oblige scientists to develop, in bottles like morphine, a kind of canned peace to preserve equilibrium. Canned peace. The toilet here is placed before a full-length mirror so that one watches oneself. Is it an *action*: the watching? Is there a photographer for such action?

I go to the bathroom four, five times a day—not so much because I must, as because it's an excuse for not working. Today's the *lendemain* of a hangover, far worse, as everyone knows, than the dreamlike hangover-day itself; reality (or rather, the habit of unreality) reappears but we're not ready for it. The skin's still too dehydrated, the head too befuddled to confront daily problems, quarrels, phones. Bathrooms then are perfect hiding-places.

30 May

Dined last night with Philippe Erlanger at the Elysée Club, a sort of superior Sardi's with a ground floor catering to after-theater supperers, and a private membership *sous-sol* for solvent artists, mostly theatrical. As we began our *turbot à la reine*, who should be ushered to the next table but Noël Coward, alone, who proceeded to order an incongruous meal of snails and hot chocolate. While Philippe ever so properly continued his ceaseless chatter (suddenly more discreet), Coward and I intensely examined each other and calculated our separate advantages. I lit a cigaret, he hummed the opening bars of "Smoke Gets in Your Eyes," I nodded *bonjour*, he spoke:

"But haven't I seen you before?"

"No," I replied. "I'd have remembered."

"Jamais je n'ai vu une chose pareille," whispered Philippe, appalled by such manners. I introduced them (astonished they'd never met since Philippe's the head of Cannes' Film Festival).

Like most Big Legends, Coward felt no need to play star; his immodesty was generous. "My genius as a composer is that my instincts are unhampered by knowledge: I don't really know music technically. I improvise into a machine and a lackey later writes it down." Or, "You like my cologne? I aim to please even at sixty-one. It's actually *from* Cologne." Or, "You want to hear about movie stars? But I'd rather hear about you. Even more, I'd love to hear your music."

We finally paid our bills and rose to go. On reaching the bar Philippe excused himself to go to the washroom, exactly when Georges Auric from his chair spotted me and Coward waiting together. He rushed over to say hello while a photographer from *Cinémonde* snapped our picture. The flash exploded as Philippe emerged from the men's room, missing posterity by thirty seconds.

Upstairs in the street while we waited for a taxi beneath the high hot elms, Coward again spoke of hearing my music. He promised to call, adding softly, "Brief encounter."

2 June

I arranged for a phonograph and on Wednesday Noël picked me up in a rented Rolls whose chauffeur squired us the half-block to Henri Hell's in the Rue de Beaune. Our honored host sang my praises as Noël stretched out on the vicuna couch prepared to listen, which he did with the careful intensity of intuitive laymen. We played *Design* (which he found "modern") and fifteen songs sung by Phyllis Curtin who he said, incredibly, was under consideration for *Sail Away*. Of the songs he was most enthralled by *Little Elegy* and declared that when I make an opera of *Brief Encounter*, it must sound like that song.

Sans date

As a ten-year-old on Chicago's South Side, safely unsafe in the arms of Hutchins' elementary school, I too, like other boys, had a magazine route to be hatefully traversed once a week on those quick winter dusks when the stomach starts to growl. My technique consisted of inquiring at strange doors: "You don't want to buy a *Saturday Evening Post*, do you?"

How, after a month or so, did I acquire a Dollar Bonus from Curtis Publishers? With that sum Jean Edwards and I one morning purchased a live goose, which none of our parents was ready to welcome. We returned it the same evening for a refund of ninety cents, the butcher maintaining a pound had been shed by the goose's travels.

(Mention somewhere the Christmas card, which in the mid-1930s Maude Hutchins sent out to the Chicago faculty, representing her daughter, our classmate, naked on the verge of puberty . . . Mention somewhere how during those years Jean Edwards and I swung high on the rings of the grammar school gymnasium, splattering excrement in some defiant homage, as on alternate days we'd spit in the holy water in St. Thomas Church. Had I been born to the golden mysteries of Catholicism, would I have become a composer?)

Meals at my home may have been tense, between low grades and high libidos, but were accomplished in cordial tones and preluded in silent grace. How disarmed I was at sixteen by the screeching mess halls of Northwestern; or at eighteen, while a student at Curtis and rooming with Shirley and her mother, when every supper became an exercise in retaliation between grown women, during which I knit Quaker brows and shut Norse ears to preserve good digestion, now knowing that such scenes are standard Jewish ritual to *help* the digestion!

Creative Impulse:

1) Much of it came from "I'll Show Them," those ignorant admired bullies who whipped me in grade school. (Yet if by miracle they were "shown," would they see?)

2) The reason for naming pieces *Symphony* was to impress Mother and Father. Symphonies were what composers composed, therefore I was a composer. (A symphony by any other name could

not have qualified me for the unemployment insurance paid by parents.)

3) How would X solve this or that problem? (X being an idol forever adored.)

Every composer nourishes his bullies, his parents, his X's. But so does every noncomposer. These hardly unique impulses constitute my only conscious motivations, and the self-expression that laymen like to hear about is all contained within them.

My sole claim to a musical individuality, in this day when claim looms high as achievement, is that I have no system and must sink or swim on expressivity alone.

9 June

Three weeks ago at dawn I smashed my right thumb flat as a bedbug in Virgil's bathroom door, was sped to a fourth-rate doctor in Les Halles who administered five stitches as I (blushing delirium) whispered *"tu me plais,"* and he replied with an antitetanus shot which, for the next twelve hours, left me hanging by a thread. (Like other chosen fools, my allergy to anything concerning horses is prodigious: to ride a horse, to smell horsemeat cooking, even to read about Swift's Houyhnhnms, I swell like a bomb.) A week in bed, shivering, finger paralyzed. Then with a few sips of Chablis and a taste of *saucisson* (which, they say, is ground donkey fat) the tetanus symptoms recur worse than before. Bulges everywhere. The antiserum contagion twists even the forehead into knots of wet iron. Return to bed, every joint aching for days, pills, pills, body a gray grub, spirit a clod, thumb sticking out like a sore thumb as I ruminate on how I bring on these dramas because "life isn't enough." Strain of sleep is no consolation and the illness is outside me—I can't control *it* anymore than I can control habit. As contrast, do not, when sober, the restraint and procrastination of logic dictate my moves? I'm insulted by the relapse. *I* want to referee even my thumb's self-cure, even my mescaline reactions, even my shitting, and my death. (Arnold Weinstein: "Life isn't everything.") The sickbed precludes concentration on books, so one thinks sweating thoughts: work going to pot and everyone capable of love but me, banal because true.

Be-bedded in Paris, I receive lost friends and old lovers. And reject each one. They speak of daily terror in the street, *pissotières* where Algerians with razors reach over to decock you with a *whack!* What of love? They tell of "the funeral parlor set" that pays dearly for union with the dead. I, for one, with all my allergies, have never gone for paraphernalia.

10 June

All I can do to write here, thumb still in a sling. Repentance—longevity is that of a hangover. I will not kick out Bacchus. Euterpe's less harmful but less social.

I am the only caricature. Why are you others so flippant? I take you seriously.

Love is cheap to the Infantile as Life is cheap to War. On the anarchist beach romps no hypocrisy. Quick photo versus slow screen.

Monotony of the needed time it takes to notate. And after one is already bored and up to new tricks. Visit this afternoon from Rona Jaffe, sent by the Harrisons. Kenton Coe came too. Set them to work making tea, changing bandages.

11 June

Visit from François Valéry.

The French language is less rich than English. French music more sparse than German. Are these limitations limitations?

Americans are jaded children. Canadians are not.
Are not what?
Exactly: that banal enigma defines them.
Defines who?

Did you ever know the so-called Groupe des Six?
Why yes, I knew all five of them.

18 June

Relapse after relapse from antitetanus shot, sweat, aches, slight bleeding.

Morris [Golde] arrived like a breath of Bronx air, immediately hired a car and took us to Chantilly. Two days ago we went to the Leningrad Ballet. Yesterday, screeching headlines announce the defection of Nureyev—*le plus grand danseur depuis Nijinski*—whom we'd thought good but not *that* good. The little friends say the defection was because of a love affair.

Too physically painful to write here.

Hyères
18 July

The summer really ends around July 15, when days die so noticeably that thought of autumn responsibility filters guiltily through the heat, and I remember never walking down Fifth Avenue at this season without pausing in the Gotham lobby where once (how many years ago?) I kept an engagement to lose my virginity. Been here since June 28. Sick: infected bronchial tubes, heel and thumb. Ile du Levant last week. Going to Cannes, chez Katchen, in three days. Then Morocco early next month. Working well, mostly on *King Midas*. Too tired to write. More later. What calm.

How much more finally rewarding for a composer to hear his songs sung by the Mindless Singer with a voice than by the Intelligent Artist without a voice.

21 July

Free of mundane distractions, Hyères, as always, is conducive to work and I'm finally recharged with that compulsive concentration of childhood. As an early teen-ager I was the contrary of those prodigies whose parents chain them to the keyboard. I chained myself. Even the call of nature was an intrusion: I would hobble from the bathroom back to the piano without bothering to pull up my pants. For hours my belt would get caught in the pedals.

The live artist's output is an animate perspective. An obituary is a static retrospective.

My obituary will be my work. That work is now in a constant flow of becoming. How can I pause to objectify the motion? What could I say about the music that the music doesn't say better? To chisel the notes onto a marble slab would be merely redundant. An artist able to assess his own work is already dead.

Is art found in the street, in human contact, in the sound of unrehearsed weeping? Such a notion finds buyers because it peddles two unrelated products for the price of one. The promotion rolls out a philosophy, cuts off the dangling edges and boxes it as art. Or boxes the art as philosophy. The promoters mean their metaphors literally: all the world's a stage, and what's on a stage is of course Theater. Now, to state there is music in the wind does not prove there is music in the wind.

Cannes
24 July

In a few hours, having again spent a few days with a few heartbreaks, I'll leave this impermanent brothel-cage and take a train for Toulon. Cannes also proved different (meaning too much the same) after the years, and I no longer like myself here. Do I hate everyone for liking themselves more than me? Am I *au fond* superficial? No. Preferring gossip to philosophy means simply that philosophers in society seek relaxation. Gossip equals maturity. Can hate be put to good use?

While the weekend weakened (*j'enviais janvier*) my head cleared enough to see Cannes as a city. "*Quoi!*" exclaimed Roro [Robert Veyron-Lacroix] as we reeled past a pretty church at 4 A.M. "*Ya-t-il vraiment des églises ici?*" My *réunion ratée* with Jean-Paul Gaël showed how liquor is stronger than love, though both are unstable, and in the same way. Love has no heart.

The dead. Ernest Hemingway and Céline (same day). Jeanne Dubost. Eddie Waterman (last year).

Scene: Ten minutes of music (Celia) without singing. She waits. She wonders. (As in *L'Avventura*). But she never opens her mouth.

How I love new Antonioni. How more agreeably troubling to watch the rich suffer than the poor; the boredom is the same, but they are *bored in ermine.* Anyway, why are the poor, just because they're poor, necessarily more likable than the rich? Father used to say: "Born of poor but dishonest parents."

Hyères
29 July

A summer similar to those long productive ones in the 1950s, minus the deranged affectionate presence of Oscar Dominguez, but plus the staunch old friends and hard new work. After a series of "refresher" lessons with the Auto-école, I failed the final exam, pique-making, considering that in high school I drove the family car some fifty thousand miles. Read *Paulina* of Jouve, which resembles this diary. *La Vieille* and *Dimanche* of Simenon. Still the weekly dinners over the hill with Tony Gandarillas. Still Saint-Tropez every three weeks, still the comings and goings of Jean Lafont and Roland Caillaud. Still the Aurics almost daily with Guy de Lesseps, excursions, movies (*Lola*, Anouk Aimée), *fêtes champêtres* on the Arnal's vast Toulonese lawn with Micheline Presle. And the Godebskis once a month. Reading with relish two books by Christiane Rochefort, *Les Petits enfants du siècle* and *Le Repos du guerrier*. Still the constant stimulation of Marie Laure. Yet I'm mostly alone, and next week I leave.

Fell in love only twice, and simultaneously. Félix Labisse now occupies a section of the property, a suite of terraces beyond the gutted pool requisitioned during the war, and never repaired again until Félix put his artist's hand to them. One morning I looked down onto the lawn to see his new guests, Daphnis and Chloé, in reality the blue-eyed Mademoiselle Claude Bessy and the green-eyed Monsieur Attilio Labis. Since they *are* Daphnis and Chloé in the Paris Ballet, and were to remain boating companions for several days, and Claude cured my foot (with razors and chemicals) of a plantar wart, then it . . . Well, the dancers have gone, and I was enamored of them both as though they were one.

Have I ever seen Sartre? I honestly can't recall—strange, given my wholehearted admiration.

I did once see Albert Camus. It would have been in June or July of 1949. He was crossing the Boulevard Saint-Germain at the Bonaparte intersection, heading toward Saint-Sulpice, smoking, self-absorbed but awfully carnal. He looked familiar which seemed natural then. I'd just arrived, and when in Paris one sees Camus. Wouldn't a Frenchman find it normal to see, say, Marilyn Monroe, crossing Fifth Avenue most any afternoon?

What makes the French French? It's hard to put a finger on what makes them French; but I know what makes them not American, and I know that they're quite as innocent about us as we about them, literarily and sociologically. From us they await other Hemingways; though we long ago outgrew (didn't we?) the phony-virility style in favor of words as poetry. Yet when I explain to even the wittiest and most cultivated Parisian that I was reared in Chicago, he points a finger and says: *"Tu es gangstaire, boum boum!"* And he insists that America's the Rome of Europe's Athens.

Robert Phelps once wrote that our view of the French (fancy cooking, Folies-Bergères, castles-on-the-Loire) is not how they see themselves. "Frenchmen," he notes, "are undeluded, self-sufficing, able to live on very little, unsentimentally efficient about gustatory and sexual satisfaction, firm about property values, keen at survival, and taking profound pride in this."

As for what makes French music French, doubtless it's precisely this essence of thrift—as opposed to German music. Basic French thematicism is often either on or within a tetrachord as opposed, say, to those pentatonic formations of the Scotch and Chinese, or highly disjunct Teutonic vocal lines.

Taste, have they? Well, I may have a sense, though no concern, for interiors, for visual balance, color mixtures, style. But taste I do not have—much less good taste—even in music, as Ravel had and

Strauss had not. Nor am I sure that taste is required for genius: it's too controlled. Surely taste is no consideration today, even for specialized audiences whose very eschewing of the attribute has come to be chic.

French is the sole Romance language without tonic accent—without a heavy fall on one syllable of a two-or-more-syllable word. So in musical settings of French (forgetting standard observances like treating a final mute "e" as a syllable), prosodically anything goes. Thus the natural rise and fall of the spoken tongue is more to be considered. In English, contrariwise, the tonic accent of a multisyllabic word is stronger than in any other language, so strong indeed that all unaccented syllables are thrown away. Consider the words *telephone* or *only* in which the *-lephone* or the *-ly* are virtually dispensable, as opposed, say, to the Italian (another strongly tonic-accented tongue) *telefono* or *solo* in which the nonaccented syllables are nonetheless granted their fair due. The few English exceptions that occur to me, in which both syllables of a two-syllable word are given equal stress, are in the numbers *thirteen* through *nineteen*—doubtless so that the ear may distinguish them from *thirty* and *ninety* wherein the suffix is, of course, nearly inaudible.

Linguistics has always intrigued me as much as God, both having been unavailable before reaching France in 1949. If my inclinations had been volatile, my Quaker worship had been mute. The first proper contact with a Parisian man of letters was in Julien Green, bilingual by birth, Catholic by conversion. To whom a more natural inquiry: "When you speak with God, do you speak in French or in English?" He only answered with his eyes, in silence.

Rabat
7 August

So here I am in Africa again, after ten years. And like two Augusts ago on finally returning to Chicago (where I found the initials NR childishly imbedded in the hard cement of adulthood before our former house) I am disturbed. For the past thirteen weeks I've sought love on three continents, and found love elusive, because you can't go back, although nothing has changed but you, etc.

Nothing affects me. Yesterday Guy's friend, young Docteur Michel Blanquit, for my general education took me to the Salé morgue and there displayed the svelte naked body of a dead Berber girl who had hanged herself in the woods. Nothing. Yet this was only my second corpse, the first being that "man who jumped off the Seranac" whom all we fourth-graders ran to see and were traumatized for weeks.

Yesterday in Fez I sniff once more the cedar, mint and heavy olives, hear and taste the terrible exoticism, feel nostalgia less strong than it should be, because I'm not involved (or don't let myself be), and grow jealous and lonely.

Who knows if America might not after all be the country where my realest problems, for better or worse, will eventually be solved? You *can* go home again.

Tangier
12 August

Head bowed in my Spanish grammar, too shy to order coffee on the "crack-train" from Rabat, I came here four days ago. Paul and Jane Bowles met me and I've dined *chez eux* ever since. Time filled in with reviving Morocco after so many years, and it's happier, now that I'm free to roam. What could this city do to me (a middle-class Wasp forever) if I remained: the strangeness is risky, lethargic, heady, sentimental, distant, odiferous, sensual, dangerous, and how would it alter the music? But mine's just a passing tourist's life of sun, liquor, cruising. What is a real man? The answer is here. So, by the way, is Allen Ginsberg.

Rabat
14 August

Alcohol's wounded me less bodily than mentally. A hangover's temporary, but the incessant series has produced an obligatory and disquieting Double Man. At least that's what Paul Bowles said. It's a strain now, in the long run, to recount (or want to recount) daily anecdotes, "personal relations," professional attitudes. Is that because other people have no effect? Diaries are for the worried mind.

It's hard to believe that Morocco was once my home. I take it less for granted now than then, and feel transient. Yet from 1949 through 1951, Fez and Marrakech were so naturally welcome that I understood Chicago to be the stranger. Nothing will ever remove the fact that, except for songs, it was during my Moroccan years that I composed my First Everything: symphony, piano concerto, piano sonata, violin sonata, string quartet, song cycle. . . . Had I remained then in the competitive pot of New York or ceded to the luxuries of Paris rather than to the bizarre reflective isolation of Guy Ferrand's two houses, what might . . . ?

20 August

Smoking too much. Impasse in work, one in thousands, familiar to all: "How to get *into* something, something unstated by me?" Then finally the hand is guided (by whom?) and the poem's squeezed out. What a price!

And sleeping badly. At four in the morning, eyes wide open in the dark, I go on the terrace to cool off. Guy's house is centered in the casbah, misty buttery thick with sounds rising from cubist roofs of pheasants, dog fights and the eternal ululations of the women with wedding music (yes, at 4 A.M.) of impeccable drumming and intermittent muezzins. I wonder about the Arab lovers of these past two weeks, contagious here, but where do I want to live? Always anywhere elsewhere. . . . Five: a *garagiste* upright at midnight; a *gouape tangéroise* when drunk while a mother shouted in the next room in that putty slum; another in Tangier, by name Adselem (or Absalom, as we tourists say), whom I might have loved (but how?); Abdel, of heartbreaking brawn; and Lahcen, forsaken two years back by another in remembrance of whom he now fixates on me. Triceps suppler than taffy, but I want something more. And every Moslem here a blue-jeaned rock 'n' roller, as I moodily sit in the Jardin des Oudaia musing on where my next symphony is coming from, as though it made a difference. Two nights ago, by contrast, dined chez l'Ambassadeur et Madame Seyoux. (There is more of Lady Chatterley in me than in any woman I know, yet Lady Chatterley didn't write music.)

21 August

Criminal faces, maniacal faces are determined after the fact. Would he still look criminal if laws were changed? Would she still look crazy if madness were accepted as part of man's estate?

Beauty's less variable than folly within a culture. Garbo and Brando, the two most famous living Western beauties, partake of each other: they do not eschew each other's identity but swallow it, include it: they are beautiful because androgynous. One pictures them without ridicule in each other's clothes. We don't think of, say, Monroe (the Eternal Feminine) as beautiful so much as pretty, nor of, say, Gable (the Eternal Masculine) as beautiful so much as handsome, and we can't picture them without ridicule in each other's clothes.

None of this concerns taste, much less eroticism, though a Frenchman would find in it a generality. For me, Berg's face is repugnant, though I love his work; Braque's face is beautiful and I love his pictures; Ingres' face is beautiful, though I'm indifferent to his work; Ruggles' face is indifferent and so, to me, is his work. As for carnality, intelligence as object seems almost obscene, probably because it's not physical. But wealth is not necessarily visible either, and wealth can be more than a mere goal, it can be an orgasm in itself.

Gagarin and Titov will be remembered chiefly as beauties.

22 August

Vainly working, toying at the keys, I'm struck dumb when Aïcha the maid (who doesn't read or write, was reared in the *bled*, is innocent of "Western" music) enters with coffee. As though she knew I were cheating! Impossible. Yet I'm obsessed that the so-called common man perceives loopholes in a form he nevertheless ignores and could never appreciate.

Later. 10 P.M. and very black. Outside the quiet milling of Morocco through a maze of tight streets. Alone and frightened. A while ago, like whistling in the dark, I began practicing a Debussy *Etude*—then heard noises behind me, and saw a brown face in the window.

King Midas is finished. The *Suite of Pieces for Easy Orchestra* is half done.

23 August

The beige and black lithographs by Norris Embry, which casually twelve years ago I gave to Guy because they meant nothing to me, are again shining down from these African walls, and God, *qu'elles tiennent le coup!* They're exactly the same as before, but exactly different. I still, as with Rorschach's cards, find the same images revealed—bleeding bats, dead embryos—but the images are no longer literal, because they are art. Which brings the surprising hope that change *is* possible, and I can thank Norris.

To my astonishment Jane Bowles calls my plays better than *Huis Clos*, and says they discourage her from her own writing. Had I one tenth her specialness, I could count myself talented.

Practicing Haydn sonatas joylessly. They don't evolve from day to day. The lack is mine, but change *is* possible.

25 August

Tomorrow we leave for a weekend in Marrakech, and next Thursday off to Spain, then New York. Telegrams from Audrey Wood call me home to do music for Brecht's *Simone* this fall.

Yesterday, a holiday, Mohammed's birthday. Amidst the confettied mosques lit like Coney Island, a young Rabatois appears at the clinic to register a daughter's death. His calves are muscled, his armpits wet. We are thirsty, and *he* offers to go buy pineapple juice. His suffering excites me, opulent squalor of North Africa. My desire is not complex: still, the teasing child, knowing I could if I wanted, is almost enough for me. (My head is all bleached again.) To sleep with the pained *because* they are pained, yet to offer no aid!

Still I do nothing, reticent vampire.

Scattered notes in Tangier ten days ago:

Jane Bowles: the comforting depths of *entente* between her and Cherifa to whom she says little, with whom she has nothing in common but surface, that is, the depths of getting through the day.

Allen Ginsberg, who breakfasts on éclairs in the Socco Chico, who inhabits a shack-penthouse at the Hotel Armor with Gregory Corso, who takes strong pills with William Burroughs (*The Naked Lunch* has power not through order but through accumulation only) and who announced "all" to the *New York Post* two years ago, in short, the original obstreperous Beatnik, tells me middle-classedly to "hush" when I ask Paul, in the Mahruba restaurant too loudly before other diners, if the dancing boy is queer.

Speech is man's most confused and egocentric expression; his most orderly and magnanimous utterance is song. This quasi paradox is demonstrable by cocktail-party (or even organized simultaneous) talk versus "pitched" fugatos. Consider how our ear at a noisy gathering can select, can distinguish and *focus* more nimbly than the eye; how we hardly wait for *him* to finish so *we* can start; how nonpitched voices become a babble of words which at best are weak symbols for ideas; how "ideas" in music are more than words can say; how boring singers speaking are; and how cohesion lacks in any coinciding speech, even when purposefully planned as in *The Young Among Themselves*. Then consider how any group singing, by virtue of precalculated tones, immediately makes sense; how a singer loses his identity inside a greater identity; how the thread of a frugal notion weaves itself into a vaster fugal frame which in turn turns and shifts so that idea as Idea grows negligible within the fact. . . .

Slide off her irresistible ski-jump nose into Drossie's Restaurant during the war, or into the Hôtel de l'Université where she, Jane, who needed shelter, sheltered us during our first days in France. Where (never) in this book are those other Americans, all dear? I speak only of a country I'm about to leave again, where people write backward (those who write). Or is it *we* who write backward? What natural law decrees that eye must move from left to right, up to down? Surely somewhere some nation is predominantly left-handed.

The handwriting, the tone of a person's voice can be interpreted only by another of the same nationality. Imagine an American seizing the hidden sense of an Englishman's utterance! Or the hash some German analysts deduce from our script.

Is it *truth* to say "yes" when, though "yes" is the fact, you know it will be taken as "no"? For instance:

"Were you unfaithful?"

"mmmm . . . *Yes.*" (Coyly, to imply "no," though "yes" *is* true.)

How far to Casablanca, Monsieur? Ninety kilometers, fill up your tank. Similarly we need preparation for listening: we must know the length of a piece (like a book) before hearing. Otherwise, having paid for a Nocturne, we risk getting stuck with a Passion.

29 August

If on the outside I'm in every sense a blind musician, it is because I'm internally visual; but can this make for opera? My discipline avoids the actual. Whenever I pick up a newspaper the mind wanders. On purpose? Still *Mamba's Daughters* is actual, though of the past, and the mixture at once intrigues and bores. . . . It's time to pack up and go home to America, quit the composer's obligatory isolation, start working on the libretto with Arnold [Weinstein], head toward that heady horror of preopening nerves preceded by rehearsals with soloists separately, with pianist, with chorus, never never enough, with lighters, with dressers, with orchestra, never enough.

Finished, daily visits to the pedicure who, with black acids, burned out my *verrue plantaire.*

Tomorrow, leave for Spain with Michel Blanquit.

Granada
6 September

This afternoon I sent Bill Flanagan a pornographic letter of the kind we've been exchanging for years. The Marquise de Sévigné's epoch is past, and now only self-conscious musicians discuss music by mail. Unlike intellectual laymen, artists together talk either money or sex, art being for working hours. My letter may scald the posts of this fascistic zone where for five days I've been confusing the cities of Andalusia without much zeal. Tangier is a dung heap with a view onto paradise, whereas in, say, Heidelberg you're caught like an ambered fly whose long stare freezes upon human squalor. (What a sentence.) Spain's neither heaven nor hell, merely Italy out of focus. Who lives here? People, not persons, and they're cross-eyed, blond, flat-assed, with the thinkers all in jail, nonflirtatious, and Michel was rolled the first night in Seville, though next day the young thief was found and imprisoned (for how long!) while we the guilty eat in cool, Fallaian gardens.

We the guilty set a tone with which to wind up this ninth notebook. Toward evening as I slurped a lemon ice at the filthy café, a nymphet, next table, watched with hazel eyes each jiggle of my Adam's apple as though to say: "I know you, dirty poet, straying through our land like a gypsy writing obscene letters to America." Still, she couldn't spoil my motionless appetite: I've never had a taste for travel. Actually, for once New York looks welcome in three weeks, older and dumber, as I write here in this dusty country without a wish to comprehend. Around each corner there are no longer possibilities for love. So much spare time is nerve-racking and I long to work as I worked in Rabat. Meanwhile here's a menopause that refreshes. Tomorrow we leave for Madrid.

Hôtel de Lille
Paris
15 September

Returned to Paris Monday. *Cuite écrasante,* rolled, sauna next day, *rencontre de hasard* with whom I dined at Lipp's, rather depressed, damp streets, buggy hotel.

Stopped by Virgil Thomson's today, our first meeting since I'd sublet his apartment last spring. Irving Drutman there too. After tea with honey and cookies, Virgil began:

"The bathroom curtain seems to be stained. It wasn't that way before you came last April. I was wondering—is it jam? Or liquor? Is it coffee? Blood? . . ."

"It's blood, Virgil."
"That's all I need to know. Milk will remove it."

Retrospectively embarrassed about certain of my earlier works, notably the *Second Quartet* and the *Second Symphony*, I ask Virgil if I should withdraw them. "Don't worry, baby. Some pieces just withdraw themselves."

23 September

That Berber boy's head haunts me harder than any fixed master-piece since seen in Spain, a Spain detested two weeks back, but now (sitting, waiting in the Hôtel de Lille, wondering how to spend the days until Virgil and I fly to New York) considered differently with an affection easy for past things. We can be nostalgic for prison once escaped.

Conclusions on Spain had been drawn through French music which it resembles, though French music does not resemble Spain. Gardens galore, hot nights, late meals beginning with summery gazpacho, thin icy tomato soup sprinkled with shredded onions, tomatoes, celery, peppers. No books in Spain. I could live without music's sound (heard silently it needs no confirmation). But without books?

Which brings us to Paris. Not that I'm devouring books here, only beer in a sordid room in a pretty city, waking at dawn to scratch phrases on the wall: "Hate jews, niggers, blind people, hate the deaf (a little less), can't stand fairies, dykes, the Chinese, the French. Rather like Arabs and Italians (though only to sleep with), hate people. *My sober life is an act.*"

The English in Morocco call Gibraltar Gib (pronounced *Jibb*). "I'm naked in Tangier. In Jibb, dear, they confiscated all my jew-els"— those two final syllables being granted their full value in that contradictorily strident mutter produced through constricted jaws common to upper-class Londoners.

Tedium and trials of truth. Even the quickest of us are afraid to admit opinions. Because I love cake I am guilty for loving. Because I

love Ravel I'm admiring when Bill Flanagan *admits* he loves Ravel.
Today again in Paris. Sunny mist, warm, alone.

Sans date

> *Le plus grand poète français? Hugo, hélas!*
>
> —André Gide

> *Gall, amant de la reine, alla, tour magnanime*
> *Galamment, de l'arène à la Tour Magne, à Nîme.*
>
> —Victor Hugo

> *Chi troppo in alto sal cade sovente*
> *precipitevolissimevolmente.*
>
> —Ariosto

Anticonstitutionellement
Incomprehensibility
Judge a country's character by her longest words.

An eighteenth-century crab canon which the French so love:

N'A-T-ELLE PAS ÔTÉ CET OS À PELLETAN

Like Ezra Pound contemplating the first issue of *transition,* and
then, reading backward: *No it isn' art.*

$$\frac{P}{Venez} \quad à \quad 100$$

Venez souper à Sans Souci

To know a language just well enough to miss the point.

The female peacock? A peacunt.
Far better to be sad and rich than sad and poor.

Why not,	Ifit	There I am	The aim
on those tests	snot	trying for babies	of life
of Szondi,	onet	with men of vanilla	is
Mohandas Gandhi	hing	Under chincilla skies	to
or	itsa	by the bay of Manilla.	seek
Elissa	noth	Instead I catch scabies.	life's
Landi?	eroh	Should I go to Siam?	aim.

And I sat even, sir, tea-book, blue-bass, spur-tins,
Sandy at seven thirty took two aspirins,
Bland by mat heaven, dirty hook, stew mass stir, pins.

—Corneille

Titles: He's Quite Crool
          He's So Good
Story: The Deligny Baths
          The Delicious Nightmare or the Pleasures of Terror

The Deligny pool (along with scab-picking and park-cruising, specialties which combine pain and joy) belongs to the category of *delicious nightmare*. Delicious for its opaline waters, lithe tourists and troubling fragrance. Nightmarish by the same token. The Terrors of Pleasure.

17 September

I always think old friends or new will suffer a sea-change from year to year or sometimes in a minute. They don't. Last weekend in Noizay chez Poulenc his famous chauffeur Raymond sat looking very masculine. After a while he went out to get some Vichy water, and came back still looking very masculine. No revelation had altered him inside or out as none alters me except the slow knowledge that no one person makes much difference. Poulenc says the orchestra is my *vraie nature*, not songs, and his reasons are simply understood. Talk of Vichy makes me thirsty, being still dehydrated from night before last (voluptuous joy of Vichy), a *cuite* with Jean-Claude. Night before last was inevitably followed by yesterday, a day inevitably thirsty, blurred, sexy. Made love as I haven't for years with someone I'll never find again. The beauty of La Touraine, of Tours, the troglodytes and posies, yellow grapes and sun. Yesterday. A *para*, moustache, an old dashing maroon plush béret of *paras*, memory of odors. Today again in Paris.

Despite what Freshman English discussions of Character Development conclude to the contrary, people don't change. I haven't changed since the age of reason, and I know no one who has. People do go steadily downhill, of course, but that's not personality change, it's a static fact of life. Those who "change for the better" simply inherit money, or feel they've made a breakthrough in their therapy and so, for a few weeks, behave charitably. But when we see old people behaving cantankerously when they should be settling with God for a bit of final grace, it's because they were always cantankerous. (Somerset Maugham, for instance, or Marya Freund, or maybe me.) *Les vieillards terribles*. Nice people die nice.

Poulenc: *On met en musique les mots, mais il faut mettre aussi en musique ce qui est dans le blanc des marges.*

No pederast he: military gerontophilia's his ice cream. Can one be arrested for seducing a major?

25 September

The Hôtel de Lille, where I try to avoid seeing the stained wallpaper as, for three years, I used to avoid bedbug smears on 13th Street. Trying to get through the days. Missing Morocco. Friday I'll be in New York, but will never be at ease except in backward countries. I drink from shyness, subdivision of boredom. On the wagon, feeling good, I grow jittery, not wanting responsibilities of sexuality. Damp naps of hangovers make a sham of fair weather. Present difficulty is that I've no access to work, caught in the hotel prison between two countries, Marie Laure's still in Hyères. No sooner off the plane than work will begin (Brecht's *Simone*). Where will I stay? for how long? Should I buy a house in Tangier next spring and return with the crocus? Morries writes that Bill Flanagan's back in Bellevue.

The inability to get out of yourself, coupled with exterior

tediums of Paris (fascism, conformist youth, and once you've seen old friends you've seen them), results in disaster. Saturday without a particle of sentiment I walked past 75 Rue de Vaugirard where ten years ago I leaned from a window in the night, as I leaned five years earlier from a window on 12th Street, and lean now from the Lille.

26 September

Every time I leave Paris she dons the old whore's look and says, Stay: today your discomfort recedes, you're avid as always for manufacturing souvenirs, walking alone, café-au-lait Rue Mouffe-tard, le Jardin des Plantes. This morning Marie Laure called from Hyères, and also Nora, making me feel "wanted." Who young replaces them? or me? Porpoises once had a culture as refined as ours, but gave it up for the joy of living.

Is it wrong not to look your age? Doda Conrad said today my music had *hardened* for the better, adding I still look the age I was on first arriving in Paris twelve years ago.

Dead: Marion Davies, Dag Hammarskjöld, Theodore Chanler. Raining. Half-packed baggage all about the room. Speechless yesterday we bade goodbye to Versailles, the Eden of the civilized. Too nervous to write details.

29 September

If I weren't a musician I'd have more time for music. Far more informed than I is the Music Lover, the amateur; nor is his information necessarily more superficial. At a time when it counted —before the age of twenty—I did learn the piano catalogues of Chopin, Beethoven, Brahms, Mozart, Debussy, Ravel, and a bit less of Liszt and Schumann. But most of these weren't mastered. To hear them no longer tempts me. Seldom at a concert don't I feel I should be home writing my own music. It's hard now to get lost and die, although *Pelléas* still destroys me as *Lucia* destroys you. Last night, as a farewell gesture, Nora took me to the Olympia to hear (see) young Johnny Halliday, and for the first time in years I experienced *enthusiasm*. Ironic, that my first exposure to rock 'n' roll should be filtered through a Frenchman on the eve of a departure for an America whose contemporaneity has evaded me.

Yet the nearest horizon seems obscured by my navel. I've made a list, culled from my datebook, of people and places I've seen and been, during these six months. Did I here never mention the Prado? the utter Frenchness of Manuel Rosenthal's home? Maya Pliset-skaya's *Lac des Cygnes*? the tone of returning to Fez after a decade? the stimulus of the impossible Noailles (who and how rich and what age is she?), my reactions to those hundred books I read? How I Spent My Summer Vacation is not for nothing the safest assignment of English teachers. Well, if I missed that boat at least I'll catch the limousine which in an hour, thanks to the indefatigability of travel-agent Bill Taylor will pick me up, then Virgil waiting with his Lanvin luggage on the Quai Voltaire, and conduct us on a red carpeted highway to Pan Am flight number 115 for New York.

New York
19 November

We took that plane six weeks ago, Virgil and I, from France at the start of summer's protracted finish, and swept over a mineral Greenland of fjords and glaciers without a vegetable or man for forty hundred miles, and a place to think of dwelling. Arrival and sleep. Then wake up and stagger stupefied to the St. Mark's Baths, pencil in pocket, hoping there'll be an exchange of addresses which there never is. Instead, casual talk about building fallout shelters, where only yesterday acceptance of unprecedented horror was unthinkable. (Note: you will legally be permitted to kill any neighbor attempting to enter your shelter, as at the baths we murder cubicle trespassers.) Rougemont's sick Western love is no longer a concern even, and every romantic malady's now forgotten in our hemisphere. So, on returning, I stay for a month at Bob Holton's up on Riverside Drive, eating corn flakes in his darkening kitchen while watching the glamorous SPRY sign in Jersey light up, and think of how in those surrounding suburban bright-night honeycombs everyone's fucking but me (fucking without love's nice illness, perhaps, but I'm not even there at all).

Rosemary had her sixth child, a daughter, the day after my thirty-eighth birthday. On my twenty-eighth I told Elliott Stein that a certain mirror, Rue Saint-Benoit, used to be very flattering. He replied: "The mirror hasn't changed." On my twelfth, when parents forbade me to see Garbo in *Queen Christina*, I drank iodine (three drops). With that blackmail I gained majority. With this birthday, after a hot Halloween, winter came finally, and back on 13th Street I edge slowly eastward with the same discontent. Ignoring the danger of parks (certain parks), innocence permitted safe orgies; then with birthdays came shyness and look at me now. Yet I'd do it all over again. Even the drinking, in spite of Bill in Bellevue, in spite of most friends contradictorily *en ménage*, of eternal boring liquor traps or a lovely commission to make an opera (with Arnold Weinstein) of Dubose Heyward's *Mamba's Daughters*.

Dead: Maya Deren, Jack Wilson, Guthrie McClintic, Joan McCracken, Esther Berger.

23 November

The world today's bored because scared. Instead of orgies for the end of time there's murder. Everyone's killed some. (Stalin: One death's a tragedy, ten thousand a statistic.) Except in Morocco where one risks less now than in the streets of our great cities.

The doubts on starting a new work. The greater doubts on a new collaboration. The greatest for a deadlined commission. Everyone hopes we'll stub our toes next year; and Arnold's late success has gone to his head more than is usual with friends: he quotes his own publicity when praising his unwritten words.

Mrs. Heyward's death, says Audrey Wood, causes complications because she never signed that to which she verbally agreed. Since I've learned that the worst is often possible the Ford Foundation might easily go down my drain and Arnold's.

This afternoon visit to Tom Prentiss. How sobering to peer through his botanical eye at the wonders of Central Park and to observe the Metropolitan's new Rembrandt which cost only $2,500,000. He advises: why not, while waiting, write *Lions* to go with my *Eagles* and *Whales!* Where is my old poem *Lions*? Who has one? Do you?

I have lost my portrait by Larry Rivers, as, five years ago in a Paris taxi, the portrait by Dora Maar was lost. Things. Are art works things?

Here exhausted I write. Across the room Roro practices my piano (Frank Martin's *Trio Concerto*), and I calculate how strength gives out every three days, and how those days (as in the old days) blur together as though I lived in a piece of snotty Kleenex. Thirty-six hours ago I dined delightfully with Georges Auric (who's in America for ASCAP meetings) at the Veau d'Or. When he tells me that in America he drinks all day, taking his first shot at 10 A.M., I exclaim, *Mais c'est le début de la fin,* he replies, *Au contraire, c'est le début de la soif.* So I take him to Jane Romano's and we all get drunker and Auden ignores me, and I tell Ellen Adler, whom I've always liked, that I loathe her, and later that night I'm robbed by an *inconnu* as though in punishment for bad breeding. So yesterday, after a *triste* Thanksgiving (chez Bill Flanagan) of pheasant and sparkling catawba juice which I can hardly swallow from numbness, I patronize not surprisingly those baths whose partitions shake at the lonely slurp of avid tongues, while Paris and Rabat have the shit bombed out of them, and Roro practices, So for relaxation I find myself wathching for the tenth time *A Bout de Souffle,* and remember how with my own ears I heard Rachmaninoff play in Chicago thirty years ago.

Hardly one day after identical day drags innocuously by that I don't consider suicide, not romantically as on those snowy nights in the '40s, but with a sordid practicality. To say liquor or fallout are already suicide means nothing. Hardly one day drags nastily by that I don't consider: "Will I tonight?" then usually do. And feel certainly no more buoyant. Yet tomorrow Billy Budd hangs while I remain alive and only think on dying. I will have spent so much time being sad. To say there are enough friends and I've room for no more—what of those alienated through alcohol (Sonia Orwell, Ellen Adler)? I'd prefer clear-headed alienation, as with Krips.

3 December

This morning at 2:30 while waiting to cross Sixth Avenue at 8th Street with Edwin Denby, a man near the stoplight examines me, but by the time I negotiate a goodbye to Edwin and find myself free, the man has disappeared. I purchase the *Times* (anticlimactically retrieving Edwin at the newsstand) and come home.

Today is Sunday, and I've returned from a matinee and American supper with Maggy.

Take a match and strike it to light my . . .

The verb *to die*, in whatever context or conjugation, disturbs me more and more. Last night proves once again that I simply can't share a bed. With all my moaning about lonely nights, the slightest contact snaps me awake. I long for the luxury of loneliness. Just as I know all about life except how to live it, so with love. If to strangers I now give my age as twenty-eight (lie by a decade and you won't fall into arithmetic traps), perhaps it's from shunning adult responsibilities. But when I inspect an "adjusted" person, his limitations repel me. Mention an idea rather than a fact and his interest wilts visibly—the essence of rudeness. Do the splitting headaches that hit me at orgasm indicate a need for help?

Mamba's Daughters is, for the moment anyway, off, leaving me *désoeuvré*.

Tuesday I leave for Pittsburgh to see the parents, smell the yellow fall and wish it were apple flesh, eat red apples and wish they were human, and feel blue. Morris Golde joins me there Friday. We saw *The Apple*. In his gifted incompetence Gelber misses the point—on his own terms. Fabricating anger he produces *ennui*.

Sans date

Jennie Tourel, Joe LeSueur and Libby Holman come to dine, the four of us in my small room with a huge sirloin, salad, and a lemon Bavarian. Toward midnight Libby goes home. Whereupon Jennie asks: "What's Miss Holman doing these days?"

When just finished with a piece, or between pieces, my focus blurs into wandering and aimless temptation. It's hard to know how to "live." Maybe knowing would be stupid. Working is not living. Life is community, the taking of time, whereas art, at least the making of it, is antisocial, for art exists outside time.

If the art results from strokes of luck, it follows that an artist is someone who controls his luck. He orders chance. An un-artist (John Cage) is one who chances order.

I am the key to my simplicities, but the lock's painted over. I have been faithless to me in my way, having been taught as a child to avoid the pronoun I.

The virtues of evil, Escape into horror, White devils.

A concert: is what precedes a party.

None but the fair deserve the fair.

He'll be a real heartbreaker when he grows up, said they of the handsome eight-year-old who, being a prosaic-minded poet, recalled the phrase by attempting to put it sadly to practice in later years.

A meal: is what precedes a cigarette.

Am I right in the head, counting (but how do you count them?) the hours or years between this and the instant of agony? Not despair but dejection, not wars but puddles of sun.

13 December

In Pittsburgh to hear Steinberg do the twenty-seventh and twenty-eighth performances of my *Third Symphony*.

A photo of me at the telephone.

Is there not something contradictory in writing down the fact that life is meaningless?

1962

The . . .
—Henry James

. . . the . . .
—Honoré de Balzac

. . . and the . . .
—Thackeray

Brevity is next to godliness, as those authors who provide the epigraphs for this section were not the first to realize.

Mere Notions to Develop:

1) "Who, Marie Laure, is the most beautiful woman you've ever known?"

"Tillie Losch. Et pour toi?"

"Ellen Adler."

2) One fall evening of 1952, in an empty room somewhere on Columbia's campus, Douglas Moore played and sang all he had then composed of *Baby Doe* for me and Mark Bucci and Peggy Bate. . . .

3) In 1937 (or was it 1938?) I gave my teacher Leo Sowerby two favorite books: *Aphrodite* of Pierre Louÿs, *Growth of the Soil* by Knut Hamsun. He liked the Hamsun. . . .

4) Last summer on a wharf in Tangier I saw, from a distance, the painter Francis Bacon talking with a young Arab. . . .

5) In 1954 (or was it 1955?) Germaine Lubin turned and said, *"Alors, mon grand ami, Monsieur Hitler, m'a conviée. . . ."*

The same year(s) brought a recorded radio discussion between Roland-Manuel and me, which I have somewhere. . . .

6) And there's a written interview with Florent Schmitt, circa 1953. . . .

7) And Monsieur Anne de Biéville. . . .

Did the mother of Valentine Hugo exist? Everyone heard about her, no one saw her. One afternoon at Valentine's Marie Laure announced, "I think I'll say hello to your mother," and was shown into a room, which she later told us was empty. When she emerged, Valentine asked:

—*Comment trouvez-vous Mère?*

—*Plutôt fatiguée.*

In 1952, when her mother died, Valentine phoned to request of Marie Laure a huge sum for the funeral.

—*Je m'occupe des vivants,* replied Marie Laure, hanging up. One week later the florist delivered a wreath seven feet in circumference with the message attached: *Des morts aux vivants.*

They have never made up. Yet I learned it was not Valentine who sent the wreath, nor did she know who did, nor could she have afforded it, nor would she have. The rift was over another principle.

Once a set of principles is established it becomes immediately obsolete. A hero can be a coward—we are the makers of manners. At what price have we killed Victoria!

7 January

While in Pittsburgh an anonymous letter arrived threatening mutilation, not because I wrote bad music, but because I supposedly wear a girdle. The "proof" lay in a *Post-Gazette* photograph of me holding up a large score which, as I examine it more carefully now, indeed resembles a whalebone corset.

The holiday season came and went, and with a grand nontheatricality I abused it by sliding through gin-soaked weather like a Van Vechten heroine and living to complain and continue. Maggy and I saw again the marvelous *Play of Daniel* during which, two years ago, the young angel vomited before a thousand spectators. Is it love or just the idea? as though love could exist without its idea? In the night I awaken to scratch my face which nevertheless does not itch. JB asks: Why are you so bloody-minded? But Elliott Stein hitchhiked to Detroit just to see a vampire movie he missed in the '40s.

When I assert that Elliott's madness derives from his obsession for detail precluding the vision of anything whole, shall I conclude that my sanity comes from a vision of the whole precluding details? Have I seen history, being witness in 1945 to Eisenhower's homecoming passage through Washington Square? Did Norris Embry see history when, five years earlier as a *rescapé* from St. John's College, he offered gin at Djuna Barnes' doorway, waiting then for hours to see that spider hand emerge?

History, or the wisdom of hindsight. If Stravinsky laments that the seventy-five-year-old Schoenberg was denied a grant from the Guggenheim Foundation, why did Stravinsky himself not come to the master's aid? Do I, with *my* Guggenheim grant, reprimand Stravinsky who, being Stravinsky, is right even when wrong, who belongs to a race apart? A race of one; not that undifferentiated collection of Orchestra Men, nor conductors who also form a breed apart, nor their wives, still aparter.

The Big Symphony Orchestra Player, that most skilled of musicians, is of necessity amorphous. Unlike the actor who's only too willing to be seen on stage without a fee, the Orchestra Player pertains to a benevolently fascist mass. He is absorbed, anonymous, so his trade union is strong; he speaks not of Dohnanyi but of dames, cards, dough. Everyone knows he's a frustrated soloist. (Reverse the image: he never made it as an orchestra man, so he became a soloist. Or: the composer as critic *manqué*.) Conductors? They are at once doting mothers and spoiled babies, amiable, gregarious, susceptible to flattery from young ladies. Their wives long ago learned long-suffering, keeping their cool by observing you with eyes exclaiming: He may be yours now, but not for long! Yet finally their mates are faithful, having little time for indiscretion. As everyone else thinks so little on art, small wonder.

Have I lost any friends here? Unlikely.

Start again like a patient spider to rebuild the web, weave and break, weave and break, in an endless sequence of expressly dropped stitches, JB (of all people) is the first in fifty months with whom I've had an *entente*. How different from the others: A father ten years my junior.

Discussions with Rudel. *Mamba's Daughters* is definitively dropped and, in all likelihood, I'll do Jascha Kessler's *Charade* (with another title, let's hope) for the City Center's next season.

Savez-vous pourquoi j'ai bu au début? Parce que, me trouvant beau, mais sans paroles, le regard stupéfié des autres m'était insupportable.

Ornette Coleman: "It was when I realized I could make mistakes that I decided I was really on to something." And: "You can play sharp in tune or flat in tune." And: "An F in a tune called 'Peace' should not sound the same as an F that is supposed to express sadness."

P still calls from Pavia in a voice that ignores the eight last years. I'm now too old for flights of the heart with peasant boys. The bridge's other end is in sight, there's not so much time.

7 February

For seventeen years I've been intermittently keeping these diaries. What will I ultimately *do* with them? The earliest ones are doubtless more—well—*engrossing* for their reportage, but the rest are mere self-exposing massacre when *au fond* I am (as Maggy says) a hardworking *mensch.* (Hardworking? At least this jornal is not concerned with work. And today I say that work means balance without pleasure; my collaboration with Kessler and our opera for next season I anticipate with only boredom—yet what masterpieces have not sprung from even less.) The other night at one of the biweekly domestic evenings *chez moi* I read the "Cocteau Visit" extract to Morris and Virgil, and everyone was impressed and said: print it! But where? Oh, the energy I had for observative journalizing in those early fifties! But as I wrote then, we spend most of our lives repeating ourselves, so now I save time by notating telegram-style. Well, if tomorrow I died, I suppose there'd remain a sizable and varied catalogue. (Am I advancing? Yes, but the scenery's stationary.) And die perhaps I will, though astrologically it should have happened to our whole world three days ago, February 4.

8 February

Bless the unseasonable weather's dependable power. Every morning comes an icy stream through the window and, with all its faults, New York's winter's more electric than Paris'. That stream declares "another happy day!" like Beckett's lady, and days *are* less melancholy now that (again) JB, with faults like those of New York, acts as AA. How different, what we write and feel at night from what we feel and write next morning. Daylight ridicules lament.

Edward three Thursdays ago for three hours read me his unbearable *Who's Afraid of Virginia Woolf?* I don't know what it's about, but neither do I know what Mozart's about. It's far from boring, *ce qui est tout dire*. . . . I now address Edward as Ralph. He calls me Harry.

A man and his work are divorced. Nothing's fixed but the props.

Newly hanging on his wall is a huge poster, found in the rubbish heap, with merely the two words *RUBY FALLS.*

12 February

If when we remain jealously home at night while our loved one's out fornicating, how much more achingly gaze the dying man's eyes from the hospital window to one walking by and vanishing into an alive tomorrow. To an alcoholic, crime and punishment occur simultaneously.

Cocktails for Richard Buckle chez Taras earlier this evening. (Assemblage of caricatures. I too am now a caricature.) Stuart Preston comes up with the somber news that last week George and Elizabeth Chavchavadze were killed together in an auto crash. All of us harbor anxieties on what seems an eternal trip amongst the living, so the sudden accident becomes more ironic than scary. We wait and wait and tediously question and wonder. Then in a flash, there, across the ocean, George and Elizabeth seize quick the unexpected answer. And we relapse into lethargy.

Afterward dined midtown with Clair Leonard who is (have I the right to say it?) pathetic. At sixty, he has missed every train, and I (unborn when he was twenty-three) am embarrassed to command his respect, I who to him represent that distant world of "success" (*si vieillesse savait!*). The temperature's down to 10°. Yes, we *can* alter taste, or rather our opinions, no, I mean our biases. Who would have dreamed that Beckett (for ten years on my shit-list)—that his *End Game* would now appear as a chef d'oeuvre? Beckett, Brahms and cats. I adore JB's cat Patrick. JB suffers a slipped disk, and I don't know how far I could wish to be *engagé*. Is he capable of accepting what I anyway can't give?

5 March

I play at being alive. My dreams are not concerned with champagne, rather with cakes, with oozing frosted pastry floating to tempt me through the sky.

Drunk or sober, death goes on: Fritz Kreisler, Ibert, Bruno Walter, and good old Kurt Seligmann who did my first cover, *Alleluia*, in 1946 when covers still mattered. Now our young Jane Romano, hospitalized for God knows how long or short. Death arrives off schedule but unchanged. Still, one changes. I've grown into cats and Brahms. As a child my final word at bedtime was magnolia; on awakening, gardenia—thinking thus to lead a "better" life. As children, Jean Edwards and I, one Saturday matinee, ensconced ourselves in the Chicago Palace Theater balcony's front row (the film: *Captain Blood*) and sprinkled pepper into the orchestra from which rose a chorus of sneezing paroxysms. Apprehended, again the police. Nor have I put away childish things.

Famed conversationalists are inevitably monologists. A fair exchange between two famed conversationalists is a sketch, a duet, from which only the spectators carry away something new. (Duets, sketches must be rehearsed.) A fair exchange without spectators is not a conversation but a discussion. A discussion instructs the speakers themselves, and is not meant for entertainment.

The improvised Interludes in Lukas Foss' *Time Cycle* should rather be named Intermissions: one talks during them.

Elliott Stein now wears contact lenses. He also has erogenous eyeballs. Therefore, when he requires that his eyes be licked for joy, the lenses risk getting swallowed, after which he must wait interminably to inspect the stool of his beloved, with whom he may no longer be on speaking terms.

Thirty minutes after my first meeting (1943) Lenny Bernstein, he announced: "You are such a combination of sophistication and naïveté!" Still true. I am sophisticated by knowing my role, naïve by bothering to write it down here.

Two Sundays ago Bill and I (with fair David Lloyd and surprising Veronica Tyler) gave the fourth in our series of Music for the Voice by Americans. This was preceded by the daily arrival of a crank letter—or rather, crank drawing: copies of our circular (featuring an informal photo of Bill and me) were returned, one by one, day by day, with my face mutilated—lips reddened, cheeks rouged, a pair of pear-shaped breasts appended to my shirt and a wig (each day huger) superimposed on my head. Bill's likeness was left unscathed. What was first funny, then eerie, now seems a menace.

Then JB and I spent a week at Danny Pinkham's in Cambridge where I gave a similar recital in the Gardner Museum. JB got drunk, when I'd wanted proudly for him to give a pleasant impression for David Sachs whom I found and adored again after all these years. I don't mind JB's behavior except inasmuch as it limits the conversation. Dark Ezra Sims watches inscrutably wearing one earring.

29 March

The weather has been so clean and warm. Yesterday (like fifteen years ago) I sat shirt-sleeved in Abingdon Square composing a little portrait of Don Bachardy in return for his of me.

Repeated annoyances accepted (eyes heavenward) with a patronizing sigh: they say I look so sad, or petulant, or arrogant, but never piss-elegant. Now, with my new Brooks garments?

Nostalgia but not poetry comes from inventory. Frank O'Hara's movie-star verses succeed as happenings but not as art.

Alcoholism is psychosomatic from outside-in as hemophilia's psychosomatic from inside-out.

22 April

Stunning Easter. Life is a postcard. Received yesterday another commission from the Ford, this time to invent a vehicle for Regina Sarfaty.

Whether cycle or unbroken narrative, the end must be *for*

voice alone (i.e., many measures—even a page—for song unaccompanied, like the device that concludes *Madécasse*).

Texts: Cotton Mather, testimonies on witches.
A Mass in English
Song of Deborah (Judges)
Marcus Aurelius
D. H. Lawrence (incl. *Love on the Farm*)
Talk to Me Like the Rain (T. Williams)
Rosetta's thoughts from *The Age of Anxiety* (Auden),
     p. 122
Millay Sonnets, if one yet dare again
(Recurrent pattern: a short smear of rain)
The Queen of Sheba Says Farewell—Leisel Mueller
John Hollander poems
Poems about Love and Rain (Pitchford, Barbara Guest,
     Ashbery)
Open: and immediately show the whole voice

Titles: "Requited Love—A Tragedy"
"Slave Wants Master"
"The Closet Queen"
"Cheetahs and Redwoods"
"Drunk in Paris"
"The Casual Cadenza"
"Various Fairies"

Goodies   (some of these must be listed elsewhere, around 1950?):
Fauré   "Pavane"
Chabrier   "Idylle"
Stravinsky   "Pastorale"
Rorem   "Barcarolle"
Poulenc   "Pastorale" and "Nocturne"
Satie   "Gymnopédies"

27 April

First real spring in years, ironical, like those hung-over noons in Cannes (*ces midis du Midi*) where I'd awaken into gold. Ironical, because we were to go to Bard chez Clair Leonard for this weekend. JB has gone alone. NO RELIEF IN SIGHT, a summer headline that makes my heart leap: I love heat. Could I, from inside, be rejoicing at the "no relief" on every level? The joys of suffering are not nonetheless those I seek consciously, as fog clears to reveal drying skin witnessed by whorish skies that refuse to rain while the pain intensifies. God forbid eighty more pages of poesy as in Claude's day. Am I, as they say, more guarded? To grovel! To be receiving now the pain I prayed for in five unloving years! Dumb recriminations. JB condemned me, *not* for trying, but for not succeeding. He's a sadistic pig. Retraction is quick. Were I to call in the country now as often as I think, the phone would not stop ringing.

30 May

More than five months have brought the inevitably ugly end. Though I dwell on withdrawn habits shared, I still say with W. C. Fields: "I may be drunk, but you're crazy. Tomorrow I'll be sober and you'll still be crazy!"

Artists and their nocturnal emission, the agonizing midnight brain-storm that keeps them awake and constantly turning the light back on so as to notate notions in notebooks by the bed, mind on fire and far from sleep, prey to the ugly necessity of inspiration.

But the pang of no inspiration! How do we change? Need we? Each new work is undertaken not from experience but from scratch. The last work, like the last love affair, teaches us only what not to practice in the next; too late we learn that precisely the new avoidance of what then went wrong makes things go wronger now.

After becoming someone through work comes the problem of remaining someone, not through work but through the special responsibility of self-promotion, dear or cheap. Which precludes the work that made someone someone. The someone he remains is not the someone who first worked to become. So he now has become two ones, not working always, but playing at cat's cradle or at tossing a coin. No one knows him ever, not even himself anymore.

Where from here do I go, confronted by a clean sheet of empty staves? What notes inscribe? To state I will not follow electric paths rather than lead down my own pungent ones does not, for all its high individual intent, render me a leader, or even foster ideas.

To reread the old diaries does show I'm different. Today I couldn't be less interested in hanging out—taking the *time* to hang out—with the Great. Yet the change that not hanging out implies doesn't fill those staves. So the musical change necessarily provoked by isolation has brought so far just a blank sheet to my lap. For refusal to jump on the safe bandwagon leaves nothing, nothing unsafe, to fall back upon, beyond the dubious praises of rarely inspired laymen.

Inspired laymen tell me that composers today are solving personal, not musical, problems by working toward, not within, an expression. Young musicians, with their overdose of choice, don't know which way to compose. My laymen then lose interest on discovering the composer isn't writing for them, or even for himself, but in order to solve an essentially nonmusical question—intimate and/or mathematical.

Critics, too, today write around rather than about music. But they do write about themselves. The same holds for me. Yet when I reread those first notes-without-music as depicted in that ponderously derivative essay on Morocco which Cecil Smith requested for his *Musical America* back in 1949, I feel the present volume to be a bit more farsighted. Perhaps it's delusion, the fact being, as all my friends know, I've worn glasses for myopia since age thirteen. But better to be shot for an eagle than a mockingbird.

24 June

Four weeks ago today, the outburst with JB, weeks of regretting that the poison's too deep to extract, that no logic could warrant a reconciliation. Today was a Sunday again, steaming with thundershowers. Itching with dehydration, I nevertheless arose, aching, to fetch Eugene at his hotel and then taxi on toward Ward's Island to visit Norris. In that antiseptic penitentiary it was difficult to distinguish visitors from visited, the former being illiterates walleyed with terror at our bureaucracy, the latter being lions docilified with Thorazine, denuded of madness' glamour. Poor Norris, quickly donning the ill-fitting (but clean) clothes I'd brought, asking and asking again when he'd be let out, despite my attempts at diversion by announcing I'd met Myrna Loy in the flesh! Rain started then, the heat exploded, and I returned, depressed, to an AA meeting (for the thousandth time, O Lord?). Alcohol flows like a Xanadu of low-grade fever permanently governing every action and outlook. Tired. Do I drink to avoid the moment? from the wish to attain those notorious "hangover hots," to be able to fuck next day, to take *time out to fuck* (since normally fucking's something to be gotten over before resuming, quickly, work)? As I smoke for the joy of filling and dumping ashtrays, so I drink for the irresponsible dream in which the body is all that matters. (Though I never smoke with a hangover.) I don't like sex, only the idea. Oh, the drinking I don't enjoy, to avoid the life I don't enjoy, to forget the boredom I juvenilely can't accept—then get drunk, I repent, then instead of stopping, I worry, and lament lost love. Then I'll reason that drinking is my way (it is, after all, one solution)—and then drink. No logic or lesson instructs. Those reasonable pages of Updike's on a woman and booze merely precipitate a binge. The difficulty of honesty: it's hard to know honestly if one honestly desires, or could face, honesty. The difficulty of loneliness. Am I honest in hasty music? A meal like last Monday's with Lukas Foss gives me a guilty conscience, though retrospectively I'm bored by his self-justifying gimmicks of musicalizing expounded via diarrhea of the mouth. When I wet the bed, when I damage my body and soul, when I suffer for yesterday and every yesterday. Can I honestly say I long to stop drinking, which, like sex, I don't dig.

Nor do I dig poetry. Surprising in one known mostly for songs? I never read poems for enjoyment (as I do novels) but with the sole motive of finding song texts. Often as not I don't "understand" the verse until long after I've set it.

That final Sunday afternoon at Bard four weeks ago before the rift we took a stroll in woods oozing life, bursting, pulsing, shouting chlorophyll, rocks screeched. Suddenly, there in the hot Hudson hardly flowing a dead bass floated past. Joy stopped. What did that fish mean? How have I felt, behaved since then, indifferent Nature?

Can short pleasure equal long remorse? Are my friends, myself, the world really so boring? Will I appreciate late my childish style?

Is there no other way to look at things? We live within our self-protective circles, and when life proves us false we invent other circles, more or less large, but equally limited. Still, I am not the patient spider (nor its cousin the sexy horseshoe crab), weaving a one-pattern web forever. Prove it? Am I willing to support two wasted days a week? Must every day be exceptional?

Two more old friends have died: Bill Berney from pills and Franz Kline from a heart attack. Death and sex are so confused it's no wonder I mutter, like Chaucer, *je meurs* at climax.

Although I don't dig poetry, I've nonetheless accepted three commissions (wouldn't you?) from the Ford Foundation: besides the opera for Rudel, and an "extended" piano-vocal piece for Regina, a television choral work for Danny Pinkham. Three at once, where am I? The *King Midas* cycle, as John Myers glibly pointed out, was all about money, and you don't write music about money. If only it all could be composed and become the past: but what to do with spare time? On Fire Island three weeks ago Edward Albee and I (while gluttonously eating sunlight) chatted of our old age, rocking together crocheting and crotchety before the crackling grate, grinningly held alive by the miracles of geriatrics but minus gerontophiles, and complaining of our works in Public Domain, writing poor imitations of those triumphs of our heyday, rising on old feet in saddle shoes to perform a rickety Big Apple and just never dying.

8 July

Late Sunday afternoon, a muggy 100°. Next Friday the thirteenth I fly to California. The "geographical cure" may work. No more vows.

Robert Phelps says that Glenway Westcott says that what I say sex-wise here isn't enough—that a man's bite should exceed his tongue, or what's a journal for? Which do I fear more: police or parents? The former hurt me as I hurt the latter. Letters and plays compromise more fatally than novels or sonatas. Yes I'm shy, though nobody ever believes it. Recovered, achieved, relapsed, and learned despite all. If shy, I too heard Hofmann play and shook hands with Faulkner who died yesterday overrated. Marilyn Monroe is also shy.

She was not this year at the Arts and Letters festivities, but she was in '59 when, in the cocktailed patio, Marianne Moore and Saul Bellow and Robert Frost and seventy other of America's dignitaries ignored each other and climbed on statues to catch a glimpse of that shy blond one.

Sans date

Being in love precludes knowing about being in love. Conversely, a critic of music may often resemble the man who, never having known love, becomes a marriage counselor. Filled with sensible advice and wise dissection, he still never quite puts his interpretive finger on the exquisite malady's sore spot. Because there is no interpretation of love (though there may be successful formulas for marriage). By the same token, inasmuch as a great piece resists analysis, opinions about (even physical reactions to) it are worthless. Masterworks can't be taken apart like watchworks; what happens within them is what happens, that is all; not what a musicologist tells us happens. Meditation more than analysis will take us toward the heart of music, but to reach that heart is paradoxically to kill it.

How long does love last? As long as anything lasts—a lifetime.

Once I thought of beauty and greatness as absolutes. No longer. A musicologist may "prove" Beethoven to be greater than Debussy, yet to me Beethoven sounds outmoded. Am I not the final judge? But let's concede he's greater than Debussy—he remains less great than Ravel.

Kids today can't take Beethoven as a master because they don't think in terms of masterpieces.

A composer learns nothing about himself from thoughtfully comprehensive studies describing creative phenomena. Even Tovey and Langer end at that crucial point at which the composer begins. Probably long after we've uncovered the very secret of life and the source of our universe, the puzzles of the "artistic process" will still be with us.

7 October

Recall of Los Angeles. The evening after she died I was taken to dine at George Cukor's, and the whole recollection is colored by that meal: mediocrities swallowing, belching, digesting the bland American foods, while a few blocks away Marilyn Monroe lay with her heart stopped. Hard-boiled Hollywood guests, cold Cukor speaking of her as a "dizzy cunt." But whom hasn't she haunted daily since? Summer of death I could not write upon because my hand ached from opera-composing and copy. Today spontaneity's gone and I can just piece the recipe together from notes. (Thumb's still numb, still flattened from the bloody accident seventeen months ago.) Yet I loved the West, the casual friendliness of a Spanish colony with indirect lighting. Meanwhile in the East friends died: living, living Jane Romano's quality gone, humor forever smothered, the same hours as Marilyn, Irving Fine, young Roger Nimier, while the old live on. But yes, the old too: Dinesen and Cummings, and even sweet rich Arturo Lopez—or so Barbette (Barbette!) told me at a La Cienega vernissage. California is the state where you hear of deaths elsewhere, a summer state which gossips of others' winters, a place so buzzing, oozing with chlorophyll, living, living, that these ironies strike fiercer. Only four clear seasons can show us how time passes. Now I'm back in New York and it's cold.

California Memories and Notes:

A drunk has as many binges in him as a soprano has high Cs. In the West Coast climate they are less ravaging.

Similarity between a hangover and the end effects of psilocybin. The first of eighteen California binges began (chez Charles Aufderheide) after eighteen sober days, and began mescalinianly. With that first amber drop my Other Eyes saw me *as I would be,* across a room.

Today in the East I have for two weeks been on Antabuse. For the first time, sanity without anguish: because the pill, not me, makes the decisions. Sobriety permits more carefully the delineation of *la fuite du temps.* For with periodic binges (unlike seasons) time stops. I explained to Christopher Isherwood how, last February, time had stopped. I likened it to the painful length of suicide: the underwater battle between the living carnal and dying rational selves of someone overdosed with sedatives; the lifetime that flashes between the detonation and the bullet's penetration. So, time being a trickster, if one jumped off the Empire State, Christopher surmised Britishly: "My! You'd quite die of boredom before hitting the ground."

In California the whiff of a rose brings back Rochas' cologne, just as Spain reminds one of Falla's music (never the contrary).

With Antabuse, am I then (still) *playing* at being alive? Drunk I react only to the unexpected, which is to say I never react, yet horrors occur. Despite the literal-minded. "Will you marry me when I grow up?" was my theme in California—or so said Jack Larson and Jim Bridges with whom I fell jointly in love as the other summer with Attilio Labis and Claude Bessy in Provence.

Growing up. What first stunned me about it was less the contradiction between what we'd learned in Sunday School and "what life was really like," than that geniuses and janitors become the same fool during love affairs.

It is pleasant to recall the almost daily lunches with Colin McPhee there at the Huntington Hartford Foundation, amid invisible rattlesnakes, and playing his records as we munched our cold chicken.

General discussion on how John Rechy should title his new book. "How about *The Four Hundred Blows*?" says someone. Another suggests *Somebody Down There Loves Me*.

New York's trees are growing bare, their leaves so scarce you can count them at a glance. Maggy, to celebrate the autumn, has given me a jar of her raspberry jelly. Tomorrow I'll buy croissants at the new bakery on Sixth Avenue. In two weeks I'll be thirty-nine.

10 October

Wyatt Cooper requests: who are the three most famous people you've slept with? Without hesitation I reply.

Dress rehearsal this afternoon of Carlisle Floyd's *Passion of Jonathan Wade*, to be premiered tomorrow. He is an unpretentious and good boy—yet how could I wish him well, since his and mine are the only new works this winter at City Center? At least his is. Mine seems to have been stillborn in California and no one knows quite what to do with the corpse.

At four went to Virgil's for a *New Music Editions* editorial meeting (sterile) with Henry Cowell and Frank Wigglesworth. Virgil offered lemonade and cookies and then (it being the kind of autumn only New York can provide) I walked home to meet Father. A good calm talk. We dined at the Waverly, because despite my years in the highest homes of France, my sole dream is of old-maid American cooking. And whom should we meet there? Virgil. So the three of us sat together as we did once eighteen years ago at the Waldorf. Afterward I took Father to see Kenward Elmslie's house on Cornelia Street, then Kenward took me to a party on 9th Street where everyone was twisting and I knew nobody except the Gruens, so, being on Antabuse, left after twenty minutes; bought grapes, oranges, coffee, Jello, yogurt on Sixth Avenue, walked home slowly (someone was following my black T-shirt). So here I write: that was a sober Wednesday without work, and procrastination is thus more drastic since the industrial fever that comes between hangovers may ultimately accomplish more. For the moment, I want to live without climax, without contrast, with boredom and a steady schedule. So little time, so much doubt about the opera which looms, and how many hundreds of pages to orchestrate? Yet my next days will be similar: tomorrow Floyd's opera; Friday *dîner* chez Tourel; Saturday Edward's opening; Sunday Judith Malina at the Living Theater. Judith!

At a party one year ago, I amicably puff smoke down Judith's throat whispering of prolonged abstinence from women, please come over tomorrow at five. Next day while on the phone with Joe LeSueur I'm jarred by the doorbell, and who, forgotten, should slowly mount the stairs (flaming wig piled high and lacquered) but Judith, sure enough. I must think fast, though hung over, so as she lights a reefer I say: But don't you get a confused time-sense? No, she answers, because I've learned that three hours for me is twelve minutes for you all. *I have adjusted!* I reply: but I haven't; what I whispered yesterday I'm unprepared for this afternoon. She: but Ned, I'd always thought you a sophisticated bitch, find you now innocent; how we never know! With that she pulls from her wallet my photo which it seems she's carried for years, a picture from my sixteen years when at Northwestern. I sat in the front row for a lecture of Thomas Mann hoping he would see me and be defeated like Aschenbach. (He never looked!) So forlorn, Judith's hopes broken break my heart—but I only take her out for a cup of tea and she leans her head back and closes eyes. While she dozes I am free to think of today, and what do I do about things?

23 October

Eventually I'll look back at thirty-nine as young. Today it's traumatic.

27 October
Saturday night (3 A.M.)

Une actualité, before (unhopefully, romantically) the world stops. On Tuesday, my birthday, started Cuban war threats. For forty-eight hours each moment seemed sacred, the air (our last breathing) turned to cashmere, the smell of the final bread was unique, a glimpsed smile grew into a treasure of the perpetual Now. Then Bertrand Russell eased us, again we became blasé: smiles, bread, breathing were once more dispensable. But tonight the fall is here, set clocks back an hour, tension reappears (we will invade Cuba), yet that tension is passive and passionless. Unhopefully, romantically we all ask: What trick or privilege placed me, *me,* the center of the earth, on Earth today when Earth finally dies? For whom then do I write these words? How soon might this page be radioactive? Will the wind blow tomorrow? Next year? In a century will it blow across a human face?

17 November

Father's sixty-seventh birthday.

Discouraged by rejections from small recording companies, Thursday on a wild chance I presented myself at Columbia Records. Schuyler Chapin said: "Describe your dream." My dream is to record as many songs as make a good cross-section of my total output, with four or five terrific singers, accompanied by me. Schuyler Chapin said, "Your dream shall come true." I love him forever.

Drove up last evening with Bob Holton toward a blaze of Indian summer—as only in America. Panic before winter of work, paralyzed, wasting time with a diary.

The older I grow the more, as Jane Bowles would say, I enjoy the simple pleasures, immediate fragrances, immediate silences, ice cream, the calm of sleep.

Meanwhile, libretto problems, endless revision. Rudel, Kessler, Ball and I don't see eye to eye. May postpone till next fall.

Lee left Willa Cather's stories on the bed table, so I read *The Enchanted Bluff*, delicious. It's about people's postponement of fantasy, or grown-up procrastination about childish things in favor of Madison Avenue. What do I regret?

5 December

Déprimé. L'envie de pleurer. Nulle raison. Ou plutôt la raison habituelle.

28 December

Tears for what? Well, for W, of course, who for fifty-two days has occupied my sober thoughts. Terms are never satisfied because no one can enter another's mind. So I shall "break it off" during intermission tomorrow at *Ariadne*, along the red velvet of Sherry's lounge. *Ariadne*, which features Gianna d'Angelo, "the Shirley Temple of coloraturas," who is featured on my song record, as will be Eileen Farrell who, when I asked her if she *divulged* her phone number, answered, "Sorry darling, I do."

30 December

Production canceled. But Rudel has convinced the Ford Foundation to extend my grant. So I start again *à zéro*. With what? *Brief Encounter*? *Shanghai Gesture*? *Frankenstein*? *Nightwood*? *The*

Children's Hour? I'm sick of opera prospects and want to get into other regions, away from the human voice. If I died today it would not really be—well, *incorrect.* Now, in the shadow of forty, looking back, I've obtained the best of all I've sought, and produced of myself (through fever, shame, terror, dignity) an artist and a person—not perhaps to other eyes which see shreds, but to myself at least. What remains between this moment and my death? For though I announce that my advancing age prefers the urgencies of pure nature to urban ambitions, it is a lie. Where and what can I go or do that I've not gone and done better? Henceforth I see only declined flesh inanely coupling with reason, sputtering, a dimming of commitment, a pointless ending, a silence which is not even silence. Yet to kill myself now would be less from not caring as from a certain sadness which after all I suppose *is* caring.

1963

Ma douce Jouvence est passée,
Ma première force est cassée . . .

—Ronsard

Not that a love affair failed again, but that love failed. No matter how I insist that work's the only faithful friend, tears streak the stupid staves. Earlier this windy evening after leaving James Purdy's in Brooklyn I detoured to Pierrepont Street and looked up at W's window. A light shone, but no shadows moved: I felt cold. (Antonioni, in depicting such cold, becomes the most interesting artist today.) Yet it's less for W I die than for them all.

The maddest torture is noise (for musical ears), but the subtlest is silence (for janitor hearts).

As a dispassionate experiment in order, am making a list—in French and in code, times being what they are—accounting for my sexuality during the year 1963. Dreams, desires, fruitless cruising will not be included, just cold facts, *des actes accomplis*. At the generous underestimation of two a week, or 104 a year, there've been just over two thousand different people in the past twenty years. This excludes *les rencontres des bains de vapeurs*, four per visit at an average of once a week. Including, then, masturbation— averaging twice per week since age fourteen—I've had 4,212 orgasms. (Yet when I'm affiliated I'm the most faithful of lovers.) When the year ends we'll see how this appraisal tallies with statistics.

The goatherd misled. Anteroom. Molester. Night Candy. Afternoon Candy.

Undoubtedly most of my life will have been spent alone, but though I am unusually impelled to "be seen," to "leave an impact," to disperse parts of myself (hair, ideas, fingernails, face, sperm, loveliness and uncharitability) in shunning anonymity's terrors, nevertheless I treasure talent for solitude as luxury, higher even than those best years passed in instructive exchange on the soft *canapés chez la Vicomtesse de Noailles,* seven years with the wrong kind of woman.

29 January

There being a strong possibility that Farrell will be on my song record, I went at dawn to a rehearsal at her sunny Staten Island home. I hardly know her except as America's grandest soprano, as spouse of an Irish cop, and as devout Roman Catholic.

Her approach to my songs is engrossing. Like many a last-generation diva she excels at rote more than at solfège. As her accompanist plunks out the vocal line, Eileen grasps the notes independently of the text which she replaces with such personal phonetics as "Fuck your sister and your brother/ Fuck your father and your mother." Well, my vocabulary contains these words too, but I'm startled to hear the melodies with verbal substitutes.

My sweetest surprise comes when she is about to interpret *The Lord's Prayer,* her favorite of my settings. "My dear" (she speaks in hushed tones), "it's one *heck* of a hard song."

Philadelphia
30 January

Here with Valerie Bettis, for the local premiere of our ballet *Early Voyagers* tonight at the Academy of Music.

Francis Poulenc has died. It was Rosemary who, without warning, read me his obituary in *The Inquirer,* and my heart sank. How little time is left? And who is left?

13 February

That which I don't include in this journal seems the most urgent, yet that's wanting it both ways. My stamina *is* admirable, what with the amount of sociability piled upon the amount of necessary conferences (are conferences ever necessary?) piled upon the only thing that makes a difference, music, which at least figures on the bottom of the pile rather than on top like the reject of a gang bang. *The Village Voice* has asked for a souvenir-portrait of Poulenc, which I've compiled between "takes" at the Columbia studios, the song disk being well on its way, under the charming guidance of A&R man Paul Myers. Norman Twain wants music for his production of Dumas; Terrence McNalley has a new play; Shirley's husband George Rhoads has a vernissage; exquisite Gloria Vanderbilt, to whom Wyatt Cooper's introduced me, gives parties I can't resist (could you?), although I'm ill from Antabuse and supposed to be making an opera. . . . Herbert Rogers premiered my *Third Piano Sonata* in Town Hall last week: I didn't attend, because although Rogers is excellent the sonata is not. Weekend in Boston where Danny Pinkham beautifully recorded my *Two Psalms and a Proverb*. Exhibition of John Button and of Rosemarie Beck, my two favorite painters; and Bill Inge's new play, *Natural Affection*, attended pleasurably with Jane Harrison. This entry, only too typical of, with endless omissions—what do you, don't you, omit?—is addled—not really addled, apparently addled. . . .

3 April

Overworked and underpaid again these past five weeks composing for the opportunistic *Lady of the Camellias*. Forty minutes of well-planned original music has been slaughtered, artlessly dismembered, made inaudible so as not to obliterate the Strasberg girl's babble, she whom I'm required to tutor (though it's not in the contract) in the ABC's of song. Zeffirelli is overestimated, being at best a *stylish* director: what, after all, has he ever sought out, "created," encouraged that's important or timely—what chances does he take? As for the producers: is all the piglike-agent-Broadway-bickering even vaguely near what in the heart I hope for? At these moments I admire Paul Bowles' quick return to Araby. I swear off; but "when I awake I will seek it yet again." That boozy phrase *par contre* gave me the joy that Jennie Tourel will give next Tuesday (when after waiting seventeen years she'll sing *Bedlam*), as I heard the Pinkham chorus perform my *Two Psalms and a Proverb* last month in nice Boston. Which counterbalances a composer's horrors.

(P.S. Miss Strasberg could be classified as profoundly untalented.)

The play—fortunately for it, unfortunately for me—closed last week after four sorry performances. I was not asked to the opening night party.

23 April

I've moved again: right next to my home of the forties (285 West 12th Street) and nothing's changed but me. Last night on Sixth Avenue a very young man asked, "Where's Greenwich Village?" (he was in it), and I remembered twenty years ago on weekends from Curtis my same wondered question. Today the magic's gone, or different, with nine sunny windows at $150 a month, when at 285 I paid $25.

Perhaps, after all, this diary (like the scrapbooks) no longer interests me because I'm no longer anonymous: because (such as it is) I've achieved a stature, so no longer need to invent, no longer *need* to write here, even though I feel even more acutely the approach to the end. Yet words or keepsakes or letters mean more than actual experience. When I experience—allow—enjoyment it is only, in a sense, a storing up of future reference. Agee felt his letters were insufficient and wrote good ones. I prefer letters to flesh, but write bad ones.

People are more or less the same; I invent enthusiasm, play at having fun. Childishly I ask do people bore me, or I them? I've had (childishly) the joy of hurting people, people who'd taken scented baths in anticipation of what never materialized.

Boredom and Sex. Everyone knows achievement seldom equals anticipation. During the act I'm often (not bored really, but) preoccupied with other things, a song, a laundry bill. Having no regular lover it's seldom now I arrive at that self-forgetting idiot-babbling state of Good Sex. Sometimes during a hangover when all concentration is on the body, during a hangover when I feel so fevered. The lays I've been cheated of, being drunk! Could this have been otherwise? Sex and Perversity. Desire for a person can be so strong that the fantasy image remains constant for years. When, in reality, I finally sleep with that person, I require the former image to excite me. Perversity and the Past. I used to take my own breath away. . . . Have been sleeping well and rarely have colds.

I will give up Antabuse. Who knows? Like Thalidomide it may later produce babies with fins.

I suspect all of my friends of insanity. Some I am sure of. Insanity means being unaware of insanity.

Perfect sex is best found in chance encounters. Fallacy: that promiscuity is due to dissatisfaction, to a seeking for the (impossible) ideal partner. On the contrary, perfect sex is so easy (in the anonymous meeting) that afterward there's nothing more; once an intellectual give-and-take is assumed, the sex is depreciated. Hence *the satisfaction of promiscuity.*

26 April

Do I say different things to different people? Is that only different ways of speaking to myself? Do I exist, indeed? Am I even what others think I am? Have I my own opinions? Has anyone? Do I just parrot? Despite lamentations through the years, do I really not care? Because God knows I want aggressively to live. Someone should tell pop singers that if you must use mannerisms use them with a reason. Billie knew most of the time, and Sinatra some of the time. But the others: *oh là!* When Sinatra is "wrong" it's still his *way* of wrong. (A dog accosts me. If animals have no empathy, as Michaux says, why do they always come to me who don't like them instead of to those who do?) Depressed. Have taken Stelazine.

29 April

Ten days ago: gave housewarming for eighty people. The vanity-assuaging didn't equal the effort and expense.

Ruth Kligman tells of the famous auto wreck. It's easy (feminine hindsight) to say that afternoon was fraught with premonition. Nevertheless, at 10 P.M. she "came to" on the black grass and a few yards away lay Pollock dead among the searchlights.

Today, an aching cold. Have finished Regina's cycle and now am bored to tears. The coming weeks look to be more of the same. The same could be said, no doubt, were I sitting in Bali.

So-called dynamic women are more memorable than dynamic men (like John Latouche, Jean Cocteau or Lenny Bernstein) because such women are *monstrueuses.*

No time left. Depression is the same for all: what have we done or do we do that makes a difference? how can we learn to know we're alive now? or is that learned, or rather unlearned? A pigeon on my window stared at me half the afternoon, asking himself (probably) none of these questions. It's snowing lightly. Three weeks of premature springtime have stopped.

30 April

Brigid Brophy characterizes herself as a "religious irreligionist," just as my father used to refer to a "militant pacifist." My father whom I love. But in the educated sixties we Americans learn more and more that fathers are hated, mothers voracious, this country's unweened, alcoholics sublimate, nonalcoholics sublimate, that one fucks only to avoid being fucked, etc. Quite simply, I had a happy childhood and I like my family. Still, one ends up believing those intelligent bromides because they're repeated so often.

Yet take a look at such French ladies as Ninon Tallon or Colette de Jouvenal, next to whom the American editress or female agent becomes a recoiling Red Riding Hood. We hit upon a pretty generality, then force it into an equally pretty preconception. Paul Goodman is guilty of this. I hate myself for accepting someone's clever demolition of another (Partisan Reviewers), accepting from envy, because I am not "as good." My own denigration of, say, Albert Schweitzer is opposite: he just is not "as good" as his glorifiers make him, whereas Paul is not as bad as his detractors make him.

Monday after Easter and beautiful. Am between works, awaiting Kenward's libretto. Have only now to write two songs at $200 each for Anne Ayer. The weather resembles twelve years back when Heddy and I would drink rosé all afternoon and wind up at 4 A.M. playing *Daphnis et Chloé* on the piano at the Boeuf sur le Toit. I love my new place. As for society, I'm now able to offer little suppers—which degenerate into expensive orgies—*et je tiens à mes amis tant bien que mal.*

May Day

Cafard. Toujours la même raison.

11 May

Numb, low, thoughts of suicide.

14 May

Very depressed. Nothing helps.

15 May

Death is the end of illusions. Or could it be the ultimate illusion, the great rewarding illusion when we thought there'd never be another?

21 May

Edward Albee stops by in the afternoon to leave tickets for the huge Varèse dinner this evening. He interrupts the composition of a Salvation Army song for Purdy's play. We chat. His parting remark is worthy of Noël Coward disguised as Jane Austen: "Finish your hymn now, and I'll see you tonight at the Plaza."

3 June

Sobriety as a spider web, as carefully made, as perishable, a slight breeze, one torn strand, the house collapses.

In my spacious kitchen, I now cook. Orchestrally. Like marriage, this is playing at being grown up. It's raining, and Shirley sits in the other room considering divorce. Are we ever really old enough to have children? I'm not a man myself yet, yet more than half our life is gone. In that room friends sat laughing last year who today are dead, Jane Romano, Clair Leonard; and who nameless in the night, that I'll never see again? Jane Wilson: I'll tell my age, but not how much I smoke.

Bastille Day

Last night, defeated after seeing Fellini's *8½* I heard again the recorded *War Requiem* of Britten, and what am I but a midget! This morning in the bathroom mirror I found my first gray hair.

Another heat wave.

Am composing backgrounds to the Purdy stories which open in September.

8 July

Last week in Philadelphia (where little Paul had his fifth birthday) I realized that as I increase in age I grow less sad, sadness being a "thing" of the young. In spite of these schmaltzy diaries my life has been, well, *good,* I suppose, and certainly busy, nor do I want to die, having enough projects *en tête* to last three hundred years. Again, over the early July holidays I went to Bill Flanagan's at Fire Island Pines, the subject being the inconceivability of our deaths. My first "scrape" with death was during second grade when in that vacant lot we saw the disemboweled horse unburied. My major allergy is to horses, serum, proximity, meat. Then in Sunday School I learned to love neighbors and believe in the goodness of grown-ups. How do we accept so simply the contradictory headlines? Any calamity caused by thinking of neighbors as numbers?

21 July

For years at all hours on the west side of Sixth between Greenwich and Waverly, there has been an accumulation of drugstore cowgirls who just hang around. Last night one grabbed her friend and threw her headfirst through Prexy's window. The friend was killed. To be alive, then next minute dead against a hamburger-bar is more sordid than any liquor-bar stabbing. Male homosexuals don't act that way: not because they are too witty but because those with stamina just don't *care* enough while others (when not committing suicide) resort to tongue-lashings or, in a pinch, weapons like telephones or cut-glass vases, never plate-glass windows. Tomorrow we record the music for *Color of Darkness.*

Bridgehampton
28 July

Here for a weekend chez Stella Adler surrounded by those young Hampton couples, superior artists, prettiest of ladies, all *au fond* as *bourgeois* as the *milieu* of Peter De Vries: *les ménages* Oppenheim, Gruen, Matthews, Rivers, Foss, Hazan and Koch. Gravel courtyards, like Poulenc's at Noizay. . . .

(I never know quite what Stella is talking about, but it always appears perfectly sensical, like Chopin's *Barcarolle.*)

4 August

In the morning, a bus again for Yaddo. Mother and Father will move in as I leave. Earlier this evening we attended *The Second City* after which I walked them back to the Quaker hostel near strange Stuyvesant Square, then returned home slowly without glasses (since I'll be a hermit for eight weeks, it seemed I should cruise; but I didn't). Meanwhile I'm alone in the kitchen with the summer night wind creating a solemn cross-ventilation over a dish of blueberries and skim milk that I consume with three Pepperidge devil's food cookies and a gleamy glass of soda. Theodore Roethke has dropped dead in a Seattle swimming pool. Is no one immune? Who will write my songs now? and those others he'll never hear?

We dined at the new Keneret, a second-story outdoor Syrian rendezvous on the corner of Seventh and Bleecker which recalls that restaurant near the entrance of Rabat's *médina.* New York increasingly resembles Morocco. Days when the sun beats and eating meat is out of the question (especially the meat of Greenwich Avenue) I turn my nervous promenades westward instead where just two blocks away are the foreign piazzas of Little West 12th, Gansevoort Street, then lower Chelsea and that unknown marvel of 21st beginning at Ninth Avenue and ending at a church (*toujours vide*) conducted to the glory of our stevedores. How inviolably sweet is Manhattan in the hours before we quit it!

Self-doubts increase with the days. In this period of low ebb for all art, at least I'm still writing *music*. Yet with little incentive. In two months I will be forty and my glamorous past is already offered up for today's children who aren't even obstreperous. Meanwhile like a plodding turtle I'm composing away, walking through the woods, not drinking, but smoking thirty-five cancer-causing cigarettes a day, and exercising fairly regularly, for whom? in this celibate valley.

René Bouché has died, and Odets (heart and cancer). Yaddo rhymes with Prado. The mascot here is a female dog named Ralph. Very cold weather.

28 August

Because I have no income, and Elizabeth Ames knows it, she has offered me a token allowance of $65 a month for a year—and I've accepted. At her ripe age she remains more stimulating, more *aware*, than anyone here, and I look forward to the generously inhibiting Quaker Sundays in her company.

This morning Leon Fleisher's recording of my *Barcarolles* finally arrived. But as though God wished to dampen the pleasure, I found in today's *Times* a spacious picture of Bill and Edward posing to announce their *Ice Age* for City Center. My heart sank in envious panic, not so much at Edward's celebrity (we're used to that) nor at Bill's overdue and official "arrival" at forty, as at the premonition that this—this *rise*, signified, for me, a descent. I've grown "to be out of fashion like an old song"—and *my* opera is far from announced. Yet I must continue joylessly to compose: what else can I do. Have felt unquiet the whole day.

29 August

In default of a libretto for eight months, I've begun here two works, *Lions* and *Whales* to accompany *Eagles*, in neither of which I have the remotest confidence. They're all color without content, and oh, how vastly hard are always those first days of launching into something big when not even the skeleton can yet be perceived. Without work as a guide, I am, in music, not only a cheat but a loss. *The discouragement of any beginning.*

How I hate Berlioz! Beethoven I don't "like" (i.e., need), but I appreciate his power and understand his genius, whereas in Berlioz I cannot even objectively find what others find. Therefore, in inverse ratio to his overratedness I must deny him, as I deny Dr. Schweitzer.

As always, when routine is imposed and far from sexuality, the days blur anonymously together, distinguishable only by changes of weather, occasionally a Scrabble game as climax. In the calm country one dies less conspicuously than elsewhere, for how can you read your own age in the mirror of daily faces? Last evening, to alter the pace I sat alone at the marvelous Steinway in the mansion parlor playing those Debussy *Préludes* I've known (and faked) for a quarter century. When I stopped, the room was filled with silent people, entranced (so they said) and appreciative. It truly never occurs to me that my pianism gives pleasure to others than me (there's seldom an opportunity), nor do I quite realize that others cannot play for their own pleasure. Yet if my "touch" is satisfaction, communicative, it's because I lack *the technique which stands between performer and audience.*

30 August

To assuage my jealousy, this morning I ran across this in Camus (*"L'Artiste et son temps"*):

> *Tout artiste qui se mêle de vouloir être célèbre dans notre société doit savoir que ce n'est pas lui qui le sera, mais quelqu'un d'autre sous son nom, qui finira par lui échapper et peut-être, un jour, par tuer en lui le véritable artiste.*

Art, sorrow and beauty are perhaps useless, but no more so than the earth itself. What is useful? Useful for what?

Labor Day

Should I feel guilty at the ease with which certain music (exclusively vocal) comes to me? I am thinking most recently of the song *Poulenc* (on the gentle poem Frank O'Hara made for me and Alice Esty) and of *The Ascension* for brass and chorus which I'm now copying for Paul Callaway's cathedral. Both were composed *d'un seul coup* without censorship or revision: my first ideas were notated unchanged. Yet such efforts have usually turned out more purposeful than my labored (i.e., structured and "thoughtful") instrumental pieces.

12 September

Shortly after writing the preceding words twelve days ago, I shattered my right ankle in a bicycle smashup. That morning at breakfast, it being Labor Day and many friends returning to New York, I admonished those taking the highways to be careful: on holidays wrecks occur in the afternoon. At exactly 3 P.M. I had my pointless accident. At the emergency ward my foot, the size of a football, was cemented into a cast which I still drag like a millstone. I was given crutches and a heady dose of codeine. Hysterical pain. Next morning, drugged and sodden with nightmares, I was in the ideal state to read the letter delivered from Paul Bowles in Asilah. It did not contain the hoped-for libretto about which we've been corresponding. Rather, it was the report of an LSD trip which makes my own seem childish; and again I am in admiration before that cool, original mind which, unknown to it, has so influenced me for ten years and which *functions for itself.*

14 September

These journals do not solve, or even pose, pertinent problems. Though I often complain at a quotation out of context in a paper (how easily one is misrepresented), I've come to believe that my whole biography *could* be put fairly into twenty pages. Like sopranos who are graduated from the role of Sophie to that of the Marschallin, we all play musical chairs. This morning I received from Cocteau the design I'd requested as cover for my Elizabeth Bishop song. The drawing itself sparkles with his habitual youth (he features Ezra Pound more than me, and spells "Elisabeth" *à la française*), like his other cover a dozen years ago. But the handwriting of his accompanying note is disturbing. Back in the

'40s—was it in *Maalesh?*—he spoke of having received a letter from old Gide whose *écriture* troubled him. (Indeed, the only letter I ever had from the ailing octogenarian, in 1949, ended: *Je n'ai plus la force que de vous serrer la main en pensée.*) And now it's my turn to say the same of Jean's famous orthography twistedly inscribing: *Avec la tendresse fidèle d'un pauvre malade dont la convalescence sera très longue et très lourde.*

15 September

In certain rooms of the hemisphere, as in all cloisters, I am at peace and at home. The hexagonal *salon du rez-de-chaussée* chez Marie Laure for one, and for another this long pink chamber here at Yaddo. Light decides. Already the day ends early and by six the room drips with suave September russet sent through the red red leaves. The hour for reading.

Yesterday, Friday the thirteenth, my cast was removed, revealing the maimed extremity which, depending on how you view it, looks monstrous or splendid. Swollen like a python, the skin's over the ankle tight as tanned marble which hemorrhage has laced with lilac veins, and stains of jet and deep cobalt. The foot aches awfully. But I must apparently hurt myself.

Everyone's gone, and for a few days I'm alone, poor cripple, in this far room on the second floor from which regularly at 4 A.M. I hear chains dragging up the stairs, approaching as far as the locked door, then crumbling with a whimper. Without glasses I see myself in the mirror across the room, texture and pale yellow hue of tapioca, sweat and no exercise for weeks now.

16 September

Am I too literary for a musician? At work on a piece of any length I'm distracted before it's half written. To see the bridge's other side eliminates the need for arriving there. I'm too logical. Yet I *réussis* short songs best, which is illogical, song specialists (dealers by definition in poetry) being the least intellectual of composers.

Manlio Miserocchi has mailed his new novel *Mala vita* among the last pages of which I figure as a drunk American at Bestiqui's

Venice ball in 1951. (—*Mi chiamo Ned Forem* [sic] *e diventero un grande musicista americano. Ma adesso voglio dormire.*) Manlio I've always despised: perhaps indeed he's cultured and suffers, but without charm, like a scorpion on fire. Too charmless to know he's despised, he features me in his book.

26 September

Early, sunny, cool. During the day Kenward will come to drive me and my crutches back to New York. Despite the broken foot there've been a good seven weeks: Composed and orchestrated sixteen minutes of music, read thirty good books, made seven new friends, wrote two hundred letters, mostly to the family, and "communed" with nature. Who today recalls Claudia Muzio's record of *Beau Soir*? In *Lions* I incorporated the blues tune from the Purdy plays, not being one to let a good thing fade. This is the program note:

> Twenty years ago, one morning after a dream, I wrote a poem called "Lions." That poem is lost but the dream remains clearly still. It opens into a room of adolescence where I discovered music, the sound of my time before that of the past. (In such a room—ignorant of Bach, Chopin, even Tchaikovsky—I used to hear recorded screams of Varèse and Milhaud, tangos of Ravel and Stravinsky, blues of Mildred Bailey and Billie Holiday.) Now that room grows vast as a cathedral, strangely cheerful, agreeably foreboding. I reenter there, nervous, obsessed; the old blues disks are turning again. Somewhere in the night a clock strikes three. Drawn toward the closet door, I open it and behold! on the dark little floor a litter of lion cubs purrs, furry-gold and rolling. Watching them, I want to play. And do. . . . But their parents must be near! Indeed, I turn to see the male's head, great, the King framed by a sunburst halo, a desert, approaches, roars. Terror is joyous, the yellow light too much, I am swallowed, drowned in fire, in the mane, a peaceful martyr. In the howling elation I die, and dying, am aware of purrs, of blues receding, innocence dimmed, hearing the force of an obsession like motors under water miles away.

Today I reconstruct the forgotten poem in orchestration.

Next year I must compose about the Sun.

Not the least effective element of *Color of Darkness*, which opened
Monday at the Fourth Street Theater, is the music which plays
almost constantly, even during intermission when the taped saxo-
phone wails into the washrooms reminding me now more of *Lions*
than of James Purdy. Gloria Vanderbilt was my "date," a fact duly
noted in the newspaper which neglected to mention my artistic
contribution to the production.

Last night the Rémys came to dine, with Shirley and Marc
Blitzstein. Marc gets pugnacious after two drinks, interpreting
virtually any remark by anyone as either approbation of or a threat
to some dream version of the common man who hasn't existed in
thirty years. But the Rémys were bewitched, having never encountered this particular breed of American, probably because Marc is a
breed of one, who, like John Latouche in the old days, when on his
best behavior, is the most irresistibly quick man in the world.

15 October

At Rouben Ter-Arutunian's this evening: the first collective informal conference for *The Milk Train* during which, inspired by
Rouben's maquettes, we were all meant to separate into pairs or
threesomes and discuss Art with our prospective colleagues. But
from the moment Tallulah Bankhead arrived on the arms of two
youngish gentlemen (and looking so surprisingly short as to seem
stunted, like a gorgeous rat), she began so ceaseless a flow of non
sequiturs that all sensible exchange was precluded.

My Columbia record is well under way. The singers are Phyllis
Curtin, Donald Gramm, Charles Bressler, Regina Sarfaty, and
Gianna d'Angelo. Me at the piano, cover by Bob Cato, liner notes
by Bill Flanagan.

22 October

Antabuse daily. Daily (unneeded) conferences with Tony Richardson.

Began music for *Milk Train*.

Cocktail this evening at James Lord's. Dined later at Glenway Wescott's with Truman Capote in whose mouth reality becomes the verity of Scheherazade as we listen rapt to his tales of research on two assassins, now awaiting capital punishment in Kansas.

23 October

Fortieth birthday. I can no longer die young.

Party last night at Kenward's with my credentials in crystal paper cutouts festooning the walls, and records of the Supremes as background to our wit.

One indication that a thing may be good or "real" is that we become acquisitive, preemptive: we don't like people we don't like to like it, we want it for ourselves (and maybe certain friends) alone. This applies to literature somewhat, but mostly to music of "both sorts." It was true of the taste for Dostoevsky, Artie Shaw and Prokofiev in the thirties; for Kierkegaard, Billie Holiday and Berg in the forties; for Genet, Gerry Mulligan and Ives in the fifties; McLuhan, Joan Baez and Wolpe today. It defines In, Out having been let loose to the masses. When he whom we disdain loves our loves, those loves fall Out.

The point is relevant, though the examples may not be.

To criticize an example is irrelevant, since it belittles taste rather than challenging conception. To say that so-and-so's example of a said point is okay but incomplete shows only what *we* would have given as example of that point, not the flaw in the point itself.

5 November

Since returning from Yaddo I have been rather even-keeled. Certainly I don't accomplish more than previously, and the smooth days fly on more irretrievably than when punctuated with hangovers. But at forty with death in mind, it seems a duty to examine clearheadedly the anatomy of tedium. At Bruce's three weeks ago Eve Auchincloss' liqueur ingestion triggered me despite an Antabuse thirty-six hours previous: I had a purple heart attack and died while conversing bolt upright. Since then my nights have passed in sober tête-à-têtes with old friends (Virgil, Marc B., Morris, of course), new ones (should I speak yet of Harold Brodkey?) culminating in Kenward's party uniting them all with their worthy birthday gifts such as the mere fact of this age deserves.

The Milk Train Doesn't Stop Here Anymore adds up to little more than a sonnet's first line; but Tony Richardson seems a civilized (for an Englishman) collaborator, though what's in it for me, besides a little money, when I'd rather concentrate on a piece to be remembered when I'm . . .

Augy Sauer is dead, and poor Frank Merlo, both my age, and both having shifted the world's weight. Cocteau has died, and little Piaf, both leaving France lighter, but without light: *les pertes noires*. My Cocteau epitaph appeared in *The Village Voice* last week, with minimal reaction, and that quite stupid. So ever present was he, with effervescent letters and eternally loud despair, that it seems impossible our last meeting was so long ago. It would have been June of 1957, at Hervé Dugardin's after the Paris opening of Poulenc's opera. We talked of *The Poets' Requiem*, performed by Margaret Hillis earlier that year, and featuring a large chunk of Jean himself dressed in my music. I remember him that night as subdued, standing, standing constantly, with Dermit at his side, not talking much, the rooms high and stony, a table covered with cheeses, and Marie Laure, who hated the music, attempting anticlerical wit at Poulenc's expense.

18 November

If I am not placing notes on staves, it's that I no longer want to put just anything down, no longer want music to be easy. Nor am I anymore interested in word settings or formal operas, nor do I want to compose about other people's problems. What's left? A chant with shrieks, a minimum of talk (this diary reduced to lowest terms), cue words like *Marilyn* and *vas-y* and *help* and *ouch* and *ti amo* and *I hate you* and *jonquil*, all in the various tongues I know—or don't know—and cut into four parts: Praise of Spirits, Ecstasy of Hate, Praise of Carnality, Ecstasy of Love. Name the authors but don't locate them in the form: they are just an excuse. Also several poems (or truncated aberrations of verse) branching out, arching away in differentiated counterpoint from the firm core of sexual horror. But there must be the human voice. For if music is the one art to which all others aspire, the human voice is the instrument all others seek to imitate (that includes trombones, maracas, piccolos, kettledrums, pianos, tin cans and electronic belches). Therefore those composers who today treat the voice as a "mechanical" instrument are exercising as vain a contradiction as that practiced by women who now tease their real hair so that it will resemble the wigs they can't afford. An instrument is a human voice *manqué*, that's its beauty. And the only timely definition of music free enough to be all-inclusive is: sound notated. (Use St. John of the Cross, Marvell, Christopher Smart.) Another definition: Music is what composers write.

Last night at Gloria Vanderbilt's after a YMHA reading by Purdy, my supper companion was Hermione Gingold. She lacks humor.

19 November

Noon at Tallulah's. Complete read-through for entire cast and production members. The hostess, disheveled and handsome in gray silk pajamas, sat cross-legged on her sofa flanked by Ruth Ford and Tab Hunter. The rest of us fanned out from her through the large clean room: Audrey Wood, Tony Richardson, Tennessee (who arrived an hour late), Marian Seldes, Rouben, flunkies, a Negro maid serving hard drinks. The reading was intriguing only inasmuch as it was chaos. Tallulah, to whom the role means everything, and who knows it already by heart, was all but ununderstandable with her out-of-date accent. The others were listless, except Ruth, who tried too hard. Tennessee laughed loudly throughout, seemed touchingly out of control, and I wanted to go to him with condolences about Frank Merlo. But it was hardly the time. Instead, as I was learning nothing, surely nothing about possible music, I left at two to come home and *write* the music. But the play can't work.

Tennessee Williams knows all about life except how to live it. This could be true of all poets, good and bad, except for the implication that the way they don't live is the right way. So the *bon mot* only

demonstrates a suburban principle: Tennessee's laments portray
him as unhappy, and isn't unhappiness wrong? No. Anyway, he
produces and gets produced. Who needs more?

Six years ago he wondered if he should change *Suddenly Last
Summer* to *Music in the Twelve Tone Scale*. "I think 'twelve tone
scale' is such a pretty term, but I don't know if it means anything."
"The term means nothing," I affirmed, "neither in itself nor as
reference to the contents of Anne Meacham's monologue." "Well,"
persisted Tennessee, "can't you at least write some background
music in that scale? I just love the sound of those words."

His approach to music is not instinctive so much as plainly
visual, or, at best, literary, associative. For instance, he asked that
Anne's entrance be accompanied by corrida trumpets; he *sees* what
bullfights connote aurally as connected to the dark death of his
unseen demi-hero. We tried it out musically, but the connotation
was too personal and too "poetic" to work.

26 November

Kennedy last Friday was murdered. That whole grand and gratuitous passion has come and gone since last I wrote here: chain-reac-
tion murders and funerals, and Aldous Huxley's death entirely
upstaged. My own drama has been more in focus than all that
carnage, but colored by it. Procrastination from writing, but what
do I want to write? HB has come into and become a part of
my—my what? schedule? He is concerned, *engagé*, what more can
be said? When a person dies, all of him dies. That's what's so
appalling about Kennedy. It's not as though he'd had his last
erection.

*Pittsburgh air terminal
en route to New York
30 November*

What concerns me most? Sex, alcohol, insanity (of all kinds: it's
poetry), being loved.

What I most like? Sequences and cloisters, movies, cherry pie,
air travel.

What I loathe most? Mediocrity (in every domain), women's
purses.

What concerns me least? Politics (I'm ashamed), eating, the theater.

I despise actors, agents, press representatives, producers, managers, directors, stagehands, and all other money-grubbing second-raters linked with "legitimate" theater which, at best, is expensive child's play employing genuine musical talent as mere decoration. This outburst depicts relief at finally having taped the *Milk Train* score (Broadway's most distinguished music in a decade). The month-long confabs with Tony Richardson have been artistically a waste, which the minimal fee and dubious prestige do not restore. I will never do another play except for thrice the pay: the nervous energy and sordid interplay exhaust, it's suicide too soon, for the real end seems daily so sooner with our President felled just now. Who are Tab and Tallulah up there dressed as grown-ups and acting silly? And who the hell am I, stuck off in the bleachers? Not, to be sure, the composer of *Miss Julie*.

Tennessee's writing no longer interests me; or rather, it interests me only inasmuch as *he* wrote it (like those last pieces of Stravinsky which interest by definition). Whereas my music interests him only inasmuch as it's divorced from me and married to his plays (a shotgun wedding at that). Because he used to be interested in my *self*—and one can't collaborate with what makes one vulnerable, except insofar as people can self-impose schizophrenia. Music disinterests him. He's said his say. I haven't yet. *Voilà!* . . . As for Tony R's displeasure with the *Milk Train* music, if it doesn't jibe with his preconceived directorial notion, then why didn't he write it himself? If we don't see eye to eye, or hear ear to ear, it's because I'm no maker of hack cues but a musician with personal contributions. When Gertrude after ninety hours of posing finally saw the portrait and exclaimed, "I don't look like that!" Picasso replied: "That's all right, you will." So if Tony feels the music isn't right, let him try it, it will fit.

Miss Julie. The music must betray—contradict—certain sentiments of the speech. If John states: "I lied when saying I loved you," the music makes *this* statement a lie: he *had* been telling the truth, he *is* in love. But one must protect oneself. Mustn't one? That question is the drama's crux, but human speech can clarify nothing (alas). Only art is true. Yet all art lies. (These are human words.)

How can I go too far and still get back? Over the cliff on the Jersey shores? No. In conversation with Miss Julie? Let's hope.

At the beginning of a love affair, like dogs they sniff around for strengths and weaknesses, seeking how they can go too far and still come back.

If a composer of background scores, in being overworked and underpaid by cohorts who couldn't care less about music, is low-man-on-a-totem-pole, with opera he becomes High Man—but at the price, now condescendingly inverted, of identical grubbiness.

13 December

Friday the thirteenth. Dinah Washington has killed herself.

Sometimes, anywhere (at work, in church, a grocery store), like premonitions of death, there comes an urge so strong that my tongue curls like a burning leaf, all orifices start twitching like the ears of a doe in danger, an erection spouts yellow like a lighthouse beacon, and I must stop everything, stop living, to search out the passion of anonymity, the anonymity of passion which, when it works, is the ultimate excitement. I could wish otherwise. (To HB tenderness and intelligence are a stimulation.) My libido and energy go all the way in all things including boredom and cigarettes, so now I'm at a low point, a bottom even. Before, I made them love me to camouflage my own dreariness in their eyes. Today I love them to hide their dreariness. (By them I mean HB.)

What's always bothered me about Ben Weber's music (as about Bill Flanagan's) is an absence of direction, hence it's untheatricality. At any given point it is beautiful, but from start to finish the same *kind* of beauty obtains: should fast sections be inserted they aren't inherently (kinetically) fast, but slow music played rapidly. His pieces are one vast ending. (Bill's twenty-minute *Lady of Tearful Regret* has a five-minute exposition, no development and then *continues to end* for a quarter of an hour.)

Diametrically opposed: Debussy *Préludes* which open in mid-stream and stay there. Or even so "formal" a contraption as the first movement of Ravel's *Sonatine* which begins as though eavesdropped upon—it is already happening.

. . . a child overheard sighing.

21 December

We talk too much. What is, is. Why define it with inaccurate words? Why throw it out because it won't fit recipes or satisfy our (probably imaginary) requirements? Love strangles by inadequacy of language. What is, is only in silence: trees growing, rocks, hearts fluttering underwater (where they say there's a hell of a racket we never hear!). With speech comes definition and that feeble concept, Truth, which gnaws at love affairs as though bromides of "mutual consideration" and "human respect" couldn't better be practiced with actions. HB, all disordered (he suffers: is even this the "truth"), says I've choreographed my whole being, including my pain. Theater of my pain. Much later, when the pain evaporates, can we safely know the pain could have been avoided had we held off? What's more painful (worthwhile): to resist or to accept?

All of which has been undergone sober. Pain is more painful with a clear head because it is undeserved. Hangover pain is presumed. Though suicide's closer then, it's not real. Nor has this allowed work. Anyway what *is* art today? My art today? It must from now on be no less than . . .

Yet (estranged) if I were to use words suggested for music by HB, it could kill me. Is it I, Ned, writing this, who have always maintained that love and art are unconnected?

Andy Warhol is making a movie of Kenward's days. As part of one day, I become Guest Star talking (silently) on the couch. Kenward sits motionless in the motion picture, like a movie of a table, on which I am the ham, gesticulating, screaming in silence.

As a child I longed to be accepted. Today, having a certain *carte blanche,* any tinge of rejection becomes not a brush-off but a misunderstanding.

27 December

Born in 1923. That fact in relief: just forty years previous Brahms and Wagner flourished, Gide and Satie were hardly known, Darwin was dying, and Stravinsky was a toddler. My parents however were unborn.

The year's closing, I feel low. High at Gloria's wedding party Christmas Day after three weeks on the wagon. We're in that blurred fortnight of undifferentiated parties, snow, whisky, fudge, carols, relatives and worklessness. I did spend twenty-four hours in Philadelphia where again I admired Rosemary's indefatigability. Never idle: with all her six kids and husband John she reads more than I, and while she converses (intelligently and without excitement), she knits pretty mittens, never dropping a stitch. John Marshall's the definitive American Father, manly, wise, industrious.

From Rosemary's cedar chest I recovered reams of notebooks placed there long ago: poems, stories, articles, *pensées,* not to mention a novel written between 1935 and 1939. For several hours I've been rereading all this and am struck by three things: the burlesque misspellings, the gloomy perversity, the energy. My orthography is still imperfect; my ten-year-old obsession (confusion) with passivity and cruelty remains today; I've always been prolific.

CHINA AND HER WAYS

Tibet is one the greatest countrys of China there is. China is great and important for its rice. The chinese people are interesting because of the life they live. The Chinese people worship there ancestors as if they were gods. . . . The Chinese people have dances just like we do. There dances are not like ours. There dances are with masks and things of that sort. They live upon tea and rice. China is quite close to Japan. Here are some of the names of some of the countrys of China. Hong Kong; Shang Hi; and many other countrys. China is a very large country. It is in the orient part of the world. The Chinese have black hair and almon shaped eyes. They dress in komonas with wide sleeves, they whare there hair in braids. Chinese people play games just like we play games. There games are not like our games, some of there games are these. The water nymph and the nightingale. There complexion is usually a light yellow or bronze. In the warm parts of the country the people wear wooden sandals. In the cold parts they wear heavy leather shoes with padded coats and trousers, which resemble quilts. China is on the other side of the world than ours. Japan is a grupe of islands quite near to China. China is the next to the largest country in the world. The Chinese people eat with chop sticks in a very hard manner with one hand. Their are two rivers in China Hoang ho; and yangstse river. (There are many rivers in China.) The Chinese people are sometimes called Mongolians. One of the Chinese customs is to bind the baby girls feet so that they would be small when they grew up. The Chinese people live in houses made of bambo. The way they get from one place to another is a ric cha.

(Ned Rorem, Jan. 22, 1933)

29 December

Hindemith died.

1964

In matters of love it is easier to overcome a deep feeling than to renounce a habit.

—Proust

A week ago I gave up smoking for the first time in twenty years. Result: wound caused by an old friend's death. I refuse the visits of an old friend who, like an innocent dog, I punish for nothing. Feel lousy. Rationalize that God will tell me on the Judgment Day that I'd never have died of cigarettes. Result: tonight I began smoking again. The first puff was purely voluptuous. (Whereas sex, anticipated, when realized is never as good as.) Because of the gory publicity, cigarettes seen now on the street seem not tempting but repellent, gleaming with radioactivity.

Have been living *à la roulotte* since the bedroom ceiling caved in five days ago. Two-thirds of life is spent in reinstating pointless broken statues, rectifying blunders.

Tonight chez Rose Plaut, Denise Duval was a charmer, eyes like Garbo's, twice bigger than eyes have a right to be. She would be perfect as Julie.

Dream with fever: I am two parts of a sandwich held together not with butter or blood, but with fire.

HB says beautiful people suffer most. Without request they are loved, are held responsible, are abandoned.

The fact that HB is Jewish makes me feel a certain advantage. Is that a despicable phrase?

Those dying generations—at their song. . .

—Yeats

Poetry is not concerned with thoughts, but with words.

—Mallarmé

Man was given the Word to hide his thought.

—Malgrida

Musical tempo depends on the tempo of living, as the tempo of living indicates that of language. No one is sure of speech's speed in Chaucer's day; philologists surmise it to have been radically slower than ours. In a hundred years we will speak more rapidly. We perform music of the last century faster (and more strictly) than it was probably played then. Similarly, a performer's instinctive choice of style is dictated more by the sonorous shape of his native tongue than by a conscious attempt to penetrate the composer's mind.

Nor are performers necessarily qualified interpreters of their national music. Subjectivity is detrimental to execution. The Germanic Gieseking played Debussy more "comprehensively" than any Frenchman I ever heard.

The speech of a nation originates from its music, not the other way around.

Consider how the generous Italian ripple is so like the Italians, and the guttural Arabic sensuality like Arabs themselves; how the suave, smooth, logical, arhythmic French tongue is like the French, German like Germans, or the somber Flamenco spurt resembles Spanish. And how Americans have altered English to fit their irritable jazzy innocence.

The musical public of a nation resembles its performers, as the performers resemble the composer. An Italian barber knows his country's music better than our typical opera queen. Everyone sings in Italy: audiences identify to such an extent with the stage expression that they must be suppressed from audible demonstration, whereupon they rise to dance on their seats. Dance in Spain is the germ of Flamenco song; the grave, harsh howl results from a bodily spasm. The Spanish sing with their feet as Italians dance with their throats. Cocteau: "The Flamenco singer spits out flowers of fire, then extinguishes them beneath his heel."

The French are more visual than aural, and have an unequaled sense of painting, flower arrangement and food preparation. They *see* their music. They too are verbal during a concert, but in discreet Gallic commentary *on* the music rather than loud Latin association *with* the music. Germans, contrariwise, have little innate visual sense (their architecture, their grocery displays are unappetizing) but, in their weird way, have the highest auditory appreciation in the West. At concerts they are mute as marble; nothing stands between them and the composer (if he's German) except the performer whom they psychoanalyze on the spot for a deeper understanding of the sound's secret sense.

Americans, like their music, combine Italian extroversion, Spanish kinetics, French discretion and Teutonic neurasthenia.

The art of translation lies less in knowing the other language than in knowing your own.

Fauré, when asked the ideal tempo for a song, answered: "If the singer is bad—very fast." Composers haven't necessarily preconceived ideas of interpretation. (A composer has the first word, never the last.) When a singer is good and has worked, that singer's concept is usually "right" on some terms, so the composer has little to suggest; if the singer is bad, nothing the composer might say will help much. A song, more than any musical form, is subject to varieties of legitimate interpretation by virtue of the performer's sex and vocal timbre. I'll accept—and be pleased by—radical variants from a singer which I'll refuse from a violinist or conductor.

I feel guilty about what I do best—setting words to music. Because it comes easily (meaning naturally), I feel I'm cheating. Still, it isn't *my* hand that has wings but another Ned Rorem's; I sit back impotent watching his hand err and triumph.

The hand works to fill a void. Whether the work is good doesn't matter.

I know music—I don't know *about* music. Yes, I write songs. This does not mean I *know how* to write songs. I can show you how to make a perfect one, but not a good one. (Oh, I *do* "know how" to compose, but that's all. If I've anything to "impart," I'm unaware of it.)

Yet I was once arbitrarily named the best songwriter in the world. For me to agree would be to take the way of movie stars who believe their own publicity; that ends in suicide. Not to agree would be the way of humility; humility isn't for artists; it leads to complacent mediocrity, another route to suicide. The right road, then? No one is ever "the best," they are all absolutes. One is only better. But by whose definition?

Composers may be profligate but never stars. Singers may be stars but never profligate.

Speech, the human voice, is a gramophone record. Some records are longer than others, but our mechanisms ultimately set back the needle. Sooner or later you've heard all your best friends have to say. Then comes the tolerance of real love. The same holds for music.

Once I said that the Sonata was a legitimate form, but that Song was a bastard progeny of two mediums. Amendment: Song is a mule, the sterile product of the union of two species. No song can duplicate itself, each has its own rules.

Poulenc's carp, like those spawned under Louis XVI and still swimming at Versailles (minus their rifled gold collars), is a jewel with a single perfect facet illuminated by that slow-flipping tail in the left hand.

My predispositions are French. People sometimes show surprise that I, being a songster, feel no affinity for Schubert. His *lieder* leave me absolutely cold.

I was more moved by the death of Billie Holiday than by the death of Landowska. For if Landowska was closer to the world in which I move, she was farther from the time in which I live, while Billie was part of my day. During twenty years I *felt* her more than any classical performer. Bill Flanagan says (and I say it too about him) that I plagiarized Billie's spontaneous inflections and froze them into compositional idiosyncrasies.

23 January

All music is a sung expression, and all instruments attempt to emulate the human voice. Yet instrumental composers have gradually ousted lyrical ones, so the latter impose their talents elsewhere —notably on high drama.

Now it doesn't follow that he who has fashioned singable songs will also construct workable operas. Opera's main challenge is theatrical, not vocal. Yet, no one writes songs anymore and everyone writes operas, but few of those operas come off, despite all sorts of wild electronic invention. Possibly it's because the proscenium arch (except for framing dancers) is finished. A brand new outlet for the medium itself is more indicated than the constant refurbishment of musical devices. That outlet will be through a projector. Because the future of opera lies in the movies. What the static area once achieved on stage the mobile close-up will accomplish on film, with an additional introspection that our age demands. We will no longer avoid poets as librettists: their every explicit, even fussy, word will be understood.

Europe's idols are historical tragedians, ours are recent comedians. Yet even Italians today have forsaken "legitimate" theater and take Marilyn Monroe as seriously as they once took Eleonora Duse. Imagine a new Marilyn, dubbed, singing the words of, say, Frank O'Hara, as set to music by . . . !

Could unheard melodies be truly sweeter? Intelligence is silence, truth being invisible. But what a racket I make in declaring this.

26 January

Of all my life this day has been the weirdest. On the 21st Harold Brodkey left for Saratoga. The following evening Marc Blitzstein was killed in Martinique. Next Saturday I too am off to Yaddo. Marc, and also HB, will never talk with me again, not at least with the same voices. Days soggy with tranquilizers. Saratoga: we had complicatedly arranged to be "together" there, a sour foreboding, and I'm as low as in the days of Claude. Who of our friends can dispel the image of frail Marc pleading for help across the swamps of that ugly country. I've heard twelve times a day that Marc is dead. I haven't yet heard from HB. The absences like pus accumulate into this drab unexploded Sunday, the hurter and hurt, who, being Jews, should have learned better. It's I who feel Jewish, put upon, dreading, unable to wish my work is more important. I miss you till my stomach writhes.

Colin McPhee has died as well, and Carlyle Brown in Rome from no alternative.

The commonest misspelling of our name is *Roren*. It outrages Father with whom last week I lunched at the new Hilton, a skyscraper I love but they hate, and Father, like all his age (sixty-nine), thinks on death silently, yet speaks of "being forgotten." How long does "forgotten" take? days? months? (Checking a library card catalog once to see the extent of their holding of Rorem music, I found only several of my songs, but every book and monograph Father had written.) Are we already *used* to Kennedy? Did he take the edge off Blitzstein? I've not forgotten the songs of Charles Naginsky who drowned twenty years ago at Tanglewood before we met.

Except for Bill Flanagan whom I see every day, Marc was the only composer I frequented *as a composer*, someone to compare notes with. When we'd finish a piece we'd show it to each other, as in the good old days, hoping for praise, getting practical suggestions. Our language, on the face of it, would seem to be the same (diatonic, lyric, simple). In fact, we barked up very different trees. Marc was nothing if not theatrical, and precisely for that he showed me how the element of theater was integral even to remote forms like recital songs.

Malamud is an author with whose subject matter (Jewish poverty in Brooklyn) I'd seem to have little in common, but with whose *Assistant* I identified wholly. It's discouraging to realize that Marc's best work was his last, *Idiots First*, which he played me just weeks ago. Malamud would have continued to be his ideal collaborator.

My charm, if I have any, is economized for occasion. Marc's was squandered freely. When as a Juilliard student in 1947 I first knocked on his door for an interview, Marc Blitzstein received me with a—a sort of Catholic Impatience, worn like a cloak, as he sat at his piano criticizing Cocteau for being chic. Have been going through my diary of that period, which talks of the slush in the gutters, Marc's postwar indignations, etc. . . .

I've always felt it, of course, but more and more I've come actually to see that happiness not only precedes but accompanies calamity.

31 January

Tomorrow Yaddo. Since HB went, the twelve days have been unfocused. His absence for a while was confused with Marc's murder. Then of course my involuntarily disarranged apartment (the collapsed ceiling and the place still a wreck) blurred with a demoralizing visit Tuesday to the dermatologist. If indeed the mole beneath my left tit became malignant . . . Knowing this I entered the Met museum across from his office but saw no pictures, only felt the dead painters (*Corot, tu es mort*). Tearful and suspended down through the thawing park and at the zoo stared and stared at a young deer: *toi aussi tu mourras*.

Yaddo
8 February

Ellen Faull, tonight in Town Hall, sings the premiere of my Tennyson poems.

I don't want what I have, want what I can't, yes I do want what I have, and I will have what I can't. The Bible—any book—gives solace only when not needed. HB says that his two qualities of awareness are sensuality and intelligence, while mine are nostalgia and wit. He feels I lack playfulness. My two needs: to be treated as great beauty, to be treated as abject slave. Seeking to emulate Lea or the Marschallin, I end as Norma Desmond. Haunted now twenty-four hours a day, frustrated as a blind Peeping Tom.

Seen from Jersey, the polluted air descends upon New York like a giant tea cozy. I wonder today if, anymore than Miss Julie after an ample screw, I'll survive the coming summer. Wintertime again at Yaddo. With the opera, all I can think of is death. Approaching quickly in any form. Or formless. Am I working too well? Am I so content? Or abandoned? Snow is all over, the room is white. And I dream.

What is Julie about? Me, carnality and dying.

18 February

The presence of HB makes for as much unrest as the absence. Love seems as inexorable as those summer Paris dawns coming up like thunder long before they should (why, it's not even closing time!). HB has the last word, seems right for the wrong reasons, is hence exasperating, since I'm defenseless. Could I wish it otherwise? No, why?

Meanwhile, time to draw conclusions and document the 1963 sex list completed seven weeks ago. During the year 1962 I had 205 orgasms, 85 of them with people I know (not 85 different people, however). Of the remaining 120 about one-fourth was masturbation and the rest anonymous. The leanest month was September (9) when isolated at Yaddo; the fattest was July (22) when I was *about* to be isolated at Yaddo. The incidents seem to increase steadily therefore to the center of the year, decline, then rise again in November. Self-examination produces smugness not art. Most of us most of the time don't know we're happy until it's too late (though of course it's never too late: recollection is sweet in itself). For happiness, unlike pleasure which is a briefly conscious Now, continues indefinitely like a low-grade fever.

I want no more hands on me: they bore and frighten. Each day my mind slips farther. Cigarettes are a satisfying gamble, Gee Whiz, Whee, Gizz!

The record of songs is finally issued and I'm proud. The vocalism is mostly right (nonoperatic) and my piano surprises even me. While listening over and over to these thirty-two moods, I can recall like yesterday the circumstances of each writing; since all were made *d'un souffle* I remember the weather, the heart, the country, each of those daytimes lost in the last eighteen years. Elizabeth Ames paid me what supposedly is the supreme compliment by requesting that two of these songs be sung at her funeral (Spenser's *What If Some*

Little Pain, and Stevenson's *Requiem*). Accomplishments though don't elate or inspire me—they bring death closer.

Washington's Birthday

Kenward comes up to Saratoga for another conference. We're deep in the opera. Yet I've other commissions to fulfill, notably the Marvelous Silver Suite for Sweet Sylvia Marlowe. Called *Lovers*. Program note: Whenever I'm writing a long piece I simultaneously compose shorter ones which feed on it as pilot fish feed on a shark; they serve also as guides and diversions. Such is the suite called *Lovers* contrived in the shadow of *Miss Julie*. Subtitled "Narrative in Ten Scenes," it depicts experiences in the day of a young couple. The scenes are songs without words; events will be guessed from sonorities—sonorities chosen hopefully as pleasant contrasts (a marriage of opposites, if you will) for Sylvia Marlowe's harpsichord. I like tunes, sounds, sometimes love when it's happy and brief as this piece means to be, allowing my opera the extended sadness it must have.

What will occur in the time that's left? A change of heart, of attitude? of habits, or taste? any massive revelations? Perhaps, though, nine-tenths of my life's been lived: within a month couldn't I be dead from a road accident or a hidden pox? In this remaining period would I produce a work to obliterate the others? or acquire an interest, hitherto feigned, in people? My youth's obsession with music, though not sterilized, has altered. No longer is an open grand piano a Pegasus, that winged horse to all versions of which I am allergic and love like the lions I appeal to and desire frightfully.

10 March

Wonderfully snowbound with our healthy meals here in West House, and for a digestive we play Ping-Pong. Glamorous Galway Kinnell who's translating Villon, aloof Jean Garrigue with her good legs and Connie Bennett gaze, Vassarish Mary Durant who writes fiction called *An End to Patience*, smiling Nell Blaine who gives me drawing lessons *à la Redon*, and sympathetic Dilys Evans who admonishes us, in a Welsh accent, not to smoke. And of course HB in all stubborn glory. Tonight in Boston and in Los Angeles my *Eagles* is being conducted simultaneously by Mehta and by Stokowski, while in Louisville the *Eleven Studies* sound.

Practicing *Poems of Love and the Rain* which Regina and I will premiere in Madison next month. Reading: *The Wapshot Scandal*, Polly Hanson's poems (one of which I just set, and will offer to Nell Blaine in exchange for an aquarelle), *Among the Dangs* (George P. Elliott), *Middlemarch* (George Eliot), Mary Durant's *Quartet in Farewell Time, Portrait of a Lady*, the Bible, *King Lear*, feeling sick, there are flies buzzing around the thermostat.

21 March

Seven weeks. They've all gone away, my artful companions of the country. The first day of spring, and Christ, I'm bored, the hours pass at a snail's pace. Being left here, in what I used to term the luxury of loneliness, brought no self-sufficiency. I invent anything to keep from working: sleep, meals, some reading, walking, anything to avoid the rare advantage of freedom. Yet next week in New York I'll bitterly miss this time I could have used better. Am I using it so unwisely? Is not nervousness due to not having smoked in two weeks (who says you forget the habit?)? Am I not appreciating more than ever (since those *échanges crépusculaires* with Denise Bourdet in Hyères) the aching sunset when it finally comes and everything seems about to collapse? Is it not healthy, as people say, to be for a while without HB? Except now I work still less, being too calm, not proud of past hysteria and current anxiety. Power for concentration seems ever more difficult. Or do I just now feel nothing's worth reading and why bother composing. I'm *not even* depressed. (But I am.) Alone in the big house and a bit scared at night. Love isn't enough, but neither is art.

Palm Sunday

With Elizabeth this morning, Silent Meeting, or rather, Noisy Meeting since we both talked constantly, while watching the cardinals in the sunny snow. The clear intelligence that comes, presumably, with subduing passion.

Slovenly reading of an article by Lionel Trilling (whom I've always admired); I was under the impression it was by Diana Trilling (whom I've never admired), and so found it bad.

Truths notated become lies. Intelligence alas can't keep up love.

Compose duets à la Dvořák, Schumann, Mendelssohn, Monteverdi, for two women.

I sense and am uncomfortable by a certain sensuality between Elizabeth, age eighty, and myself.

New York
April Fool's Day

The effort to write just this!

Madison, Wisconsin
12 April

With David Stimer and Regina Sarfaty for the under-rehearsed premiere tonight of the *Rain Poems*. Tomorrow, helicopter into Chicago's loop, to spend afternoon on South Side, weep over U-High, fly back to New York after three nights' absence which seems like years. No one improves. We accumulate and water our catalogue, and live on. Death of Gerry Devlin.
    The effort to write just the effort to write.
    The effort to write the effort to write.

New York
14 April

Yes, yesterday I returned to high school halls for the first time since graduating a quarter century ago. But having properly laid the ghost in 1959, Chicago this time seemed less sad than boring, an unrotted corpse, recognizable but bloodless, at least without *my* blood.

Our premiere was a triumph so far as noise went, yet not a single intelligent question was asked by students or faculty after the concert. Example: "Mr. Rorem, what's your opinion of so-called *cerebral* music?" (Cerebral, of course, means whatever the questioner doesn't dig.) Or: "How do you write a song?" (Despite the fact that I've written two articles on this, why should I, just because I compose songs, necessarily *know how* to compose songs? One doesn't *know how*, one *does*.) More and more I'm weary of philosophy, of generalities, of talking around the thing rather than becoming the thing. If I'm unique as a composer, it's not for my wisdom but for my gossip. Enough of an artist's theories! let's hear his voice, only *he* owns it. Enough of advice to the lovelorn! tell us a romance, recite anecdotes; what are your favorite desserts, colors, vices?

Plane conversations. Regina Sarfaty, forever Jewish, is as naïve about me as Christian, as P (forever Catholic) was about Quakers. She questions unanswerably: "If a nun is married to God, is she not jealous of her sisters who, like harem wives, are married to the same god?" Then Regina vomits into the sack provided by the airline for this purpose. She is, after all, four months pregnant, and more released than she knows from the tension of our "first performance" which moved us so far beyond rehearsals.

The hardest of all the arts to speak of is music, because music has no meaning to speak of.

For whom do you compose? . . . Art for art's sake is hardly fashionable, though is there a better sake? But even should such a motivation exist (it probably doesn't), it would apply more to meaning than to purpose. Actually, composers compose for someone, but they're not always sure for whom. Alexei Haieff says we write for the friend we love. Or is it an imaginary listener we search for? A person from the past, or ourselves in the future? In any case, not for ourselves in the present. Just as diaries are always made to be seen by other eyes, so all composers write for an audience, if not necessarily what the audience wants to hear—or thinks it wants to hear. They also write for commissioners; assured performances plus palpable pay counteract their dreamy apathy. (Good dreamers make bad artists.) In fact, all of my musician friends agree that money is their chief stimulation.

Does writing music help to get things out of your system? . . . Self-expression, as people call it, is not a purge. Artists obviously express what's in them, but the fact of clarifying it on paper doesn't mean it's no longer in them. Besides, any living thing can "express" itself; an athlete in action doesn't *think* of his muscles; a robin fashions, without knowing, the tone and life in her sky-blue egg. Murder may be provisional medicine to a maniac, but a few months (or days) later he'll not seek new releases, he'll commit another murder. A woman having borne a healthy child won't necessarily say she'll never have another (mothers don't join book clubs until their children leave for college). Similarly, an artist, having said something, has really only found a *form* in which to say it. Many great ones spend their lives repeating themselves in different colors.

I'm not convinced that artists ever advance, much less grow. What they know they know from the start; each work is a new way of saying the same thing. Their obsessions don't change, only their modes of emission. Nor do they always know what they've said. Corot once answered a lady who was searching for hidden meanings in his work: *"Non, madame, la peinture est plus bête que cela."*

Good music? . . . It depends on where you stand (one man's meat, etc.). The point used to arise through confusing art with entertainment. They've now been fused by intellectual and commoner alike. The only bad rock 'n' roll is that which doesn't distract delinquents from switchblades. Nobody cares about posterity anymore.

Nevertheless art (as it used to be called) is an aristocratic affair. One cannot demonstrate that the average man experiences—or can be trained to experience—those reactions which make up a work of art, or an appreciation of that work. For the first time ever he can have it all free, and rejects it. The world feels an innate suspicion and jealousy of the artist, for the artist has ripped open a protective curtain to display what outsiders most resent: himself.

Are you your work? . . . Am I my work? No, I was it.

Not even while in the act? While in the act some poison part drains off forever while I now remain paradoxically weaker and stronger. So, yes, while working, I'm it, or at least it's *in* me, but while inside it's unhealthy. Once notated, interest lags (and this very phrase could never attract me again—I'm cold to compliments on bygone tunes). But spirit lags, too. Empty now, but not enough: dregs stay. My life was and will be spent in scraping clean such stinking residue to create a vacuum. Yet to create a vacuum is, in a sense, to fill it. An artist is slave to irony.

An artist is no more self-involved than other people; he just shows it more.

Am I of the earth? I am not you, nor them, nor even my work, for it becomes it. What can I leave? I am only my name. . . . Art, said Braque, is made to disturb, while science reassures. I might be content that years from now my song could act as a balm, though that song today leaves me, its maker, dry.

Do you do your own orchestration? . . . Why is this an enigma? Because study of musical notation is not a Liberal Art. All collegians should learn instrumentation, though, conversely, composers don't need the Liberal Arts. (Yes, I do my own orchestration.)

Where is music going? . . . Nowhere at present. Eventually, though, it will follow, as it has in the past, wherever a great monster leads it. His way will not be one of invention but of synthesis, a gathering of trends into a communicable whole. He will write not for vogue but from necessity, and he will *get the necessity over.* His voice will sing out, avoiding theories. For art's not abstraction of ideas but incarnation of ideas. We talk all around it, but only the thing itself explains the thing itself. What music "should" do is nothing next to what it does.

That monster is not yet around. Meanwhile, music's definition —for the first time ever—requires expanding. Among the young it has come to fill logical, not emotional, needs. I cannot object: one may resent evolutions but not deny them. My own language, however, remains one of "expression," a damning word today.

There's no real audience (emotionally pleased) for contemporary music now. Concerts serve a new purpose for their little public: what's played is not important, what *happens* is. Boredom too has become an art. The reaction music is supposed to produce is the reaction it does produce, so any reaction is the right reaction.

How much time did it take you to compose that? . . . I don't know, ten minutes, eighteen years. Would you despise me if I said it was easy? I can only tell exactly how long it took to put on paper, though what difference does it make? But then, what difference does anything make?

27 April

After a near half-year HB and I are, as they say, *through*. Since as is the case with so many novitiate analysands, the choice is to defenestrate nearest and dearest without sweeping the shattered glass. I'm not dancing with joy, having learned (if nothing else) that grass is no greener, etc. If, however, HB achieves the Nirvana he presumably seeks, then I too will have curiously. . . .

The Vogue of Death. I'm giving you the worst years of my life. Having been born to an "enlightened family," is my weakness therefore in never having had to come to grips with Vital Issues?

The trouble with letter-writing is that the act defeats the purpose. Feelings expressed are no longer feelings, yet strive to transmit the untransmittable. The heart changes a dozen times while the letter's rigid contents wade inexorably through the mails. We still *mean* what's written, though with shifted emphasis. Still, conversation seems impossible, exploding in recrimination as though that had been the subject. The pleasure of each other's company is its own payment. So-called noble virtues, as you once pointed out, are all we work toward, but love, as we understand or practice it at the moment, is not one of them. Power of silence.

29 April

A note on diction. The solitude of notation began early: I started to talk and to compose almost at the same time. The first music, and much of it since, was for that impure medium known as vocal; impure, because it conjoins two arts by setting words to tones. Why I was initially attracted to songs, and why that attraction continues, is unsure. Certainly I can't sing; perhaps that's the answer: composing expresses the invisible singer within us all.

The first words I set as a child were those of my own language,

English. Over the years I've composed in French, Italian, Latin, even in ancient Greek. Never convincingly—though I speak and think in some of these tongues.

It was not for a long time, during the cruelties of growing up, that I realized the generalized world about me was not made up of composers like me. Nor, for a while after that, did I realize that the particularized world of my profession was not formed of musicians writing songs in English, or even songs at all. I did learn quickly, however, that singing in English was considered, by American teachers of that time, somewhat low-class. Which is one reason that the art and practice of the song recital are now dead issues. Yet the only thing bad about songs in English is bad English.

Later I learned bemusedly how many of my colleagues considered the writing of songs "difficult." Now, writing music—the doing of anything well—is difficult. Of course, song-writing is a specialty within a specialty, so some composers are drawn to it, others aren't. I'd always found word-setting to be as natural as speaking; that very naturalness, plus love of verse, drew me to song. No matter what language we are born to, we each, as individuals, speak that language in our own special manner. I set words to music as I talk them: which is what makes my songs personal—if indeed they are.

As to the diction business in the interpretation of those songs: inasmuch as I feel the settings to be natural, or rather, inevitable (for art isn't natural, it's art), I've never understood why singers aren't understood in English. Doubtless they're primarily concerned more with the sensual (meaning sound) than with the intellectual (meaning verse). Maybe there's also a question of embarrassment when they sing in their own tongue. For while self-expression through song is something all desire but few fulfill, interpretation of songs is more than self-expression: it is self-commitment, and hence somewhat compromising. To be put on the spot is embarrassing if we don't know what we're talking about—or singing about. So, many singers rely solely on beautiful noises to pull them through. (This is truer between the coasts than in California or New York where the preponderance of Italian and Jewish vocalists possess, through ethnic extroversion, no shame at word sense.)

Certainly I'll take the blame for blurred diction if in making a given piece—a coloratura vocalise, for instance—I decide to sacrifice sense to sensation. But mostly I conceive within a tessitura that will gratefully express the meaning of a poem—at least its meaning as I mean it.

As to my own physical reaction while listening: I am constantly torn between which is more outrageous or less satisfying: the gorgeous voice mouthing words not one of which is understandable, or the mediocre voice of absolute intelligibility. The ideal combination, a gorgeous voice with clear enunciation, even among our most respected artists, is strangely rare. Strange at least for me. Because if the words are well set, and if the concert singer spent more time in deciding what those words connote (like the pop singer does) than in quibbling over consonants, I as a composer would think his battle three-fourths won.

3 May

Friday at 4 A.M. as Julius' Bar was closing Edward Albee invited sixty zombies to my house where they scattered beer cans until late morning when Tom Prentiss evicted them. Such parties hardly help. What have I done of consequence with my silence? Visitors appear, because they're hard to discourage. The most recent, an Episcopalian priest, came calling Thursday. He desired to "share ideas." But why, because he likes my songs, must he know me?

Called Aaron out of the blue because his *Organ Concerto* on the radio pleased me, and what does anymore? With Edward then, and Bill, he too came to dine and was touching about being left like a burning ship by rats. Though would he see it this way?

Bernac also came, but a note in my mailbox told him I was unavoidably called away. Alcohol invents feebly. Do I care about old friends? Truthfully HB's image is all that shows me I'm still alive. Arnold Sundgaard appeared with requests (was it in 1946 we last met, with Alec Wilder?). So much for names. Unavoidable horrors: the surgical removal of a nevus mole sprouting beneath my left tit (the stitches have been removed, a Mayan sacrifice). Rudel is quite unsatisfied with the libretto. Yes, where now?

5 May

I entered a room where HB was supposed to be, and it was empty. The dream this morning awakened me with a damp face. Tonight I phoned HB and went to visit for three hours. Undone and relieved. In time it will be the impossibly tacky past.

7 May

To Washington this morning, with Lee Hoiby and Stanley Hollingsworth, and the inauguration of the Cathedral's new bell tower for which we'd each written an Ascension Day piece. Paul Callaway conducted nobly. Lovely weather. Bad sore throat. Arrived home in time to eat my perfect homemade peach ice cream which this morning hadn't looked as though it would jell.

19 May

Virgil asked for my new song disk, invited me, Doda Conrad and Maurice Grosser to dine. After supper we arranged ourselves neatly to hear the record's thirty-two tunes. By song number five Maurice was asleep and snoring on the purple sofa. By song number seven Virgil too was snoring in his corner. I shot a smile of complicity to Doda, bowed to the sleepers and left, hurt, but not very, and anyway I had a date.

Virgil's best recent song is on Kenneth Koch's *Prayer to Saint Catherine*. Curiously, five years later, in my song to Polly Hanson's *Tree of Night* there are phrases identical to those in Virgil's *Prayer*. How could he have known I was to write this music, and then plagiarize in advance?

Golly, I've composed a lot! But am geared to make a change. Will it be to speak the same ideas in a new tongue, or new ideas in the former language, or both, or some combination? *Poems of Love and the Rain* (already seventeen months old) may indicate an answer for outsiders, but not for me: they sound, they came, so naturally.

Long brandied evening with John Wingate, unchanged in

eighteen years, still dominated by Christopher Lazare who nevertheless so far as he knows may have expired in Vienna.

24 May

Society forces us, in Cocteau's words, *to neglect our solitude.* Yet in friendship I do not "go out" (or do I?). Still, the point of living lies in the hope of one more revelation.

Devoted the day to sex, its search, discovery, abandonment. The temperature rests at 95°, but at the baths it's a good deal hotter and there a Baltimore football player (*soi-disant*) administered a skillful massage. Back home I ate, ate, ate, compulsively as with hangovers, cabbage and Coca Cola, when Jim Bridges called and came over and we walked in the crowded presummer square and then had hot fudge sundaes at Howard Johnson's. Sex increasingly dominates sleep and waking hours, claims priority over friendship, work, ambition, repeats itself undistinguishably and has no issue, no construction. Sex and posterity *chez moi* ironically contradict; but what *is* waste? The past revisited is flat as a pancake; Chicago showed this. That I shall never know those who died before and those who'll be born after my life on earth literally stuns me! My new filing case grows heavy with the past, contracts, and all the love-and-fan notes—heartbreaking because they're of a past which is flat. Left to my own devices I'd fornicate seven to nine times weekly and compose only songs. But the world wishes otherwise.

10 June

Over nine months ago I broke my right ankle at Yaddo. It remains weakened and I limp. This is written (I'd write *n'importe quoi*) to avoid work. But there's nothing to say. A rainy low warm Sunday, shrill boys play handball downstairs, voices in the hall, heels clicking and Goodyear tires skidding fifty feet away near Abingdon Square where during the war I used to sit hung over eating sherbet and feeling much as I feel today as though two decades between had taught me nothing.

Monotonously HB repeats: "At least I'm never dull." He fears he is, probably because his output is small.

I drink because: The streets scare me. My looks are a sorrow. To break the very rhythm I've set up. To be able to nurse the physical wounds, to avoid nursing music.

Midnight, tired, discouraged. The temperature's dropped twenty degrees. Dined with Morris and Bill F, discussion all politics, the Negro revolt, and the festering of this greatest of all possible lands. In two weeks I go to France.

On my birthday were born: Franz Liszt, Sarah Bernhardt, Maurice Grosser, Miriam Gideon, Johnny Carson, and Margaret Bond's daughter Djane.

Reaction to "intellectualism" came in the '50s through the purple pleasure of nearly all painters retreating from methods of obscurantism by no longer avoiding *communication* as a dirty word (the same painters who now eschew the easel in favor of film-making and choreography), through the poems of Ginsberg and Kenneth Koch, and through the novels of Durrell and Nabokov. Music, as always, lagged behind like an abandoned child, a lost but pompous Fauntleroy nobody cared about anymore.

11 June

Two or three times a year I dream anxiously of being pregnant, my belly swells with child. The anxiety lies not so much in how the child got there, or that it *is* there, as in how it will get out. . . . Before giving birth I awaken.

I average two to three fair-sized musical works each year.

Ran into May Swenson on 8th Street, looking like a newborn pixie. We've not met in two years. For five minutes we each breathlessly listed our recent successes, then quickly said goodbye.

9:30 P.M. An hour ago HB strode out, after staying only fifteen minutes during which his *propos* were unclear. He prearranged a misunderstanding so as to leave, full of Justice, his eyes in fever. My own fever (though I still shake—from what?) has dropped now more suddenly than yesterday's temperature; I am free, and *can* go to France. So I ate alone the meal I'd prepared us, liver and peas, salad and babas au rhum on ice cream, while through my second-story bevined kitchen window I watched the summer sun set on the muscled youth across the street as he repaired his motorcycle which he's been doing loudly eight hours a day for three months.

HB had phoned me this morning to quote *Time* magazine: "Since the death of Poulenc . . . Ned Rorem is probably the world's best composer of art songs." His reaction was more fearful than my own (he'd admonished me to be "humble"—meaning physically debased—this evening). Down with posterity! To be alive today!

20 June

The heart bleeds for those girls who stand singly on Greenwich Avenue shouting up to their friends in the Women's House of Detention: "Who's being nice to you, baby?"

Can any American just do nothing? Can any American just watch Blue Jays, or shadows shifting on Poison Ivy leaves for hours?

Quite often I think of how seldom I think of HB.

Limbo. Because I've been gone from America psychologically for a week.

Paris
Fourth of July

Paris. Everything is the same except everything. I'm a month too late, have a cold, most old friends have gone for the summer. A feeling of not belonging, emphasized by the city's beauty.

8 July

My seventh day back, but only my first really back. Already anxious to leave for Hyères, to get to work.

Surrealist plane trip with Morris. Miles above the Atlantic Ocean at midnight heading east, on our little movie screens we watched *The Pink Panther* run its course, when lo! at 1 A.M. the sun began to rise, and the thirty Orthodox Jews who shared our aircraft put on caps and prayed in the aisles, exhausted.

Old passions resemble *Un Carnet de Bal*. Henri Fourtine, a balding fifty with three superb children; Claude, balding and prosperous and *de mèche avec une dame du monde*; Jean Leauvrais, thick-haired and thick and full of theater. Less painful than dull; thought hurts more than reality.

It's raining as I dress to go to the opera with Nora Auric and Raffaello de Banfield. How will they look? . . . I've had my two *cuites* and will leave for Hyères Sunday. Isherwood's new novel has been my sole reading matter, deep and icy, saying we can only go forward, and then only to death.

Supper last night with George Bemberg who says I've never found an ideal love arrangement elsewhere because I've always had it at home: a lifelong affair with myself. He's relieved at not wanting what he knows he doesn't want. Yes, nothing has changed except everything.

> *Château Saint Bernard*
> *Hyères (Var)*
> *13 July*

Yes, again in the country where everyone (authors and otherwise) keeps such fragrant diaries that I feel like one of the mob. In twenty-four hours here I've tried frantically to revive everything. No, nothing's different, like living in a photograph which, though it yellows, remains unchanged—as Marie Laure finds me, and I her. Frantically, because in just a day I've *redone all*, including trying to finish *Miss Julie* in three hours, including writing here. But Provence is where we learn in time to take our time, where one day's like the next. Usually I enjoy others less for their contact *now* than for their contact anticipated or in retrospect. Here a stroll in the paradise hills breaks your heart on the spot.

20 July

Art for me mustn't be difficult, music must come easily. It doesn't now. . . . A song cannot have padding. Opera has almost nothing but. . . . My work today?

Plump Lily, the concierge's daughter and hardly what you'd call a heavy thinker, for some reason asked to borrow the record of my songs. Her sole comment: *"C'est pas mal, vous savez,* but the singers make so much noise you can't hear the music." From the mouths of babes! Now of course the singing *is* the music, but Lily's attitude is held by many a layman more involved than she. An opera queen would inversely remark that because of the music you can't concentrate on the voices.

The cramped thumb aches from the eternal copying of *Miss Julie.*

Supper at the Aurics'. The insect season has begun. We speak of sex and bestiality. Georges ends the discussion with: *Eh bien! moi, cette nuit j'ai couché avec un moustique.*

Everyone remains silent about my choice of opera subject. The French naturally feel that Americans should musicalize only Hawthorne, Thornton Wilder, or Marx Brothers' movies. They have a point.

28 July

Each morning on Marie Laure's lawn a flock is brought to graze, wearing a dozen different-sized bells. We awaken to this gamelan of goats. The twelve-toned group, like Santa's sleigh, fades pleasurably each evening as the animals are led tinkling to the hills.

I'm scared of all dogs. Why? Simba and Jeffrey, the collie and cocker of our childhood, were good friends. True, they both went insane.

The French: None asks about America. They ask: *As-tu vu telle chose à l'opéra?,* never: *as-tu entendu.* . . . With the melting off of God, psychoanalysis takes hold. Who would have guessed? this country which disdainfully defreudianized me in 1949! Then only the rich dabbled. Today their chief analyst, Lacan, is an avant-garde "thinker," while the young are "into" therapy. I used to think France had left America behind, but the opposite is true. I've changed, France hasn't, but we're still in love.

Saint Bernard society. Not easy to shift frequently from work to play, nor to talk when everyone is talking.

I could no more help being forty than HB could help being Jewish. Here dispute tightens friendship, there dispute destroys friendship.

Love implies a soldering anonymity which repels me. Or did.

Edouard Roditi, honoring the music he admires but cannot make, has sent me a silver baton. Did he forget he gave me one two years ago in New York? Has he trunks full of them?

Marie Laure speaks of modern chicken-breeding: *Ils naissent dans leurs cercueils.* Born in the coffin.

No, Europe never took American "serious" music seriously. France still doesn't, but that makes little difference since France has surrendered to Germany her role as musical tastemaker. Naturally today the only music taken seriously by anyone serious anywhere is that of Elvis Presley.

Yes, the revitalization of dodecaphonism recommenced not in Germany but in France. One doesn't think of France as latching onto "systems"—schools, perhaps (Impressionism, Surrealism, Dada), but not systems. Though, of course, it is not countries but individuals who make rules in art.

Cannes
1 August

French popular song has triple meter with narrational subject matter in A-B-C form. ("When our love was young he looked at only me; then he slept with my best friend Annette; now, though I've killed him and await the guillotine, I'm content knowing we'll soon be together in heaven.") American popular song has duple meter with static subject matter in A-B-A form. ("He doesn't love me, maybe he will tomorrow, but he doesn't today.") The American relates a state of mind, the French a state of body. The difference between America and France is, in the largest sense, the difference between Protestant specialists and Catholic nonspecialists.

What is the Beatles' genre? Being English they straddle the ocean by describing little situations, or storylets, which develop, which "happen" (but which are certainly less than Piaf-type sagas), and they do it in both duple and triple meter. The genre is seminarrational.

Passing through Cannes were thirty American beatniks (do they still exist?) with beards and stringy hair, guitarred boys and dungareed girls all with copies of *City of Night*. How sweetly nonresistant were they to the police! how like silent gypsies their shadows crouched at midnight on the public beach, how utterly casual were their almost-no-movements, how very young, how pretty!

I always come here as a reward after every two weeks of work. Yet it's never a reward, this time more sordid than ever. *La prison de luxe.*

Less a need for self-expression than for self-justification. There *is* self-expression too, but with more métier and less earnestness than twenty years ago. Besides, what else should I do? Not to mention work's being a detour from death. Time stops when work starts. But possibly my best work is over.

The unquestioned assumption that the best work lies ahead!

Hyères
15 August

Mornings are satinier, French fruits sweeter. Having by choice no love, I feel free. Being steadily at work, have a minimum of desire beyond the evening odor of black petunias in the park along the *Avenue des Iles d'Or* which occasionally I cruise halfheartedly. Since I can only live excessively, I am excessively moderate today as I compose to the accompaniment of Marie Laure's brush strokes in her atelier next door.

Tonight I'm alone for once in this fifty-room castle so familiar for thirteen years. Plump Lily has served the evening meal on a silver tray and I consumed the cold cuts, artichoke salad and peach-surprise, while watching the sun fade over the walls of medieval brick and cypress which hide the house from the town below. Now in the darkness I take advantage of the "freedom" to write a little here.

What shall I say? In six sexless weeks the least "good" of the twenty or so French books I've read is the diary of the youngly-dead Jean-René Huguenin (all the rage), because it lacks gossip and carnality, the very stuff of journals.

Marie Laure praises my physicality in front of others as if I were twenty. Uneasy-making. In nine weeks I'll be forty-one. In three months there could be nothing left to praise. What can the guests think? Yet how I've taken that physicality for granted! The Ugly don't change in aging, while the Beautiful (by definition dumb) have a double problem. The problem doesn't lie in whether I was once beautiful, but in whether I thought I was once beautiful.

I am with all people as I was when I first knew them. (Two weeks ago in Saint-Tropez I saw P, and shouldn't have, after eight years, and was stunned, not by my reaction but by my action. Active indifference.) When with, say, two or more people I've known from different periods, the frictions produce a composite comportment not always successful.

In America my friends are mostly younger. Here older. The reason is not general, such as that in the States we ignore old age. It's because in France I see my old friends. They're mostly Marie Laure's. She says that I'm *un solitaire*. It's probably true, musically too, for I've never been part of a group (why be *part* when alone one is *all*?), nor cared enough to sing the praises of a cause. Besides, composers have more paper work than anyone, and it's lonely. I spend fifteen hundred hours a year *attablé*, writing music, orchestrating it, copying it. This results in an annual production of two hours of music. My first draft is my last: I revise en route. I've listened to no music (except Labisse's dreary records of Flemish jazz, or that gorgeous Johnny Halliday) in six weeks here nor do I miss or need it. I'm inventing it. And how I love to orchestrate!

No, I'm not now suffering personally. Only for the America of Goldwater.

Nobody writes about New York as about Paris: a place of parks, street names, alleys and odors, a décor. It's either all (Dos Passos) or nothing (McCarthy). Never Frenchly taken for granted.

Sulfurous afternoon on new beach with Henri Boutillier. First day free of work in weeks. Felt like a seal in the clearest water since Paestum 1957.

Auric prefers me today to fifteen years ago when we first met at the Reine Blanche, because now I'm an American musician living in America, a settled specific rather than a drifting generality. He implies that I know who I am. I don't. It's he who knows who I am.

Tony Gandarillas stops by for twenty minutes. When he leaves, Auric and I recall how in the summer of 1951 through the telescope on our lawn we saw him being flogged by his chauffeur in the Château Saint Pierre five hundred yards away.

The horror of prodigies. Cocteau in 1955: *Tous les enfants ont du génie, sauf Minou Drouet.*

Autumn uncertain, even for lodgings in Paris. But I must cross some border before October to get passport stamped. Work smooth, little diversion (though we plan Saint-Tropez for tomorrow), reading Ramuz, nights with unexpected cool streaks, and an occasional creepy breeze which makes Marie Laure go on, quite seriously, about haunted houses, and about how her own portrait, by Balthus, once spoke to her from the wall. For the moment I'm caught by her oratory which, however, is pure fantasy *pour se faire intéressante*, and one runs out of conversations as the summer draws to a close.

The future cannot be read, for it does not exist; if the future existed it would not, by definition, be the future. Most successful artists aren't much concerned with mysticism or extrasensory perception as subjects of conversation. The meaning, whatever it is, of such things is concentrated within art forms; its discussion seems relevant only to laymen.

Wednesday in Saint-Tropez. Takes longer to shake the shakes, nor has there been sunlight for days. Finished the first act of *Julie*, so I felt obliged to prove that liquor and love don't mix. As a result that beautiful town glows like a *bidonville*. Next week I'll stop for a day in Marseilles to see PQ, then fly north, how I dread it! Here Marie Laure *malgré tout* is a protecting parent, but who'll change my diapers in Paris! Have I reached the point of saying with Natalie Barney, "I like all men from the neck up"? Stars that haven't existed for millennia burn still for us, like masterpieces, bright as day. Couldn't I be the exception and, like the wandering Jew, never die?

Saint-Tropez was a nightmare, Cannes a nightmare, wherever I don't work is a nightmare, the "opening" in St. Paul de Vence with a hundred buffets and champagne à la *Dolce Vita* was a nightmare. My reading and writing have been peaceful and noncompulsive. Daily visits with the Aurics and François Arnal (the latter's still down on the terrace with César, who couldn't be more delightfully a painter) and Roro, Micheline Presle, les Achard. My twist made me the star of the *Fête des Boules* here—the French don't know it's out of fashion. But I'm too tired for either generalities or philosophy. My hands hardly move, eyes are closing, legs numb, *bonsoir*.

6 September

Lunch today with Wolfgang Fortner, brought by Madame Gidon. Also Ines Leuwen and Ennique Beck. How can the Germans, almost without exception, be such boors?

La Piscine Berriau with Nora and Roro. Lunch with Cascella and Daniel Milhaud. Perfect weather. Premature end of a season. *Julie* well under way. The end of a beginning. Too soon to leave for Paris tomorrow. Too soon to die: I haven't eaten my quota of cherry pie. No clouds, sound of the birdcages, sheep's bells, lawn mower (operated by Maxim, the gardener's son). The azure coast. And in just thirty-six hours I'll be a groaning mass of Pernod, presumably chez Roditi surrounded by the Arabic.

There's no alternative to Black as there is, in theory, to Queer. Black's static, Queer's behavior. (Black behavior is secondary to being Black.) One does not refrain from being Black. In theory,

Black has the more cause for complaint. In theory, too, it's wronger to discriminate against Age than against Youth, since there is an alternative to youth.

Criminals are saints *manqués*. Saints are artists *manqués*. Artists are criminals *manqués*.

If poetry is criminality or sainthood gone astray, as in the case of Genet, it is also childhood regained, as in the case of—Genet.

Since conservative poets feel the same as far-out poets about their poems (wanting words, if not meanings, understood), since experimental composers are seldom drawn to conservative poets, yet since audiences have a hard enough time just *getting* the words to anything sung by a "concert artist," one concludes that all music dealing with words must necessarily, to communicate, in the strictest verbal sense, be simple.

Of course in grand opera words have always been more or less dispensed with—long before McLuhan's literary incomprehensibility of deafening rock—and the music becomes more than human speech can say. But this is not babble, nor tribal, but ecstasy organized by one man.

> *Montredon*
> *11 September*

Not at all in Paris, but chez Lily [la Comtesse Jean] Pastré near Marseilles. For once I acted on impulse rather than inertia. Thanks partly to Roro who's here too I can grab another week of free sunlight, thick meals, unhampered work before we drive north.

The tone is luxuriant, ramshackle-formal (as opposed to Saint Bernard's expedient bohemianism). A thousand acres and an ancient house governed by the affectionate Countess in baby-mauve silk from vast stem to stern. A herd of female offspring, high-pitched, ample and pretty like fawns or fruits. Besides us, the only male guest is refined-to-extinction Jean de Gaigneron, and the only distractions are high tea and croquet.

Courage occupies a low rung on the ladder of virtues. None but the dull deserve the brave.

If I lean far out of the window I can see the Countess on her private terrace each dawn. She stands and sits *en négligé*, nervous and ungraceful, answering her mail as she fills a giant tumbler with slugs of Noilly Prat. From eleven to eleven-thirty she vocalizes, and practices scales on her violin, which sounds I remember hearing with fascination fourteen years ago when she was maybe sixty (it was she who first "sang" for me Poulenc's *Le Disparu*). *Sympathique.* She loves, needs music, even if undiscerningly. But who'd have believed that Lily tippled? She who for ages kept Boris Kochno on a leash.

After-dinner conversation consists of enthusiastic bromides about art. To say that the French speak in generalities is already a generality, as disdain of the Middle Class is a middle-class sentiment.

During the day, eat too much, work a little, go swimming at Cassis, recounting to vicarious Jean de Gaigneron imaginary encounters from the evening before. This notation of company and detail is less interesting than what *should* be said of the life I live. I no longer keep this journal from sorrow but from boredom.

Yes, every midnight when the household sleeps, Roro and I creep into town to a square quarter-mile between the Canebière and the Opéra seething with big-assed whores, small red barrooms, and *hôtels-de-passes*, a district freer than the one in Hamburg a decade ago when prostitutes were on display behind plate glass. Here finally, with our desperate flair, we discovered a *boîte-de-folles nommée Le Paradou*. When we opened the blue door it was like a sting chord on a Hitchcock soundtrack. *Enfin les voilà toutes!* Young bleached queens with gold eyelids sway in the arms of the *forts des Halles* as I, in the shadows, drink apricot juice, listen to the records of Johnny Halliday, and think how it's been a quarter-century since I first swayed in identical bars of Chicago's outskirts. Meanwhile Roro sighs into his Bok, his mind far from Couperin's mordents. *Mais rien!* When one considers the thousands one's had, why, at the present moment is it always so difficult? Today it's less from shyness than dread of getting involved, even for an hour. I'd rather waste an evening *looking for* than *making out*. Nothing happens: we're interlopers in a southern family. The answer remained No, although we hung around the Paradou until 3 A.M.

14 September

Despite not having had an orgasm in nine days I want either Love or a *partouze*, not a sappy flirtation with someone from the "tedious vocation as engrossing as bee-raising and as monotonous to the outsider." They still, the world over, raise their eyes to heaven lisping in unison accompaniment to the jukebox with accents Brooklynese or Provençal. (This season it's Dionne Warwick's "Anyone Who Had a Heart," sung by Petula Clark as *"Ceux qui ont un coeur."*)

Doubtless the same in Burma.

Every binge is that much less music written, or every pleasant conversation or page in a diary. A poet cannot not. He can't not speak truth. Sherban says Oscar Wilde was a hypocrite because the "frivolous" letters at the end of his life were in contradiction to *De Profundis*. Sherban is a Catholic. Surely the church knows the power and width of contradiction. Artists grow, and growth in any direction is Truth. Rimbaud and Sibelius (what a pair!) stopped short because they had to.

The French—those I know—are making the identical comments on the identical music they were making fifteen years ago. The arts are produced exclusively for ears and eyes (never for tongues, hands or noses). Northern countries are preoccupied with ears, Latin countries with eyes. We are not *au fond* all the same, but deliciously different. Yet the French persist in linking the arts without stopping to realize that not only are poets and painters temperamentally far apart, but their publics are as compartmentalized as night and day.

15 September

Anything, sunlight or night clubs, to keep from work. Yet this morning in one fell swoop I wrote Julie's mad song for act two.

My summer reading? Erlanger, Beaufort (history and nice trash), *A Moveable Feast* of Hemingway (the genius whom, with Faulkner, I loathe the most), Simenon (three books), Benoist Méchin on Alexander the Great, Julien Green's *Mille Chemins Ouverts* (only Europeans keep journals and his, alas, is the best: compare it to Huguenin's who's humorlessly amusing only because he died young), Beckett's *Oh Les Beaux Jours* (the Boulez of theater), Roditi's *De l'Homosexualité* (thorough, nonerotic), *Chronique d'une Passion* of Jouhandeau, *L'Inquisitoire*, a sort of masterpiece by Pinget, Baudelaire again, and Christiane Rochefort who, finally, is an unsympathetic bitch. *Les Mots* of Sartre is the French favorite, and I too place style over content.

16 September

9 A.M. In two hours we leave for Lyon by the Avignon route. This minute the air is clear as a diamond, the view over Lily Pastré's field blends blue air and sea and the brutal little rock islands just off the Corniche, hot icebergs. It seems stupid to leave the Midi. Last night with tawny PQ and the best Chinese restaurant this side of New York. And well now I must tip the servants.

Chez Roditi
Paris
25 September

While waiting for John Ashbery and Roy Leaf to pick me up for supper I'll write. A week ago today after a hilarious rainy car trip with Roro (and a somber night in Macon) I arrived at Edouard's who's in Delft for two weeks, but whose Algerian welcomes me *comme il faut.* The weather has been contradictorily bronze (to match the new-cleaned buildings), warmish and clean, as opposed to the unseasonable *temps maussade du Midi* all summer. Nevertheless Paris somehow doesn't delight. Yet in this week I've worked, made fugitive friends, and performed urbanities—in other words, behaved as always before.

Yes, I did get drunk forty-eight hours ago and spent yesterday loathing the world, too full of hate even to mingle with strangers, but eating cherry tarts (Rue des Carmes, and in the Eglise St. Victor, of all places) which tasted of ambrosia. At four I swore I wouldn't go to Marie Laure's dinner party feeling her insult to be crowning: *"Nous allons chez Jouhandeau; toi tu peux te promener dans la forêt de Malmaison pendant que nous montons le voir"* as though I were a *pauvre cousin.* But I went.

I mean to her party. And found Iris Clert and Harold Stevenson irksome because I'm jealous of those who work harder at publicity than at what they're publicizing. Tonight I fled to my first French AA meeting and as usual was too shy to speak to anyone. I don't react to people so much as I try to provoke a reaction. So I walked back, hating the French, and the Rue Saint Benoît was seething as never (it's Saturday), and at the Flore I looked for friends without wanting to see any. But there was Robert Levesque with a young Moroccan so I asked them home (home?) for a *verre,* and told them about the Opéra's Chagall ceiling. Wednesday it was inaugurated at the Palais Garnier and Auric had sweetly provided me and Roro with seats in Box 24. Auric sat in a *loge* with Malraux and Chagall and flashbulbs and we all craned our necks toward heaven, but only after the sensational *défilé du corps de ballet* (who dreamed—not I—that the Opéra stage is a quarter-mile deep?) was the ceiling finally lit. It's a Yiddish skirt sewn with scenes of Tristan and seamed with pasty blue and red ribbons studded with goodies from Pelléas and the odious Berlioz. Nobody's used to applauding what's silent, yet people were there to clap and they did, desultorily, while the ceiling remained inanimate and the painter rose in his box. But how long do you clap for a picture? Well, the spotlights remained fixed while the orchestra played (not badly) the last movement of the *Jupiter* which was meant to *accompany* the image, to *give time* to the observation. So everyone talked during the music (including Auric) and clapped a little more, and then a lot more when the music stopped and the lights were turned out, which signified the mural was finished. Then Attilio Labis and Claude Bessy danced *Daphnis et Chloé,* the first suite of which is patchy but the second a masterpiece I knew by heart at fourteen and I'd never seen the ballet in any form. Décors by Chagall, *bien sûr,* and choreography of Skibine. The dance scene in France is lamentable and they don't know it.

They don't know it because they of all Europeans travel least and their vulgarians, like Maurice Béjart (whose name soils these pages), sneak American choreography across the frontier watered down as their own.

6 October

Despite the drizzle I can perhaps tie up this tenth journal begun three years and thirteen days ago in this same provincial city.

Thursday was fatal. Lunch at Marie Laure's where finally, I met Marcel Jouhandeau whom I charmed like a bird off a dead tree (if not his wife Elise). Jouhandeau, who admits to seventy-six, says: *"Le bonheur ne vient qu'avec la vieillesse"* to which Georges Bernier instantly retorts: *"Alors vous serez triste pendant encore bien d'années."* . . . Over dessert (a succulent crusty *Charlotte*) Emily Faure-Dujarric surpasses herself with a *gaffe* to Madame J.: *"Au fait, Elise, si vous n'existiez pas il aurait fallu que Marcel vous invente. . . ."* We go upstairs for coffee and Jouhandeau is able for the first time to come straight toward me (*vous parlez un peu français?*) to the annoyance of Marie Laure who wants him to die for Jean Lafont, Lafont the rival: it shows on every face. Jouhandeau minces no words in telling me he swallowed poison on three occasions for unrequited love. I told him about the iodine when my parents forbade me to see *Queen Christina*. "Ah," says he, *"vous êtes à la fois frêle et très dur. J'aime les gens frêles . . ."* but Jean Denoël interrupts us, surveying, always surveying as they all do. . . . Jouhandeau gives me his phone number (but doesn't write his name on the slip of paper) and I'm to visit him next week *"pour que je vous apprenne à être plus optimiste."* Elise observes all this with a serpent eye. They then leave for the Cimetière de Montmartre to visit the new plot they hope soon to inhabit. . . . (How many have told me I'm soft and hard! How else should one be? Have I not sighed that I wish another great Frenchman would die so I could write how sad I am he's dead?)

That same Thursday Marie Laure and Jean Lafont came to dine here at Roditi's, the first time ever that ML's been a guest *chez moi*. They brought four bottles of champagne and Marc Doelnitz whom I dislike. My other guests were Guy Ferrand, suave Jeanne

Ritcher, and Sauguet, each of whose glib Gallic wit forced me to silence and wine. Yah-Yah had prepared a massive couscous and a caramel cake, devoured by candlelight which softened the dusty corners of this Art Nouveau (which the French call "modern style") apartment. By the time Claude arrived (uniting my ex-lovers forces me to wine and silence) with the worldly Charlotte Aillaud, I'd alone killed two champagne quarts. Toward 1 A.M. they whisked me to Régine's in Montparnasse, the latest black-and-red-plush boîte where the Jet Set has an excuse for bad conversation because of the ceaseless deafening rock 'n' roll to which I twisted half-naked. Was it four hours I spent trying to convince Françoise Sagan (whom I'd never met) to marry me? Three obsequious arguments to ingratiate myself: 1) Frank Merlo is dead (meaning we have the same friends); 2) have you read Brigid Brophy's praise of you? (meaning I'm an intellectual who takes you seriously even if no one else does); 3) the French wouldn't know it, but back home I have a reputation (meaning: so don't think you're better than me). I then ordered drinks from her handsome ex-husband whom I mistook for the waiter, and who forbade further conversation. If masochism underlies such detail, how much more did it precipitate me from the ridiculous to the sublime! At 6 A.M. a North African stole my 500 NF in ready cash plus traveler's checks amounting to $1,900. On awakening to reality I recalled only my reiteration to Sagan: *Si toi tu ne veux pas de moi, est-ce que tu m'offres au moins ton mari?*

The upshot: *les petits amis* spread the news, Marie Laure has "dropped" me, and all *her* friends are "very busy." People in the street, bus drivers and cops are of a rudeness classical, and the red tape of borrowing just enough to live on! Sheets and bathtub are filthy, I feel alone and hate and seek it, and feel too that—as they say—my life is not in order. All night the jukebox across the street howls, and hammers and accordions at the Carrefour Buci prevent my sleeping all day. In a month, in a year, my present nightmare of squalor and a dry tongue may grow into one of those gentle souvenirs of excess which only The Young can survive. But for the moment my ankle, broken a year ago in Yaddo, still hurts, especially mornings.

Well, things will fall back into place, they often do. Menstrual cycles have also their happy curves. In two weeks on my birthday

William Steinberg is doing my *Third Symphony* in Barcelona. Perhaps, then, I'll go to Spain, Spain whence I'd just returned when I started this notebook, and this notebook will then have the fortunate shape of an hourglass.

9 October

Edouard Roditi, blessedly back from Delft or wherever, lends a mad teacher's sense of respectability to his own household, exuding a haughty intelligent warmth that makes us all feel wanted. We have adjoining rooms. I have given him this diary to read. But my comportment being what it is, he's continually overhearing precisely what he's reading about.

Hearsay reports that Francis Poulenc's cook, Françoise, committed suicide by throwing herself down a well. His niece Brigitte, to whom he bequeathed his copyrights, has also died. Another friend to whom he left a certain sum used that sum to open a bar where he was arrested for serving minors and sent to jail. Crowning irony: like Gide, Poulenc once sired a daughter, who, not being legitimate, inherits nothing.

38, Rue des Epinettes
16 October

Alone in Guy Ferrand's *garçonnière*, near the outer boulevards. Spic and span in the Moroccan furnishings that surrounded us fifteen years ago in Fez, same plates and pillows retrieved now, so removed in space and time. I read Roditi's article on Morocco and realize that I don't care about the politics or fate of any country, but only about my contact with the country's individuals. Khrushchev was dethroned last night. If the bombs fall on Paris or New York, let it, Lord, be after I've left or before I arrive. I suggested how the world could go, and who listened? So have come to this: and the cycle is closed with the joining of Guy and Edouard who have never met.

Street of spinets. From the window one looks through branches to the biweekly market and beyond to the corner bakery, then on to the street of the Jonquil Girl. Still farther, on the Avenue

Saint-Ouen, is the world's most famous pastry shop, Vaudron's, where this afternoon (on my way home from Florence Gould's monthly literary lunch at the Meurisse) I purchased orange tarts and huge cherry *clafoutis,* all of which I consumed tonight. Behind me, though, Billie Holiday moans on the phono, so where am I except far away (from where?), and worried about her and Marilyn, Americans both, who never knew this seventeenth zone of Paris? Individuals, yes. Chaplin's boring book has just appeared. Perhaps like all great comics I have no sense of humor. But more and more I hate the French as French.

Jean Leuvrais in *Hamlet.* Shakespeare is more comprehensible in French. By definition, it's modern translation. What the language loses in poetry is clarified by contemporaneity. The "understanding" breaks even.

20 October

Sad dreams, low despite sunlight. The reason's irremedial, yet the "mere" act of *not* drinking renders me happy, so that I feel too good to go on. Avoid adult decisions. During dreams: there's one day less in my life, was it wasted? What's waste? It's hard to concentrate on other people's art, Mozart or Botticelli, and isn't it bizarre? here in the village of the seventeenth *arrondissement* with wooden shoes and kitchen gardens, to be listening to Billie and remembering how twenty years ago at Chicago's Three Deuces I put my hand between her legs and she smelled like the Catholic Church, oh old Paris.

Well, in forty-eight hours I'm off to Barcelona for the first time since our ballet there in 1952, and I'll see the same people—Mompou, Montsalvatge—and walk the streets, and be with French-speaking artists.

Hotel Manila
Barcelona
23 October

As birthday gift I offered myself the Picasso Museum in Calle Moncada and there for a while was content. The view from windows between pictures illustrates narrow streets where I've never lived, a pleasant pang, while the pictures between windows ask again *Who can aim higher?* So vanity was humbled as always since I never choose between life and work, and today, forty-one in the sun, but yesterday a rain torrent welcomed me, no taxis, and the mute subway ride in a strange town didn't help to be a man.

26 October

A city's pride can be a tourist's shock. Gaudis are cow pads.

Because during four days involuntarily I lived a miniature adulthood: as composer, as *mondain*, as tourist, as lover. After the concert, at which Steinberg conducted my *Third Symphony*, I had promised Bernie Goldberg to go barring. My pair of pleasant guests (young playwrights Enrique Ortenbach and José-Maria Segarra) had never met a flutist. Backstage we realized—already woozy from the intermission champagne—that all 125 members of the Pittsburgh Symphony shared a single dressing room, namely the wings, where their instrument cases were stored. Bernie asked us to wait while he changed. So we witnessed a hundred hurried hairy musicians in long underwear packing their cellos and white ties in great cases, joking loudly *à l'américaine* beneath the impassive gaze of the Spanish firemen. When the lights went out! The whole city's current failed. The vast bowels of the Teatro Liceo reeked of sweat, panic, wet clarinet wood and our winy breaths. Firemen's flashlights sparkled like glowworm phantoms-of-the-opera as we three made our legitimate escape leaving Bernie in the lurch. Emerging onto *Las Ramblas* the sole illumination of the flower-and-bird kiosks and autumn palms was from moving headlights. As it happened my friends left me at the Copacabana (it opens at two) where four hundred gents and three women stand upright in a room 20×40, ignoring fire laws and witnessing a shabby floor show of queens in soiled tuxedos, spike heels and feather boas, swishing through mock bullfights. Unlike Anglo-Saxons, whose humor is vicious (in the true sense) and objective, Latins are comic in themselves. With Italians the point of departure for camping is *bel canto*, with Spaniards it is the *corrida*.

At five, with two newer friends, I returned to the Manila where (despite warnings from Paris) the personnel was delighted to deliver us trays of coffee until 9 A.M. . . . X spoke perfect French. We discussed Peyrefitte and Kafka while Z (who was cuter, but just spoke Spanish) gamboled amongst my colognes while taking his apparently first bath in weeks, a two-hour process. Spain was a success. Only in such somber colonies of Mother Rome could the Torero and the Inquisition take hold, remain and fester.

Barcelona is provincial. Since that's the classic term for any large agglomeration, what city isn't?

Paris
1 November

Jouhandeau again. He'd invited me for three weeks ago but I lied, went instead to the Aurics' in Freneuse. So then last Sunday with Roro we drove out for a *visite-hommage* which I relate less for myself than for Robert Phelps:

Got lost in Malmaison park: it took as long from there to the sacred home as from the Etoile to there. Still, the *maison* Jouhandeau is worth the trip. Deep in the castle forest, it has a sign *chien méchant* outside the garden wall. A clanging bell, the author himself opens the gate followed closely by Elise in an all-enveloping housecoat (it's 5:30 P.M.), bandana, and distorting her ears are a pair of massive crystal spheres heavy as barbells. We are not introduced to the three other guests, for Elise quickly rips us from her husband *pour faire le tour de la maison*. Beautiful because habitable: to die among those huge crannies crammed with Laurencins! a second, a third story, unexpected studios, grand bathrooms and books, books, winding stairs, stone walls, a terrace over a *potager* (the domestic version of a cloister which, with musical sequences, gives me most pleasure), and beyond, a peach orchard too satisfyingly peaceful.

Downstairs now in a small room piled high with huge cushions (really huge: a yard wide), an organ, a fire burning. The others turn out to be a protégé of twenty-six, the third volume of whose autobiography has just come out (that's all they write now in France) and who spoke of it loftily before shutting up for the rest of the evening (silenced by approaching dazzlement), and an obsequious couple of early middle-age who contributed nothing more than interjections of *Sans doute, maître . . . Je suis tout à fait d'accord, maître*. The *maître* produced a tray of alcohols, I distributed heavy doses, crossed myself.

What a sketch, that Jouhandeau couple with their public quarreling, their vying for attention, their visibly nasty need for each other which is slightly less-visibly sweet! Given his self-castigating introspective writings on purity and her past as an imitation Ida Rubinstein, they are really quite *mondains*. (Gide, for instance, would have never dropped the *sort* of names they drop.) (Am already too bored with this hard-boiled *récit* not to want to cut it short.) Conversation led nowhere. I was drunkish on an empty stomach and three fat whiskies, when Jean-Michel Damase arrived. . . . Well, Roro and I did all the talking. Jouhandeau asked questions (a lot about Levesque) and Elise monologued on the good old days. The current rage of Paris is Shirley MacLaine's *What a Way to Go* (*Madame Croque-Mari*) which I said was an inverted *Candide*. They all clapped. None of us said anything he hadn't said before, and all I had to "glean" from Jouhandeau had been gleaned two weeks before: namely that he broadcasts his pederasty in dear terms, and that only a *tête-à-tête* could be sentimental. (Like Poulenc he called me *mon enfant*—and—"we must see each other soon again." *L'air complice*. But why? To *emmerder* Elise? That's a Parisian game I can no longer play.)

As I had a date with Jean Leuvrais back in Paris at seven and it was now eight (*"Dites à monsieur Leuvrais que son Hamlet était plus que beau"*), I swallowed a final sumptuous slug and returned in the dark to the city with Jean-Michel to drink muscatel until dawn.

What of Jouhandeau's writing, his value? Can I only retain reactions of others to me, not mine to them?

                                                                    5 November

A bord de France.
First day:

Indeed, I was given the Table Alone I'd requested. There I sit, solitary and grand, reading. The others regard me as The Mysterious Passenger, or so I imagine.

So I imagine. Because last week I asked Roro what the

Jouhandeaus thought of me, expecting to hear, "He's appealing and smart," or even that they'd said nothing.

"*Ils te trouvent étrange.*"

Am, then, I weird? Still a child with dreams of homework incomplete, meditating the beauty of young fathers embarrassed with Sunday baby buggies? To see ourselves as others see us will require another million centuries. Now, away from land self-exiled in this luscious jail, is a time to witness my own weirdness and how my work could at least equal it. For I no longer liked my symphony in Barcelona, all frills and show. Back in Paris unpacking blades I sliced my thumb at the self-same spot that was slammed in May 1961. These last ten days in France tore like furies at each other, loving and despising. Impatient, all irked, resentful yet lonely, hearing (still!) "*je t'aime*" (for how long?) but not needing it.

Glad to be going home (home? did I say it?) for one less time in my life. To New York which will be new, where my parents now reside two blocks away. Will I occasionally reel drunk down 4th Street at 8 A.M. and encounter Mother emerging from the A&P? That is the risk I run in leaving the Paris which is not now new, where I've finally sorted out whom I need. Nora comes out highest.

Always I've allowed living to be governed by a swarm of feminine details. I'm half-woman and half-genius (the *dishes* they break in quarreling!) with a vacuum between, a vacuum which elsewhere is Male. Compensation: women at least aren't geniuses. Am I any longer?

Second day:

There's nobody on this ship (at least in First Class where I'm lodged for the first time ever) worth knowing. So I'm free of speculation's strain and can abandon myself to ocean air. I speak only when addressed by the steward (*Vous avez passé une bonne nuit?* which is not his business) or headwaiter (*Y a-t-il un plat précis que je puis vous commander pour ce soir?* which leaves me in a quandary, the listed quails' tongues being quite sufficient). The cabin radio has two buttons, for jazz and classical, the latter emitting, curiously, almost exclusively Ravel.

Third day:

Why notate disordered notions when all about are books

clearer by real writers? Yet ironically it's through need for order that this disarray continues, so cold. I can't speak here of my musical problems, though possibly they're all I "know" about. But how to sort the other scramble? Chronologically? in retrospect? anecdotes? What's a lie? To state that no one on this ship intrigues me, or that I'm indifferent to the fate of any country, is contradicted by the very statement. Does Sartre sense that contradiction when he utters those old-hat truths in his last Situation book? Really does he care? At least he can *write*—while Simone de B. . . . (Not unsurprisingly her choice of epigram for *Une mort si douce* is the same tired "Do not go gentle" verse Stravinsky and every high-school girl has overused as though Dylan Thomas had penned naught else.)

On the boat I've read *The Group* with fascinated respect. By chance I fell upon HB's last story. He'll never be the author he sees himself as until he forgets to accept his "bad points" as *part* of himself simply because they're in print. Admitting to mediocrity does not make one less mediocre. He hasn't begun to command the objectivity of professional art. McCarthy's book is the model for what HB's means to be: the good old days disciplined by a zoom lens, modern by its very datedness of speech, not to mention the nervy aptness of metaphor and a swell feeling for spinning a yarn (what's going to happen next?). HB is still *in* the good old days so his formless poems (they *are* poems, really) lack tragedy. And they lack tragedy because they lack a comic sense.

Let me also complain of Regina who, with Juliette Greco (how can I love these girls so long? *seule Billie Holiday tient le coup,* perhaps because she's dead), turns out her feet of clay. Installed now in Paris for years with her fatuous mate, she lives within that insulated self-righteousness of newlyweds. To "survive" in this city they must avoid the French! *Dommage!* When I suggest that the French at least make good conversation, the husband answers that he was weaned among the brightest minds of our time (Harvard class of '53) "—and let Denise Duval top *that*. I wouldn't have her in my house!" She meanwhile warms the baby bottle without batting an eyelash, finding me superficial, and proud of her man. (Neither of them, incidentally, speaks French enough to greet their concierge.)

Fourth day:

Gosh I get scared on awakening at 4 A.M. to find the boat capsizing. Fantasies of the *Titanic* until dawn when I drop off again. Yet I stuff myself with the famous saucy meals, am not in the least seasick—nor have I been since 1936 when Rosemary and I vomited across the North Sea to arrive empty and famished in Stavanger where aged relations (but young Ragner could still be living) fed us carrot soup and plums in clotted cream as we watched the midnight sun.

How could I yesterday so smugly criticize Sartre and Beauvoir? The latter's little book on her mother's death turned out to be disturbingly solid. The former's the best of what there is, who, from all standpoints, can afford to turn down a Nobel Prize. What am I but a condescending undisciplined mediocrity?

Fifth day:

So we have a new president. (That is, the same, reelected.) A summer of observing in the French press before my French friends the infantilistic slanderings of grown men campaigning for the earth's most serious job not by announcing How good *I* am, but How bad *he* is! I'm ashamed—all the more that the French are only too quick to point up our childishness at the expense of our originality.

Reading Maritain's *Réflexions sur l'Amérique.* Surprisingly obvious generalities with a minimum of examples. The European seeing America through the small end of a telescope (can one ever dismiss completely one's preconceived ideas?) ends up more innocent than us. As for that American tourist who complains of French toilet paper (and I at this moment am inflamed down there: even Marie Laure wipes herself with newsprint), can't he seek the atmospheric *différences,* which really count? If I've learned one thing in fifteen years of journey it's that despite international milk shakes and penthouses, we're all quite, quite removed. Opposites attract, but only with the eyes open. The Congolese conscript and the American Negro airman, the Yankee Dane and the ruddy Copenhagener are wonderfully enough separated to marry and live happily.

A week ago this morning we docked and the New York that I'd for the first time been missing has more than fulfilled expectations: everyone's in a state of emergency. M has semiconstant tears and punished nerves. G today has his vocal cords incised (his brother died of throat cancer). T, a nonsmoker, has a lip growth removed. Nell, penniless in Washington, seems hardly recognizable, pleads for aid, her lungs devoured. And poor Bill in Towns Hospital for another cure of pills and booze and a broken heart. I avoid professional dismay (i.e., Hoiby's jitters at his opera's cool reception), but the sun, the American sun, blesses this confusion with the sweetest electricity. Jay and Jane Harrison too have fled it, feeble and fired to California.

That I've never been a whore is nothing to be proud of: bigger than I have been. But that I've never offered my soul free to the devil sometimes seems cowardly.

At Sylvia Marlowe's rehearsal Elliott Carter sits on one side of the empty hall, I on the other. We acknowledge each other with weak waves, no words, much less bravos. Next night at "the party," *même jeu*: Helen Carter does congratulate me, though Elliott addresses only Edmund Wilson (their superior minds meeting in communion) whom I'd found incommunicably tight. Next morning the press praises Carter, strangles me. Yet his piece isn't pleasant, mine is. Which is what I mean by lack of wit. We've all been brainwashed, me too, and Casals way over there basking in sanctimonious self-approval.

I've simply never taken to either harpsichord or pipe organ, the one because it can't sustain (the pee-pee raindrops make mockery of Bach), the other because it sustains too much (the pompous blur sounds like Go to Church). Obviously I'm preconditioned to the pianoforte, not censoring, just taste. However, what a temptation to compose for organ *and* harpsichord together: their separate vices would be canceled into virtues! With *Lovers*, Sylvia's silver keyboard blends with the vibraphone's gold and, when cello and oboe are added, produces a velvet homogeneity I don't need to complain about.

31 December

Sylvia yesterday recorded *Lovers* for Decca. But the premiere write-ups were so appalling (right for wrong reasons) that I can only feel: we are no longer new! (we being the post avant-garde). Don't feel like doing anything. Have only sedentary wishes to "redeem" myself through *Julie*. The long days fly past.

1965

Music revives the recollections it would appease.

—Madame de Staël

Influenza. Canceled everything including tomorrow. Lukas Foss
will nevertheless fend without me. If he protests too much, I protest
too little. An author called upon to explain his work in other than its
own terms knows the work has failed. Edward doesn't bother. My
only complaint with *Tiny Alice* is that he gives the Universe more
credit as an evil rather than as a banal concept. I despair less for
man's wickedness than for his ordinariness. However, I don't *care*
enough to understand. The reasoning of others will suffice, be it
splitting the hairs of Alice or analyzing the music scene. Today no
audience, nobody cares. It's not that people are outraged—they're
bored. Sick as a dog, muscles in crumbs, America's winter's
overheated.

Visit from one Charles Choset who would like to commission, as a
gift for a loved one, some songs. In Ancient Greek!

During intermission last week after the Copland-Taras fiasco *Portals*
(I mean, they're both so much *better*), Lenny B. tells me he'll
probably premiere *Lions* next season. But my excited tears are for
other concerns.

   Miss Julie's done. At five this afternoon Rudel and I will decide
upon the final orchestration and discuss singers for next fall. So
tired.

   Have finished proof-corrections on *Poems of Love and the
Rain*, already two years old and technically not yet launched, only
previewed (or preheard) in Madison and Muncie. It was an
"Antabuse work" written during three months' sobriety, proving
that my best vocal music's made from silence. (The snow-emerald
color of music galleys is so satisfying one could wish they be printed
that way.)

Full of antibiotics. Sick all January, during which sex closed out all else. Canceled debate with Lukas (John LaMontaine furiously pinch-hit at the last minute) and everyone thought I was shamming, as perhaps I was, though until today I've hardly smoked for three weeks. Nor since returning to America have I worked. Those five days on the ocean I spoke to no one: I'd been talking all summer and *would* be talking all winter. We each have two or three or maybe seven hundred things to say in our vocabularies of a few thousand words (no matter the order). Then we repeat ourselves into a comfortable old age. Delirious for two months. What happened? Well, Hilda Mary, the first girl I ever slept with was killed in an auto wreck (could all that flesh die?) with, necessarily, some of me. I tried to read on the perspiring sickbed, but Berenson bored, and Bowles and James too. Only Jean Harlow held my attention as, lying ill, phalluses floated through the sky, you know how it is. Christmas Eve I deposited my last opera check in the savings bank which, for the occasion, had hired an ugly middle-aged virgin in organdy to play carols on the organ "with a beat," a beat to send clients skipping, she *smiled* at me (it was "that time of year") and Oh, America. . . . And, well, Sylvia recorded *Lovers*, after which I got drunk at a bar called Skelly's (just next to the savings bank), too drunk to recall why I was evicted so violently, forehead black and blue, flat on the street. A Negro picked me up and we went to The Bistro which usually doesn't serve me (but if you're with a Negro these days they *have* to serve you!). He stole my wallet which contained no cash. Two days later it was returned, special delivery, with a note "good luck on the music." If I were him I'd have flung it to the Hudson.

Bill's back in the booby hatch: for him his plight is absolute: anything I can do, he can do worse. His drinking, so much less but so much more concentrated: is it more damaging? In his absence, I've corrected his choral proofs and returned them to his publisher six months overdue. This as a pat on my own back, since good deeds are easier than good thoughts.

27 January

It's difficult to care how to go on. Still I care enough to write. Now Protetch reports not only on anemia but on liver damage. I allow the negative to defeat me, without allowing the positive to elate me.

My music is a diary no less compromising than my prose, though nobody hears it that way. A diary nevertheless differs from a musical composition in that it depicts the moment, the writer's present mood which, were it inscribed an hour later, could emerge quite otherwise. I don't believe that composers notate their moods, they don't tell the music where to go—it leads them.

Why do I write music? Because I want to hear it—it's simple as that. Others may have more "talent," more "sense of duty" (Lukas now admits this). But I compose just from necessity, and no one else is making what I need.

Yet we're all afraid of being misrepresented, as though we didn't misrepresent ourselves every minute.

To start writing about your life is, from one standpoint, to stop living it. You must avoid adventures today so as to make time for registering those of yesterday. Of course, musical composition is also the sacrifice of social living; but though it too is possibly autobiographical, it is not necessarily retrospective—at least no one can prove it to be.

31 January

Cold Sunday night. Just returned on Lee Hoiby's motorcycle from the Waldorf where in bow ties we were honored guests at a hotel-type (breast of guinea hen) dinner for Julius Rudel. I sat between Mrs. Robert Ward with whom I discussed raising children (she has five), and Rita Rudel who like a Sargent model was gowned in vermilion velvet from head to foot.

In love I've reached a turning point and refused to turn. During extreme moments I'm incapable of what our grade school teachers called self-reliance, nor can I call for help: no friend's the *right* friend when love fails, and Valium merely alters an obsession's angle.

5 February

Clear cold yellow electric winter never felt in Europe. Sober a week, doctor's orders, and the scare works better than any Moral Decision. But I feel—well, *pointless,* as though I'd fallen for slogans of absurdity. Having all to look forward to, I look forward to nothing, and hate to be alone, having no ideas. Oh, my head's full of thoughts—musical and literal—but when I'm seated to inscribe them (as now), a "why bother" lethargy sets in. *Murder by inertia,* the supracontradiction pointed up in *The Young Among Themselves.*

Wednesday, I gave a big dinner party, wishing it were over before it began (which doesn't make for a hostlike tone). From nerves I got drunk despite what the doctor warned. The potatoes were underdone, the roast overdone, the salad too spicy, the wine sour; but my mint cake and strawberry mousse were divine. Frank O'Hara went too far in insulting Menotti (the guest, I suppose, of honor); Bobby Lewis in doing an imitation of Mary Garden broke my best glass; John Taras was here for hours before I said hello; John Pritchard arrived after the bourbon had given out. And Bill Flanagan, fresh from another incarceration, arrived five hours late with sunken eyes. I retired alone at dawn with tears and a tranquilizer.

Tonight, sad again. Dined at Shirley's with the Goodmans whom I hadn't seen in years. Sally, no less pretty than in the San Remo days, has become a compulsive talker, and speaks to me with the martyred complicity of one Gentile housewife to another. Paul, looking like a comfortable Jew, is more pontifically cocksure than even Virgil, and asked me nothing about myself.

Between these two occasions I've been to ballets and bars and am learning nothing. How do *other people* manage?

17 February

Bathroom to icebox to bed to icebox to bed to bathroom to icebox day after day and little else.

The phone woke me this morning: Newell Jenkins to say that our Nell was dead in Washington. She'd lain lifeless for days before the police broke into the room. . . . With sad relief I felt: so it's finally happened! And for hours now involuntarily I've been reviewing our seventeen years of on-and-off friendship. Curious how my elephantine recall declares I've not led a life but *lives*: each overlapping strand with every friend completes its separate trip and, like muscle fiber, never joins except in a diary's blur. Nell Tangeman was the first to sing my songs Big Time, establishing us both as "recital dealers" in an age when the recital was through. But in examining our mutual adventures (through Town Hall, Turin, Hotel Bisson, AA, Denver) until her gloomy long-distance calls for help in an unrecognizable voice six weeks ago—was this the mezzo that launched a thousand fans?—I see that each was punctured (I meant to write punctuated) by a state of stress; states which to others might occur four or five times in a lifetime were, to her, weekly. While wondering, "God, did I do all I could!" I add in fright, "There but for His grace go I!" For Nell was no longer in my life when she died. But for a time she *was* it. Today the sun streams through all my rooms.

20 February

In a large parlor at Bobby Lewis' Katonah house for the weekend, to see and smell changed fruits and air, the morose air, far from the angular city I already miss and love.

Is there being born today someone I'll ultimately sleep with? Long walk in woods, hearing stillness, listening to American sun.

In this journal I notate less about routine (reading of magazines, writing of music, arithmetic of lovers, sallying forth to social functions) or about those I see daily (Morris Golde, Bill Flanagan, Tom Prentiss, Joe LeSueur) or monthly (Maggy, Shirley, Virgil, Frank O'Hara), than about emergency, exception, self-imposed obstacle. Yet the banal eventually tells more. The banal seen through dark glasses. And retrospect. Father reads the Sunday *Times*; from across the room I see an ad for a TV revival of Edward G. Robinson's *Night Has a Thousand Eyes*; Father doesn't see it; but I'm carried to Fez of 1949 where this film was dubbed into Arabic; carried to my Chicago childhood where Paderewski and Mary Wigman played and danced (yet they say, How young you look!). Shirley invites me to hear Ornette Coleman, but I'm wafted back to our high school weekends where at Wabash Avenue's Tin Pan Alley we danced with Baby Dodds and Lil Armstrong, reporting hung over for final exams. Tonight? Tonight back in the city where JA waits to be surprised?

My frequent thoughts of Nell are more pleasant than sad, doubtless because I saw so little of her during the last three years of her life. What is revived is the happy début. To recall her is to recall her repertory, those many works we all heard first through her: Schoenberg's *Gurrelieder*, Stravinsky's *Oedipus Rex* and *Mavra*, Milhaud's *Chansons hébraïques*, Chanler, Mahler, Fauré, Copland's *In the Beginning*, Messiaen's *Poèmes pour Mi*. Reading through the Messiaen again took me to his other cycle, *Chants de terre et ciel*, which in turn, like Proust's bite into the madeleine, brought back rehearsals in 1946 with Janet Fairbank on the banks of Wisconsin's Lake Geneva. In those postwar years Messiaen already was what he remains, the most interesting composer in France today.

4 March

JA is apathetic (in the style of the times—though what times weren't? we know only our century) because he can't break the block between ambition and work questions. Work questions, because he needs to be right, before the fact rather than after. Like Auric he's hamstrung by logic. A real artist (if you like generalities, and who doesn't?—though how an artist should work provides the sole axiom in the universe without laws) is unafraid of vomit, of decontrolled shrieks, doesn't fear being bad. He *doesn't not*: he *does*—and judges only results, never possibilities. Blind before risks, he can run only correct ones despite himself—that's his definition; chance and choice to him reverse their accepted meanings. But JA, not wanting to be wrong, ends by not wanting.

Taste, like intelligence, can stifle the abandon needed for "getting on with it," although intelligence and taste are not akin.

Hotel Sheridan Cadillac
Detroit
7 March

Flew here yesterday with Morris for Bill's *Narrative* which the orchestra premiered. Detroit's the asshole of a mediocre planet where I'm obliged to remain alone for twenty-six more hours before leaving for Utah, of all places. Which puts me in a no-man's-land, time to kill, movies to see, diaries to catch up on, in the blizzardy Middle West of my teens where I no longer recognize home ground. Dine alone, walk the wet streets, see *My Fair Lady*, shower (never take more than two baths a week), go to bed and read. Tomorrow I'll lunch with Howard Harrington and persuade him to persuade Ehrling to play *Lions* next year (since Lenny, after all, won't be doing it), then go to the museum, pack and quit Detroit forever. But having written it, how now to live through it?

11 March

En route to Salt Lake City, Last Thoughts, on supposing the plane will crash, center not on unfinished manuscripts but on an end to sex. Choice or chance. On my arrival they offer me $18,000 to teach six hours a week for eight months.

It seems Braziller will publish parts of all this. You mean I'm writing for real readers?

8–9 April

The first spring evenings are here, wet and warm. Tomorrow night with Regina Sarfaty, the New York premiere of *Poems of Love and the Rain* which Tuesday we recorded for CRI. . . . The spring nights are here, dry and cold. We performed to SRO the *Rain Poems* which were what in New York one euphemistically terms a success though nobody "understood" including the singer and me whose heart still bleeds and I'm sad that I'm happy and nothing remains. (Ruth Ford on Regina: "I liked her less than I liked her.")

Adjectives for music (velvet touch, golden tone, delicious) are tactile, visual or oral—but not aural, how can they be?

Poets are worse off than composers because they earn even less, and because their craft does not demand the hackwork of copying that eases tension. A poet's main problem is what to do with those other twenty-four hours a day.

10 April

Bill's out of the hospital (again!); Edward, Noel Farrand, the analyst, each talks of sending him "away." Our impotence here. I too revolve in melancholy, but *function,* whereas for Bill a tree is a Cyclops and no jest or chastisement can make him see otherwise. He cries softly, doesn't read (much less write), and the shining intelligence seems waste—if ever we can know what is waste. Sad for other things, yet all goes well. Too tense to speak of what's most concerned me these last weeks.

The chore of beauty. Maybe what's worth writing can't be written. Why try? As a frame of reference. Art isn't *that* important!

Fame brings more pleasure than the so-called creative act it irrelevantly celebrates. Fame while it lasts is complete, while creation (how I despise that ill-used word!) is often unfaithful, always imperfect.

Perfection is no more a requisite to art than to heroes. Frigidaires are perfect. Beauty limps.

My frigidaire has had to be replaced.

13 April

So Bill Flanagan's at a "home" in Katonah. I'm sad that I'm happy and nothing stays. During illness those things most dear make no further difference.

Diary as Publication: (By the naughty nearsighted Norwegian nun.) These notebooks were written before I knew how to write.

JA says (mouth of a babe): "I don't see why your songs are so great. After all, you didn't write the words." He's got me.

I gave a dinner party of JA's chicken paprika to guests-of-honor Aaron Copland and Lenny Bernstein, the former lethargic since his dethronement, the latter comparatively subdued since the weekends away from Curtis in 1943 when I used to vomit in his bathroom. (Other guests: Virgil, Ronnie Welch, Tom Prentiss, John Gruen, Morris, Edward Albee, Joe LeSueur and . . .) Andy Warhol brought as homage *Fuck You: A Magazine of the Arts*, an audacious sheet mimeographed by a mass of postadolescent popsters. Toward 2 A.M. Lenny started to read aloud from *Fuck You* as leftovers all rolled in the aisles. All, but Edward and X who, they say, holds Edward in a high moral grip, divorces him from old friends and has him pray nightly at the foot of his vast mahogany bed. During the reading they exchanged pained looks, lips firm, then excused themselves and vanished. Is this so far from my remarks on Allen Ginsberg in Tangier four years ago ("Shhh! people will hear!")? The most terrible *enfants terribles* are, if not prudes, at least decorous in the parlor: it's the ribbon-clerks who balk at nothing.

19 April

Yesterday, Easter Sunday, Morris, Jeff Apter and I drove to visit Bill at the expensively seedy loony-bin near Katonah. We escorted him through the gloomy drizzle to an *auberge bretonne* for a long lunch. I found Bill more optimistic than I find myself, and his article on me is off to a good start: an apologia for the "noncomformist" music he and I write during this academic epoch.

Black sky. Returned to Joe LeSueur's party for Joan Mitchell, but JA was (is) constantly in mind. I can't be alone, have none of the security needed for art. Except that I do. The only new thing about these old complaints is that I'm older. Soon all spoken of will be dead and more forgotten than last year's meals or sleep that kept us breathing.

Morris' parties. What do his five gorgeous Negro maids think when, year after year, through the mist of twisters, lady painters, and middle-aged couples, they observe *boys kissing*? That these are the *mœurs* of white upper classes?

Stravinsky, being a great man, is always right. The Great don't make mistakes—or what makes them great? Like Marlon Brando's changing physiognomy, all that Stravinsky does is right, even when we know he's wrong.

The Great don't innovate, they fertilize seeds planted by lackeys, then leave to others the inhaling of the flowers whose roots they've manured. A deceptive memory may be the key to their originality.

Why don't I sort out that trunk of old letters? Not from regret, apprehension of the dead, remorse or joy of living, but because it takes time. I prefer wasting time destructively. And because this implies a momentary removal from the future: the past is awful if it blots out, even for a second, what is to come. I'm nervous about editing with Robert Phelps these journals. Once written it's fixed. But the past fluctuates. My life as I've lived it has always contradicted what I've written about *how* I've lived it.

Sans date

It is integral to singers as to terminal cancer patients not to believe in their own decay, no matter how authentic evidence may be shown to the contrary. But whereas such "disbelief" is, for the sick man, self-protective (a compassionate foliage offered by God), for the singer it is arrogance purely.

My magnanimity cannot compare to Frank O'Hara's charity. Frank writes blurbs (for me, incomprehensible) on Morty Feldman. Poets comprehend musicians more than musicians each other. It's that I'm unable to turn a felicitous phrase; I mean no one ill, especially not Lukas Foss. Talent? He has and is it: a performer able to build a sonorous arc in a manner that will affect our bodies and minds with satisfaction. No need to define terms—terms fluctuate while the definition holds.

An idea in itself is not enough, it's what you do with it. Most of us don't get more than two or three new ideas annually—that's more than sufficient for our variations. Lukas' new piece after Bach, *Phorion*, is an idea utterly unready for release to the public, like tubes of rare oil in search of a canvas, or a sexy farm boy seeking urban employment. It is incomplete, not because, as he thinks, it is supposed to be, but because it is really part of a mixed-media process, of which the other media don't exist.

Phorion is the Greek word for stolen goods—says Lukas. Tom Prentiss says only the plural *phoria* means stolen goods; *phorion* means damning evidence.

He used to write what singers liked to sing. Maybe they've come to like what he now writes; I wouldn't know—they no longer come my way. But Adele Addison did *Time Cycle* as though it were a master's piece; and years ago Nell Tangeman performed the little songs as though they were Schubert. And so they rather were. Though today his vitality seems conformist, he is a square dynamo.

His *Echoi* is a depressing masterpiece. It contains much that since childhood I've precisely thought of doing but never did.

Like *The Blood of a Poet* this diary fulfills a need no more self-exposing than Paul Goodman's most reasoned complaints. But oh the energy it takes to call off a date: keep it, *kvetch* later, repent in haste; whereas Paul complains about being stood up.

Hellish moments however are seen through friends. Nell, after her initial triumphs with Robert Shaw and Messiaen in the late forties, and the marvelous review from Virgil, observed hell in the shape of undesired death approaching. And did not keep a diary.

She assumed the privileges but not the responsibilities of a prima donna. If she lacked the bigger-than-life presence of a Steber at a party, she did have a brazenly appealing Irish laugh—at least until the seventh martini when (eyes blurred and mouth flowing) she'd make a pass at host or hostess. But she retained too little stamina for work, too little natural voice or temperament to carry her through. It was intelligence and novel repertory that made her briefly—too briefly—an important mezzo.

Nor did she receive a single dignified obituary. Thus the performer, though represented by no matter how many dazzling disks, cannot lug his glories—as presumably composers can—past the pearly gates.

Lukas lugs his glories through life, through well-directed

energies Nell also possessed and misused. The pearly gates of posterity are beside the point today. The young, even the middle-aged or Lukas, cannot sing their music anymore, while carnage escalates in Vietnam. For all I see, then, his talents are wisely employed, he who, like me, came of Quaker philosophers, plays the piano better than anyone, composed his *Time Cycle* while subletting my New York rooms when I was in Buffalo paving the way for his current influences in that city. Yes I see, then, his talents, of inexhaustibly juicy breadth, more talented (if talent still counts—and it does) than, say, Bill Flanagan whose qualities are elsewhere and otherwise. More than—but who am I to judge? *Echoi*, whatever my petty generalities have at times enviously implied, is a master-piece (that word again! now, when no one cares, when care is only for now), and how many masterpieces can we hope for, we composers and audiences alike, during one lifetime?

20 April

Jealousy? The Love Goddesses? *The Love Devil* makes an apter title. Hairless I border on boredom or hysteria.

Tonight at 8:30, to be pleasant, I am to attend a meeting of the New York Singing Teachers Association to be elected an honorary member. At 10:30 I'm due for supper at Stella Adler's. Then at midnight will cross the park to Bob Holton's who's giving a party for Henze. Henze: Naples again. There, during August of 1957, not knowing him, I rang the doorbell and said: Here I am. De-German-ized, he offered his afternoon and evening to show us his city as though he'd been born there, which, in a sense, he was. (These are meetings for diaries. In themselves uninteresting, they provide biography. I remember every hour but am too lazy to record it. Today we're both older and I guess fatter.)

23 April

I *did* go to the Singing Teachers meeting: it gives mediocrity a new meaning, is everything I've been fighting as a composer. Aged male vocal coaches with dyed copper hair accompanied (with much hand crossing) inept sopranos who winked at the enthralled audience while singing songs in German about cuckoo clocks. My own song was slaughtered, and everyone rightly praised me for the wrong reasons. These shams dictate the singers' taste across the nation!

Fled to Stella's. Now I had mentioned to no one I'd be there. So later when the doorbell rang (interrupting converse with her twelve selected nonbohemian guests, she in lamé pajamas, they in graying temples like all authors of best sellers), I was nonplussed to hear that my "guests have arrived." In the foyer stood Andy Warhol with four disheveled sidekicks, all silent, glassy-eyed, placing me in a false position. Without waiting to ask how they knew I was there, I slammed the door. Whereupon Andy phoned intermittently to the party for the rest of the evening. Picasso would not permit himself such dreary liberties. Party-crashing stops at seventeen. Had I let them in they would not—with the spirit of a Gregory Corso—have romped about goosing actresses, but stood like statues. It's the new style. . . . I crossed the park to the reception for Henze who never showed up. . . . These mysteries were preceded that morning by my call to Mother. The phone rang thrice, was removed from the hook with a dull crash, then silence. Having the key I ran to the building on Charles Street, opened the triple-locked door, and there in the sunlight irony of an absolutely empty apartment was the telephone receiver, off the hook, squeaking at the end of its cord which swung from side to side. The doorman said no one had been there for an hour.

Do I reassure JA that we are not competitors, because in fact we're not (though for reasons other than he thinks)? If indeed I had a lover as "successful" on his terms as I on mine, could I stand it? Could I stand to be Socrates to one who'll take my place? in any field? What is my place? One of never having sold myself for rubies nor been interested enough (perhaps alas!) to write in other than the only way I know? (Yet in the days of Marie Laure I used to be called "that playboy musician.") I *am* in love again while knowing every silver lining's cloud.

After the first little decade what are we yet? Yet we've only five or six more to go, at most. At most I've eight thousand nights ahead, at most alone. Or, at least, a division of mere moments: each one—no matter how it's sliced—linked in a chain pulling me (and all alone) toward the long coffin. Ouch.

12 May

The burden of true love. Joy's painful. Fortunately, like sorrow, it ends.

Though not actually dependent on, I at least need other people's opinions. (That which we recognize as a masterpiece is largely due to conditioning.) I'm not afraid of my own ideas which aren't my own. I'm afraid of my own ideas. I fear other ideas which are my own. I'm clear and open now as to what bores me.

All we do is eat and fuck and work, it's heaven. All we do is fast, procrastinate and quarrel, it's hell. Even with a lover reading quietly under the lamp we aren't wholly at ease. I used to be purposely thoughtless, now I force myself to pay. Do repetitive laments imply that through the years I just haven't learned? At least I've learned that I haven't learned.

Have I heard all I have to say? If death as you say is a joke, it's on you.

2 A.M. and JA still not back. Miserable.

13 May

God, I'm happy.

Dangers of happiness: nobody's much interested. Weep and the world weeps with you. David Smith has died. And Franklin Giddon, Judy Holliday, Carl Van Vechten. You can't do everything. Yes, you can.

Intermittently I continue to receive obscene anonymous phone calls, and refer them all to Joe LeSueur. I narrow concepts and definitions through sedentary fear. Adventure has grown to bromide. I'm only what I've decided I'm, delimiting possibilities, barricading dimensions. As much from discipline as from laziness.

Gaffe: Boosey & Hawkes requires the parts to *Lovers* which are at Sylvia Marlowe's. But she is in Guatemala and has sublet to Nicolas Nabokov. So I make a date to pick up the score from him whom I've not seen for years. We chat amiably, and I ask: "What are you doing in New York?" "Well, last night I attended Balanchine's premiere of *Don Quixote*."

"I hear it's terrible. Who wrote the music?"

"I did."

Am reminded of another *faux pas*, still more insulting in its implications. Fifteen years ago, when Cocteau's film *Orphée* was released, I congratulated Georges Auric on his background score. "What I loved most," I told him, "was that marvelous tune when Death turns on the radio." What could he answer! I was probably the only person on earth unaware that this particular music was a verbatim quote from Gluck.

In Saint-Tropez last summer, when I saw P, white had become black, yet I had not changed. Today JA is as dependable and generous as people need be; probably I'm no more dishonest than people must be. Some days are built or broken on a word of yours (you angel, you puppy). *Il est si beau qu'il me fait peur.* Now who'd have dreamed I'd come to that! How long can it last? One always asks. For once I'm "the older one" (though it doesn't alter my sexual landscape) and can look away, at how youth, with all its worries, claims priority, without even knowing it (yet knowing it so well). In the street people see JA, not me. I am, thank God, not so displeased, holding as Marie Laure held Oscar: with the bait of superiority. As Robert points out, it's not my physique but my capriciousness I'm shaky about. My infidelity is alcohol, and even that, he adds, I do, not as a lush-proper, but to show people I'm mean, not all peaches and cream.

Friends lose their worth before the fact of a lover, but regain their worth when love is gone.

2 June

Seeking Miss Julie in our decade, Kenward and Nikos and I visit Semitic Elaine Malbin on East 52nd Street, and find her ideal for Swedish Julie.

Yesterday Rosemary, her husband John Marshall and their six children sailed for Uganda.

Bill Schuman phones. Will I accept five thousand dollars to compose a piece for the Philharmonic in 1967? Will I! It's to be called *Poems of Hate and the Sun*, for voice and orchestra.

18 June

Against the better judgment of my mother who wished that I, like Robert Lowell, had taken an open stand against Vietnam, I accepted the gold engraved invitation to Washington on the 14th of this month.

Of the four hundred guests at the Festival of Arts—a first gesture of this kind by our current administration—I was, quaintly enough, the only long-hair composer. (Hugo Weisgall represented the American Music Center.) The thirteen-hour day began at ten. I walked to the White House from the Carlton, weather paradisiacal, my pretty invitation relinquished to the first of a thousand white-garbed aides, and I was instantly struck by the two impressions that remained all day: 1) Who were all these intimidated celebrities? If it weren't for badges reading Saul Bellow, or Dwight Macdonald (who, as self-proclaimed "black fairy" was, perhaps tastelessly, rather vainly—the occasion being ill-chosen—soliciting signatures for an antiwar petition), etc., it would have seemed a convention of classy salesmen. Of course, artists are no more physically beguiling than "real people"; but, in fact, few artists were present. 2) How unostentatiously clean, the White House, with its neat unobtrusive flower arrangements, its groups of military crew cuts performing chamber music in corners! Wealth in Europe is luxury, in America it's order.

Mrs. Johnson, the First Lady (this nomenclature was the sole bow to formality), greeted us individually in Southern tones beneath a barrage of flashbulbs. Faithfully she smiled all day, disappearing only at five to change from dark blue print into pale blue sequins. She's younger, prettier than her pictures.

In the East Room she first introduced the writers who read for an hour, and only Hersey caused a stir, handsomely, in a no-nonsense reference to "wars have a way of getting out of hand," quoted by noon in Washington headlines.

Then we had forty-five minutes to "view" the pictures (Rivers, Jasper Johns, Wyeth, Man Ray; no one was screened either politically or carnally).

Buses deposited us on a red carpet before the presidential entry to the National Gallery where we lunched: a so-so chicken in jellied cream, cold asparagus, salad, strawberry meringue. At my table: Phyllis McGinley who spoke only of her *Time* cover story, Mrs. Roger Stevens and the head of the Smithsonian Institution, a Mr. Ripley who was unable to answer my perhaps ingenuous question about implosion (does it make a noise?). A wise but too long speech by George Kennan.

Return en masse to the White House State Dining Room where Marian Anderson tonelessly introduced Roberta Peters and praised American music (making no mention of me, or of any composer) and the Louisville Orchestra then played my *Eleven Studies* (cut version). On my right sat the president of the Indianapolis Symphony who talked to me all during the music; to his right, the First Lady in meditation; on my left, Catherine Drinker Bowen scribbling notes on how divine my piece sounded; on her left, George Kennan. And me, heart pounding, because the presumable cream of U.S. culture was obliged to presumable silence for twenty minutes by my presumable music. . . . Concert over. Kennan leaned across Mrs. Bowen to congratulate me, receptivity well marked upon his sad intelligent features.

Mass removal to Ball Room for The Art of the Stage introduced by lovable little Helen Hayes (holding back the tears). . . . Plays over. Mass removal to the movies presided over by Charlton Heston whom I'd not seen since our work together on Iris Tree's comedy in 1948. (He didn't seem to remember.) . . . Movies over. Gene Kelly spoke of choreographing my piece, showing he'd really listened, really heard (which is true of one in three hundred), while screen directors Zinnemann and Wyler praised me (genuinely or not), doing wonders for my ego.

But now I was (and am) bored, my contribution having come and gone. Five o'clock. The schedule allowed us, like grammar school inmates, two hours of recreation, again to *view* the paintings. I considered leaving since I missed New York already, but decided to fly back on the nine o'clock shuttle, since after all . . .

Tour of grounds. Giddy sculpture on Protestant lawns. At seven, cocktails. No one drunk. (I shuddered at the thought of an Oscar Dominguez there, surrealistically goosing the First Lady or disrobing among the saxophones. Aren't artists *supposed* to drink?)

We now found ourselves seated on hard-benched rows amongst the roses, where promptly at 7:30 our President appeared and spoke for ten intelligible minutes, then descended into the throng and (do my eyes deceive me?) was assailed by autograph seekers. "What are we doing here?" some of us asked, as he shook our hands without seeing our eyes.

The evening buffet, consumed beneath lantern light, consisted of shrimp creole, roast beef, mushroom salad, champagne. To my right sat the Kansas City Symphony's president. I remarked: "Virgil Thomson is from your town." "Ah yes? And what's his line?" This exchange illustrates the tone of the day. Whereupon I departed for Manhattan, missing the Joffrey ballets and Duke Ellington who, it's said, played far into the night (which Kenward, when I told him about it by phone, heard as: foreign to the night).

Postscript. Paul Hume, as always, granted me a pretty review. . . . Next day a gleam of joy. In the Museum of the City of New York I arrived on the second-floor landing at the moment a five-year-old nymphet in slate-blue dotted-swiss emerged from between two glass cases filled with pewter, and flashed me a grin brighter than the sky through that dark window behind her.

Old Lyme, Connecticut
18 July

Ten days ago JA in cap and gown graduated from Cooper Union. Here now we are for a farmhouse weekend. I'd forgotten to bring orchestration paper, so mostly we've been quarreling. Until we found the attic filled with costumes in which John Gruen (as Stella Dallas flanked by his eight-year-old Julia) photographed us all. Our host was Mother Hubbard, JA a toreador, the local cowhand a mandarin. But I, bedecked in a shoddy *décolleté* bridal gown, one strand of pearls (no wig, no makeup, *toujours simple*), and a posture to-the-manor-born, resembled a youngish gloomy sapphic literary baroness of prewar Berlin. Such is the way of our leisure class.

My music needs no explication. My Boswell could only be a sentimentalist. I see my sillier self objectively and now in books, too early or too late. People aren't people until they're stimulated—two or three times in a life. Meanwhile they're vegetables in a stream drifting.

> *At Tom Prentiss'*
> *Fire Island Pines*
> *10 August*

Away from city pollution listening to various recordings of *Jeux* and observing squid eggs through a microscope. Haven't written or read a thing in four days. Sunburn. Forty-five years ago today Father and Mother married.

Last night I wrote THE END on *Miss Julie*'s orchestration. It's like completing *Crime and Punishment*, like losing old friends, left at loose ends. Eighteen months' work, a thousand pages, half-a-million neat notes. . . . Now it's delivered to Arnstein for extraction, six copyists working nights to whom (to the nights!) Boosey & Hawkes will pay five grand. (Numbers, numbers.) Then building of sets, hasty rehearsals, collision of composer with conductor, director, designer, costumer, sweat, soloists, choruses, numbers and money and time, time, all for an opening which will fail November 5 and one additional performance seven days after, fireworks and obscurity. But it's my biggest piece ever, out of my hands, and now what can I do? Write something else.

> *16 August*

Finished *Pudd'nhead Wilson* and am reading *Zuleika Dobson*. Seeing movies but not enough.

"A little too much is just enough for me." Actually it is no longer. Here's where JA finds disappointment when he should rejoice. Our thirteen years' difference underlines my change. He lives visually in the present (the artisan's immediacy) while I live aurally in the future (the artist's posterity). He is sensuous, reacting to kisses and food and the color of a room. I'm what he calls a limited poet, reacting to sex and the past, the blindness of music. The difference hurts him. He needs understanding, I require conflict.

Urban heat wave. Without society, routine summer days are interchangeable except that each draws us nearer. . . .

What's worth writing can't be written. Why write? As a frame of reference. (Or: the greatest moments [thoughts, ideas, etc.] have no expression [lingual, visual, etc.]. Then why Art? As a point of reference.)

25 August

Order and Late Joy. Am between two works, like between day and night, *entre chien et loup.* Looking for poems—poeming I call it—for Carolyn Reyer's cycle, and for words about Sun for the Philharmonic commission. Guilt, that good old word. Feeling guilty about looking for poems to set to music, feeling the time should be spent in *setting* them to music. Feeling guilty about feeling guilty. Yet not feeling guilty about wasting time.

I am never really convinced that cities don't disappear when I leave, so I'm surprised to find them intact when I return. I'm also surprised to find them no longer intact. Perhaps the world *won't* stop when I die (if I die). But please assure me it will change—I mean that it won't be able to change (except for the worse).

3 September

Mass meal with Julius Katchen, the Graffmans, and hangers-on. Pianists talk of fingerings and food, and nothing else—oh, travels maybe, or anecdotes about audiences (underplaying how many people walked out on them in Singapore or somewhere because an earthquake made the chandelier a threat). Never ideas. But they are good-natured and, like singers (who speak of food only), more relaxing and less bitter than composers.

Too busy to work! Out of the question that I compose any music for the next six weeks. Julie's rehearsals are all-demanding, plus visits to Father in Beth Israel, then Utah in a week for a week, then interviews, essays, broadcasts, diary alterations for Braziller. Too busy to work, but not to worry. . . .

Attending a party for oneself after a flop is something to avoid. Though maybe Kenward's right, maybe such parties are funerals whose arrangements must be professionally attended to. We are, after all, the survivors. . . . These are preopera thoughts, I feel put upon. . . . *Lions* is to be premiered by the Detroit Orchestra at Carnegie, just one week before *Miss Julie* opens.

Is love settling for second best? What is important? Philosophy and war? Or the sting of heat on garbage cans in early spring?

Réverdy maintains there is no love, only proofs of love. By the same token there is no poetry, only proofs of poetry. There is no universe, only proofs of the universe, and those proofs are art. . . . People are suspicious of an artist who will not verbalize his work: they feel he is evading the issue. Yet a phrase like "let the music speak for itself" is corny only because it's true. My performers, in singing for their supper, may starve. Still I'm beginning to miss the solitude of work, the silence of my own sounds.

15 September

JA "accuses" me of never having suffered; if I *had,* he says, I'd have told him about it. Well, have I? What, indeed, has this diary concerned for twenty years? What of the death of friends? The winter of Claude? The operation for piles? What about the making of any piece of music? Or just living? What *is* suffering? Who's to say who has or hasn't? Is it important? Can it help work? Could the *effort* toward happiness be termed suffering? No, rather, the *ability* for happiness—not for sorrow—is *the* achievement. A last beginning.

JA's need for independence is something I should encourage if I myself were more securely independent. Yet if I don't allow him to love himself how can he love me? Mozart's pain is no more acute than the hatcheck girl's. Love and logic: a meeting more impossible than bees with humans. Instinct and reason: their collision explains stars.

It's New York and late summer. The strongest remaining pleasure is, toward seven in the evening on our way to supper at the Waverly Inn, to pass beside those molting Rose of Sharon trees that hang over Bank Street.

23 September

Last night, City Center gala of *The Flaming Angel*, the season's one other new production. When it was over, Copland smiled slyly at me through the crowd and said, "You're next!"

Salt Lake City
28 September

Here for a week briefing my mild pupils on what to expect in '66 when I return to stay. As a professor I'm getting a foretaste, with an identical loneliness felt a quarter-century ago this month when my family deposited me as a freshman on Northwestern campus. In the early cold I dine alone (the cafeteria closes at seven) among the sexy students, and the sole friendliness is a glow on a vat of boiled spinach. Missing JA. Wondering when I'll die. Peaceful.

Abravanel (a Jew—hence a Gentile for these Mormons) seems a civilized ray of hope.

15 October

Are not the Beatles, at first sound, like a choir of male nymphets? like the long-silent castrati of Handel's day evolving through Tom Sawyer via Balthus? or like Tchelitchew's leaf-children come to life with androgynous cries echoing all through the tree of Hide & Seek, not asking but forcing us to listen again?

The Candide theme (Herlihy's *Midnight Cowboy*, Genet's *Querelle de Brest* or Southern's *Candy* versus Britten's *Billy Budd*, Bernstein's *Candide* or the Purdy-Albee *Malcolm*) makes good reading but bad theater. The beautiful but dumb cipher-hero plunging down a narrow path causing distress and destruction to intelligent victims—whom he ignores as victims—is inherently undramatic, being unclimactic. Meanwhile, the unlikely play *Fortune and Men's Eyes* works musically and thus works theatrically (over and above its "theme" stolen from *Haute Surveillance*). The author's quartet is composed of solos for each instrument, duets and trios for the possible combinations, and ensembles for the whole with an ingenuity all true climaxes imply and comprise.

If Winter comes can Spring be far—*behind?* But Spring's ahead and waiting. Winter overtakes, dissolves into and is excreted by Spring. Then do seasons arrive before or after each other, or spiral about, intertwining, contradicting time?

So where do we go from here? To boredom. There's no beginning and end, and boredom's integral to it. Though one can vainly ponder as to how boredom, as we know it, might be a part of Eastern Art and Music. Twain don't meet.

Toward the middle of *The Chelsea Girls* I turn to Jack Larson: "It's a masterpiece, isn't it? And shall we leave now?"

1 November

The past month has been wonderfully tiring. If only I'd kept "A Julie Journal," I've learned so much. The production coordination of the inexorably cold union schedule with the interpersonal heat of hate and hysterics. Daily coaching with the admirable principals, Elaine Bonazzi, Donald Gramm and Margo Willauer. Everyone working for me, on my trillion little notes. The assistant director at odds with the conductor, choreographer in a blend with costumer, the three leads drowned in the chorus, the supers lost among the orchestra men who look at their watches, the management gripping the whole, and the whole pseudodeferentially looking to me for the last word which I cannot speak. (A composer has the first word, never the last.) The climax was reached in the huge publicity of yesterday's *Tribune* and *Times* with my photograph adorning complacent interviews by Allen Hughes and John Gruen, and the cast dressed fit to kill. Thursday's sold-out premiere will come as an almost letdown. Meanwhile the Detroit Symphony with my *Lions* arrived and roared and left.

No leisure for reading or writing, liquor or love, only for nursing the nervous throat obsessed with cancer, and I've had another birthday, the forty-second, on which JA moved in, and Paul Tillich died.

With Robert, I edit my diary for Braziller. Excerpts already appear here and there in cool print proving again that anything frozen onto paper becomes untruth. Truth is fluid, invisible, nonexistent even, like lines in space. It implies shifting emphases of standpoint and the Now, never of history. So my diary is all fiction.

3 November

Catastrophic dress rehearsal. Ridiculous spoken preamble by me for the invited lady Friends of City Center. Margo, vocal cords frozen with anticipation, merely mouthed her role, while Donald's decapitation of the bird caused laughter and had to be restaged. Question of firing the conductor (Rudel, at this late date, envisaged memorizing the score himself overnight), but settled instead for an extra orchestra rehearsal tomorrow afternoon. Kenward and I profoundly dissatisfied with the gauche lighting. The printed libretto arrived, seething with errors. (Boosey & Hawkes has hired JA to design the covers; for this purpose he has bought a canary which he intends to photograph—after wringing its neck.) The fact of a lousy dress rehearsal does not—despite Broadway superstitions—indicate a glorious gala. Tuxedo back from cleaners. In twenty-four hours it will all be over except for the party.

12 November

CRASH! Margo lost her voice, whether from fear or fever, and portrayed Julie half-spoken throughout—which few reviewers remarked. Now, professionals at crucial moments just don't lose their voices—or what makes them professional? Yet I also endured misrepresentation on other sides. For instance, there was Prokofiev's *Flaming Angel* in whose lavish shadow my opera was economically given short shrift. Had I been more experienced, or more aggressive, perhaps I could have imposed righter terms; but how was I to know that finished sets don't resemble maquettes? that lighters won't take last minute advice from composers lamenting what seems a peasant cottage in cheap blackness instead of in a wealthy midsummer haze? My sour grapes growing from the stage's scraggly poplar might have ripened were I less concerned with just the music. And the critics were blinder than I. So, until an ideal production is one day mounted and *still* reaps bad write-ups, I'll continue to pass the buck in retrospect.

Time magazine:

> Ned Rorem is tall, dark, handsome and undoubtedly the best composer of art songs now living. "I can put anything to music, including the encyclopedia," he once remarked, with an engaging lack of diffidence. The Ford Foundation believed him, commissioned him to write an opera. Last week Rorem's opera had its premiere. The overall verdict: Rorem would have been better off with the encyclopedia—and the U.S. is still looking for its first major operatic composer. . . .
>
> Rorem, who was raised a Quaker in Chicago, spent eight years in Paris working most of the time in the 18th-century mansion of the Vicomtesse de Noailles. He returned to the U.S. in 1959, taught at the University of Buffalo. "It was a juicy salary," he says, "but I hated it. Most of the students were such clods—and I was jealous of the rest." In January he plans to accept a similar post at the University of Utah, where he hopes to create an opera for cinema. "Utah is such a boring state," he explains, "I know it will be good for my work."

Time then quotes me as "hating" the sets. Needless to say, I sent off a note to Buffalo apologizing for the out-of-context reference. *Time* has this week printed my "letter of retraction":

> Because I do not want to bite the hand that feeds me, I'd like to amend (or at least amplify) the phrase that "Utah is a boring state." No state, by definition, is in itself boring. As for The State of Boredom, to me it is synonymous with tranquillity, i.e., lack of distraction, which most artists will concur is the first requisite for getting anything done.

Yet I must still go off to live in Utah soon, and doubtless be lynched. Meanwhile a final performance of *Julie* took place

Wednesday (in the wake of the blackout!) which proved in nearly every sense superior to the opening. The principals, Willauer, Gramm and Bonazzi chewed up the dubious scenery, while Zeller's orchestra glittered and soared toward appropriate shrieks. Too late. No one came. And thus, the demi-elaborate preparations trickled away like those of the actress in *Diamond in the Sky*, like those of Balanchine's *Variants* so succinctly adumbrated by Edwin Denby, or like the taciturn *Bartleby* of Flanagan who, less grandly to be sure, expired, but no less sadly.

1966

The man who really knows can tell all that is transmissible in a very few words. The economic problem of the teacher . . . is how to string it out so as to be paid for more lessons.

—Ezra Pound in *ABC of Reading*

Hard to write here now, two months later. But if I don't write here
that I can now live without writing here, who will? So I will. . . .
Partly it was *Miss Julie*'s failure—the publicized flop (shall I admit
my heart was never in it? that I, too, never believed?), followed by
the complications of leaving the heart behind and coming West;
partly also the imminent publication of these Diaries that inhibit
the hand. Doubtless the prose will receive as derogatory a press as
the music—but for different reasons. (Why different? I'm saying the
same thing.) Music reviewers who put me down evaded the
problems I solved by inventing other problems and stating how *they*
would have solved them. Literary reviewers will stab me for
insolence, though insolent I'm not, just the diary is, its form (at least
in America) having no standard of comparison. None judges a work
on its own terms. Nor do *I* judge, but simply, like Valéry, condemn.
However, I am not a critic. My music is a diary where no one sees
the dirty words.

Miss Julie, during the eighteen months of her making, never
really concerned me. And during those ninety preparatory days I
grew removed from *their* excitement, intrigued only by the
complexities of transfer from paper notes to living breath. For
nearly fifteen years I've not been *concerned* with what I've done.
(This dates back to the post-Moroccan days when I began regularly
to be played, to be a "professional.") I compose because I know
how, that's all. If I've anything to impart I'm unaware of it. Yet now
Salt Lake offers me a salary precisely to impart what I presumably
know. What I know then comes forth exclusively in citing friends.
At least it's I who select the citations, and doesn't that grant me a
certain claim to individuality? Or does it?

The archness of the preceding paragraph is just what I predict
the critics (if there are any) will take at face value. When does a

diary say what it means? The same material two hours from now would have emerged otherwise. Of course my music concerns me. *Julie*'s failure was stunning!

9 January

Meanwhile, ensconced in a new apartment building, *genre môtel de luxe*, surrounded by the Wasatch Hills, I won't be able to say fuck, much less do it, for months. (*Je baise, donc je suis*.) I know no one but the University President and the Symphony Conductor. Abravanel is good and more than considerate of my first week here, partly, no doubt, to serve as buffer for those who (justifiably) resent the remark that "Utah is a boring state." Certainly we have points in common (as though points in common matter anymore: I lament there's no one to talk to, but when there's someone to talk to I'd rather be alone.) Wasn't it he who in 1932 gave Kurt Weill his first French hearings in the *salons* of Marie Laure? Yesterday he generously interviewed me on an hour-long program of my pieces for the local radio, after which we lunched at the Alta Club with none other than Henry Mancini who—though he may lack Abravanel's verbosity and my pseudosophistry—is an ingenuous sexpot and makes two hundred times more than just me put together. . . . I record such *minutiae* (or however you spell it) by way of demonstrating that though I've taken up residence in this "boring state" I still manage to rub elbows with The Great, and the town's matrons have already let me know that if things get too dull they'll provide me with pretty girls.

Not a perfectionist. A polisher, yes, but not a perfectionist.

In an excised portion of his forthcoming review of Susan Sontag's essays, Robert Phelps hits the nail of Camp squarely on the head: the middle-class homosexual mocks himself before anyone else can (Wilde's sunflower, etc.). Camp's of necessity middle-class. It was not featured in Shakespeare for whom a bourgeoisie didn't exist.

10 January

In six days here how has solitude settled? I've begun and completed a whole little *Votive Mass* for unison chorus and organ. And of course teaching conscientiously (how they hang on my every rehearsed word! and how I give all, knowing nothing will come of it but their memories), reading (Arbasino and Kleist), and socializing —mostly with a Jewish milieu.

In the student cafeteria yesterday I was astonished to hear two tawny youths speaking Arabic. It seems that this state contains the largest Moslem population in America. Mormons, having found Iran to be climatically identical to Utah, made converts who returned here, bringing their anti-Semitism along.

How many more days have I? What will be "said" in them? Is my best work behind me? Is anyone's? If I do die, does that prove I'm mortal? that I didn't invent the whole thing? I think of your arms and odor and lips and brains and friendship and go crazy.

13 January

Late last night, alone—or so I thought—in a studio in Music Hall, I was reading through the Purcell *Fantasias* at the piano. Gradually the music grew out of focus. I grew scared, stopped playing, yet sound continued. Wasn't I alone? Stepping into the hallway I heard more clearly what seemed a distant wheezing tuba. I peeked into the concert hall and witnessed this: eight women, each armed with a double bass, were performing unison exercises under the tutelage of a ninth. My ear had heard brass. Unexpected sonorities aren't always identifiable: middle-C on the piano, caught and sustained electronically after the ictus, is acoustically identical to the French horn. Pop a green grape into the mouth of an unalerted blind man: he'll think it's a soft marble or a butter ball.

Does sound come to our ears, or do our ears go out to sound? Earshot is a meaningless word; our ears go out to the horrible beauties all about. Or *should* go out. Really we hear just our heartbeat, taste just the tongue, contemplate our navel, smell nothing but our upper lip, and feel not even our own fingertips. Perhaps they're all we have.

Apparently it's been dark and cold in the East. Here, after ten days of abnormal Spring, it finally snowed heavily this morning. I was speaking to my students when, between parentheses, I turned to the window and gasped at the blizzard. Yet now, at four in the afternoon, the city is clear yellow and warm again with no trace of the earlier whiteness. Days growing noticeably longer.

Outing in the mountains with the Abravanels (we speak French: she's *parisienne*) followed by a *poulet au riz* at their house, and then to see *The Red Desert* which I liked even better the second time. (Antonioni is beyond definition, like a beached whale.) None of which relieves my eyes which ache and quiver from surplus of composing and reading. The composing is on the cycle to poems of Kenneth Koch. The reading, which is Janet Flanner's wise and, in its way, thorough *Paris Journal* (so unlike mine), inspires me mostly to dream of whomever I was regularly sleeping with during the periods she depicts, although to her (at least in print) those years were less sensual than political. Was it already fifteen years ago that Marie Laure, in the Bagatelle rose gardens, was starting my French education? Today I can no longer *hear* that language because I understand it; it's hard to listen to a tongue *as music* when you know what it's saying (the same might be said for the over-familiarity of "real" music). Today in New York I loathe going into streets of unfriendly visages, traffic masses and pollution descending like a mat. Today in Utah I find friendly faces—perhaps that's all that need matter. We have time (and space) for only so many people. They must be treated gently. I can no longer "play" with them all, a certain detached remorse forces me to *pay* for my past relationships.

Artists don't seek reasons. They are all by definition children, and vice versa. Like children, alas, they are always showing you rough drafts.

During three weeks here I've written twenty-seven minutes' worth
of music. And detest every note.

When Gide's wife like Hedda Gabler burned his letters he told
the world that his greatest effort had been destroyed, and the world
believed it. Why believe in the invisible? Gide's statement was a
tour de force, but those letters could have been pap.

An author grows inclined to disdain his more successful works
(they lead their own life after all) while retaining a fondness for the
less appreciated ones. Maugham preferred his little-known *A
Gentleman in the Parlor* to *Of Human Bondage*. Cocteau used to
ask, "Why don't they read my poems instead of *Les Enfants
terribles?*" These tendencies demonstrate more a testiness on the
part of the author (he wants to be loved for himself alone, i.e., his
whole self) than a lack of discrimination on the part of the public.
The public's been trying its hardest but, in a sense, can't win. (That
joke about the mother who gives her son two ties. When next she
sees him, he's wearing one. She says: "You didn't like the other?")

Two more old acquaintances—old criminals *manqués*—have died
this week: Giacometti and Noah Greenberg. Their lives taught me
more than their heart attacks. Smoking twice as much. In Utah
what else is there? Yet this city demands more and more. I'm
neither a professor nor a celebrity but a composer. Being a
composer has here transformed me into the other two, leaving little
time to compose. Tomorrow Copland arrives, bringing air of the
East for which I long. This evening Gary Graffman plays a recital of
a kind I'd never attend in New York. Old Home Week. To see our
friends, we must leave the town we all live in.

Aaron here now to conduct two concerts, and to receive an
honorary degree during which I too will sit on the stage demurely in
cap and gown. The first person in whom I've been able to
"confide," he adores gossip without being a gossip, unlike Virgil,
with whom we still relate (if not compare) him; they're our fathers.

He too's at a loss with his spare time. So last night after rehearsal I invited him (he paid) to Bimbo's Basement Pizzeria, the only place which seems to be open after eight in campus regions. Bimbo's turned out to be a basement high school hangout, and as Aaron and I chatted (about how to conduct, about his recent trip to Poland, about David D's talented complexes and Edward A's flop which somehow satisfied me, about the Mormons who inhabit an unchallenging compound from which they never emerge, about how I feel current privations less than I feel I should feel them and about the continued drought in New York where water is a subversive beverage)—as we chatted to the tune of the jukebox, our bulging eyes cased the room which in the hour had filled with model juveniles. Aaron's remark: "I can see why you're demoralized. There's not a soul here *our* age." On the way out we paused before the glass partition of the open kitchen to regard a dark young saint with sturdy forearms knead the dough, flatten it, smear it with tomato paste as though preparing a canvas, sprinkle it (first with chopped peppers, then anchovies, hamburger, saffron, truffles), and pop it into a white-hot oven, only to resume the procedure from scratch with another wad of wet pasta. There was flour in that almost-blue hair which curled sweetly in the heat while, with an occasional glance our way, he pursued his assembly-line duties, presumably throughout eternity.

At nine tonight we're to have supper with Maurice and Lucy Abravanel in the mountains.

23 January

Besides letters, JA phones twice a week. Today again the news was death. Noah Greenberg's mother, learning of her son's attack, expired a few hours later. Now Ruth Yorck too has died, at the theater while watching *Marat/Sade*. We loved everything she attempted, nothing she produced. A final cruel irony—the theater audience mistook her dying agony for yet another directorial excess and looked away, embarrassed at her amateurish histrionics.

Sapphirine weather continues inviolably. This morning, on the lawn before Music Hall, there were robins, a regular invasion of red plump robins. Ironically I'm comforted by his depression (known so well and often, though he for the first time) which takes me out of myself while giving the force to guide him by remote control.

Last night, yes we did dine in the mountains, and tonight I'll pick Aaron up again at his Hotel Utah (a De Mille set) and go to a Japanese restaurant.

Twenty years ago after the premiere of a Ben Weber work at an ISCM concert I asked Lou Harrison: "Was that piece of Ben's twelve-tone?" "Sure. Couldn't you tell by the way he avoided saying so?" Imagine such an attitude today!

Of course I was part of that serial movement—the part that talked against it.

They're all writing the same piece. At the moment that piece is for intoned speech with small chamber group, and resembles—according to the instrumentation—*Pierrot Lunaire* for parties (Boulez's ice-cubey xylophones), or *Pierrot Lunaire* for barnyards (Berio's cackling woodwork), or *Pierrot Lunaire* for Sunday School (Babbitt's organish loudspeakers). Pieces that evoke—as these do—extramusical rather than intramusical stimuli are always preferable to vice versa, i.e., those point-blank imitations of the above three B's that grow indistinguishable from each other.

The difference between Reactionary and Conservative is that the former uses traditional devices unchanged, the latter uses them freshly. Within the catalogues of, say, just Barber and Moore, both tendencies exist. To name only vocal works: *Knoxville* and *Baby Doe* are conservative, *Vanessa* and *Wings of the Dove* are reactionary.

I could hope for my music to be thought dateless (like much of Satie—his *Gymnopédies* sound as new today as in 1888), not astonishing for when it was composed (like much of Ives), or pleasantly nineteenth-century (like much of Menotti), or quickly *démodé* (like much of the current Academy). But without Time, unmannered. . . . They tell me I'm gazing into a mirror of the past. But mirrors are faithless: if they reflect the truth vertically they inevitably lie to breadth, since right and left are reversed, and become wrong and left. Am I right to be left and wrong?

24 January

Last evening the young girl operating the elevator at the Utah Hotel confided she felt feverish. Was she coming down with chicken pox? On reaching the ninth floor a few moments later I recount this to Aaron who answers that *his* elevator operator had *recognized* him and was coming to the concert Wednesday. Then he showed me two fan letters from innocent youths (one in Michigan, the other here in Salt Lake). The Father of American Music preens over such tributes. On television they ask what I think of Copland "as a man." (What Aaron thinks of *me* "as a composer," after twenty-three years of acquaintance, is uncertain, since he never comes to hear my music.)

We walked a cold mile to the Pagoda for second-rate sukiyaki (I paid) and three hours of talk, mostly gossip. But what were his reactions to being a performer: guilt at spending a week here rehearsing an orchestra in his old pieces, instead of staying home to write new ones? Yes, he said, but there's always the chance that if he'd stayed home he'd not compose. Well, the performer's life! Four thousand people cheer you, and an hour later you're in your hotel room alone. So we walked the Sunday streets at 10 P.M. encountering *one* pedestrian in the whole downtown area: a drunk Japanese. I showed Aaron the Temple and Tabernacle. We examined a group of sad soldiers piling into a bus at the depot. Their departure left us alone at the Do-Not-Touch magazine rack which displayed mostly movie rags featuring Jackie Kennedy. That was our night. Aaron is given neither to philosophizing nor to overt self-pity.

Returned home to finish Truman Capote's new murder book which, though it scared and engrossed me (so does Agatha Christie), is all I disadmire in writing: the author is invisible.

Tonight at 8:30 Aaron received an honorary degree in the Humanities, bestowed by Abravanel and by James Fletcher. I and around thirty colleagues sat with them on the stage, dressed

appropriately, and gazed into the huge hall which embarrassingly
contained around thirty spectators. This was because, despite
yesterday's robins, the first heavy snows have begun. A car smashed
up outside the window this morning, and now, through the same
window, the surrounding suburban mountains are staring in,
blindly, not caring. Off to bed.

30 January

Sunday noon. In three hours I must introduce an all-Rorem concert
at the University. Will I survive? It's not timidity but bronchitis.
Penicillin has disguised all but a sleeping sickness. Canceled classes,
but I have been able to read. I'm lost without a book. Thursday at
the doctor's I was required to wait for twenty-five minutes alone,
bookless, in a room with nothing but bottles and a flexible bed.
Utterly blank, unable to cope, no thought beyond one of resentment
at having no thought.

The three works being featured are "representative" inasmuch
as they are as distant from me today as they are from each other.
Mourning Scene (1947), like youth, is sentimental and serious. *Four
Dialogues* (1953–54) is Pre Pop Art and vulgar. *Flute Trio* (1960) is
"uncompromising"—at least as uncompromising as I can be.

Midnight. . . . Concert jam-packed and televised. Reception afterward (cherry punch, brownies) at which the receiving line consisted
solely of me and President Fletcher who said he "liked the music
but didn't understand it." Later, Robert Browning brought me to a
strange party in the outskirts—the hostess (a Mrs. Allen, queen of
Salt Lake's Bohemia) resembles Tallulah and owns thirty cats which
wander among masses of lacy armchairs and debris and the
too-witty guests treat me well, too well.

31 January

Stanley Kauffmann has published an article titled "Homosexual
Drama" echoing the commonly held untruth that since homosexuals
hate women they can hardly be expected to write compassionately
about them. (Most males are socially antifeminist, but homosexuals

less than most.) How can heterosexual comportment be, to the homosexual playwright, "a life he does not know" (as was suggested) when he has been free to observe it openly since birth. Certainly the emotional adjustments of the average homosexual are immature; indeed, his infantilism is equaled only by the average heterosexual. The international success of recent domestic dramas by homosexuals is due less to a frustrated *double entendre* than to a public which "identifies" quite literally. It never occurred to me that *Who's Afraid of Virginia Woolf?* was about queens in drag—and I'm in a better position than Kauffmann to intuit the playwright's intent. As for Genet, yes, he *is* an admitted homosexual—but homosexuality is not a subject he deals with *as such* in his plays. Art can't deal just with "problems." And what about Pasolini? His film *Saint Matthew Passion*, though hailed as a masterpiece, has not even secondary dealings in homosexuality. Or rather, it deals in all love. (As to whether it *succeeds* in the movies is another question. Christ, like Kafka's K—or even Dorian Gray—is too personal to each of us ever to be satisfactory when given theatrical flesh.) The homosexual's Sense of Responsibility, of course, differs from the heterosexual's who has a marriage license and offspring. But that issue too often stresses longevity at the expense of tenderness. A relationship should be judged by its civility, not by its length. A homosexual is not a Grown-Up. Thank God. But regarding his claims to artistry, let us lament them. Because it isn't the homosexual but the childlike components retained in a man which make him an artist. All children harbor homosexual properties, but that's incidental.

10 February

To *Saturday Review*:

Capote got two million and his heroes got the rope. This conspicuous irony has not, to my knowledge, been shown in any assessment of *In Cold Blood*. That book, for all practical purposes, was completed before the deaths of Smith and Hickock; yet, had they not died, there would have been no book. The author surely realized this, although within his pages it is stated that $50,000 might have saved them—that only the poor must hang.

Auden, in his libretto *Elegy for Young Lovers*, portrays a poet who, for reasons of "inspiration," allows two people to perish, and from this act a masterpiece is born.

Now I am suggesting no irresponsibility on the part of Capote other than as a writer: I am less concerned with ethics than with art. Certainly his reportage intrigued and frightened me, and certainly he presented as good a case against capital punishment as Camus or Koestler. But something rang false, or rather, didn't ring at all. His claim to an unprecedented art form gives cause to wonder.

An artist must, at any cost, expose himself: be vulnerable. Yet Capote the man, in his recent work, is invisible. Could it be that, like the Ortolan-eaters so admirably depicted in Janet Flanner's recent *Paris Journal*, he is hiding his head in shame?

15 February

Another day.

16 February

Another day.

19 February

Another day.

25 February

One less day before . . .

26 February

Still another day.

28 February

Another day. Gray hours blur and merge, they *blurge* interchangeably. Said it before, will say it again.

What constantly struck me as I read her original book were less Susan Sontag's strong thinking and wide erudition than the possibility of rain or sunshine while she wrote: that water would have inexorably fallen onto the summer of Washington Place whether or not she was writing; or rather, that she would have inexorably filled those pages with her helpful ideas whether or not the sun shone.

As for writing here now, it's been six weeks. It could have been six hours or months for all the difference between these Salt Lake days. They vary only in length as the equinox approaches. Moderation has been excessive: nothing to drink since our Farewell Party nine weeks ago. This is not "commendable" inasmuch as I've had no kisses either: sex and liquor go together—their strain producing life (and I've been larval). Smoking for the first time in a fortnight. But neither was this abstinence commendable inasmuch as I've had pneumonia: tobacco and health go together—their contradiction producing good works (and I've been sterile). Okay, I *have* finished *Hearing*, the cycle of Kenneth Koch poems, but with no blind giving of myself. (Would this—were I still capable—have made the songs better or worse? I'm not an actor.) What can I say that no one else has said better? Utah provides everything but the essential. The past *is* us.

So I caught pneumonia. And so, instead of spending a long weekend in Frisco with Mother and Father, they came here gloriously to nurse me, bringing the touch of home-out-of-context. Now, after ten days, they've left as they arrived (in a taxi with a lady driver), having cured me, having "served their purpose," and pursue their post-retirement survey of relatives in the West.

During their stay I corrected for Braziller the galleys of what now seems my rather silly *Paris Diary*. The good pages are canceled out by the mass of toneless lists.

There are inertia and anticipation. If I have lost enthusiasm (if not conviction) about music, I still can *look forward to*. In seventy-two hours I fly to New York.

James Merrill's *The (Diblos) Notebook*. I liked everything about it but it. The idea—so obvious, like anything good, now that he's revealed it—is painfully newly clear. Yet so dull. He couldn't have it both ways.

I hadn't realized until rereading my earlier journals (now to be publicly christened as *The Paris Diary*) how much Boulez troubled me in the fifties. The words strike now as about someone feared. Yet my reaction to his music remains constant, that is, no reaction.

28 March

Returned from three weeks in the slush-filled, obscenely dirty and now second-rate borough of Manhattan. Saw everyone, did everything, still love JA, but people are alike, and I cherish the solitude that keeps me sober.

Janet Flanner invited me to a three-hour *déjeuner en tête-à-tête* at a midtown French dive famed for its *soufflés* which turned out like slumping mounds of pus. Her conversation, on the other hand, surges with health and light, if a touch reactionary. She hates "pornography" (her reference to the galleys of *The Paris Diary*, for which she reproached me with a hard monocled gaze) and apparently ignores present-day American writers. The pretext for our meeting was her pleasure (and mine) at the idea of musical settings of chunks from her own *Paris Journal*. Robert Phelps confected a suite of extracts and the composition's already under way, for chorus and small orchestra. But Janet's writing interests me more than her living words. I'm reticent of contact and comfortable with but a chosen four or five. In terror of the diary's June publication, I would prevent it if I could.

Salt Lake by contrast is tenth-rate, but God! the welcome change. In three weeks the thermometer's soared to summer, the kids are all in shorts doing homework on the campus lawns among emerging crocus and forsythia, boys and girls with hairy thighs, and the sky is daffodil-colored. My mind is half on work.

31 March

Black hot March night, the last of the month, and the older I get the less desperate. Yet I've just returned from a choral concert on campus during which—for twenty minutes or so—I was assailed by pessimism. Sitting alone in the front row, concentrating 100 percent on the music (performed with a fair accuracy), I was concentrating also 100 percent on the choristers whom I pictured naked and exuding a gamy young smell as they e-nun-ci-a-ted with clear eyes riveted on the conductor's "sculpturing" gestures. Such children, such believers, so eager. I imagined them dead. Which one would be the first, no longer to hear, to see or feel his companions, turn to rot, leave his grief-stricken parents? Who would be first, and when? This year? The boys were in tuxedoes, the girls in sea-green evening gowns. Those (of each sex) who are to graduate (to graduate!) in June were privileged with red carnations, like Marguerite Gauthier. One soprano stood delicate and intense with an angular beauty and a good crop of hair as satiny as Rosemary's in adolescence; I could not refrain from seeing her in the coffin, her mother's tears as she clipped those locks for the cedar chest. Well, the necromantic bathos of these fancies was also the musical background: some setting of Christina Rosetti's *When I am dead, my dearest*. But it made me cry.

Energy of foreboding urges a composition of feeble phrases which nevertheless outlast the morose self.

10 April

Raining this morning, first dark day in months, ironic, since it is Easter. So I've decided to go to Friends Meeting. A molar though is killing me, despite Demerol, and tomorrow doubtless I'll have it pulled.

Early afternoon and raining still, harder than ever. Got back just in time. As I slowly write here, clouds are amassing with the wind, and on the hills across the street the weeping cherry trees and baby-green willows wave for dear life. It's really starting: that stuff looks thick for rain, maybe it's sleet, but there's lightning. Now it's actually snow with thunder, quite quickly cold, and the window's grown too misted to see through. Only an hour ago I sat in the clammy heat of a Quaker meeting unattended since Saratoga with Elizabeth Ames. Not as a child, nor in Saratoga, nor yet in Utah today, have I ever felt the Inner Light communally. The sweet conjointed silence brings yawning revery, the itemizing of overdue bills, or, at best, concentration on the wren's cry there from the apricot tree, or on the far tinkle of spring's first Good Humor wagon.

Now I'm home, have had lunch. Tooth still hurts, but the rain's stopped.

Writing is self-conscious now that it may be published. Graphic exhibition would be inhibited, or even to write of inhibitions, period. Because now I'm *choosing*. But none of it was ever me. Like Colette I used myself as model, made a novel based on parts of me, but it was never ever all of me, what could be?

Yesterday, to ease my sickness: a box of the season's first strawberries, huge ones now ripening on the kitchen table. The whole apartment giggles with their fragrance.

William Burroughs maintains that readers are distracted by what occurs on the visual periphery of the pages. He justifies his cutouts by having them incorporate that periphery. But isn't there, in turn, *another* periphery, forever—like Chinese boxes? He is categorically wrong—like Kinsey researchers (themselves a category) who *categorize* behavior.

Early evening, raining hard once more. Back from the dirty baths, quite upset, took a Valium, molar maddening. Can't chew. The rain, the rain. To get through the evening . . .

17 April

One week later. Raining again, as it must on Sundays, a welcome change after the near nausea of too much perfect weather, the almost insulting silk of daily dawn air floating into the kitchen as I boil coffee, alone, and dot soya bread with icy butter, and look out onto the flowering quince and crab bushes of colors unknown in our East. At night the useless crescent moon like a bone-colored slice of melon slits my curtains and invades the celibate bedclothes to freeze the crotch. Utah is uncanny in this season, beautiful because, alone, I know I'll leave (thank God) forever soon. But there's no thrill to it, like Morocco. Why? Because it's my own country.

Because, despite the ever-present tone set by Mormons, I'm in my native land whose only mysteries are those which don't intrigue. Ten years ago I found the American enigma aphrodisiac.

I'm just not unhappy now. No urgency, no need to lament. Still, though I can't give my "best" to anything, neither words nor notes, I have more commissions than I can handle, mostly for churches, ironic, since who gives credence anymore to "religious texts." Nevertheless, this rainy afternoon I began and completed a four-page song on words by, of all people, Mary Baker Eddy, whose benefactors granted me a goodly sum. (Last week it was a Psalm for chorus and organ, *Truth in the Night Season*, to be sung in Houston.) Juxtaposed on these sanctimonious verses was the reading of Paul Bowles' new novel. His others I'd swallowed gluttonously. This seemed more of the same. Yet don't we all always just produce "more of the same"? Who gets better? Name one! Broader, longer, maybe. Not better. Still, "more of the same" must maintain its life. Paul's preoccupations seem dead as mine here now.

An advance review of *The Paris Diary* refers to name-dropping, and to life in French Café Society.

A name is dropped when not attached to something, to the reason for speaking it or to an anecdote about it. A person whose name you drop is someone not speaking of you although you speak of him. Dropped names are those which cannot be picked up. I have never dropped one.

As to Café Society, were Nadia Boulanger, Balthus, Honegger a part of it? Or Guy Ferrand in Morocco, or P in Pavia, or Edouard Roditi? Artists in France are a dignified and integral part of the whole, and so much the worse for American society.

How can we be sure of how well you really knew all those dead French people? "To know well" means an exchange between two participants of permanent portions of themselves. In the four or five meals I had with Eluard, in certain street encounters with green-eyed strangers who took me by the hand to painful hotels, in chance tearful meetings with Tchelitchew or a hilarious single supper with John Latouche, I felt a contact, a generosity, a participation, a heat, a curiosity, an indelibility which permit me to say I knew and know and will always know them well. Meanwhile

I'm indifferent to some people seen daily for twenty years; they offer neither growth nor anecdote. To know has to do with intensity, not habit.

24 April

Icy skies have made their point and gone away killing every fruit crop. The city's in spring again, all bare legs. Time is precious, yet I can't wait for it to pass, to quit the slow calm of Utah for the quick horror of New York, to catch up with moments anticipated (as though they were worth it), to be with the parental son.

Music? What can one *say* with it? Anything anymore? If others are moved, I'll have said it, though I'm never moved. What kind of music will I be writing in six years? Still the kind that's paid for? If I've never sold my soul, is that because nobody's offered to buy it?

Does Milton Babbitt like listening to his own music? Ravel now, and even Billie Holiday, leave me indifferent. Yet performers —at least classical ones—remain the same, keeping up their enthusiasm, year after year, for the few old chestnuts.

John Browning, Gary Graffman, back in the days when we all Had Time, played to me alone for hours as I sipped vodka martinis; they needed no booze to enhance a manifest ecstasy in controlling that winged horse (the grand piano, a tree skinned alive and lacquered), an ecstasy provoked by *other* people's music.

A week ago, visited Provo to represent "my" Composition Department in a symposium of Western music schools. What amused and finally wearied me was not so much the Berkeley beatniks versus the Brigham Young conservatives (the smokers versus the abstainers) as the evidence that *within* their representative groups they *cared*—it all *made a difference*. The same goes for *Perspective* magazine. I've no complaint with what's written there, I even agree. I'm just not interested anymore. Oh to be young and split hairs again! But Milton Babbitt's not young and he, I suppose, cares.

Still, I read about Schoenberg while thinking less on him than on what his ghost coughs out. The mere mention of his name (this has been going on about a year) evokes a dark green park, beautiful and murderous, traversed *en famille* somewhere in Europe during

1936. But where? Arnold Schoenberg's main problem was that with all his technique, his knack for invention, he wasn't very musical.

30 April

Afternoon Saturday. Can only retrace my thoughts during those hours preceding the moment that ended all thought. As if by examining each mental progression before catastrophe was caught in time's eye, we can this once, please God, blink, and it is gone and never was. Tomorrow is May Day. In a week on the 8th, Mother's Day and Rosemary's birthday coincide. Day before yesterday I wrote to Rosemary for the first time since she, John and the six children left for Uganda last June. . . . Yesterday noon a heavy package—having been forwarded all over the globe—reached me here in Salt Lake. It was from, startlingly, Prince Louis de Polignac in Paris, and contained an expensive volume of *hommages* to the memory of Marie-Blanche. . . . My letter to Rosemary concerned mostly Mother and Father—how they both appear healthy, "adjusted," with their new roles in retirement. I also mentioned the not-so-casual coincidence that we two children, each on a separate path, had migrated from Chicago to the African continent, and I enumerated certain differences between Fez and Kampala. . . . Last night (after returning from a meal at the Country Club with the Abravanels and later attending the Czech film *The Shop on Main Street*) I opened the pages about Marie-Blanche, opened them onto the irretrievable past and consumed them cover to cover. Eulogy after eulogy, for hours, souvenir on souvenir, gradually shed a modern light on that gentle pampered Countess, dead nine years. I was so moved by the *tendresses*—somehow unlike the French, even when writing epitaphs—that my three dozen or so meetings with that lady revived themselves: how she made us each feel like her sole *confidant;* how every weekend she received us in a fresh Lanvin *création* (the first was of diaphanous apple-green chiffon through which one glimpsed her handsome limbs—not legs—as she crossed the room, or rather, staggered, as I cruelly pointed out in diaries, not knowing it was illness and not opium murdering her); how she would collapse beside me on a satin couch, left hand poised lackadaisically with a cigarette holder dripping ashes in slow motion onto a mother-of-pearl tray, right hand planted firmly on my thigh as we (she) listened intelligently to Février and Auric playing Chabrier on her two black Pleyels; how her *maître d'hôtel* would then pass a *plateau* of champagne (manufactured from her father's grape groves) or *cerisette* which so admirably quenched my dehydration, this being always Sunday and I having been always up late at the Pergola the night before. . . . I went to sleep and dreamed this: Trying to reach JA by telephone—he had disappeared leaving only a number which didn't work—Rosemary then got on the phone: her monopoly, my frustration, and we quarreled as we did in childhood, she mocking me about JA . . . At 6 A.M. I awoke and for two hours lay thinking about the dream, then again about Marie-Blanche. The dream had shattered a security *vis-à-vis* JA and renewed an ambiguous incestuousness *vis-à-vis* Rosemary, while thoughts of Marie-Blanche were brighter than last night. I recalled my premieres in her salon beneath the Vuillards; my bringing the uninvited Julien Green (shy, but dazed with infatuation) to a *réunion* where eyebrows soared; my telling Marie-Blanche that if I were wrecked on an island with but one recording it would be her *Lamento della Ninfa* (how many others had said the same! yet it was—and is—true). There, in that now-demolished mansion of the Rue Barbet-de-Jouy, and not chez Marie Laure, I first knew Nora and Roro. Then, I found that the French, as opposed to Americans, if they were rich, *knew how* to be rich. . . . At 8 A.M., wide awake, these reveries (what else shall one name them?) were interrupted by the telephone ringing. It was Father in New York telling me John had been killed in an auto crash. Rosemary is preparing the children. They will come back to America. . . . By noon the sun was blazing, summer is here. I allowed my legs (my limbs) to lead me on a stroll through the campus. The quince and forsythia bushes are already a thing of the past. But I paused for a while to examine a bank of perfect white pansies. I watched them there, growing, *visibly growing,* sweet faces praising the sun. Suddenly they looked hateful and stupid, and a wave of nausea washed over me as I whispered to them: "Just wait. You'll find out!"

San Francisco
(*Californian Hotel*)
18 May

After writing those words I went over to school to work some. It was hot, nearly 90° (Utah has a mild climate, I shall miss it). Kept thinking of John Marshall, waste of his worth, the always-so-unexpected fragility of life, this first Death in the Family. All my friends have died, but never (since early grandparents) a close relative. How in such heat could I compose, imagining Rosemary's attempts to compose herself in Africa? I paused at the concert hall where three girls were rehearsing Debussy's *Trio Sonata*, the coolest of medicines. Listening, it became clear that *we are supposed to die*. That fact, which everyone accepts, made sense for the first time. Three weeks ago. Today I'm ever more aware of decay, of the ultimate disappearance of these words too, my music, the planet, you.

The night before I left for San Francisco, Steinberg conducted *Design* in the Tabernacle. I will not defend my children. I will betray and mock them and acquiesce to their opponents. (These words were written not by me but by another Ned.) I hate to attend even glamorous performances of yesterday's works when I should be home orchestrating tomorrow's.

Today, though, I'm in Frisco which I'm about to leave after six days of sightseeing. The city is self-contained: you don't feel (as with Los Angeles) that you're in California. It looks like Boston, New Orleans, Tangier, with super-clean one-story white structures pierced by lanes on dizzying hills, sunlight of England, Chicago's insufferable wind. Los Angeles four years ago had breeds of birds and posy new to me, raccoons, snakes and above all space, canyons, slowness. Frisco is less slow than casual, insular, oblivious to cinema. In L.A. I was depressed by those beauties in their bars. Here I don't go to bars but to baths more plush than funeral parlors. Would like to live here, hate to visit; time far from work grows abhorrent. Everyone's been cordial, especially friends from the really vintage past: Gary Samuel, charm itself, has made the Oakland Symphony the only rival of that irascible Krips; the Pitchfords here too on a visit; while writing JA I wait for Lou Harrison to stop by for lunch;

and tonight Charles Mather, a nursery chum, will drive me to the airport.

Nothing much else to write of. I do like being alive and it's tiresome to keep repeating. Tiresome to speak of the young composers here whose bodies intrigue me more than their theories. Tiresome to read diaries like those of Nemerov who confesses (proudly) the wickednesses he's *thought* of doing, while I relate those I've *done*. Nemerov's intelligent and uninteresting, but you don't go to jail for dreams you've had. He has nothing to leave himself open to.

> *Salt Lake City*
> *26 May*

Haven't lived by impulse or madness, but by restraint. Even in ecstasy, even when drunk, a lazy ambitious logical armor inhibits. I move in a personal cocoon. As for Life—the fact of it—I've never learned how. Nice, no doubt, as one fades farther from early disorders. But all that evolution—for what? Some cherry pie, the moon? Were we made for no more than this, than just wisdom, archaeology or love?

Secretaryless hours (perhaps forty a week) spent in a calligraphic craft keep mischief at bay.

Seventeen years ago today the now-destroyed SS *Washington* had chugged twenty-four hours into the ocean toward France. Shirley met me at Saint-Lazare, took me to the Flore. The Bal des Beaux Arts was in preparation. A flock of naked students painted yellow invaded the café in broad daylight, swept the Pernod from our tables and poured it over the laughing policemen. This was a first impression. Utah is hardly that.

Even New York now is a "closed" town to which San Francisco provided blazing contrasts. Lou Harrison (bellied and bearded), during my final hours there, invited me to visit the Mattachine offices, where I learned that local legislation will permit seventy-five queer bars within the town limits. Since now only forty-seven exist, everyone's very busy.

Tuesday I return to a summer on 12th Street. Salt Lake couldn't be more tranquil and I dread the cheerless panic. Dread JA who seems to have suffered a sea change. Haven't *I?* Dread this book coming out next month with George Plimpton's party where famous friends will stand around trying not to look as though they'd missed a bus. Here I take a more innocent pride in the concert of my students' music beautifully done on Tuesday night. Things will work out. They always do, unless we die, and probably even then.

30 May

SIR, YOUR NUDITY DISTRESSES ME. These words, inscribed in red Magic Marker, were slipped under my door last evening as I sat orchestrating, quite naked (as is my habit in heat waves), near an unshaded window. At first I found the note to be—well—civilized, and phrased with care. Later I took offense. The spectator (a young male Mormon? a frustrated spinster?) *could* choose not to look, my home is my castle, etc. It is not agreeable to be spied upon. Tomorrow, in any case, I'm flying from the castle to New York. And so, with these words (which I write while naked by the unshaded window) I take leave of Utah.

31 May

Airborne, on the 12:40 United flight, Salt Lake to New York via Chicago. Midafternoon. Arrogant sun rays sift through the first-class cabin, resentful of humanity so high up. Lunch (hot beef, shrimp salad, cherry-cream tarts, all consumed with the same fork) has been cleared away, and I'm now deep in Mishima's *Death in Midsummer*, more dazzling than anything since Mann's *Stories of Three Decades*, which I've not read in three decades. The seat in front is occupied by a large-headed bespectacled lady one yard tall. A couple of hours ago I observed her in the waiting room, upright and wreathed in those smiles of false optimism which only dwarfs or the blind can afford when approaching strangers, safe in the knowledge they'll not be accused of lewd importunity. I have to pee. I am in the bathroom combing my hair and have removed my glasses. When, on returning to my seat, I will pass by the little lady who will gaze bravely at me with impossible discomfort. . . . I am back in my seat, she did not look up. Engrossed in Mishima. We are all smoking. I am forty-two.

Fire Island Pines
7 June

With Tom. Fawn-green dawns of The Pines enter his new house architected by Horace Gifford so that you live simultaneously indoors and out. New York was dirt and sound. Here one regains the sedentary grace of the Far West.

At a party to honor Robert's *Colette* I say to Janet Flanner, "Have you heard? Doda's mother finally died." (Marya Freund, at ninety, had been a raucous burden to many.) "Yes," answered Janet. "They say she passed away. Very quietly. For a change."

My settings of Flanner's *Paris Journal* are nearly complete. Her turn to set my diary to music.

That diary's out now in store windows. Great men's names, sometimes their faces, are often seen in public places.

10 June

George Plimpton's party last night, to launch the book. Proustian. Those present who were featured in the diary no longer resemble the people featured.

Cambridge
19 June

At Danny Pinkham's. We've come to Boston, JA to visit the massive Matisse retrospective, I to talk money with the Christian Scientists. There seems less desire, even friendliness, between us: he sits in one corner puffing pot between smirks, I lounge elsewhere swilling ice coffee between thoughts of death.

Danny asks if he may put passages from these pages to music, for spoken voice and harpsichord.

However immortal I may feel, October 23, 1923, remains a finite date, though I cannot recall it. Doubtless all of me will have been contained within the twentieth century. Why the twentieth?

Things go well, nothing's denied, yet I feel unachieved. Organized fragments of my past are requested by libraries, by publishers spread over this country and century. I want only to squat and watch grass sprout, having said all I know. Yet those giddy stacks of unfinished business! commissions, anecdotes. Only to spawn yellow roses, yellow yells. And yet . . . They complained I never mentioned Marie Laure's Goyas. What we omit is our art.

In ten days I go to Muncie to be treated as Hoosier-Boy-Makes-Good (claim me who will) and where *Miss Julie* gets her second chance. Lost interest.

Muncie, Indiana
30 June

Heat wave in the birth-state, where I relax to the smell of wet hay and smile at the drawling tripthongs. Not amusing, though, are rehearsals of a work as complex as *Miss Julie* so obviously unprepared. Not that I mind being misunderstood, but I'd prefer to be misunderstood with intelligence. The staging is farcical. Margo Willauer, imported for this occasion, is tense; the baritone playing John looks like at least her son; and the woman who sings Christine has rearranged Kenward's text because her husband won't have her uttering "certain words" onstage.

Meanwhile, seeing that Herb Gold is also featured at this Arts Festival, I leave a note in his box. On emerging from the elevator he approaches exclaiming, "I see you're still handsome, which means I'm still young." (If he only knew, he's the handsome one. Twenty years ago I'd have been titillated at Jew admiring Gentile, like bass a soprano.) We take meals together in the air-conditioned cafeteria of the Student Union. Occasionally Margo joins us with her raw hamburger and conversation no heavier than any singer's next to Herb's glib hip wit. But she's in superb voice—far better than last fall—which is all that might rescue the absurd production tonight. (Absurd, for example, because the chorus of SATB contains no TB's.)

Now Herb, who names Muncie the Paris of the Middle West, has flown back to Frisco. Tomorrow I'll leave for Chicago to promote

The Diary with Robert Cromie as I promoted it Tuesday with
Arlene Francis: Braziller has me behaving as my diary indicates
I'm supposed to behave, but it makes no sense when it's business,
selling what's unsalable. I don't wish to peddle the past but to
construct that which can be peddled. Yet Distribution is Art's
primary function today. The book sows dissension, or at least new
values, between me and my friends and family. It has castrated
JA (who reacts as Dorian Gray to Huysmans) and he is moving
away.

This end to another love affair wraps up former years in a cool
wind. I now refuse to be unhappy (misery's a privilege of the
young). When in love you don't observe or react *for yourself.* Out
of love you're lonelier but more aware. Free of love you are free
to perceive. Perception is not a shared experience despite what's
said about the emptiness of solitary travel. Honeymooners are
blind.

JA was fine about keeping me from wine, not through cajoling
but through disdain. Fine too about opening eyes (literally) and
palate, and emphasizing the present in things sensual. Stubborn
however about learning from me of things past and future. So we
came to the same dead-end I reached in the city of Paris. Not
outgrown so much as grown off. In years to come we may all need
each other again. Rereading the printed diary fascinated, touched
and finally bored me: what doesn't exist or has died grows dreary,
watching the brash youngster shrink into a microbe on a monotonous horizon.

By the same token my opera tonight—even if it were the ideal
performance—will be something to sit through, get paid for. I didn't
write it, *he* did, and *he* no longer exists. I marvel at Margo's (or any
actor's) continuing enthusiasm for a role she must re-create time
after time.

Henri Fourtine back in Paris writes Yes to send him the book
so he may recapture *"le bout du chemin qu'on a fait ensemble"* and
goes on to speak of family problems and an arthritic leg. That
response at first annoyed me: why tell of *his* trials or sentimentalize
coldly (Frenchily) about our *bout du chemin* as if *I* were no longer
his sole concern? But it *was* just part of a trip taken together and
which ended, as JA today ends. His problems, not mine, *are* the real

ones. The diary thus is useless, having recounted what is no longer true. I smile wryly at an historian led up blind alleys.

Where does one stop? Complaints edge off, dissipate, will finally vanish after this brief reeruption of the opera in Muncie.

But a beautiful edition of *Miss Julie* is soon to come off the presses of Boosey & Hawkes who will send it to the world's various opera houses, one of which may eventually present it with love and money.

Bitterness abates. I'm interested (somewhat) in opera again, even stage opera. With Gavin Lambert, have been thinking in terms of Frankenstein, not so much because psychedelia is the rage, as because the tenderness of a non-oedipal father hang-up has never been exploited—especially today when it lurks beneath every bomb but never bursts itself. There's also a question of writing a childhood fantasy with Maurice Sendak. (My mother wonders about Sendak's having no children. But I explain—as to a child—that it's the child within him which speaks for him.)

The all-knowing Colette ended thus one story about an old lady lamenting her young lover's disappearance: When a still older lady consolingly suggests, "Why not take another lover?" she dries her eyes. "Another lover? I never thought of that!" . . . A new-lover-as-opera can be in every manner bankrupting, and by definition a bastard who usually brings along no dowry. Yet it is tempting once more to think of reshaping another form into one's own image.

Does that image really change so very much? John Cage with inconsistent logic suggests we need fresh food now, and asks that he not be asked to vomit up and eat again a steak he ate ten years ago. I am no more of a petrified coprophagist than he, yet I do not banish steak from my diet of today. That diet consists less of words as words than words as music. I long to return to it.

Chicago
1 July (evening)

The heat wave goes on with the thermometer soaring to a deadly 101°, dry and breathtaking. I love it. There's Chicago again.

Kenward showed up unexpected in Muncie last night for the opera
which ran more smoothly than anticipated. This afternoon I was
delivered here in a timpani-sized plane and have been laying the
ghost ever since. After a dutiful visit to the Art Institute (Magritte
retrospective), I traversed again—as in '59—the whole of Hyde
Park, again was struck at the lack of change, again awakened the
sleepers, recalled which streets were best for roller skates, again
cried that no one I knew arose from those too-familiar patterns: like
Magritte, the identical décor without the actors (whereas in Paris
we meet the same actors with whom we now play new roles).

What most hit me was how, in the University environs, there's
scarcely a street without at least one house whose ghostly *voyeurs*
yell of my adolescent sexual discoveries. Supper—a ghastly tuna au
gratin—alone at International House (unchanged, unchanged), and
then—why not!—phoned Gertrude Abercrombie, beloved of us all.
It was still light when I knocked on her door. There she stood,
unchanged too after all the years, still a bit drunk, the same tears in
those eyes, uncombed hair and frayed kimono retaining a Bohemianism long since replaced elsewhere, and I welcomed her kisses.
While the sun set we smoked and talked in the heat of a great parlor
surrounded by her blue self-portraits listening and contributing—
Magritte being coincidentally her spiritual father. Also staring from
corners, and from between dusty photos of Dizzy Gillespie, were
the eyes of live cats which never emerged into the room. Three
times Gertrude explained rather plaintively her own fascination
with the outlandish black scab on her knee (from which a
surprisingly long hair protruded): "I am a surrealist. I am *still* a
surrealist. Dizzy gave me the wound"—but she didn't explain if it
were from a kick or enforced genuflection.

Then we were silent. Then we talked again, less spontaneously.
Then I said goodbye, a trifle undone, and have come back to this
hotel dead tired.

Well. At George Plimpton's on June 9 I did predictably get
drunk. So much so that in the homeward taxi Virgil said, "Baby,
we've had that number. You're not supposed to drink at a party
honoring a book about how you used to drink." He's right.
Nevertheless, though I still love and learn from Virgil—I'm not sure
that on that score he has my number as patly as, say, Morris or JA.

With those two, a few nights later (sober), Virgil expounded authoritatively on my high-potency ratio of the past decades although he has no practical knowledge of this. Now a reputation is not a fact. Marie Laure, for instance, does not discredit tales about her nymphomaniacal incontinence, though in truth she's quite naïve. Like silent sirens or talkative sexpots, she's suspect, needs constant peripheral proofs more than occasional central screws. I'm similar, but being male require hygiene more than invention. Despite a colorful love life, once they're snared, my attention turns to the future. Sex is of the present, being the past (i.e., anticipation) made flesh.

What do I like to do? I like to write about what I like to do, but I do it too, and can't write about it, am afraid of the law.

For two months I've been raking my tongue across sharp molars; it bleeds with a wish to escape. Robert says it's the advent of my book: we oral types at the Moment of Truth would bite off our tongues. . . . It is the next day, I sit at the air-conditioned airport preparing to quit Chicago where Robert Cromie conducted the interview at the Petit Gourmet of my childhood over fruit salad, cold tea and peppermint ice cream.

New York
8 July

Heat continues all through the East. Returned last Saturday night to find JA slumped in darkness, shuddering with pain. Forty-eight hours later his appendix was removed at St. Vincent's, which is to say at The Isle of the Dead. Already he is home, an eager convalescent. Robert was a salvation throughout the ordeal, as we spent hot evenings between the hospital and Howard Johnson's ingesting orange floats and discussing money. Cities in summer are dejecting and provocative, devitalizing yet sensual, with JA all ill and Rosemary all widowed back now in Philly, and me so unproductive, a healthy poison. Celebrations have come and gone unnoticed. A Sense of Proportion is never more lacking than in firecrackers on the 5th of July.

21 July

I had been invited by telegram for lunch today at the White House again. (Why?) Didn't go though. Not so much for their Vietnam policy as because the plane strike makes travel inconvenient. Besides, I've already been.

Like the last disks of Holiday my diaries have grown flaccid, self-imitative. Like the last disks of Piaf my diaries seem brittle, hard-boiled. That simplicity I've always worked for in music is more difficult here. It's hard to be easy: spontaneity must be calculated. The published journal doesn't help matters. I'm unhappy to be publicly known as unhappy. That *Paris Diary* does provide an impotent power—strangers write of their obsession with me, but how can I profit? They tell me protectively how they could have helped, if only they'd known me then. (But if they could have helped, the book would not have been written.) They "identify." They try to contact me to see if I'm as pretty as I made out. When satisfied that I am not, they're reassured. Or they phone at 3 A.M. and simply breathe, or suggest I stop writing music. Fame, though irrelevant to the product it celebrates, is more satisfactory than the product.

On 4th Street, by his new house, I run into Kenneth Koch. Although my whole spring was spent with him invisibly while composing *Hearing*, I hadn't known that in reality he was growing heavy. "Ned, make your diary into an opera." "But it has no plot." "The New Theater's no longer concerned with plot but with action." He's probably right, he who a year ago, introduced me to Scopitone.

Fire Island
13 August

Here we are at Fire Island again where three weeks ago Frank O'Hara was struck and destroyed, quitting this world with the same intensity that he lived in it. Need for comment lessens, time passes and Frank left a harem of literate widows each of whom has already composed epitaphs less compelling than those he wrote for movie stars. But what a need for phoning Frank to get his opinion! I've reread the several letters he wrote to Europe during the '50s (none after: we grew apart once we lived in the same city), and was impressed anew not only by his intelligent humor but by how urgently he seemed to want me to be a good composer. How many artists care, really, about their friends as artists, except for instruction? Frank was the exception, until it killed him. . . . It always used to be my habit at gatherings to ask Joe LeSueur: "Who in this room will be the first to die?"

His poems were, among other things, conversational, elliptical. Frank O'Hara died in the middle of a sentence.

"Sing us *Hôtel* again, Ned." The request referred to my notorious moans resembling a cow aborting which Frank nonetheless found musically rewarding.

I did not choose my profession, it chose me. Since childhood it has grown between me and people. A strangling protection. My music is all one love letter, but to whom?

Frank O'Hara knows this but reacts otherwise, calls his poem by another name: Lucky Pierre. That poem itself is gratified, being squarely between the poet and his love, instead of between two pages. And it exists, remains, can be referred to (which a phone call can't).

Yet Frank is estranged and growing more so. Because—not despite—of his art.

Strangling protection or Lucky Pierre, whatever you call art, that art takes, drains, thrives, empties us forlorn.

All's in a name. A fuck by any other name would feel less good.

To make a masterpiece was not Frank's pursuit. A masterpiece is for the future.

X, robust and appealing, speaks with poignance about always having found him sexy. If Frank knew that now, he'd turn over in his grave.

We met on John Latouche's floor, December 1952, toward the end of my first trip back to America. Sonia Orwell was then new in New

York, and John gave her a party. Vast carpet, Manhattan-type wit I'd forgotten, of course piano tinkling to support divine Anita Ellis whom I'd never met either, who clutched her red satin hem and threw those closed eyes to heaven screaming *Porgy!* while the room exploded with applause that only Streisand, secondhand, commands today. Today, when half those guests of John Latouche, and John Latouche, are dead.

Pushed by John Myers, Frank edged toward me, and placing the ashtray among our feet, exclaimed in that now-famous and mourned Brooklyn-Irish Ashberian whine I didn't at first take to: "You're from Paris and I think Boulez is gorgeous." He meant, as they say, well; and I was surprised that a poet then already knew Boulez' sound over here; but gorgeous seemed hardly the word, even from that poet, for that composer.

Snow, and the year was closing. I sailed to France where Bobby Fizdale suggested I write something for two voices and two pianos. What words? Why, those of his friend Frank O'Hara. So a friendship was planted over the ocean which blossomed into our *Four Dialogues*, originally titled *The Quarrel Sonata*.

Here I'd hoped to quote whole letters. It can't be done in diaries—that's for grandiose epitaphs and homages he's everywhere receiving, more than his more famous peers, Jarrell and Delmore Schwartz. Nevertheless, from May of 1955, plucked from their generous context, come concerns about opera after witnessing my *Childhood Miracle* on Elliott Stein's libretto:

> Surely we must do an opera together. Something terribly sweet and painful, maybe? . . . I am prejudiced by my longing to have you write the significant modern opera I feel about to happen in music. There is no social, dramatic or sensational contemporary situation you couldn't deal with in your characteristically beautiful fashion, I think, and that is true of virtually no other composer now, saving perhaps Marc [Blitzstein] who has other ideas and other gifts from the ones I'm thinking of. . . . When you think of yourself in relation to the work I imagine hearing from you (and remember this is because I love what we already have and don't mean to be overbearing or overstep the bounds of discretion between one artist and another), think of Manon and Louise and 3 Penny and Lulu. Why deal with a melting snowman when a cocktail party would be a great opportunity

for great music? I don't mean to harp on modern subject matter; of course the subject counts for little or nothing sometimes. But it doesn't hurt a great gift to have a significant subject either, whether it is the liberation of Flanders or love à la Onegin. And I really believe that an artist cannot be in his best work more mild than the times. . . .

More mild than the times. . . . I do not, like Styron or Blitzstein, pretend to deal with the times' Big Issues. Yet by definition my prose and music are of, and hence concern, our day. Who can say that narcissism or the forgotten themes of romantic love are less timely, less indigenous to our health or malady?

But when Stravinsky states that "artists and 'intellectuals' can be as dangerous and foolish as professional politicians . . . about matters beyond their competence," smart Mary McCarthy concurs, but points out that artists do possess a higher intuition and are good at smelling rats.

Frank O'Hara smelled rats. And from the common rats about the house he made his poetry.

Yaddo
2 September

Lovers fade from these pages like Anna from *L'Avventura*. Paroxysms of hay fever, sinus, unbearable toothache. How work? Two hours of music to be composed and orchestrated by Christmas, I freeze! Heat and mosquitoes don't help. Could it be that if I'd forgo success I might, as people say, begin to live? Jane Bowles, asked if she'd been writing lately, replied: "Oh no, I'm much too busy." Well, she lives in Tangier. Boredom like suffering is unattractive, but that's no more helpful than saying age is unbecoming to the old. What shall I do now? Perform today, comprehend tomorrow.

They. They are stronger than I, because they still care. And though maybe smarter, they confuse the fascination of a work's analysis with the work itself, interpret the intricacies of that analysis as the work's virtue, and hence produce false evaluations.

13 September

There is no fun in assaulting nonresisters. Which is why drunks are less vulnerable than is generally thought. Elizabeth Ames tells of her "new" Quaker meetinghouse in Easton, inaugurated 200 years ago. The vicinity at that time was under constant Indian attack. One Sunday morning tribesmen stormed the building, tomahawks raised. The congregation remained quietly seated. After a suspended moment, the Indians relaxed, stacked their weapons in a corner. Then they too sat down to join the silence.

14 September

The most painful pleasure is nostalgia. Nostalgia arises through those two senses with which no art primarily deals, taste and smell. They can't be channeled, intellectualized and passed on (to avoid the word communicated) as sound and sight and sometimes touch can be. Tongue and nose single-mindedly burrow through diamond-hard culture-barriers to—I guess—instinct. When I landed at Rabat five Augusts ago it was my first return to Morocco in a decade. Even before I reached customs inspection, the indigenous odors of tea, mint, cedar, dung, olives, hot flat bread, burning wet leaves (here too, as in grammar-school days) and new tanned hides walloped dormant responses, and my mouth told me—even before I'd embraced Guy—that Morocco was (though things never are) still better than before. The pain of this pleasure now is in recalling the pain of this pleasure then.

Norman Podhoretz is here, and acts, in a manner of speaking, like a Jewish Lenny Bernstein. Literally in a manner of speaking. Those self-assured inflections! Since he and I, for the manner of speaking, are the only ones around who know how, every night he gives me an education, since I've never been offered satisfactory explanations of what a Jew today is. Certainly Semitism or Belief no longer obtain. Norman maintains that Jewishness finally is a *consciousness,* though he's not sure why Jews still wish to survive as a distinct group. As to his famous Negro Problem, I cannot naturally include myself in the seemingly all-inclusive category of those who react as he does. I was not raised as this poor Brooklyn boy at swords' points with Negroes, but as an upper-middle-class gentile whose parents often "asked Negroes to supper." I took them for granted. Rosemary doesn't even take them for granted, she merely takes them, living, as is the case, in a neighborhood her presence helped integrate. She is no Liberal, nor no longer knows (in the best sense of the phrase) *what a Negro is*—he just is. She's a "better" person than I. . . . Norman, in citing as his authority Jimmy Baldwin who states categorically that all Negroes hate whites, hesitantly agrees that whites may have a feeling of sexual inferiority—hence an attraction—to Negroes (the reasons suggested for these sentiments are too famous to reiterate). About the first assertion I wouldn't know—I'm not black—but I wonder. As to being attracted to Negroes, I simply am not, though I love dark hair—there are different sorts of opposites. Much as I deplore personal criticisms of a writer (as know-it-alls do with Albee's "fiction"), in the case of Baldwin's nonfiction it's pertinent. He is black, of course, so he should and does speak about that. He is also plain. If his color is indisputable, benevolence tells us that plainness is a matter of taste, and anyway beside the point. But what *is* the point? *Giovanni's Room* (fiction, of course) opens with the author's appraisal of his own blond beauty. Jimmy was always partial to white boys, at least at La Reine Blanche, from what I observed. Unobservably perhaps today, by a process of inversion, or of conversion to his own prose, he too has become spellbound by the Negro's Superior Virility. The fact is that, however unstable their generalities, both "races" (indeed, like current Catholics) have reached the urgent point of self-examination, a turning point from which their rationale nonetheless remains: Negroes are superior because they have suffered, Jews have suffered because they're superior.

17 September

After forty-eight hours of black rain our sky's turned a glacial white with petunias again releasing the pollen which sends me back to asthma pills. For seventeen days I've entertained that mirthless sinking feeling we all know at the start of a new work. From recent darkness I've been presumably manufacturing my own *Sun*, that being the title of the music I've intermittently dabbed at for child-soprano Jane Marsh who this afternoon is being driven to Saratoga for our first confrontation. But what shall I show her? ("What Can I Tell My Bones?")

Once I wrote that I wasn't too lazy to work twenty-four hours a day, but too lazy to make it good. Now I'll do anything—read, walk, smoke, eat, die—to avoid putting notes on paper. Gone that childhood urge to "express" myself. Remains only that childhood urge to be recollected. But we can't be remembered for what we haven't done. Babette Deutsch raises her eyebrows as I explain that I no longer need poetry itself, only the words to distort, to musicalize; that I'm left cold by a *sound* of poems, nor can I hear the music of language once I understand what it's saying.

Am I a thinker? Other composers here (principally Nicolas Roussakis with whom in the evenings I play clarinet sonatas) seem impressed not only by my total recall but by my erudition. Erudition! A slipshod peripheral training it's been. Education comes solidly only for Jews and Jesuits. Yet I love my undisciplined reading, or what is time for? As to total recall, why experience and then forget? Am I a thinker? But there are no Doers anymore who don't look silly. I am a Doer, and I look silly.

Miss Marsh has come, spent the afternoon, gone. She wants more high notes. Music after all is made for instruments with practical limits. We lunched on red grapes and oatmeal cookies, spoke of her Moscow prize, walked around the lake, and agreed that *Sun* must be sung in a dress (a gown, as singers say) of gold chiffon. She shall have her high notes.

18 September

Sunday. Silent Meeting with Elizabeth, afterward lunch on the lawn. We spoke for two hours of those blue fir trees surrounding her house, nothing but the marvelous trees which, like weather that dictates every mood, are really the only things worth talking about.

Reactions to *Paris Diary*. Press mixed but not bland. Aggravation, admiration, pity in equal doses. "Taken seriously," though always for different reasons. Segments quoted out of context collectively add up to the entire book. Conclusion: there's something in it for the whole family. A hundred fan letters of which not more than ten are sarcastic, some intelligent and touching, a few enclose photographs (monstrous), and three or four engaging enough to answer.

France preserves stony silence, except for nice notes from Philippe Erlanger and Robert Kanters. Not a peep out of Marie Laure despite the fact that she read and encouraged it as it was being written, despite her written permission to "include all," and despite her now being placed (for the most part favorably) on the map of America, or at least of New York, where, whether she knows it or not, she was hitherto invisible. For it seems that of the two printings and 8,000 copies sold thus far, 90 percent were in New York; the diary, they tell me, is a Big City Book. Unfearful of that book's first phrase, barflies inquire if I'm Ned Rorem. I answer: "Well, somebody has to be, but you'd better ask my friends here, I wouldn't know." And I'll always have friends, some people just do, *malgré tout.* (More disconcerting, a stranger wheezes, "You look like a poor man's Ned Rorem.") Others wonder if I still keep a journal, and if so, have I changed much, or my preoccupations, am I still so gloomy? No, I've not changed, music and death and the body and love still attract and repel as much, though with different emphases. I'm now forty-two. ("They say I don't look it," I exclaim coyly to Norman Podhoretz, and wait. He draws slowly on his sixtieth cigarette of the morning, and replies, "Yes you do.") As to gloom, that's the keynote of diaries, but like liquor it represents only 10 percent of our self-pity, albeit the most flamboyant. The rest of the time we're home working.

John Cheever arrived this afternoon looking more than ever like David Wayne, which renders incongruous the cultured pearls rolling from his tongue. This evening we heard the tapes of one Peter Skullthorpe, a mustachioed Tasmanian whose musical canvas is soaked in novel color providing a gorgeous background on which he does not yet delineate a subject. Heavy rains keep up, blending the days into a soggy cake.

21 September

Yes, naturally I compose "contemporary music" because I'm living today. Since the age of twenty-five, two-thirds of my life has been spent (and three-thirds of my music been written) in communities nobody's ever heard of: Fez, Hyères, Saratoga, Buffalo, Salt Lake.

23 September

At nine last night John unexpectedly appeared at my door with a fifth of scotch. Three hours later, filled up with liquor, never having stopped talking, beginning with humoristic labels (he calls Lillian Hellman a BMOC), continuing with his recent three-month psycho-therapy, going on to how he drinks, how he equates writing and fucking (which is why he's better than his colleagues), etc., etc., etc., he reluctantly left, but not before making a date for us to bring our lunch boxes to the swimming pool at noon today, which we did. We went for a ride in John's red roadster across the battlefields where autumn has prematurely sprung with the maple trees wrongly peach-colored and the apple trees blue, and he talked of his Russian travels and Yevtushenko whom he admires.

28 September

Generalities given to Kinsey eighteen years ago (but times have changed) *re* homoerotics in the male sex. Composers in the '40s: 75 percent (and conveniently, three of the Top Four). Composers today: no more than 50 percent—the musical style doesn't lend itself. Of the leading youngish composers singly representing America, France, Italy and Germany (I don't know about Scandinavia or the Orient), only one: the German. . . . Pianists, then as now, about 50 percent. Organists: 90 percent (not because of attraction to the word but their sissified Protestant background—though in France it's otherwise). Harpsichord: 95 percent. Violinists: no more than 10 percent (the solid Jewish family). Soloists, though, of course are more neurotic than the orchestra players for whom music is a living wage and who are 99 percent heterosexual. . . . Harpists: fewer than you'd think. . . . Abstract expressionists of yesterday:

almost none. Pop artists of today: almost all (a question of humor; they don't drink much either).

Of wet dreams (which the French proprietarily call *faire une carte de France*) I've allowed myself only two. One was twelve summers ago during the night before flying to visit P in Milan for the first time. The second was last night and involved Jane Marsh.

New York
1 October

Visit from Francis Steegmuller. He plans a biography of Cocteau and wanted to ask about the poet's spoken language. Tall, anglicized, gentleman and scholar, tactful and consecrated, Steegmuller, graying at the temples, is the very definition of the biographer. With carefulness he touched on Cocteau's sexuality, had I ever (pause) been to bed with him (no), and what were his tastes? Well, his tastes I know from hearsay, and divulged them all, as I probably should here, but am too lazy.

   Hangover of return. Jane Marsh at the Farrs'. Baths. Total fatigue. JC, Jean Cocteau, Joyce Carey, John Cheever, Jesus Christ, Joan Crawford.

   Tomorrow I fly back to Utah.

Salt Lake City
16 November

Five weeks ago this morning I evicted JA. That is the word, *evicted*. He thought I was raving. The scene was a healthy amputation. Depletion set in immediately, an inert month during which I drank, got flu, collected injustices, was lonely, relieved. JA already last spring had begun gradually to withdraw, socially first (he derided me before friends), then spiritually (the priority of acid-heads to whom superiority, not charity, is the key) and finally bodily (he just wasn't there, even when he was). Said he didn't understand me, but who understands whom? I don't want to be understood so much as not to be misunderstood. JA the perfectionist is always right. That's his tragedy: He misses out on poetic alternatives, and the very missing out is restricting. Perfection is as dull as a flock of identical peacocks which year after year and never out of step strut the pavane to which they've lent their name. Art, like youth, is unfinished. JA's an old man. I've not much time left to spend on unhappiness.

The preceding (what shall we call it?) assessment reads coldly. But for a month in my head I composed a *lettre à la Claude*. The truth is I still miss and love, but miss what was and isn't, and love what (classically) "could have been."

Forever we await a sign, to learn only that the waiting itself was the sign. Neither another's life nor another life are purchasable. I do have a style, don't I!—at which nevertheless I can laugh, but which JA took at face value. HB used to say I'd provoke situations wherein I could play both criminal and victim. Who doesn't? Certainly I justify and protect myself and so, like JA, miss out. But I *choose* what I miss out on. If I'm no longer anxious to gather rosebuds while I may, it's not that the flowers seem prone to shrink and die leaving me intact and holding the bag. It's that I'm just no longer interested in rosebuds.

(JA trying to persuade me to his world-weary fancies brings to mind the Pope's rejoinder to Mrs. Luce's pressuring: "But Madame, I *am* a Catholic.")

Have completed the book reviews, the Cocteau preface for Joe LeSueur. *Sun*, unorchestrated, still looms like a nude zombie whining for clothes! Am well into the *Water Music* for Robert Hughes' young symphony.

24 November

More sound-alikes, each derived from "Goodbye Old Paint": Delius' *On Hearing the First Cuckoo*, Françaix' *Piano Concertino* (last movement), Rorem's *Design*, Copland's *Billy the Kid* and Chopin's *Nocturne* in G minor (Op. 15, No. 3): the second half of the opening period.

If we steal we're also stolen from. What's new? The sun? Who's to judge? The good grasp what *is*, then shape it. For musicians no less than for *littérateurs* (oh flagrant Shakespeare!), plagiarism is a prime prerogative.

My *Sun* is new, and so is television. At least they're new to me. But while my sun was robbed from a Pharaoh and Byron and will continue shining, television dies forever every day. So television cannot be art, in our understanding of art as lasting—lasting like movies. Nor can television be a *medium* for art, either in itself or in retrospect (the late show), being by definition actual, reportage. Immediacy is television's power, and immediacy is a lesser ingredient of art. *Amahl* is far better onstage than on camera. To pretend that TV can be meditative is as fallacious as the recording companies' justification of stereophonic sound, a sound that keeps composers awake and raging all night long.

28 November

One critic speaks of my "unorthodox" love life. But whose is orthodox? Ava Gardner's? The Pope's?

Others speak of the *courage* in publishing this diary. But since they all agree, where's the risk? Where draw the line, in poetry as in battle, between courage and exhibitionism? However, none pointed out that *The Paris Diary* was what it was: a self-portrait of an artist as a young man. As such it should have been condemned or not, not as a book of etiquette. At least everyone disliked a different portion. (Of those outraged, few were writers. Writers see *trouvailles* more than ingredients.)

Why pretend that the present words are more "mature"? We don't grow up, we grow down, become narrower, and when the moment of illumination comes, it's too late. Too late for what?

Or why pretend to have a neck smeared with fresh hickies, bloody proof of desire, what the French call *les petits bleus* (a *pneumatique* in the time of Colette being the color of bruises), the dark blue telegrams of those in love. Nevertheless today, five months after the printing of a book which brought me more *réclame*, for better or worse, than twenty years of semirespectable musicalizing, I still receive nocturnal phone calls, silly or lewd, written proposals of marriage from grass widows and to date about

400 letters. But where's the help? I credulously feel that another person (another person!) might soften the blow. Not *one* other person but *an* other person, and there's no such thing. Soften the blow? The blow of solitude? Harden it.

29 November

From my book, the most quoted (even in *Reader's Digest*) phrase is "Nothing is waste that makes a memory." The pentameter imposed itself subliminally: it was inadvertently printed twice, on pages 126 and 234. That's having my cake and eating it.

A published diary is such a cake, presenting, then retracting evidence, saying nasty things and apologizing, changing its mind with impunity. Eventually even the diarist cannot keep his cake, for if he doesn't eat it, his readers will, and judge his recipe on their own terms. Americans don't allow themselves to have it both ways, to lead two careers.

To publish a diary is to have it two ways, but not three. (A third way, if it existed, would be to retain ability to write without inhibition while knowing the writing would be read by strangers. That way cannot exist except through pornography, which, however, is the most inhibited of all writing, being anonymous.)

Another person's childhood is tedious, our own is engrossing forever. Yet on rereading certain pages I find it hard to recognize myself in hard-boiled postures, over-preoccupation with sex, self-indulgent sadness. As though the infant within me had drawn his honest aquarelle, then a meaner fatter older brother carefully applied a medicine dropper, smearing meanings, heightening colors, overblowing narcissism at the expense of compassion, blotting out charity with sequins. It's not for me to say I'm a "nicer" person than the diary indicates (yes it *is* for me, since I'm saying it), though the proof lies in the fact of such a monster keeping his friends. Actually no one has time to be as miserable as my portrait and still get work done.

31 December

"Are any of my enemies here?" I ask my host, Norman Podhoretz, as he opens the door to Shirley and me at the grand New Year's Eve assemblage which is his retort to Truman Capote's ball. He answers proudly: "They're all your enemies."

1967

At thirteen I knew backward Stravinsky's recording of *Les Noces*: it was about grown-ups getting married. Last week I saw the Robbins ballet on this music; it was about two kids getting married. With a sigh I felt my age.

—NR

Is this actually me again in a Utah parlor on a winter evening alone, drinking hot cider and sorting the yellowing pages of old journals? How remote, love trials, when finished, while work trials hang on like Damocles' sword. The highs and lows, the breathings, of this diary appear with the scope of hindsight steady as a sleeper's. Yet tonight, snared by the details of other years, pausing at yesterday's landmarks strewn over the floor, lost episodes revive with the identical instability of their first occurrence.

The mulled cider's Rosemary's recipe: cloves, apple juice, real apple, cinnamon, squashed raisins, heat together with whatever else you can think of, add whisky. But I'm in the country of Latter Day Saints, and have been ill since the holidays (eternal illness pays for a quarter century of dissolution, or is it that in months of neither smoke nor drink a mist around the illness cleared?) so have left out the whisky and won't give myself a glass until I return East in March. The agonized love's my own recipe: the past, sentimental oils, real upsets, squashed hearts (add whisky) all whipped up into one affair. But I need it again. In all probability I'll retain that American malady long after it's becoming. And the landmarks on the floor are my dozen diaries (plus blue pencil, stapler, Scotch tape) because Braziller, pleased by the Paris souvenirs, requests a "sequel" which we'll call *The New York Diary.*

Now is the time to compile it: I've finished *Water Music* for Oakland's Youth Orchestra, my book *Music from Inside Out* which comes out in six weeks, and a liaison whose aftermath added to the noisy pollution of New York where, unlike France, we look at our feet instead of the sky. Though Salt Lake may offer diversions social and sensual more engrossing than those of last season, I shall desist in favor of a teaching schedule which I take seriously and for the freedom of coming months in the isolation of retrospect.

Isolation of retrospect? On returning here last week I ask What's New? Well, seven murders over Christmas: six by a pair of young jailbirds who flayed and castrated two adolescents, killed a cab driver, then randomly fired on three strangers in a tavern. The seventh by a heartsick swain who entered the local gay bar and shot his girl friend and then himself. These *dramatis personae* were, it seems, Tabernacle children. Ah, thought I, it's begun: the revolt of the Mormons. Last season presaged it with the advent of a not-at-all-stupid magazine, *Dialogues*, although my own students, inasmuch as they had all the answers, didn't ask questions, and that's fatal for composers. But now it is rampant with the whole docile city bolting windows. I'm only a foreigner, no harm can come.

10 January

Can an artist paint himself painting? This book becomes the suicide note of one who, in decay, feels the need for a fatal backward glance.

   . . . Last night they whisked me from this work to a concert of Arthur Fiedler. In the audience was Nigerian Ambassador Alhaji Mahammadu on a good-will tour of the U.S.A. As his midnight train for Frisco was delayed because of the blizzard, we went back to the Abravanels' for supper and talk. The Ambassador, young and personable, with blue-chocolate skin, a guarded speaker though a good listener, was like most men of politics more concerned with education than culture (there is a difference). His aide-de-camp turned out to have been resident in Uganda at the time John Marshall died there last May. He declared the death a national tragedy, since John was headed for a Nobel Prize. Which moved me, as it will Rosemary.

11 January

History concerns the present. Klimt's Judith has not emerged from Holofernes' tent, not even via King James' version, but from a bedroom in Freud's Vienna. *The Sign of the Cross* depicts Hollywood in 1933. *Henry the Eighth* is about Charles Laughton. The first Globe Theatre productions didn't pretend to be costume dramas: Cleopatra dressed like Elizabeth.

Music too is so much about him who performs it! Would Schumann recognize his Etudes as (gorgeously) played by Ashkenazy? My own music of ten years ago concerns my reactions to the world of ten years ago, caught there, like a grape in Jello. (Fact: Paderewski's heart is lodged in the vault of a Brooklyn bank, floating in formaldehyde like a grape in Jello, maintained by Poles protecting their anti-Communist reputation.)

Pasolini's taste in music (Marian Anderson singing a spiritual in his *Saint Matthew Passion*) is as intrusively naïve and wrong as Maurice Jarre's scores (*Doctor Zhivago, Lawrence of Arabia*) are intrusively sophisticated and wrong. Each mistakes history for the past, and for his *own* past.

13 January

Martha Graham I've known, albeit casually, since 1944. Having in that year run away from Curtis Institute to seek Manhattan fortunes as Virgil Thomson's copyist, I earned a few extra bucks a week as accompanist to Martha's classes on lower Fifth Avenue. She hence became my first official employer, for whom I drew out Social Security number 091–22–5307.

Immediately I came to worship with the entourage: as regular worker she showed us the model of Spartan self-denial, scheduling a class even for the hung-over blizzardly New Year's dawn; as exceptional artist she showed us how to wander from the beaten track—but only *she* found her way back. Then as now she was America's first female, yet now as then she must solicit subsidy despite that fame. That fame was such that all her girls wore their hair tight in abject adoration, their mouths slightly open, their thighs at skinny angles—but only *she* brought it off. Then like now Martha Graham was of the four most significant influences of any sex, of any domain, of our century. My dream was to compose for her.

But she fired me. Oh, quite nicely, because, as she rightly explained, improvisation was clumsy discipline for young composers. Her unspoken reason was my lack of the pianistic thrust needed to impel collective contractions and releases. Dance accompanists, to be good, must take classes themselves.

Fired me. But today, thanks to that discipline unclumsified by dance class, I've made a music which it seems, so many decades after, she is about to use.

For a quarter-century we socialized at five-year intervals during parties or backstage, fragmented moments, urgent to me, unrecalled by her. Then last fall her conductor, Eugene Lester, intoxicated by *The Paris Diary*, felt that Martha Graham and I should meet again, for business now, tête-à-tête, on the subject of a collaboration.

She approached across the immensely echoing floor of the rehearsal room, each step disintegrated the clock until her scarlet mouth was close, uttering the identical phrases of years before, the same words, but which, like those of Nadia Boulanger, took new meanings according to occasion.

"Oh, Martha," I say, "I'm feeling ghastly—I wish I were dead."

"Ah, when a dancer says 'I've hurt myself,' I answer, yes, it's *we* who hurt ourselves, not the barre."

"The bar? You mean—?"

Our indefatigable Spartan reeled. Why not reel, when still famous as before—but who sees her now and not a statue? Can statues create? Sure she reels, alone in the rarefied air, I from rum or sleepiness, her reasons are hers.

Stock-still for twenty-seven minutes she listened to the tape of *Eleven Studies for Eleven Players*; when it was over she'd all but choreographed it in her head. We shook hands, kissed. It was a deal. Already she had a title, from St.-John Perse, "The Terrible Frivolity of Hell," and I remembered that, of course, Martha always spoke in iambic pentameter. . . .

Well, I'll believe it when I see it done, for Bernhardt too was unpredictable.

Autumn advanced with inspired midnight phone calls, cubes tinkling through the wires across our city, Martha's voice accompanying them with tones again I could not understand, but understood; her ballet was evolving.

Will I, here in Utah, see it next month during her Easter

vacation New York season (for presumably she works still on it this minute)? Meanwhile (though the dream may come true—and Boosey & Hawkes has frozen the option against other choreographers), since the music is both published and recorded, other dancers *have* used it before (Valerie Bettis, Norman Walker), but Martha doesn't know. Please don't tell her.

15 January

The snow hasn't stopped. On the contrary, for a week it's piled into forty Wordsworthian inches and we're all stranded not unpleasantly in this cold I so hate. A far cry from the Mormonic heat of last May when I'd sit copying music stark naked by the open window. (The Rorems although Quakers were constantly naked: about the house, in mutual bathing, at meals even; intelligently, the nude female was never a mystery, unclothed and respectable.)

They keep me busy. I'd had a suspicion they might not want me back at the University after the wicked book. Not at all. I'm a cross between Socrates and Ann Landers on five-minute TV slots that pose such musical queries as: "Professor Rorem, what, in your opinion, is the aim of life?" (Answer: "To seek life's aim. Next question.")

Or the Abravanels arrange for me to meet Princess Irene who's touring America and adores music. This occurs at the ski resort of Brighton where I sit between the Greek Highness and her piano teacher, Gina Bachauer. The girl is pretty, youngish, cordial, with no opinions and the dowager voice of one who's never heard commoners. I toyed with the idea of asking her to marry me.

Reading hundreds of little mags and a few intelligently tiresome books on music for review. For pleasure: *No Orchids for Miss Blandish* and *Valley of the Dolls*.

Since Christmas no alcohol, no flesh, no tobacco. The last is most significant: I've never stopped smoking before. I've not climbed the wall, but it is a bit dull. Saturday, deciding to try again, I bought a holder, a pack of Chesterfields, prepared some coffee as though for an Aztec sacrifice, and finally (joy!) fired the sacred weed. Instead of the expected delirium came a nausea of dizziness, impatience to finish it off so I could get back to work. I've not smoked since. But I will.

Heard Liberace in the Valley Music Hall. Astonished by the accuracy of his fingerwork: he hits all the right notes, but in the wrong way. . . . The previous night, films by Stan Brakhage who personally introduced them (handsome, long-winded). Afterward I was too shy to go up to him—though what was there to say? his mythology isn't mine. Neither, for that matter, is Beethoven's, yet I admit Beethoven's genius. Genius is always tiresome.

The *Symphony of Psalms* sung by a chorus of 450 high school students from the foothills, the girls nymphets with hair the color of candied yams, the boys just past a ruddy puberty and mouthing this suave music with the look of lost lambs. But the experience was moving if only because they were so very young. Indeed most Mormons—even their septuagenarians—seem (as we used to declare about Americans in general) dangerously young. Dangerous, because innocence pushed too far is complacent, and complacency's a form of madness, and madness at its worst destroys.

How many musical thrills does one have any more? One or two a season? *Même pas.* Yet last June, the last piece on the last program of the last Stravinsky Festival was the *Symphony of Psalms* conducted by the *maître* himself at the speed of his metabolism. We've all heard it and him a thousand times, yet those threads of spice wove us insidiously into a heavenly hammock which rocks still this moment.

Bob Rauschenberg appears in Salt Lake. Impromptu party. He's surrounded by local fans. I enter and say: "Did you ever expect to see *me* here, out in the middle of nowhere?" Heads turn, severe. I nervously fall farther: "I mean, nowhere *geographically,* like Sodom in the desert." Silence. "I mean Gomorrah." Rauschenberg aids me: "Go out and come in again?"

9 February

Six perfect days in San Francisco. Every apprehension was survived without one drink or cigarette. Deplaned Wednesday after a long day of classes, checked in at El Cortez near Union Square and one hour later reemerged into the February summer, heading for The Club, stayed two hours, then to Dave's for three more, finally retired exhausted at four, after having done five miles on foot. Awoke at six to terrible hammering, and at seven moved to the Bellevue down the street.

Thursday Herb Gold took me and Saul Maloff to a Chinese lunch of whole crusty thrushes, my first appetizing public meal in two months, after which we toured Haight-Ashbury, so much more playful and benign than Manhattan's East Village. (Everything being psychedelically equal, at the Cafe-Drugstore even the chef's cap was, of course, rainbow-colored.) But there's a disquieting indolence showing me I've grown far away—pacifism differing from theirs, and all ambition to them a hang-up. How though can I complain beneath this excellent sunlight which blended with evening (like Barcelona's Ramblas three Octobers ago) when Lou Harrison came to pick me up in his *roulotte* carrying us off to a rehearsal of *Façade*. For I'd come to Frisco not only for the business of pleasure, but for the pleasure of business. After the rehearsal we drove, with Robert Duncan, to a Japanese restaurant where as always I had a sinus attack so took a Dristan which made me drowsy and hence irritable to the noise, the noise being the laughter of Japanese whores (for this was a brothel) flirting with pink-mousy American businessmen. The food was no good anyway and I loathe ladies' laughter so I went home to bed.

Next day, Friday, long walks again to museums, more low warm weather, high tea at Donald Allen's, early supper with Roditi who's teaching at State, and then a party in Berkeley with him and Lou (they didn't get on) and a hip little concert organized by Robert Hughes.

Robert next morning collected me for the *Water Music*

rehearsal in Oakland. Now this piece was tailor-made for his youth symphony there: a concerto grosso in the form of variations for solo clarinet and violin with small orchestra. The soloists, aged seventeen, played like angelic devils. Meanwhile the night before at 2 A.M. my entourage arrived from Los Angeles and accompanied me and Lou to the S.I.R. dance (all male) which I'd feared would be vulgar but which turned out pristine as a high school prom.

Sunday noon, Joaquín Nin-Culmell called for me at the hotel and we drove out (again to Oakland) for lunch at the Milhauds'. I'd not seen them in—how long? ten years?—and found Darius at seventy-five looking healthier, more black-haired and thinner than before despite his arthritic complaints and eternal wheelchair. We somewhat timidly reminisced while the gentle Madeleine (but with her Gioconda smile) prepared a lunch consisting of hearts of baby artichokes, heart-tender fillets and heart-shaped strawberry tarts. Madeleine and Darius are cousins: her maiden name is Milhaud which she pronounces Meelo and he calls Meeyo. Their house, at the end of Faculty Lane on Mills campus, is surrounded (in this season!) with hot hollyhocks. We played the tape of *Lions* and Madeleine and I did the talking—mostly about Stockhausen who's now on the Coast, about the trials of Darius' forthcoming *Son et Lumière* project, and about flagellation. They were delighted by a detail from my Whip Book: in eighteenth-century England when masochism was all the rage of upper classes, it became difficult to accommodate the increasing demands until a certain Master Butts invented a mechanism capable of spanking twenty persons at once. . . . Talk of radiographologists and photographic sorcery. Toward four, in the Milhauds' garden, Joaquín and I took our leave after a sweet cup of *filtre*, and we all were very happy.

That evening I débuted in Madeleine's territory as *récitant*. Donald Pippin had arranged a balanced program at the Old Spaghetti Factory on Green Street. First a Lully Suite for eight instruments. Then my *Lovers*, narrative in ten scenes for harpsichord, oboe, cello, vibraphone and tom-toms. Followed by Lou Harrison's *Jephtha's Daughters* with Robert Duncan declaiming. Finally *Façade*, deliciously conducted by Hughes, with Lou and me as speakers. This was possibly its most amusing American performance, Lou's timbre being squeaky, mine low-pitched and both our dictions impeccable. But we had too much fun performing—the audience was left out. Should only be done by the English.

Next morning Robert arranged to guide me through an LSD trip in Gary Samuel's garden. Which he did. But as I refused to go alone, the split dosage was insufficient. We reached only the suburbs and not the magic city proper as I had nine years ago at John G's. Yet it seemed familiar as a twin, and beneficial. Because there were, despite premonitions, no hints of horror, only Gary's lemon tree heavy with luminous fruit and every nerve in the body strained as a strait-jacket. We drove over to Haight-Ashbury which I greeted with more empathy than with Herb Gold a few days before. And we devoured pounds of cheddar cheese and oranges in Golden Gate Park. By six I was normal enough for a last voyage to the baths. Then packed, checked out, and at eleven met Robert and we motored through the night to Lou's house in Aptos.

To awaken at Lou's is to have the host approach your room at dawn from the other end of the house, tapping his instruments en route, first the distant chimes, then closer cowbells, then graduated silver gongs and triangles and ever louder blocks and cymbals and sky-blue windclocks are set in motion reverberating in chorus with the bobolinks outside, and finally a knocking and a human voice declaring that the sun is up.

Lou on San Francisco: "If you don't want to disorient yourself during your initial excursions of the city, just remember: Market Street" (pause) "is *wrong!*"

After French toast, Robert drove me through Carmel to the Frisco airport. And here I am.

26 February

Miss Graham in Manhattan has premiered my ballet and called it *Dancing Ground*. Everyone has phoned about its "success" and sent the Clive Barnes clipping. Possibly because the music wasn't written for her, my feeling of high honor is joined with disinterest. Next week I'll be there and, like Maldoror, will see for myself.

New York
8 March

The music *was* written for her! Before the fact.

In the past it's been shocking how dancers seem unaware of what composer they're dancing to. Not Martha's troupe: they demonstrated how I'd made *Eleven Studies* in search of an author. How unright that music was without this sight! How Helen McGehee's vibrating hops were inevitably correct against the amorphous trumpet! the group's immobility when my orchestra goes wild! or young Robert Powell's rhythmic trance behind the screeching clarinet! Virgil Thomson once wrote: "Dancers are autoerotic and have no conversation." Virgil's epigraph was incomplete: dancers never stop talking, although they only hover over facts while avoiding ideas, except when approaching ideas as though they were sacred or (what's worse) new; but they are so eloquent with their autoeroticism that speech becomes superfluous.

Because she was unliteral and knew how to design *counter* to the yet-indispensable music, Martha is my only collaborator (though she never once asked my advice) to have been right, all right, turning my disinterest to satisfaction.

Who, to share the satisfaction, did I rashly select to attend the performance? Of all people, Susan Sontag. By phone I invited her. She said sure, but could she bring a friend. I said sure. She said wait a minute. Then I overheard her explaining to someone: "You know, Graham, *Martha* Graham: she dances." The shifting generations! Next night we sat in a neat row, I in my shiny green shirt beside Susan who, with that enigmatic grin beneath a yard of tresses, offered to my achingly expectant ears no comment whatsoever.

12 April

In a letter from Vermont: "I have not much longer to live. Please inscribe a few bars of music on the enclosed sheet of paper, and say that you'll never forget me."

[These words seemed less moving when, the following year (and every year since), I received a similar plea in the same handwriting, and also learned that certain of my "public" acquaintances were regularly approached by the same petitioner. NR, 1974]

18 April

Very little response to *Music from Inside Out*. Braziller says it came too soon after the other, but actually the reason is that people don't like to concentrate. The journal was pure television. Only Paul Bowles has written to say he far prefers the new book—that he never "believed" the diary. Glenway Wescott's the opposite. His array of letters during 1963 constantly urged me to "reveal more," to go over the hill, yet contradictorily to tighten the melancholy.

Always demanding stage center. When was it—1936?—that I fell from that high garden wall in Yankton and opened my kneecap on the cement? Twelve relatives gathered to watch Cousin Lois administer iodine. The ensuing cataleptic dance devolved less from pain than from a desire to entertain.

Meadville, Pennsylvania
5 May

Spending five days here at Allegheny College as honored guest of Dr. Wright North (doctor because of a thesis on my songs), lecturing and listening to my music as performed by burly youths and Protestant nymphets. Always apprehension about such small-town stints, but agreements are signed so far in advance it seems the world can't possibly last that long. Still, though one must not say No to money or dissemination of the secrets of art, when the date does come I fall sick.

This visit began weirdly. At midnight I was met at the airport by a middle-aged ashen gent whose face bespoke no wit, who introduced himself as (I misheard) the Dean of the College, who it developed was Mr. Deane from the college, a hired chauffeur. Until his identity was clarified I was uneasy about the quality of the coming days as I observed him drawing a blank at such words as *curriculum* or *choir loft*.

Time sneaks by. I rehearse the kids, presumably knowing more than they about how my music should go. It's touching to hear them—who've had no contact with Negro or Catholic, Jew or Poet—singing the verse of Goodman and Roethke. Touching to hear them, but to *see* them, ah! As their chorus intones (so well, so well) *The Corinthians*, reason flees from holy writ to groin with love for the whole batch. This love is returned in the cafeteria when girls fling *billets doux* onto my tray and giggle. The boys stay mute. It has rained every day.

Self-absorbed is not self-satisfied.

I take myself more seriously than I take my work. Should it be the reverse? That I may be effective in society makes me wonder at society, yet who should there be effective if not I? Enquiries from those writing theses on my tunes bemuse but don't elate me. To find myself history, and not a historian, is saddening, for where do I go from there?

Always they ask if I miss Paris. Yes I do, and I miss myself there. Neither exists anymore.

New York
5 June

At Northwestern a five-day conference titled "Arts and the Press." I share a panel with Malcolm Frager and June Havoc. For two hours we answer questions from an audience of professional critics, about the artist's responsibility, and about criticism.

My colleagues instruct me little. Frager is sentimental ("Music is my life"), while Havoc confuses her "femininity" with privilege and her "suffering" with literature.

I too am sentimental and confused, though not, I hope, in work. Sentiment is found traversing the Evanston campus where I first set foot as a freshman twenty-seven years ago. Three wars, yet nothing's changed. Confusion is found in examining reports on the massacre of intellectuals in Red China. Where do I myself end? I'm in moral terror of being killed for just being me. Coincidence: that we—you and I—should have been born, after so many billion years, into this generation that witnesses the world's end.

Phoned Stephen Spender, another guest of the university, mislaid for years. He took me on a huge picnic, literally to the groves of academe, raw cauliflower and homemade cakes, wise-handsome students and their cultured faculty progenitors. Stephen, unkempt and two-track-minded (the handsome-wise students, the CIA infiltration of *Encounter*), apologizes for the "official" aspect of the *fête champêtre,* not knowing that for once I'm allowing what happens sheerly to flow over me without panicking.

Later I check into a Michigan Avenue hotel (Chicago, you are as lovely as any continental boulevard!), get drunk, fly back to New York in time to take, exhausted, Maggie Paley to still another party, another party.

Movie: the opening: a cripple hobbles. The hero walks behind, miming the hobble. The cripple turns and sees. Then: film credits. . . . Violent and ceaseless torture, followed by shots of mulberry blossoms. The feminine makes love to the masculine who lies prone. Scene ends with masculine rolling over and possessing the other as camera closes on those nude shoulders.

No matter who, the unhappy are tiresome. Sorrow, feeding only on itself, leaves no room for wit. The tiger in love is a bore.

One assumes one's friends—indeed, all thoughtful people—stand against Johnson's Vietnam policy. I question my conscience: can E remain a friend? Yet am I a pacifist only by definition (by upbringing)? Do I reach my own conclusions? or merely those of respected friends? (Though why *merely*? What's wrong with respected friends?)

No one can prove that a man enjoys the abandoned anonymity of a whore less than the devotion of his true love. The mistake is in trying to relate the two.

18 June

Midnight, and a five-day heat wave is being—as though it were a dusty curtain—ripped open by a torrent of wet blades. The first welcome slash was by a person from Poland performing on pink sheets left streaming scarlet. Then came the cloudburst. Now I am alone.

A five-day wave of heat, with it a lost midweek, embalmed in a dusty curtain of dying. Where find the will to write? Compulsive hanging around Christopher Street's docks, in the dull dry dust where an elephant graveyard is formed by those protective Mack Trucks beneath which indiscriminate vermin seethes, as I observe, unsmiling like the leathery others at this my age of forty-three. Thinking how thrice in five days I was stood up (or at least *décommandé*), while everyone else keeps nose to the grindstone which is really all that we who "know how" should do.

In two weeks Jane Marsh and Karel Ancerl will premiere *Sun* (it's raining), after which I leave for Yaddo where there's nothing to write beyond a small churchy anthem and maybe some notes about music. Nor next autumn is there anything scheduled for mind or heart to look forward to. Set in stale ways, for worse or better, and ready to die. Still the world keeps on revolving in ever-more-tremendous error, while the boys at Julius', to the noise of beer and the taste of a deafeningly inaudible jukebox kicking up the dry dust, stare coldly through each other.

21 June

> Music and wine are one,
> That I, drinking this,
> Shall hear far Chaos talk with me . . .
>
> —"Bacchus," Emerson

"Wine which music is" talks to *me* in a far Order. La Marsh and I, after piano rehearsals with Otto Guth during this strenuous heat wave, devour quantities of Schrafft's ice cream sodas (all the color of Jennie Tourel's concert gowns during the 1940s) over which we get better acquainted, mostly in discussions of transsexuality, her father being one of America's authorities on that interesting subject.

Surfacing. A flawless final day of spring, and lunch at the zoo with affable Sylvia Goldstein.

Ned Rorem, 1965 (© *Adamiak*)

With (left to right) Elaine
Bonazzi, Donald Gramm,
Marguerite Willauer at a
dress rehearsal of *Miss Julie*,
1965 (© *Fred Fehl, courtesy of
the Music Division of the New
York Public Library*)

With Virgil Thomson, Paris, 1961 (© *Alfred di Molli*)

With Martha Graham, New York, 1967 (*courtesy of* Women's Wear Daily)

With Maurice Abrava-
nel, 1967 (*courtesy of the
author*)

With Jane Marsh, 1967, at the première of *Sun* (*courtesy of the author*)

With Morris Golde, 1968 (© *Arnold Weissberger*)

With soloists Larry London and
Thomas Halpin for the première of
Water Music, Oakland, 1967 (© *Martin
J. Cooney*)

With Anita Ellis and Myrna Loy, 1973
(*courtesy of the author*)

With Gérard Souzay
at the première of *War
Scenes*, 1969 (© *Beth
Bergman*)

With soprano Phyllis Curtin, 1968 (*courtesy of the author*)

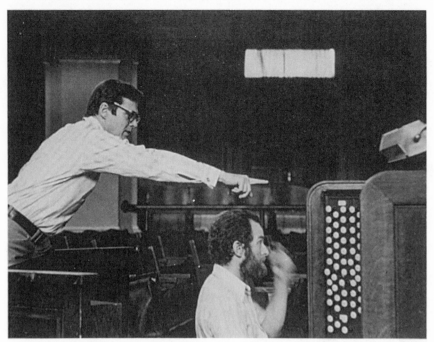

With Leonard Raver, Yale, 1977 (© *Eugene Cook*)

With Elliott Carter, Lincoln Center Library, 1973 (© *Helen Marcus*)

With James Holmes, Nantucket, 1978 (© *Harry Benson, courtesy of* People Weekly)

James Holmes, Nan-
tucket, 1981 (*courtesy of
the author*)

Ned Rorem, 1979 (© *Pach Brothers, Inc.*)

Outsiders say that steady love would provide inspiration. But love comes from outside: it furnishes, it distracts, it brings at best admiration. Inspiration is not *provided*, it emerges from inside, and no composer thinks about it. Love merely keeps us out of mischief.

Now having time, there's nothing to do. . . . Jacques Dupont, back in town to do sets for *Faust* at the Met, reproaches me for worrying. Who was it twenty-two years ago?—was it Parker Tyler? (let me refer to my 1945 diary—yes, it was Parker)—who felt "guilt" would be my end? Has it been? or more likely like love a constant beginning.

24 June

Before *Lulu*, dined (badly) at the Plaza with Morris. Next table a lady was relishing a bleeding cherry cobbler. "Delicious," she uttered thickly to her companion. (Now the word *delicious* I cannot abide as it applies to edibles. In a pinch it works for clothes or clouds, or when meaning *delightful* as the French use *délicieux*.) "Really delicious," she repeated, the adjective oozing gooily off her tongue like the pastry itself. So I could eat no more, which set the tone for the Hamburg Opera, in all ways unsatisfactory. Anneliese Rothenberger was no heroine but a soubrette, the set was murky without gloom, the gentlemen unappealing, the countess too restrained, and the murder—which should have been choreographed as a savage rip from vulva to jugular—was a paltry offstage tap donated by a pale salesman (I imagine Jack the Ripper as handsome). The music, like the melodrama, gaped at the seams.

Meanwhile the first summer days shift from dusty to tropical, smog and noise smack the streets, no question of sleep. I rock and squirm, look out at the viny bricks and try to see them otherwise, as planets or jewels. Forgive, don't worry. Dejected. Night after night dancing their hearts away at the Stonewall, decadent (deliciously), *what* would the Russians think! Intermittently reading the bearably good new Purdy and Chester novels. Vision of gold turning silver, then changing to cloisonné and bursting into nightmare. Awake! Sweet consciousness. Working so as not to work, cleaning the sink to avoid composing, so as to retire, ironing to return to China which will (they say) have changed.

People phone and apologize for wasting my valuable time, when actually I'm lying in bed with a hangover (but *that's* valuable time). People think I drink with them from comradeship, when actually it's from fear—to get through the evening. *Vous autres,* reading this, will say: how empty! You're right.

Smoking far too much again and sick with nerves about the premiere, a week from tonight, of *Sun* at Philharmonic.

The Difficulty of Being, Jean Cocteau's essays, has finally been published by Ellis Amburn, with Elizabeth Sprigge's translation and my preface. The press so far has been widespread and tastefully favorable, while not quite decided about how to take us all.

Finished correcting galleys of *New York Diary* which I reread in two fell swoops and found dreary. In literary papers now one sees ads for the second volume of Anaïs Nin's precious diary with blurbs promising a glimpse into her psychoanalysis, etc. My reaction is what others must have about me: who cares! And yet the painful need to display dirty laundry to a mostly hostile public, while the rest send letters about themselves (yes, who cares!) or ingratiate themselves by spouting noble lineage, thinking us to be snobs, or merely weep onto *their* stationery for what *we* used to be, but hardly are, not now! Literally no one has bought *Music from Inside Out.*

Compose a libretto about an autistic child.

30 June

Rehearsal of *Sun* at Philharmonic Hall. At intermission Paul Jacobs asks if his piano is "ugly enough" for me, while Seymour Lipkin (the assistant conductor who knows the score better than I) asks if the cellos should be playing A-flat instead of A-natural there on page eighty. When the music sounds again, George Plimpton arrives with an entourage, in preparation for his next public venture into orchestral conducting. He speaks to me with *bonhomie,* oblivious to the fact that I'm listening to my own music. . . . Karel Ancerl is sympathetic, musical and intelligent, if not especially energetic, and the orchestra plays like gossamer copper, which is how Jane Marsh looks. But somehow, I feel that only an English-speaking conductor should conduct a work on words in English, no matter his sensibilities, or the international hardships of his past.

Fourth of July

Sun, Saturday, received its premiere. Well, I liked it. Miss Marsh, normally six feet, added a wig of several inches, and vocally too soared to unnatural stratospheres. Later we all drank champagne and I made a pass (rejected) at Barbara Harris. Lukewarm reviews. Now I long to leave town, to estivate, to compose more and more, nothing else counts.

5 July

The Sunday *Times* printed James Lord's comments on *The Difficulty of Being*, and indirectly his attack on me. People are usually right for the wrong reason. James is wrong for the "right" reason, the reason of the old-fashioned fashionable French who disparage Cocteau for his semisincere self-contradictions, his so-called frivolity and indiscriminating modishness, as though these qualities weren't precisely what make Cocteau Cocteau, a sum of his parts, another artist, *quoi!*

James Lord's vendetta wounds me so that I've spent the day composing a classical Letter to the *Times*. But what the hell. His arguments (in many cases lies) are too limp for puncturing, and my spleen's spent.

How wonderful it would be to *learn* from a review. And I do dream of one day finding, in those columns of Replies to Replies, not the habitual hairsplitting accusations, but a clean statement like: Dear Opponent, you're right, I'm wrong, forgive me, you've shown me the light.

7 July

Is a diary, by its nature—more "honest" than a novel? Probably not. The undisciplined first-person involuntarily inclines more to disguise than a novelist does. As to whether I know less "who I am" than, say, Alfred Chester or James Purdy, neither they nor I will ever know, any more than we can perceive the self-awareness of that farmer, that nurse, that dogcatcher.

Yaddo
12 July

Knowing I'd soon be in Saratoga, I for six weeks procrastinated, stifling all inclination to compose. Allow the faithless body to cave in while faithful works grow out. Write *Air Music*.

Formerly I consumed a coffee float thinking how grand a cigarette would taste after. Now I eat in the now. Not that not smoking's not frustrating, but so is a rush through meals. Literature is defined by what an author can get away with.

Can I get away with saying that during this, my first evening at Yaddo, feeling lonesome (for what? hating New York so), no impulse either to work, to stroll the forest whose every leaf, like the stained glass and pink rugs of West House, is familiar as childhood smells? Having quit the city with all complete (galleys of new *Diary* corrected, *Sun* performed and placed in the past, final Utah check cashed) and nothing under way, I'm now required to resume from scratch. The thought of beginning another opera—even with the perfect book and a fat commission—seems superhuman and pointless, like holding your breath for a high dive onto rock. (If I began it, though, that beginning would begin with a disjunct aria bellowed before the curtain, like Riabouchinska who in gold opened *Coq d'Or*.) Yet, appraising these who will be my colleagues in the art of crime (I mean the crime of art) here for the next several weeks, I intuit, maybe wrongly, that not one can turn the trick. So I must. Why must? To consume coffee floats and smoke with clear conscience. What work? They tell me *Sun*, which cost an arm and a leg and a heart, seems less convincing than *Water Music* which cost nothing. Since "they" are always right I'll grit my teeth and pursue the artisan's track, ignore inner head and heart and follow my craft, trying meanwhile (unlike these amateurs) not to confuse conviction with greatness, nor effort with accomplishment. And I shall take sun, diet, swim, read, so as to make a firmer body for the destruction next fall.

Eleven weeks since JA entered, as an emergency patient, the Psychiatric Institute of New York. Hindsight proves that anyone's on the brink, that all our friends are mad. Yet when he turned up that Monday dawn I was unprepared for the folly which glowed forth like radioactivity. We'd not been on close terms since last October, but an act of violence is one sign of love and JA had been always in mind. My concern might have changed tone had he shown more strength. Yet despite no end of presumed passivity, social and physical, I arrange for friends to depend on me. JA no longer depended.

The following afternoon, I knew, when the doorbell sounded, that it was JA again, insane, returning up the stairs, and I felt inconvenience, victory, repentance. He entered, unslept for five days, asked for a boiled egg and peace. In a period of three hours he touched paradise and hell; I watched that so-familiar body quiver like a sick thoroughbred, and wondered how death hadn't come a year sooner, had I retarded it? By five I realized that to trust JA's sleeping there while I kept a two-hour appointment would mean returning to his slit throat. He was incapable of speech beyond calling his doctor with whom I "took charge." (The sin of treating compassion as a virtue!)

By nine we had already been for hours around the waiting room of Columbia Presbyterian Hospital submitting to farcical interviews. Ultimately we were transferred to the Institute. By midnight JA, with my tenuous advice, exhausted, signed himself in. Coming home then from 168th Street in a state of shock, rain falling thick, I consumed a quart of chocolate ice cream, phoned Robin Pitchford, collapsed in tears, frame wrenched in a purge it hadn't known for a decade.

Nothing has much sense except in retrospect. Did I want love or its illusion? What is love's illusion? During the weeks that followed, JA, mad as a hatter, proved not much madder than you or I, lucky to be not in Bellevue, showed "improvement," and I was less needed, hurt. Still the fact of him rather annoys me. Lovers exist as potentials, or as souvenirs. I'll never have another, so waiting is a waste. But what *can* satisfy? Not the most perfect performance of my music, not for more than moments. The making of music is pain plainly, and I'm sick of trying. Here is Yaddo, palms open, deadline-less. I love no one, am not interested in seeing any friend again ever (yet paradoxically suffer from love) and there's no place else on earth I could rather be.

15 July

Can't stand being alone, even to work, unless there's something in the evening to look forward to. If only. Only apprehension of being forgotten concerns me. Think I'm ready again. If only the gardener and I had reached some understanding whereby each evening he would climb to the porch and rap the window with earthy knuckles, enter and spend some time in smiles. How soon could I wish him gone, so as to write? And then not write?

Love is impossible. If it were possible, it wouldn't be love.

To define it is to miss the point. Romantic love is a mystery which when solved evaporates. Such love can only be defined after the fact—yet how define what no longer exists? Lovers inhabit a cloud, free from space-time laws. The cloudburst signals an end to the honeymoon, a start to responsibility. Decades later they recall the cloudy life, but cannot refeel, and thus cannot specify, it. Memory of intensity becomes a vaguely embarrassing treasure.

Tristan and Isolde consumed a potion brewed to last three years, and died before the effect wore off. Like Romeo and Juliet, the appeal of their fame lies in their death. Had these "immortal" lovers survived, their affair would have evolved like all affairs: into accommodations broader than carnality. Romantic love belongs to youth, and is by nature too selfish, too isolated, to burn long without the nourishment of change. To an outsider, all young lovers are boring except those who are killed.

As to friendship—what the French call *camaraderie,* or nonsexual love (if such a thing exists)—this differs from romantic love not in kind but in emphasis. Presumably it is less egoistic, more caring, and endures longer, similar interests and goals being as much involved as affection. Lovers, while they last, need nothing in common beyond their bodies.

None of this has changed since prehistory. Surely the New

integration of colors and classes, flower people on a collision course is old as the dictum that opposites attract. If their union creates explosion, that's another matter.

16 July

Air Music shall be totally *fabriqué*, with no thought of expression, much less of self-expression. Emotion, as opposed to clear thinking in so-called philosophers (and certainly in artists), is not trustworthy; if their work is good, emotion will distill within it after the fact, without having to be put there.

Although, by the clock, I work a great deal, I literally don't know what it means to concentrate on, suffer from, slave over that work. I can ache from the effort of making a long piece "go"—making it sound "inevitable"—but that's concern over scaffolding, not matter; once notated, it's never revised (revisions are made *en train*). As for short pieces, they come in one sitting, off the top of my head. Now those wise men who chide me for prolificity and hasty selection: are those works I've *thought through* superior to those I've not? I would if I could but *I don't know how*. Yet who can prove that that which is scooped off the top of the head hasn't been brewing, like bubbles, which form unattainably at the pot's bottom, then rise into nourishing foam? This all applies to my music. But the prose is no different (though perhaps snottier in texture). I'm capable of accusing a Milhaud of what others reproach in me.

Music is not a question of finding ideas, but of giving them shape. Ideas are a dime a dozen. (I had only two or three ideas in my life, and spent that life in resculpting, reknitting, refining, repushing them like a silly Sisyphus.) If I'm supposed to write easy pieces I write them, as I'm now doing in the four-hand *Birthday Suite*. If I'm meant to write more complex ones I write them, as in *Air Music*. The process of manufacture is the same, though naturally I prefer certain of the dispassionate ingredients to others. This paragraph could use some revision.

24 July

Awoke saying: *The irrationality of religion to rebreathe some fantasy into music.*

Continual rain, with mistakes all over the world, and the Revolution under our nose. Nevertheless, I'm living only, apparently, for what *will* transpire. Living occurs just in retrospect. Nothing in the moment seems sufficient, correct or useful, or even worth the trouble for our subtle mechanisms.

Yaddo meals are so to my taste! During fifteen years at the best tables of France and North Africa, my culinary dreams were still not for snails in garlic, but for malteds in Schrafft's. America's sole contribution to world culture is bland cooking made succulent, as exemplified at our Saratoga table. Greedy for sugar, I purchase at Sutter's a great glistening lemon meringue, bring it home and begin to glut in solitude, the doorbell rings so I hide the pie (not from guilt like the alcoholic with rum bottles, but from an unwillingness to share), impatiently hurry my visitor, find myself alone again, finish off the pastry entirely. Next day I repeat the process with Sutter's four-pound devil's food cake, and the following day with twelve cream puffs. In fairness let it be said that I do the same with salt as when hung over, with sex as in heat waves or with all-out abstinence as at Yaddo.

26 July

No music in me today that needs to come out. It seems impossible to compose without a deadline.

I seldom take the little stroll between West House and the Mansion without pausing at the garage gardenette to enjoy the varicolored begonias vibrating with a vitality so lacking now in me. To dissolve into the vegetable kingdom, to face for a change the problems of plants: that would not perhaps be peace, but neither would it be the war into which daily we plunge ever more irrevocably. Shame on the animal kingdom for coming to this! for preventing the begonias from growing more blazing, so thick are the wounding clouds.

27 July

What if suddenly I told the truth? There'd be a blank page. But *which* truth? I feel no different—certainly no wiser or less physical—than ten years ago when leaving France for good, or twenty years ago when still discovering New York and finishing Dostoevsky and "using" people, or thirty years ago when having in Chicago a first exposure to the magic of nonclassroom French through Marlene Dietrich's record of *Assez.*

And yet. John Moriarity, absent for years, came up in those wet gloomy corridors and muttered: "I've been teaching your songs for so long I'd forgotten they had anything to do with you!" When we get to know him, we disassociate a man from his work. We even disassociate ourselves from our former works. Nevertheless, despite what's said about the artist's work versus his life (and certainly in the past few years they've become indistinguishable), his living provides his work. Yet he never lives to his ultimate, since that is precisely where life stops and art starts. An artist can only observe from around the edges, even (paradoxically) when he's in the middle, because he can only experience in terms of *using* experience, be happy through rehearsal or icily document his hot sorrow. He must notate that he doesn't care about not caring.

It has been a very long time—a decade maybe—since I could lose myself in work. This proves nothing, is irrelevant to the *quality* of output.

28 July

For days a filthy rag of thick mist hangs over Saratoga, hiding dishonor from the rest of the solar system. Horseflies and mosquitoes forbid long walks around the lakes; the only experience is reading. Or occasionally, with Wallace Fowlie, a movie. Last night *The Dirty Dozen* which Wallace relished and which appalled me. Is it an upbringing of nonresistance that renders me squeamish to violence? Humor shrivels when each day news of riots grows. Mostly I stay confined to the great pink room. It is the second-floor apartment I have always occupied at Yaddo, sixty feet of warm rosy plush, feminine antiques, an erotic chaise longue and a celibate bed, windows on a level with the ocean of elms through which the room (a hall really) becomes, on good days, inundated with filtered sunlight, a vast porch looking onto a formal alley of red and white petunias, from which, toward six in the evening when nitrogen heightens the air, perfumes rise, mocking my sterile afternoon. Table and piano are snuggly placed in view of all this, and for a while I have no cares. Yet what am I doing? Repeating myself. The rationale is that artists have always performed but one act—in different colors, speeds, sizes, perhaps, but only one subject, since the cosmos is in a glass of water, et cetera, mirrored in every phrase, recurrent identically through the years in wave after millionth wave of pride or pity, or throughout the pages of this unclimactic journal. To my justification, where's the model for variety? Not in the outside world whose dangerous games have been wearisomely similar since before the Roman Empire. Suddenly exasperated, I don't mind if the races cannibalize, the sky erupts. Justice and brotherhood seem no longer considerations anywhere. I just want to save my skin.

29 July

Yeats states our dreads. Involuntarily I place myself among "the best" (who doesn't?) to justify lack of conviction about music. "Passionate intensity" is precisely what our poor, our rich, society is so wastefully spending as it works toward a negative goal. I'm a pessimist.

There are our hopes. Quite naturally I feel myself as one of "those that build again" (who doesn't?) to deflect foreboding of Blacks raiding Yaddo and drowning us all in the swimming pool. I'm an optimist.

Not that—Quakerhood notwithstanding—I wouldn't react precisely as every Negro everywhere, although (since I can only *feel* as white, whatever I *think*) I want to be on the rising side. Yet who *in the fact* can know what side he's on? Perhaps the world has just begun, and here is our first trial. I mean, perhaps the world's about to end, and here is our last trial.

Not that I read Yeats much, nor certainly for pleasure. Since childhood, involvement with verse has been solely through seeking texts for my manner of musicalizing. Still, there are more close friends among poets than among those others who provide pleasure. But it's "those others" who've held me since I came here two weeks ago. My reading has been, as annually, every word of every issue of every Little Mag from the past year in America, France, England. Criticism pours out the ears. Add to that all of Proust finally in French, *The Seven Pillars of Wisdom* (of all things), V. Woolf's Diaries and James' *Art of the Novel,* plus necessary and unnecessary acts of fiction by acquaintances here and abroad, and you ask why I get no work done.

Each day some work—not much. Quite bad, but I'll continue to grind, knead and bake it, finally frost it with much too much colored sugar, cool it, then eat it all furtively without chewing enough, digest it lumpily, then puke it out like a mother bird, collect it in a manila envelope to be sent off to Boosey & Hawkes who hasn't even asked for it, my first uncommissioned piece in years. Funny, how this time next year the solution, the recipe, of *Air Music* which now so fills my head, will have faded utterly and been replaced by other conundrums.

30 July

Listless, now that there are whole days and nights free. Communal meals and noonday swimming are high points; otherwise prefer to be alone. Yes, I need people, their acknowledgment, but no sooner with them than I'm uneasy. Relieved that Elizabeth has canceled our Sunday morning meeting. But tonight we go again to the ballet (Balanchine's in summer residence) and I'm exhausted in advance. Despite haughty garrulousness and social reputation, I've always (and certainly as a musician) been an outsider, a lone wolf, from shyness and disdain, from an urge not to drown.

Could these pages build upward, though fragile as a house of cards, instead of outward like dominoes always one color and aimless, a substitute for living without climax? But of course their aim unconsciously is (like Virginia Woolf's diary) the theatrical target of the author's real-life death.

A need to *construct,* not *add to.* Now Braziller asks for another music book. It shall be made from interviews on the subject of music's direction during these fatally silly times.

31 July

Last night, with Polly and Wallace Fowlie, final evening of ballet. On two occasions I'd bumped into Nicholas Magallanes doing afternoon shopping in town, and both times promised to go backstage in the evening. I didn't, he seemed annoyed. I have the Greenroom Horrors, am as fearful of dressing-room artifice as of barking dogs. So I avoid the ritual, even with good friends. Too bad, because the famous artist often finds himself alone just when he most needs to unwind at the sound of compliments.

I can walk on my hands. That's all I can do which nobody else can do.

From England a sheaf of *Paris Diary* reviews, which Barrie & Rockliff has just published there. The critical substance is much the same as the American write-ups (though snider, taking at face value the narcissism which evidently failed as irony: my prose lacks tone of voice), but now the fun is over. Dejection from any mention of that coy book. Yet I permit *The New York Diary* to come out in October. Why? Because lessons learned from an experience apply to *that* experience, not experience generically. We always repeat our mistakes. Sometimes they turn out correctly.

2 August

So rare is the sun that when a few beams announce themselves we fly between the soaking drops and look skyward with thanks: we pray for drought. Anything to keep from work. But what I don't compose will remain forever uncomposed as though it made a difference. Not smoking brings on sleeping sickness. The reason for making art *is* moral, though it has nothing to do with persuasion. Art's function is to keep the artist out of trouble. I find more pleasure in words. Wandering daily from diary to keyboard, mixing these mediums, how does it feel? Words feel better, because although they're more clearly "responsible," I sense no responsibility toward them, they're not my business.

Dined last night for the first time outside Yaddo, an airy respite with Larry Josephs who's been teaching English here at Skidmore for years. Meal of green and gold: glossy cheese soufflé, delicate sea-colored salad, a meringue of greengage plums. Larry, now a vegetarian, is otherwise unchanged. His lodgings are a mere transplant of the pristine chambers he's always inhabited. Records of Maggie Teyte and Nellie Lutcher peeled away twenty years in twenty seconds (each squeak and moan like a familiar photograph in negative), though the anecdotes he dredged from our old acquaintance were new to me. We'd known each other better than I remembered.

5 August

Asp's a slicker term than the redundant Wasp: Anglo-Saxons are by definition white.

Fined for jaywalking, we learn not to watch for green lights but for cops.

 Just as a soprano has only so many high E-flats in her, so a *ragazzo di vita* contains finite orgasms. Use augments potential, no? Exercising the voice increases the possible number of E-flats. Etc. Don't be stingy. Still, singing and sex do take up time (time for what else?), and we can smoke just one cigarette too many.

 Dream of panic: stranded on a desert island without my glasses.

News worse, though to the eye each day's the same, children play, we brush our teeth. Johnson projects a surtax, escalates Vietnam, plots war with China while America wars with herself, each day's the same but worse.

 At the Saratoga Performing Arts Center last night we and eleven thousand others heard Van Cliburn. How was he? How would I know? simply not caring whether one young whiz this week whips a war-horse gentler or meaner than another young whiz last week. Do they weary of their wee repertory of shopworn *chefs-d'oeuvre*? At their fees? (From the standpoint of live composers, William Masselos is the most significant pianist today.)

Insomnia. Anything, a spider's whisper, awakens me to ruminate for hours on far Morocco with wet eyes, or on those years of a thousand hours and ten million notes from which what remains—a few one-page songs, or not even? Insomnia precludes breakfast at The Mansion among the other inmates who bruise each other with ribaldry, or (worse) with philosophic evaluations of *structure* and *levels of meaning* at this ungodly hour. Morning's passed in slow withdrawal from dreamland, dear. Elizabeth hospitalized yesterday for eye surgery. Hortense and Curt arrived. Also Robert Garis. While Wallace and I keep up steady movie attendance.

9 August

Cigarettes. On giving them up (again) my first night in Yaddo four weeks ago, something—as the saying goes—went out of my life. Today I resumed (puffing away while writing this), yet "something" has not been reinstated; instead there's a soft burn blackening my hard resolutions. Eating and smoking have grown so intertwined that one motivates the other. The sole pleasure of dessert comes from anticipating the cigarette afterward (I've never encountered a similar pervert, just as I've never met anyone with precisely my libido fixations), so I race through the most delicate meals. That Calvinistic self-denial imposed one month ago increased the appetite, yet left it ironically incomplete (libido meanwhile nonreactive, *mais tant mieux*). With the excuse that all this provoked my recent fractiousness and bad work (i.e., no work, though I've never felt healthier), I bought the yellow pack of king-size Winstons. We'll see. I must give them a fair try, mustn't I? To what extent would one smoke or drink or screw—more or less—if assured of death by torture six months, one week, three days, or four hours from now?

A sweet envy one could feel in reading Thomas Merton's *Day of a Stranger* in the current *Hudson Review* is canceled by a sanctimonious tone. In retreating—or whatever he calls it—to a Trappist abbey in Kentucky, he reserves the right to forget about being himself, while undergoing a compulsion to publish (with a complacent chip on his shoulder) his diary about forgetfulness. Why must he tell *us*? who are we to share his special thoughts, thoughts which ipso facto can't be shared, can't even be *thought*, much less written down, if they're to remain "pure"? Nevertheless, the same reproach might be made of my journal (though I don't pretend to being either hermit or swinger), perhaps justifiably. For if I *do* have an urge to let others—family, friends, professional milieu, the whole world—in on my sufferings or scope or special recipes, ever less do I feel that I really suffer (or see well, or enjoy), or, if I do, that it's rightly written, or if rightly written that it's understood, or if understood that it makes a difference. Ever more am I sure that what "counts" can't be expressed, while plagued by a suspicion that what's not expressed does not exist.

Sans date

When we observe careers in the making, a conflict arises in both enthusiasts and detractors: they get so concerned with what *should* be developing that they grow blind to what *is* developing; they aggrandize themselves by showing what *they* would have done, while neatly ignoring what, in fact, was done. If we can already situate in retro-perspective our homegrown performing talents like Maria Callas and Ava Gardner, or creative ones like Tennessee Williams and Jerome Robbins, we are still witnessing the unfolding gifts of, say, Alfred Chester or Andy Warhol, whose works are not sufficiently distant for us to sift the wheat from the chaff. We are cruel to shrink an artistic generation to a five-year span, and to demand always something novel from our artists without allowing them to crib even from themselves.

   We've grown intimidated by bright critics, who in turn have been brainwashed by that breed of "suspiciously articulate composers." Suspicious, because they place understanding before feeling. Bright critics meanwhile, vengeful of the intimidation, hate to let an artist get too big for his britches.

They speak of the artist's responsibility. But he has none, even to himself. Responsibility's a moral question; art isn't. Unlike ethics, art doesn't seek to change so much as confirm: art renders us more so. Should it manage to change us, it would fail as art, nor could it ever succeed so well as philosophic propaganda—the lucid logic of words and deeds. Ritual, being narcotic, changes us; art, being a cleanser, establishes us. The Beatles know that art evolves from ritual, but they do not confuse art with ritual, as do lesser popsters. Politics rises and falls, but the work of art presumably goes on forever (it may change meaning from age to age, but not shape: the *fact* of it is stationary).

Responsibility? Artists feel no guilt about not giving the public what it wants, though they may feel guilty about giving the public what it *does* want (what it expects), about being coerced, entertaining, condescending. Artists, after all, are the makers of manners. The performer may have a responsibility toward the composer, but the composer has none toward the performer beyond the practical one of making his music performable on some terms. With, say, the Beatles, composer and performer are one (or four), so that particular rift is bridged. Indeed, if for the bourgeois, Artist now means so much it means nothing, for Youth, which dictates the tone of any generation, Art and Artist are no longer capitalized: art is where they find it, in museums or mountains, Buxtehude or Barbra, formed by what they call The Environment rather than by one ego signed in large letters. The Youth Public itself has come to be less judge than participant in what is no longer good and bad Art, just good and bad.

19 August

Hortense Calisher, the first "outsider" to read *The New York Diary*, returned the galleys last night with these words: "It cost me two martinis to speak to you now, and now I can't speak because, after all, more than being a work this is your life, so what dare I say? Certainly you're bitchy when depressed, certainly I've defended the other diary against attacks on its bad taste, and certainly I'm annoyed with *your* attacks on the sacredness of art—or at least on attempts toward the making of art which, finally, is all we have, is all that counts. And you do have a penchant toward what I call Biological Criticism—discrimination against women writers. Still your book holds together, at least the first half, though it seems to want to present itself *as literature*."

My life? But it's not. Or no more than 10 percent. Taste? That was admittedly not among my considerations, how could it be, in a diary, or in any work of art? As to art, that is not sacred any more, if ever it was. (Isn't it clear that I denigrate the work of others because I'm momentarily sterile?) And as to what I say on female authors, ten years ago it was true: then their writing was so feminine (overloaded with ideas, like too many earrings) only a woman could write it, or so masculine (drily to the point and no nonsense) only a woman could write it. Today the best writing in England—both fiction and non—is by women: five or six names immediately come to mind, but I can't think of any new male authors, except playwrights. The same holds in America, to a lesser extent. . . . Of *course* my writing is literature, though not, by definition, calculated with Hortense's skill. Though if I lash out against her in this paragraph, it's because she's read me too correctly. . . . Probably I regret the book's imminent publication; still, to regret the imminence of something inevitable and, in a way, grand, is pretentious.

Meanwhile hay fever chokes me, Saratoga seethes more than Israel with Orthodox Jews, and the August racing Mafia has all arrived in bleached limousines bringing that luscious cooling smell of pinecones and horseshit, while I just sit around, or read and read (Boswell, Proust and Dickens) or go to movies or play four-hand Brahms waltzes with Robert Garis or write in this diary or on reviews I've been asked to do (about Poulenc-Bernac's new disk for *High Fidelity*, about Ezra Pound's hot air for Plenum Press), but not on musical composition per se, heaven forbid, also alas, and meanwhile, too, while it continually rains I count the days until New York.

Because for the first time in fifteen years I miss the city. Could it be that despite the rural air here I'm not really living (but only documenting having lived) because there are no threats, no highs and lows? or that I need something to take my mind off the fact that my mind's not on work or that I don't care that I don't? or that I simply need to get laid? (although one would conclude saltpeter's served here). What I most anticipate is the Sutter's blueberry crumb tart! Awake nights planning not a seduction but a menu for Ruth Ford who will arrive on Labor Day Sunday with my parents to give me a haircut: roast chicken with olives and sherry, new potatoes, watercress (brut champagne), carrot cake with brown sugar and my secret formula for lime mousse (Château d'Yquem): the wines may break the taste buds but the planning's the fun.

Yet while in Yaddo I indulge a daily perversion foreign to Manhattan: reading the *Times*. Such reading becomes each hour more comic, so anesthetic in its hysteria that we only sigh and turn the page unless hit in the eye by the death of a friend. Matthew Goodman was killed mountain climbing. Killed thus, like the kin of so many I've known—and now Paul and Sally no longer have a son. Why *him*? Or why John Marshall? Why, finally, me?

Me, who guard against overdoses of coffee, like an old maid preparing for senility just over the bridge. Growing ever more peevish, all galls except the approach of forty-four of which I'm proud—who'd have thought it! Braziller sent a batch of reviews for *Music from Inside Out*, mostly equivocal, and I do get upset, for I am too hard on myself.

I am not hard enough on myself. Exactly twenty-two years ago, the month that war was finishing, I started this diary. Now young people send me dissertations on my songs, and doctors in the paper tell about cancerous smoking, allowing none of us anymore even that dear pleasure, while we all prepare the new war.

Sans date

Music must no longer be American. Boundaries are senseless now. I want my music identified as mine. Yet that creates the greatest boundary.

What made you become a composer?

I *was* a composer. I became a technician. To worry what "made" me a composer would keep me from composition. I continue from logic: whatever my gifts, no one but me can supply my needs. It isn't courage but disinterest which prompts me to be, as one says, myself. I don't compose what I ought, but what I want, for my "integrity" is woven with laziness.

I'm disloyal to my children when they disgrace themselves in public. I deny knowing them. My past is a sinking ship, and I am a rat.

Seven weeks without tobacco (almost) or alcohol. Lately I don't write much about self-denial, it seems petty in view of the world. What does that prove? What *should* one put in a diary? In several days my Lenten fast will break. And this time next year . . . I used to feel that if I didn't record each time I got drunk (or stayed sober, which is the same thing), future generations wouldn't pity me enough. Emphasis doesn't come through repetition but through economy. Besides, there aren't going to be any future generations. So let's be extravagant. What does that prove?

The New York Review of Books wants a piece on the Beatles. Amusing, suddenly, to be taken as a serious writer, to hoodwink the public as Picasso is still accused of doing. Now, if those accusers take *me* seriously, anything can happen: if I can be an authority in fancy mags (and what do I know? what can I learn from myself?), what hope then is there for the world? Like Lady Bird Johnson attending my music—has she nothing more important to do?

Being taken seriously as a composer is, however, I suppose, by now well entrenched (meaning that I also take it seriously), mostly because I get paid. Though to be taken seriously means to be grown up, and to be grown up is hard to swallow. (Notwithstanding Cocteau, who says childhood's what children seek to escape.) Those students' dissertations on me "know" more about all music—including mine—than I do, yet they ask my advice. They ask it because they've seen my name in the paper. (Modesty forbids suggesting they may admire the music.) I smile inside, yet give the advice, and am right, righter than they, for the very idea of a dissertation is wrong. Wrong, at least in this case, because necessarily incomplete where completion is all, and hence misrepresentative.

I believe in the word, even in two or three, in stringing them together. But I do not believe in writing. Not that it can't be done: it's been too much done. Ditto for notes. But simultaneous notes are more amusing than simultaneous words. Music has more potential.

Censorship's relaxing, so things will get worse (before they get worse). Pornography, they say, is of necessity nonliterature; true erotic literature does not excite. Yet portraits of Alexander the Great, of Tarzan, and Plutarch's Cleopatra all excited me plenty, and so did Lincoln Steffens, and who knows Henry James' intent? Whatever artist portrayed a nude and said it was not meant to excite (from Praxiteles through Manet to Francis Bacon) lied. Each has his collection of dirty pix. Masturbating, aged fourteen in our Chicago bathroom, onto the pages of Longus' *Daphnis and Chloë*, paper oozing where Lyceaneum seduces the young shepherd, saying, "I before Chloë, made thee a man!" Reference to this literature was of course through Ravel whose music also had us all masturbating. Yet if, as I so often now claim, music doesn't mean anything, it produced semen then aplenty. Not in itself, perhaps, the yet-symbolic book, but through association. Saturday night with the Benny Goodman Trio wowed us. Of course, music masturbation is another esthetic, and I can't imagine it to, say, Bach fugues or even to nonvocal Mozart. But I still own that book of Longus, the pages forever glued shut by adolescent sperm of yesterday.

Having read and relished *Whacking Off*, it could seem fitting to compose an Ode to Philip Roth's prick. His personal offense (or not) at such a gesture (gesture!) coming from the likes of me (or whoever) is irrelevant; vicarious interpollination among the higher orders (the élite who never, alas, meet) is all that keeps us (well, at least *me*) going. The Society of Artists has never discouraged circle-jerking but applauded that which occurs between the wretched spiting and the nonadmiring. Yet incest is "worse" than inversion. The inclination disgusts you, not because we're both men but because we're both artists. One needs a cultured waitress, the other a stevedore. Ah, but if the stevedore and waitress went off with each *other*! How touching, we'd say. Not: how wrong.

Uneasily perusing the epigrams of Malcolm de Chazal. They lead nowhere. My aversion to aphorists resembles Poulenc's to Fauré: blood ties too close for comfort. Or who owns what?

At 11 P.M., alone in a corner of this large pink room at a large white table, a single bright lamp, and the nineteen windows thrown open to the evening. Despite screens, moths arrive, flutter madly, grow calm, go mad again. Various species pause dazed on this very page and my impulse is to crush. I hesitate, lower my head an inch or two, look close into the eyes of this marvel whose gentle silk prongs and fragile onyx fans make Fabergé seem coarse. And my own eyes ache as I consider how tonight, at forty-three, I've already several decades of imperfect effort behind me, while others shout: You've had your share, withdraw. I freeze, bemused, relax, then start to move again, brush aside the moth and write this paragraph.

Labor Day
New York

No sooner off the plane than, like a victim of privation, I flew to the liquor store for a case of Montrachet, to Gristede's for the ingredients of a carrot cake, and gave a wet party for Virgil, the Phelpses, David Diamond, my parents, Arlene Heyman and her boyfriend. In one day I lost my suntan, posture, no-smoking resolutions and, fortunately, virginity. Collapse.

It will soon be a year since I've composed any music, and am now killing time while waiting for time to kill me. Hours, hours spent gazing from my kitchen window, a window of alabaster hewn—no, chiseled, no, sliced—*sliced* so thinly even hens can see through. So, gazing, crushes, even love affairs spring up and grow and are dispelled by dreams, wet dreams like those of Demetrios in *Aphrodite.*

Tricks of perspective. From my window here on the second floor, two out of three in the street seem beauties. Yet when I descend, after hours of daily gazing, I never find them.

Ice cream? I love it more than life itself. And it is all, what's more, the doctors now allow me. Doctors who—in overpainting the horrors of a nicotined afterlife yet offer no substitute beyond blandness for the thoughtfulness of hearts—are saving me from a death worse than fate.

Since returning from Yaddo three weeks ago my body has deteriorated: plantar warts, cyst on spine base, hay fever so paroxysmic I sneezed myself into throat hemorrhages. Finally had my ugly subcutaneous nodule excised from the abdomen and replaced with five stitches (the growth itself resembled an agate-sized hog embryo). While attending in the East 80th Street anteroom of Dr. Bineau who performed what he called the "cosmetic operation," who should enter there but Kenward Elmslie. Quickly we dispensed with the habitual early-fall discussion ("How was your summer?") and fell to our health, which subject, after forty, replaces genitalia. Then I announced: "Oh, maybe I'm in love!" Having got uptown early I had spent an hour in the Metropolitan, and there among thirty marble busts was one of Caracalla whose perfect mouth caressed mine across the room and over the centuries. "It's love, and oh must it, Kenward, by definition, be unrequited?" His reply was not one of wonder at my fastening on impossibilities of time (after all, if I work hard enough, either I can arrange a return to Caracalla, or he can come up and visit me, what's time!), but of pleasure that I said Love. "No one anymore says Love. They say 'I've got a hang-up on so-and-so,' or 'I've got a thing for her,' but never Love. Your romanticism's touching." Yet the Realities of Love (a contradiction in terms) are far beyond (or behind or ahead of) me. Could I know it if I saw it? except in the flawless lips of dead emperors?

While it is contrary to the "style" of newly deceased composers to be granted sudden fame (as opposed to painters whose market value, by definition, rises when they die), Poulenc nevertheless received an instantly belated quickening of appreciation. Indeed, ask the average square, or opera queen, or rock lover, whom—outside his own specialty—he most digs from the present century, and the only name he's likely to come up with (besides Gershwin) is that of Francis Poulenc.

Why? For the same reason that everyone from every class likes

the Beatles. Such music makes us feel good, makes us cry, and we're
no longer ashamed of these responses.

Like the Beatles, or like the novels of, say, James Purdy, which
give the lie to the until recently chic suggestion that criticism has
supplanted fiction, the resuscitation of Poulenc deintellectualizes
the art of music in favor of kinetic response. Thank God he's good!

Halloween

Denise Bourdet is dead. Lingering cancer, a somewhat un-French
disease. Once again, shock not only at the surprise but at the
stupidity of death. Roro says that even at the end, in her hospital
bed, Denise's stance was not one of sadness but of annoyance, of
inconvenience: death was disrupting her life. (And he tells with
distaste of Marie Laure phoning Denise a month or two ago to ask:
Est-ce vrai que vous mourrez? What can one make of such cruelty
except to hope it's unconscious. Marie Laure is a child who will not
tolerate illness and death, especially in women.)

For thirty years she survived her husband Edouard Bourdet
(lover to Marie-Blanche) whose play *The Captive* once gleamed in
our family bookshelves like forbidden fruit.

Clear as yesterday I see Denise thirteen years ago on the beach
at Hyères, her pearly skin and high cheekbones, her tawny but too
thin legs, eternal cigarette, eternal gold bracelets jangling each time
she scolded me for not being *croyant*. Hear her repeating: "I feel so
absolutely marvelous in every fiber of my body, I wonder where it's
finally going to start (*Je me demande par ou ça va commencer*)."
Another day, turning to Jacques Février, her exact contemporary,
she said, "Don't you find that life is, after all, quite long? Not too
long, but all the same, quite long?"

Tonight, world premiere of Bill Flanagan's *Another August*.

2 November

Denise taught me how to use a knife & fork as Europeans do. She
showed me how to "act" at high mass in Hyères. She took me to
buffets at Rubinstein's. Although (she said) her body didn't *comprehend* desire, she did not, for that, like American coquettes, put a

high price upon it. "If sex means so much to these men of value, why deny them what costs me so little." She loved too wisely but not well. As for liking, she wore like a coat that so-French virtue—cold on the surface—of staking all on friendship, friendship through conversation, conversation through culture. The quality is upper bourgeois, is dying in Paris, never existed in New York.

21 November

Cocktails for Luise Rainer at Arnold Weissberger's. I'd spent the afternoon with Hugues Cuénod and was to spend the evening drinking with Michael Sakara. Feeling unwell.

23 November

Withdrawal symptoms—withdrawal from society. Thanksgiving Day, it rains now, and I'm shut away, forever it would seem, imprisoned within this century. Outdoors a park, soggy and leafless. Sadness hangs over the waking life like fog on that swamp, influential yet detached from the world's mistakes. Sadness pervades the dreaming life as well, a trillion-tonned heaven descending to settle ineffably here from where we don't evade, expectations overwhelmed on a hopeless map.

Everyone's depressed and thinking little on art. Small wonder: we paddle through the digestive track of this ill earth whose poison washes us always. Waste, shame, guilt, waste. All not directly contributing to work is guilt, shame, waste, guilt. Yet most of our life goes to food and high drink, society, toilets, movies, family responsibility. Can these not be classified as contributions? No. Work is work. It isn't through experience but from imagination that art is made.

I still place hope in nearly any passerby, wondering could you love me, do you (you do) without knowing it? I still put faith in almost every new encounter, wondering. Yet they all collapse (while I sicken with envy at lovers behind blinds) because we won't learn to adore each other's differences.

It's not that we want to be understood: we want not to be

misunderstood. Nor that I have a "block," nor that I'm without ideas; I've never felt more fertile. It's that I've grown scared of the obligatory solitude of notation.

27 November

At 11:30 A.M. read portions of *The New York Diary* for Don Leventhal on WNYC. At 3 Maggie Paley escorts me to a sordid television studio on Times Square where I submit, with the cordiality of a cobra, to a puerile interview by Helen Gurley Brown who can't stay off the subject of homosexuality, as though she imagined I imagined myself in that category.

Days getting ever shorter, Maggie and I return through the black afternoon and drink sherry until dawn with Leo Bersani and Jacques Dupont.

3 December

Rehearse with Adele Addison at 5. At 7:30, memorabilia exhibit of Frank O'Hara at Museum of Modern Art. Eugene Istomin at the Mayflower at 8. With Manos Hadzidakis and Shirley we go out to dine, drink bourbon and wine, return *chez moi* to hear tapes and drink more. (At 5 A.M., *crise d'hystérie*, telephone to Glenesk.) Rereading Morley's *Parnassus on Wheels*.

4 December

Severe hangover. Prepare a meal nonetheless for Roro and French-speaking guests. *Cafard.*

5 December

Electrocardiogram, flu shots, shots for Mexico, Antabuse. Adele at 2:30, during which reaction to shots. Phone Arnold Weissberger and cancel *Walkürie* tonight.

6 December

Give party for Mother's seventieth birthday: Tom Prentiss, David Diamond, Maggie Paley, Hélène Rémy, Adele, Francis Thorne, JA and later Morris and Bill Flanagan.

8 December

Visit to Aaron Copland in Peekskill. *Dîner à deux* on perch fillets.

11 December

Sermon by me yesterday, and concert of songs (including *Mourning Scene* for voice and string quartet) with Adele Addison at 6 P.M. at William Glenesk's Spencer Memorial Church, Brooklyn Heights.

Get tourist card at Consul of Mexico. (Board of Health stamp.) Appointment with Dr. S, psychoanalyst, at 3:45. (The waiting room screeched with Muzak.) Taken by Maggie Paley to Drue Heinz' impressive reception for *Paris Review*, then to concert featuring Maggie's cousin, Alan Leichtling, at Juilliard.

13 December

With Mother, yesterday morn, to rehearsal at Met of Barrault's *Carmen*. (We leave at intermission.) Dine at Shirley's. Messiaen-Loriod recital at Hunter College. (At intermission we bump into Morton Feldman who's lost a drastic amount of weight. I mention this to him. "Yes," he answers, "ten more pounds, then I'll publish *The Brooklyn Diary of Morty Feldman*.") Reception at the Morot-Sirs'. Baths.

Review new Beatles record for *Village Voice*. Evening, to see *Mame* with Jerry Lawrence. (He laughs appreciatively at his own script.)

16 December

At midnight, visit to Elliott Stein in his Fifth Avenue Hotel pad. At 1 A.M. Susan Sontag shows up to watch *Dracula's Daughter* on TV.

(Dracula's daughter, when offered a glass of wine, refuses, saying: "I don't drink—wine.") At two I take leave, with the words: Imagine having to live with a curse like that! Susan, looking swell in boots and long hair, replies: *Et nous alors?*

18 December

At 4:30, Henri Sauguet's concert with Virgil. Shop. Bank. *Dîner chez moi* for Henri and Virgil; Arnold Weissberger and Milton Goldman, Leo Bersani and Morris Golde. At midnight, after they'd left, phone rings. *Comme si par hasard* it is, for the first time since the beach at Hyères in 1954, Jean-Lou Roussel, who stops by and sniffs poppers.

19 December

At 1:30 Josué, take vaccination card. Braziller at 3. Sick again from the shot. At five, visit from JH, a young Carolina musician. Party at Jane Marsh's. Fatigue.

22 December

The Loft Workshop on Bleecker Street with my niece Charity Marshall. At 5 Bill Archibald and Maurice Sendak come for a drink. We talk about the future of Children's Theater, ill defined and not too urgent. (Today I threw away a large supply of LSD and Methadrine.)

26 December

Vittorio Rieti and Henri Sauguet come to a leisurely lunch of fillet mignons. Joe Brainard at 5:30. Cocktails at Tcherepnins' at 7. Dine 8:30 on leftovers with JH.

My chief assessment of an individual is through his vulnerability. Finally I am drawn to him because of his susceptibility to hurt, his lack of self-confidence. Genius aside, this seems always present in good artists, in attractive people. Which is precisely what made Monroe superior to Jayne Mansfield, made Johnson less appealing than Adlai Stevenson. It renders Lou Harrison more *attachant* than . . .

The playful fallibility of Bernstein! Though certainly as "famous" (if such things are judged) as, say, Albee, he appears to have more fun at it—the *power* of glory not being a concern.

27 December

Huge cocktail at Eugene's. Later, Russian Tea Room with JH, *cuite*, a surrealist frenzy and tears at the Stonewall toward dawn.

Snow. Fire in the grate.

Musical differentiations now should be Commercial and Noncommercial. Bernstein is both separately, Weill both at once, while Cage *seems* both, though in fact is neither. Noncommercial and commercial have always been distinctions one could draw from reference to individuals: Bach's cantatas versus his piano fugues, Mozart's operas and quartets. We're told that Copland has two styles, hence two publics, one for the diatonic open spaces of *Rodeo*, another for the chromatic "urbanity" of *Connotations*. Vernon Duke—Vladimir Dukelsky—even uses two names for his two presumable audiences. But such audiences now are one. Nor have such distinctions ever been felt by Insiders.

31 December

New Year's Eve. Heavy snow. Take JH to Virgil's. Later, heavy meal at Bill Flanagan's, with JH and David Diamond. We listen twice to *Another August*.

My two articles on the Beatles, in *The Village Voice* and in *The New York Review of Books*, have caused as much reaction as any of my more narcissistic prose, no doubt because I've relieved the intellectual of his guilt about not "knowing" anything about music. But I start to get jealous of my Frankenstein monsters.

Their autonomy seems no longer required for their success, or even for their personality. The much publicized branching out is indicative, because clearly good, though as yet uncertain.

Paul McCartney's score to *The Family Way* might have been on a par with Satie's *Entr'acte* or Copland's *Of Mice and Men*; for it was not a flow of Wagnerian molasses shadowing the action, but a series of functional "set numbers" (three, I think, if a single hearing could judge) as neat as those in a Purcell opera. Might have been—but was not. It seemed clear that although the young composer provided an uncut jewel of highest quality, it remained for some "professional" to polish, shatter and set that jewel. The music was disseminated throughout the film with a gratuitously psychological "rightness," sometimes omitted where most needed (when the hero upstairs ponders, while downstairs a contrasting bewilderment occurs—a duet situation Copland dealt with so touchingly in *The Heiress*), sometimes decorative where least needed, as in the tasteless finale. Had the dirty work (i.e., arrangement, orchestration and dramatic juxtaposition of the raw material) been left to McCartney, it is tempting to speculate on his ingenuity; for if music can't actually ruin a movie (though in *Doctor Zhivago*, say, or *Baby Jane*, it tries hard), it *can* enhance or radically alter a movie's complexion, or even a movie's intent (as in *Blood of a Poet*). However clever McCartney's inventions may have turned out—given his technical compositional know-how—the ultimate result would still have proved nothing beyond his instinct for fine points of theater.

How much, anyway, should a composer *know*? Some of our greatest show tunes were composed by the likes of Irving Berlin or Noël Coward, proud of their ignorance of even musical shorthand. Such presumption, if such it may be called, now pervades the longhair world forcing definitions to change at breakneck speed. As to the age-old query about who enjoys music more, the professional or the amateur, that must remain as insoluble as: Who has more fun in lovemaking, man or woman?—at least until an auditory Tiresias shows up. For myself, I no longer hear new music except visually: if it pleases me I inscribe it on a staff in the brain, photograph that notation, take it home and develop the film which can be preserved indefinitely. This manner of musical recall is not, I think, unusual to many composers.

The fact is, I'm wearying of the Beatles, resenting the pompous elation their efforts effect in the hearts of my friends. Already wearying, true to my times, as with anything that gets too In. And need to return toward that hermitage, again to meditate upon, and then compose, something of my own.

Tomorrow: Mexico City with Morris Golde.

1968

Cecily: I keep a diary in order to enter the wonderful secrets of my life. If I didn't write them down I should probably forget all about them.

The Importance of Being Earnest

These phrases are composed on the edge of the pool at our *dolce vita* hotel. Over there are elderly American gents with money, with strident wives made from teased hair, with grayish scrota dangling apparent from too-loose Bermuda shorts. And see that local loving couple whose golden bride squeezes playfully her near-Negroid groom's shoulder blades knotted with pimples that spout like chocolate éclairs into the pool? The pool is already thick with crusts of Bain de Soleil, a soggy cake frosted with the narcissistic deposits of my countrymen whose country today indicts friends and colleagues, Dr. Spock, LeRoi Jones, in temperatures near zero while chasing intellectuals running riot, frightened, as in the German thirties. We sit here, observing a haughty pair of flamingos, swallowing weather so warm and rich it grows indigestible. Up there America floats remote yet perilous like a cloud. There's such a thing as too much beauty.

Too much beauty. And with each advantage somehow tacky, paid for by cash. Those years with Marie Laure far passed this in comfort, elegance, tact—with never mention of money. Wealth offers the leisure to work. Never before, as an adult, have I taken vacations, gone away for reasons of indolence or health.

One week ago we approached from the sky at night the City of Mexico which resembled a luminous bruise on a deserted prairie. Irony. Two weeks before our landing I found JH. Such knowledge arrived too soon for canceling this pleasure trip, yet too late for not finding the trip a waste, like a honeymoon taken alone.

Twenty-seven years ago I, crisp adolescent, came by train to Mexico (and never since) with Father for a summer holiday far from what they (parents) sensed as the first corrosions of my libido. How could they know, during the decadent war, that no one in Taxco thought Father was father (which I explained to him years later, and he was not amused)? It's said that from this impression Paul Bowles drew his *Pages from Cold Point.* Because the Bowleses were here then too, and Paul was the First Live Composer I'd ever met.

Eighteen years ago I'd settled in Fez where, with no thought of commissions, for twenty months I poured forth my first everything: first symphony, quartet, opera, name it, and how many dozens of songs which to this day stay my best.

One year ago I stopped writing music. I can no longer compose what won't be paid for, and since the publication of *Paris Diary* I've received no commissions, either because my "unbalanced" thoughts mean I'm a bad (or irresponsible) composer, or because everyone thinks I'm rich. Yet I don't miss that innocent effusion of Fez-energy which pleasurably brought forth *n'importe quoi.* My last piece, *Sun,* written with disgust, is my masterpiece. And I still do think in terms of masterpieces, yet feel guilty about not feeling guilty about not really wanting to write another one. Still, if I don't, who will? These elderly gents with hanging balls? their wives? that loving couple? The flamingos? In this synthetic summer I for once have time to think—the time we all kvetch about never having—and how do I use it? Being nervous. To live in the instant? I wish I were in New York where I'd wish I were in Acapulco.

16 January

The bullfight was anticipated with revulsion. Yet as it was taking place the effect was like a disease coursing through the body but with no effect. My one other corrida was in 1953 at Arles, the memory of which remained so pungently shocking that it acted as immunity. Now the fight Sunday was exactly as I'd dreaded, but occurred painlessly as in a dream. Nevertheless, we do not develop immunity to ourselves being tortured; on the contrary, one of the horrors of torture is the suggestion of its reoccurrence. So we have little consolation, except in injections against typhoid fever.

New York
30 January

JH suggests that I may (as is the case with amateur "stylists") be overemphasizing the mannerism of parentheses in my essays on music. Such a mannerism (adds he) is okay in the diary, since a diary is nothing if not parenthetical.

. Parenthetically, in our America the personal journal is not, as in the France of Amiel or Martin du Gard, a standard literary expression. Especially a composer's journal. But I am shy: I confess on the page instead of in talk. And admit I'm as curious as the next one about where it all comes from. Music represents my order. The diary my disorder—but orderly disorder. Though perhaps all music, too, is orderly disorder.

That which yesterday we formed with such desperate care became a fable today. Lives are not facts.

I don't know where my music comes from or what it means. It interests me to hear others analyze their reactions to my work, though I can't identify with their identification.

The shock in growing up—that everyone wasn't like me. I'd assumed the world was made of Hawthorne readers, Ravel listeners, Duchamp lookers or of little boys who cut gym class to write music.

20 March

On one side I grew up a spoiled child, but with sentiments of insufficiency—what teachers termed "a sloppy thinker." Effete yet fiercely timid, fattish (was I ugly?), unpopular with Sportsmen, coddled by the Intelligent whom I took for granted and hence didn't esteem; uncultured, nonetheless, so raped for prettiness (was I pretty?) by those more ripe, more knowledgeable. Submerged, that is, in an insecurity which may be a prerequisite of "artistic" personalities—though certainly the inverse does not hold: so many of the insecure are drab, uncreative; and perhaps I was (may even still remain) one of them. Despite an ingrained Quaker nonviolence, has my will to be a Successful Artist coincided with a need for vengeance on those who treated me anonymously? Could such vengeance make of me, indeed, an artist?

Oh, the conceit of the masochist, the sadist's vanity! An artist never forgets, and in remembering goes beyond limits. His treatment of history is no less misconstrued than a historian's.

Generations, whatever their length, evolve in pairs, as obstreperous mother and pristine child. They breathe in binary form. Inhaled impression becomes exhaled expression. Victorians emerge into flappers, action into reaction. Sacred turns profane back to sacred, then profane once more and forever. New twists are added, unraveled, reinstated, again torn apart.

For instance, in movie females: the good lightness of Mae Marsh which once vanquished the bad blackness of Theda Bara was itself vanquished in the '40s, which introduced wicked blondes like the Lana Turner of *The Postman Always Rings Twice* or the Barbara Stanwyck (bewigged for the occasion) of *Double Indemnity* into contrast with the now-saccharine brunette of the Ann Rutherfords or Phyllis Thaxters. Dark Gail Patrick was no longer the "other woman." Then Marilyn brought back the Blonde as Victim, despite two wicked roles (*Niagara* and *Don't Bother to Knock*). As a sex, wicked or not, women are Out when men are In in the movies—as during war, which overlaps with peace, which overlaps . . . Such men in their turn are pretty Valentinos superseded by virile Gables, superseded by pretty Powers, by virile Brandos, by pretty Dean, virile Belmondo, pretty Delon, ebb, flow and ebb. . . .

By the same token, the sending of children to public rather than private schools, like circumcision practice (at least among upper-class American Gentiles), alternates generations.

Similarly with music. Given eras stress length or height: counterpoint as opposed to harmony, vertical versus horizontal. The sophisticated linear represents, if you will, the "sacredness" of Palestrina, Bach, Reger, Schoenberg, Boulez; while the vulgar up-and-downness of the chordal signifies the "profanity" of Monteverdi, Beethoven, Chopin, Poulenc—who each settle neatly upon the others. We have just entered another harmonic period in both so-called Jazz and Classical, a relief for all audiences (of both classical and jazz) from the contrapuntal stress of the '50s and '40s, which were releasing themselves from the harmonic prominence of the '30s and '20s, that were revolting against the teens, that were . . .

As for *performing* musical personalities, they are just that—personalities—according to the sexual emphases of a particular epoch. Sexiness, and its projection, is individual. (Groups aren't sexy.) Collective singing, from Gregorian chant to rock 'n' roll, tends to generalities, political or religious, both in spirit and text. By definition, during the decade after the war, the nonvocal contrapuntalists (in all musical expressions) were nonsexual, that being a "social" age; while individuals (personalities) like Peggy Lee, Ruth Etting, Sinatra, were sexy *because* individual. Even Caruso or Tebaldi presented sexiness, take it or leave it.

If today is sexual, it's not sexy, being polymorphous; our trend is massive: the gang bang. The Beatles aren't sexy, and neither are the Doors despite promotional attempts to individualize one of them. Rock gangs just aren't preoccupied with sexiness any more than Nikolais' dance group canceling itself into a delicious blur. Even the powerful Paris personality of Jacques Brel, who composes both lyrics and music of the songs he performs alone, is in New York today promoted by an undifferentiatedly unprepossessing quartet.

22 March

Tonight we saw Bette Davis in *The Anniversary*. Have I more reason than she to be embarrassed?

28 March

Premiere last night of Douglas Moore's *Carry Nation* with the extraordinary Beverly Wolff. She is not exactly a silk purse, nor is Douglas' opera a sow's ear, but Wolff made something big out of something medium-sized, and I'm thrilled at the prospect that we'll be collaborating next December.

I'm 100 percent sympathetic with the language Douglas speaks through song, though he sometimes uses an awfully corny accent.

Il faut être absolument moderne, said Rimbaud, and Pound said: Make it new. The tradition of the new! Yet for three millennia before the "modern" era both male and female apparel remained the same: tunic and toga, comfort and grace.

28 May

The National Institute of Arts and Letters this afternoon, after many years of waiting, honored me and three other "conservative" composers, Bill Flanagan, David Del Tredici and Francis Thorne. For this we should perhaps thank David Diamond who went out on a limb for us all. If when winning my first award in 1948 I deserved the prize but the work did not, today the reverse may apply.

What I shall remember, however, is not the glamour of the ceremonies proper, but the appearance during the earlier informal festivities of Truman Capote, with dark blue shirt and coral tie, as he approached me with an uncharitable glint in his eye. Beginning softly, he crescendoed to a point where a crowd gathered, and finished off with frenzy: "I've liked what I've read of yours lately, Ned, etc. etc., I didn't see it, but friends told me you'd written something in *Saturday Review* against my book. Now I worked hard. You didn't go through what I went through, I produced a work of art, and you have no right to attack it. . . ." This! twenty-eight months after the fact.

Anyone has the right to attack a work of art, especially when the work is self-advertised as documentation. An author who claims his facts are unassailable because they're art wants it both ways: Don't hit me, I'm a lady.

8 June

Boom is no improvement on our play of four years ago. Later, *The Best Years of Our Lives* on TV, with the coolly experienced Myrna Loy.

Yesterday, visit to Igor Kipnis to discuss writing a piece for him.

Today, talked with John Gutman, at the Klingenstein Pavilion, about his commissioning a little opera for Met Studio students.

9 June

Martha Graham, matinee of *Dancing Ground*, which continues to please me as much as though I'd not written the score. During the intermission spoke with Mae O'Donnell, more beautiful than ever.

Avant Garde writes to ask: "Who is the most despicable American of all?" I immediately reply: "Miss Helen Hayes." Because, through her sophomoric portrayals representing class to the masses who accept her imposture as First Lady of Our Theater, she debases the already low standards of American culture.

15 June

Invited Mart Crowley to dine last week (with Shirley and JH). He is witty, intelligent, abstemious and on top of the world with the huge success of *The Boys in the Band*.

Weekend with JH at Tom Prentiss'. (My *Water Music* is being recorded today in Oakland.) Retiring to the lament of whippoorwills, awakening to the madrigal of cardinals here on Fire Island.

21 June

Last night, while dining at the Waverly Inn with David Diamond and Francis Thorne, JH was seized by the same pain he suffered a week or so ago. During the next twelve hours I saw him lose weight, change color and age by several years. At three this afternoon, in New York Hospital, he was operated on for burst appendix.

12 July

Frequent visits, during this long heat wave, to and from Kenneth Koch who has already completed two librettos, weird and tempting and hopeless.

Next month with JH I move to West 70th Street.

Finished a short harpsichord piece, *Spiders*, for Igor Kipnis.

All Saints' Day

To call a piece boring is unprofessional, for it expresses reaction rather than opinion, and does not begin to suggest appraisal. Yet last night, the sole element of Larry Austin's piece that I could draw forth and retain was boredom. I suspect the boredom was organic to the work (although unwilled by Austin) and not some chemical response meanly manufactured by me. Now willed boredom, like Warhol's or Cage's or Stein's, or like the hypnotic repetitions of African musics which entrance and alter us, is okay. It's not for me, but it works. I'm not persuaded that Larry Austin knew what he was doing. Nor did his ignorance result in the (supposedly primitive) charm of an Ives or a Satie, rather than in the mortal wish of one listener to expire in self-defense. So I can only describe his piece as boring. (Let him be warned that continued exposure of his own children to those ultraviolet lights flashing over Hunter College's stage will incur incurable maladies.)

To celebrate the instigator of this crime, Virgil gave a supper later at the Chelsea for Lukas Foss, who surrounded himself with an essentially nonmusical flesh governed mainly by Larry and Clarisse Rivers.

One definition of To Love is: *to want to live with*. This applies no less to works of art than to persons or pets. Yet probably no one work of art could suffice indefinitely without a contrast, an opposite number, an antidote. We never betray our mates with others who resemble them.

What one work is most beloved to me? The Monteverdi madrigals perhaps? Mozart's G-minor Quintet? Messiaen's *Quatuor pour la fin du Temps*? The *Saint Matthew*? . . . There's no such thing as one work, there is only an *oeuvre*. Would it be one song, say, by Debussy, or a disk of twenty Debussy songs as sung by one Maggie Teyte? Would it be Bach's ten-minute Italian Concerto or his five-hour Latin Mass?

Nor is there such a thing as first choice. During that initial visit to Alice Toklas I saw on her walls a pair of Picassos unknown to me. When I remarked on their unusual beauty, Miss Toklas replied, "Yes, Gertrude always used to say: if the house were on fire and I could only take one picture, it would be those two." . . . As usual, Gertrude's *mot* contained as much wisdom as whimsy. Like the

Greenwich Village restaurant which advertises itself as The World's Second Best, she knew there is no first best.

The ideal work exists only in theory, that is, in the imagination. When imagination is made reality it is always unsatisfactory, at least to the creator, if only because *it could have been different.*

13 December

Can a composer imagine a more satisfying experience than mine last night in Town Hall? A capacity crowd listened carefully as I accompanied three friends in a whole program of my songs. Donald Gramm in white tie sang a group of Theodore Roethke and Paul Goodman poems, Beverly Wolff in green satin sang *Poems of Love and the Rain* and Phyllis Curtin in black velvet sang a miscellany. Then together we performed the premiere of *Some Trees* (John Ashbery) for three voices and piano, and everyone clapped long and loud, after which we all went to Virgil's at the Chelsea for cold salmon, cheese, white wine and chocolate cakes (paid for by Boosey & Hawkes). This morning *The Times* is approving, while Beverly on the phone apologizes for not having come to the party because she had performed with a temperature of 103 °.

17 December

Review of the recital by *Newsweek*, which, though not unfair or exactly incorrect about the music, sensationalizes the notice with "hints" about my life. But I asked for it. On the same page, a wistful column on the death of Talullah Bankhead.

Late December

Morning sickness. I am going to write a piece.

Again this noon, while waiting in the check-out line, I became ill. At night I vow nevermore to set foot in Food City; every morning inertia and economy send me back among those mirthless housewives. Yet their faces contain the reassurance of the quotidian.

Today, to avoid waiting, I limited my purchase to six "items" so as to stand legitimately in the Express Line (more than six and you get looked at askance, even yelled at), yet still we lagged, the cashier being out of paper bags, then out of nickels, then a lady cashed a check which required the monitor's confirmation, then another lady spilled her items—plastic cups of mandarin yogurt squashing dirtily over the floor—and had to run back for replacements while we sighed. (How can people, including me, parade these private wares so openly: toilet tissues, mouthwash, peanut butter.) Still my heart went out to the little cashier, a new Puerto Rican girl, quite lovely, indeed beautiful and appealingly unprotected.

Ahead of me stood a woman who resembled an Eskimo fondling with paper-thin tentacles a quart-sized can of baked beans, the meal of those who live alone. To divert my too ardent attention from these nauseating and attractive distractions, and above all to kill time, I took from the counter rack a copy of *Family Day*. The soft colored pages opened themselves to the photograph of a goody which gave me pause. My passion for sweets begins to know no bounds, and here loomed a swooning mound of pink fluff named Iced Grape Soufflé. After perusing the recipe I stopped breathing.

> Dissolve: 1 package Concord Grape Jello in
>   1 cup boiling water
> Add: 1 package frozen red grapes, strained
>   1 cup freshly squeezed grape juice
> Chill for one-half to three-quarters of an hour
> Fold in: 1 cup heavy cream, whipped with
>   cinnamon and white of one egg
>   1 to 2 teaspoons framboise liqueur
>   1 cup blood

I "came to" on Columbus Avenue one block north of the store, halfway home and no one stared. I was walking along, slightly annoyed though far from depressed, having awakened from a short dreamless nap, or so it seemed. By the sun's rays it could have been well after three, maybe a quarter to four. Where and in what condition I had lingered between fainting and moving here now, I do not know and may never learn.

December afternoons surpass the subtlest texture of afternoons from other months, gather themselves into a formula which happily blends hot with cold to soothe our collective dread of forever losing the already vanished summer. Add to this the resilient smell of chestnuts and children, and you achieve perfection.

It's 5 A.M. Insomnia. The strangest minutes of my life have just gone by. How describe in words that which words can only misshape? Soon the lights in the brownstone across the street will twinkle through the dawn, the old man there will begin measuring coffee, as he does each morning, reassuringly.

Is it possible to predetermine my unborn child's bone structure by sitting at this Walgreen's counter, hands hard against the railing, contracting and releasing the abdomen muscles? to adjust his brain cells, arrange his force, his worth, his "creativity"? Would I work hard, apply myself, if I knew how? be willing not to cheat, if only I were aware of when I cheat? Could I, in short, become a genius? Such sacrifices are not granted to any passerby. Is it my would-be genius that must produce a child, or my femalism that needs to engender genius?

Neither, finally. I detest pregnancy for its challenge to thought and feeling. It's too unbalancing to be thrilling anymore. My life seeks to become a firm straight line, alongside but aloof from the whirlpool. If I think so hard and long upon myself, the child may be born without a thought of its own.

Nativity week has come, and so has the first thaw. Carols emerge from ubiquitous Muzak into the unseasonable warmth, while from West End to Central Park, along 72d in the afternoon grayness, comes the huckstering of hawthorn streaming with angel hair and icicles. Damp Santas exude, with the drunk Cubans, very little of what we call Christmas spirit.

The church on 71st must always have lurked among those nondescript apartment houses, but I'd never noticed it until today. Some perversity pushed me to enter it, and instantly the city vanished. The Catholic interior was as vast, as "convincing," as *beautiful* as any Roman cathedral. Not a soul, a dim incense and rhythm of my own breath as I tiptoed a thousand yards toward that swarm of candles like bees on a cake. I knelt and prayed, then rose and, turning to see if I were observed, furtively blew out three or four candles. Seated now in a pew, I awaited (in this vault more still than the moon's surface) a scolding.

From far off came a sound of weeping, doubtless an aftertaste of Muzak, for the church was sealed. Yet I was moved, and my own tears welled up.

"Have you ever killed anyone?"

"I don't know," which is the truth. (A recurring dream suggests that I may have, once, when I was too drunk to remember. I cut up a body with methodic application, then conclusively dispose of the pieces. Conclusively—thus far, anyway. Awake I never think about it.)

Again last night, toward dawn, I awoke, quickly and widely, with that common reaction of Where am I? but with a less frequent sensation, too, of: In what city and year of my life am I?

Staring now at the pointless bottle of ink through which the sun shoots lavender refractions invisible to the naked eye, and realizing that when I had been left alone and silence took over this room again, it was the ink bottle, not me, which, utterly still, seemed sad. Presumably overcome with grief we find friendliness in inanimate objects, not in roses or peaches so much as in tables or inkpots which among themselves in sunrays form a family. To love is not to understand. I do not want to be understood, I want to be loved. X understood me, and that was that.

Not that I'm apprehensive—or is it precisely because I *am* apprehensive? I've had offspring before. They ultimately disappear to die or live on their own. When they die, *tant pis*. When they survive to make fools of their puny selves, it is not they but I who am derided as mother to such dreck. On occasion I've been proud of certain strapping lasses who not only win pole-vaulting tournaments but have brains to boot, and who even now begin to reproduce themselves for better or worse. And in dreams (only in dreams) I've birthed a fully formed infant who grows to be the envy of the world. Mostly, however, I grunt and summon forth a shriveled excremental offering to some low-class god who doesn't even acknowledge the effort, assuming he's aware of it.

1969

Beauty is but a flower
Which wrinkles will devour;
Brightness falls from the air;
Queens have died young and fair;
Dust hath closed Helen's eye;
I am sick, I must die—
    Lord, have mercy on us!

    —Thomas Nashe, *"In Time of Pestilence"*

Prayer unsaid and mass unsung,
Dead-man's dirge must still be rung . . .

While correcting the proofs of *Six Irish Poems* last night I was invaded by a nostalgia that transformed a New York study into the little Turinese hotel where, nineteen winters ago, these songs were conceived. I was on a first trip to Italy visiting Nell Tangeman. In America most of my piano-vocal works had been written for her marvelous mezzo; indeed, my whole compositional outlook became for a time directed by her special sound. In Europe Nell was now fulfilling symphonic engagements. What could be more natural than to undertake my first voice & orchestra work?

She herself proposed the poetry (by George Darley) whose bleak evocation took us far from the sunny climate of our reunion, close to our mutual Nordic ancestry. Over the following months—in Florence, Morocco, finally in Paris—I completed the suite, orchestrating it in early spring. The first hearing was given the next year by l'Orchestre de la Radiodiffusion Française under the direction of Tony Aubin, on July 4, 1951.

The sense of the past comes now mostly from a memory of Nell's performances, and of Nell herself, dead four years. Thus I hear this cycle's final "Sea Ritual" as a premature epitaph, a prayer both said and sung by one whose intelligent but brief career first acquainted me with the human voice as a practical instrument which still sings in all I write today.

25 March

Visit from Jerome Lowenthal. He wants to commission a piano concerto.

And a letter from Gérard Souzay who wants me to compose a

cycle for his autumn tour. Short notice. Twenty years ago when his voice flowed smooth as warm caramel and my inspiration reeked like musk, I could have whipped up something in half a week, probably on the verses of Musset. Now we're other people. Now his art concerns me only as a steely wail through which some tough sad words could make a sharp point. What words? For never again will I write in French.

29 March

Virgil Thomson last night gave a *dîner à huit couverts*, four men and four women, all French-speaking, for Pierre Boulez, whose sister, a Madame Chapelier, has appeared in America for the first time. I sat between her and Louise Varèse. Virgil and Pierre presided at the table ends, and across from us beamed Natalie Nabokov and Maurice Grosser.

One may try to gossip with, or even about, Pierre Boulez, but it isn't easy even for prevaricators: he's all business with a smile. The few times we've socialized have been strained. For me music can't be talked, only played; my conversation centers on particulars, usually human. Boulez being all generality, even around laymen like last night with whom he talks grape cultivation or family trees, I resolved not to speak unless spoken to, nor to pose any question if I didn't care about the answer. Result: three exchanges in four hours. 1) *Comment allez-vous?*, 2) *Veuillez passer le beurre, cher ami?*, 3) *Eh bien, bonsoir, monsieur.*

But Virgil went all out with bisques, off-season fruits, and Châteaux d'Yquem served in crystal goblets whose stems represent naked females raising their arms. I found myself talking psychedelics, as I have before, with Madame Varèse (who pretends to know nothing of music, but did translate Michaux's book on mescaline), and geography with the sister whose affability flowed counter to her brother's—her cordiality invites contact, his discourages contact. Virgil was determined to know what the child Pierre was like. That would have interested me too. But we never found out.

After the meal, when we adjourned to the parlor with the arrival of all the Sylvia Marlowes, I kept a physical distance. Virgil this morning on the phone: "You and Pierre reminded us of

Gertrude and James Joyce, revolving like planets at opposite ends of the salon." (Which one is Joyce?)

We acclimate quickly to big innovations like electricity or trips to the moon. What was unheard of yesterday becomes obvious today and indispensable tomorrow. So it is with this endless war. No doubt we grow rapidly accustomed to our own death after we die.

Received the giant volume of Aldous Huxley letters (among which one to me, from several in the early fifties about The Libretto Problem). What disappointing resonance! It lacks the creator's clear hot ring. The cool body of correspondence sounds only like that of the compleat intellectual which American adolescents remember him to be. The dilettante speaks louder than the poet. Perhaps it's unfair, but two or three of these thousand letters sour me even to Huxley's intelligence. (An eyedropper of LSD will contaminate a city reservoir.) In his first message to Stravinsky, for example, the denigration of Wagner reads like a quick conclusion to curry favor. And to suggest that Cocteau is "not serious" is merely to advance a fashionable putdown, and seems petty in the light of reasoned statements by a Pound or a Goodman on the French poet's uniqueness. Still, one does gasp at Huxley's scope; his vision of the future and compassion for the present—both now so tinged with the past—do spring from a tough inspiration.

Dine with parents. *Winning*, at Radio City. Twenty years ago today I landed in France on the SS *Washington*.

With JH and his young brother to Dance Archives in Library of Performing Arts. See filmed version of Glen Tetley's *Lovers* based on my score. Drinks at five with Norman Singer. Don Ritchie there too, fresh from Japan, where he says Mishima is among my admirers. I'd like to believe it.

4 June

Pick up passport. Dwelling on the past, inclined always to melodramatize. Claude and P provoked no less trauma than did a canary once. There was, when I was twelve and avicultural, a bird show at Chicago's Blackstone Hotel where I fell in love with (premature but quaint irony) a cinnamon-throated warbler which Father thought would be one-too-many and forbade the purchase. I walked the night lanes of Jackson Park (Father secretly surveying from the family car), brooded, threatened suicide.

28 June

Intense heat wave. Rose and Fred Plaut here to dine. Saga of their escape from Laval's France.

Simenon is to be apotheosized because like all great men he hits the nail on the head with style. That's not enough, of course: Gore Vidal can do it too, and Philip Roth, and they're not quite great. But Simenon's evocations almost kill us—for whom his shock of recognition lies always in murder.

30 July

The new Piano Concerto's half done. Growing pains of the unborn.

Soon I shall have to start imparting to my infant all I know. But as I no longer know, she must grow up not knowing too.

1 August

Auto-abortion is the most courageous of acts, at least of physical acts. Morally it's my most cowardly act, having been unwilling to nurture and guide the fetus to a healthy, if not necessarily inspired, birth. Yet could he have been—no, all mothers ask that. Still, I've already proved I could drop talent. . . .

Drippity drip, drippity drop, blood trickles down, and my own life's easing away too, stop one thing too often, and . . .

2 August

To the surprise of no one acquainted with the vicissitudes of theatrical fortune, my old plays, *The Pastry Shop* and *The Young Among Themselves* (though often auditioned as private entertainments), have yet to be publicly performed. So I am bemused to discover that some rifled copies are listed in the catalogue of a Cornelia Street bookshop as museum pieces for sale by auction.

Labor Day

Bill Flanagan is dead. I write it, not believing it, but with the same impotence that every death brings. What a dumb slump! what lack of inspiration! the always brighter bonfire of those even less dear to me than Bill. Their dying doesn't add value to, it lessens the value of, our own lives. And my God, the practical anxieties.

Early last night, as JH and I were leaving to face the heat of the empty city and walk nine blocks south to dine at Eugene's, the phone rang. A tough compassionate American voice, identifying itself as that of Detective X of the 6th Precinct, asked if I were acquainted with a William Flanagan: "He's not living, you know." (The locution struck me as British.) "No, I didn't know," I answered, sitting down and beginning to shake, although in a sense I *did* know, and everything he told me seemed somehow expected. The police, alerted by neighbors, had broken into a musty disorder of the Sheridan Square flat, and found that Bill had been dead for probably days.

Hours before I could locate anyone!—Edward, Dick Barr, Judge Isaacs—the logical people all gone for the long weekend. Eugene's goulash, so carefully prepared, tasted of gall. Returned home early, phoned all over Long Island until 2 A.M. It was agreed that Edward would notify Bill's parents in Detroit (he was the only child), though as of now (twenty-four hours later) he's not gotten to them.

More calls today, principally from Theodore Strongin who's trying to compose an obit for the *Times*, and from William Anderson of *Stereo Review* who asked if I'd go to the morgue to identify the remains. I cannot.

A reasonable obituary in this morning's *Times*, containing all but the essential. JH phoned David Diamond in Rochester; the body's being sent there and the burial takes place tomorrow.

What dispatch! And after so long a term of resentment and affection, of trying to make it against standards of his conscience, of copping out like Nell Tangeman, or like his lamented Judy Garland. Too soon to reason. Bill was my only nonromantic affiliation whom I saw daily for years, and surely the only composer my own age whom I'd call a friend. Picturing him this evening brings back those bone-white hands, a sense of loss, of revulsion, and as always, the sense of What did I do wrong?

Japan Airlines
Flight # 2,
New York–Paris
29–30 September

Look at yourself all your life in
a mirror and you'll see death at
work like bees in a glass hive.
        —Jean Cocteau

When one of us dies, I'll move to Paris.
        —Paul Goodman

Not that I haven't been warned. Logic alone would indicate that in a country where most of my friends are a generation older, many should now be dilapidated. Some may snub me because of *The Paris Diary*, though surely the French have more urgent concerns than to begrudge me that light book after so long. Others will not answer phone messages simply because they're dead.

Around midnight. Airborne in darkness, this novel choice of transport provides geishas to comply with "passenger needs," while in the next seat by happy coincidence (I being the original hypochondriac) one of my many medical doctors snores a duet with the motor's purr counterpointing my wakefulness. The craft is virtually empty, though by another coincidence we find Sono Osato, whom I've known since childhood in Chicago, with her husband Victor Elmaleh, and chat for an hour over an inedible supper, then retire. The takeoff, as usual, was appalling in its rightness, purposeful as an erection, by contrast with the landing, always mundane as death. Here now are suspended hours for thought-collecting as the Japanese plane becomes a time machine retreating toward a personal French past.

This brief return to Paris is my first in more than five years, the first since reaching my forties, the first since the issue of my four books. For the Parisians, I left as a musician, come back as an author. Five years. But it's been twenty since I went there to live (*earning* the arrival, as anyone does who takes a boat). The ostensible purpose for this twenty-one-day Economy Excursion (ending with a week in England), other than to swallow a healthy draft of the past and then hush for another spell, is to compose an essay whose subject will be a comparison of Then with Now, generally in society and the arts, particularly in the musical scene. Whatever way I am received will be the right way, for as it will nourish my narrative, I can't lose. I declare it self-protectingly, being panic-stricken.

For two weeks I'll have Guy Ferrand's apartment alone in the Rue des Epinettes. Thus my original impulse was to give a mammoth party, mailing invitations before leaving America, seeing who would not come, who would bring new faces, who would no longer be alive. Some Proustian gestures are risky, expensive, vulgar. My present impulse is Dumasian, and the fragility of *Vingt Ans Après*.

Way after midnight, the horizon's aglow. Hurtling toward the future while drunk on the past. Yesterday, in preparation for the "tone," I leafed through old datebooks. In 1951, for instance, I note (among reminders like *Buy oranges* or *See dentist* or *Phone Heddy about what happened last night*) a casual mention: *Lunch chez Marie Laure with Giacometti, Balthus, Dora Maar.* I did not then know who these people were, assuming they "were" anyone. Yet if today that seems history, it is no more nor less memorable in retrospect. Lunch with the future-great is not the same as with the now-famous. With the now-famous one remembers because one is *supposed* to remember how really unexceptional, at lunch, they perhaps are, or "are."

But it is not people I have missed and now seek, nor even my own vanished self, so much as smells and temperatures, bakeries and rivers. These perfumes of the past become, when mixed with personalities grown atrophied, like fetid dinosaur breath. In a sense, the idea I still retain of France is the one I had before I ever knew that country: a France of Rimbaud, Satie, *Les Faux-Monnayeurs*, the young Jean Gabin.

More than the taste, the fragrance of *fine à l'eau* transports me. The taste therefore (the effect) takes me not to France of yesterday but to the irrevocable today. Space is possible in the kitchen. Not time. Why drink? Not, anyway, for time remembered.

If I don't go, maybe It will happen. Maybe It is happening now in Danny's bar, at Casey's, in my own parlor—and I'm not there. But has It, really, ever happened? . . . Yes.

Gravity ages us. After forty our jowls, armpits, breasts and buttocks sag toward the impatient earth. Lean over a glass table and see yourself as you will be in ten years. Now throw back your head, and see how you once were. Like every living thing always, we are all corpses on parole.

The French at least can see themselves aging. Americans can't. Yet collectively we're no longer adolescent, and individually we're less pretty than our reputation. We are prepared for nothing, certainly not for the embarrassment of growth. Children after summer vacation return, along with the oak-leaf bonfires, nervously to mark change wrought on classmates, a very sudden wonder of nail polish on the girls, and on the boys new pubic hair of first maturity. They turn shyly away—but adults *know*. Except, of course, they don't. Every return at every age brings surprise. Now I turn from the embarrassment of death stamped on the features of everyone I've known. *Les neiges d'antan,* since you're wondering, will be all over those autumn streets of France.

Tomorrow has come. Sono, over there, stretches one leg straight out like Miss Turnstiles of yore, as she waits for tea. In an hour we'll be landing in the Paris I've thought so hard upon for so many invisible years that I'm sick with joy at what I can't possibly find. In the baggage room my suitcase whispers with two little gold-plated Tiffany snuffboxes, gifts which might be refused by Marie Laure and Nora Auric. (The Aurics have preserved a stony silence since my diaries were published and Marie Laure's not written since 1967.) Will nobody care that I've come? What of the anonymous letter stating: "All but myself attend you with sharpened knives"? Could it have been appropriate that I chose the fall season, *la rentrée*, at once a rebirth and murder, for my humiliation?

The geishas fuss like gnats. I must comb my new sideburns, pee, finish the *croissants*, swoon (now is the moment) and wonder if the French taxi strikes are done. There's the city.

Final query: What does it mean when, on a last-minute impulse, you change your flight; then, indeed, the plane you were going to take, crashes—but so does the plane you *do* take?

> 38, *Rue des Epinettes*
> *Paris XVII*
> *1 October (forenoon)*

The trip from Orly airport to here covers the whole city. Unslept, unbathed and thrilled in an overcoat beneath the hot and unpolluted yellow sky, I was able immediately to see it as a telegram. Malraux's high-pressure hosing of not only monuments but private buildings was just a trickle when I left in 1964. Now Paris is a blond. If that's a cliché to the Jet Set, I quote Paul Taylor who, when chided for choreographing Beethoven because it wasn't new, replied, "It's new to me."

Guy's semiluxury high rise is located near the Boulevard Bessières, an *extérieur* neighborhood unfamiliar to most Parisians, and where I am regarded deferentially as a Martian purchasing pears, cheese, instant coffee. The apartment, swept neat as a pin by Madame Rose, transported me in time and space, welcomed me to those anachronistic bibelots I lived amongst twenty summers ago in Morocco, and to a pile of mail containing notably a letter from

Claude. *Ned, je n'ai ni l'envie, ni la curiosité de te revoir. Et je souhaite que le hasard me fera éviter de te recontrer. Claude.*

Valium, a nap, the day fades. The evening, as arranged months ago, is to be shared with Robert Kanters. In the quick-falling dark I cross Paris again, this time on foot, the few miles between Epinettes and Robert's beautiful building, 23 Rue de Beaune, directly across from where I briefly lived, and died of cold, chez Jacques Damase in January of '53.

Robert's four-room lodging is ornamented solely with that most attractive of furnishings, books: on shelves, tables, toilet, floor, some ten thousand, each one cut and perused and dusty, their owner grinning out from amongst them. He has become healthily pot-bellied and elfin, ruddy and aphoristic, fifty-eight, much the same as when we met, if more self-assured, being now a crucial brick in the critical wall which for Paris, more than New York, separates reading and reader.

My reason for wanting immediately to see Robert Kanters was affectionate gratitude; he was the only one of the French press to defend my diaries; also the first "intellectual" I knew in Paris, having met him in 1949, as I met everyone then, by collapsing at his table and requesting a chartreuse at the Montana bar where he was seated with Fraigneau, Peyrefitte and Boudot-Lamotte (none of whom inherently objected to the presence of what I then represented), a milieu corresponding to David Sachs' in Chicago a decade earlier.

Despite the international *rétrécissement*, one would conclude, judging from Robert (with whom I avoid discussing music, an area in which, like most literary people, he is lost), that American literature, including *Portnoy's Complaint*, is no more in vogue here than ever. But he asks a few polite questions, mostly about the theater, that being the domain in which writers' names are better known than their writings, at least in the United States. Tennessee Williams and Edward Albee, for example, are certainly more famous than their works, while *Myra Breckenridge* is surely more famous than Gore Vidal. But where Albee and Williams have *peaked*, as the saying goes, Vidal remains stable, he being also a mind, an *idea* mind; idea men, for better or worse, are more adaptable to changing weather than are poets. Williams and Albee, try though they might, have never produced idea plays like Sartre's or even Giraudoux's, they are sensualists with good ears. They may ultimately be revived or forgotten utterly. Death brought oblivion to Gide and Hindemith, stardom to Bartók and Poulenc. Meanwhile, home is represented here by an apparently hideous production of *The Boys in the Band.*

At ten we go to dine on the right bank, again on foot, meaning I have to guide Robert, who is losing his eyesight, over the perilous Carrousel bridge. In my recall, Paris' plan had become a maze: what Avenue led from one *quartier* to another? Once here, the reorientation's so immediate, so exact, I've almost no need to visit old haunts, knowing just where and how they'll be. When, then, at the sudden encounter of an eyesore—Saint-Germain transformed into a circus, Gare Montparnasse a gooey hole like an extracted wisdom tooth—I recoil.

Fillets of sole in a bistro off the Rue Sainte Anne. Of course at the next table are Bernard Minoret and entourage exactly as I left them, sleeping beauties gossiping, years ago. Eyes closing from thirty-six wakeful hours, I made a date with Robert to see Alberto Moravia's play on my final French evening (Monday the 13th), then taxied here and went profoundly to bed.

Now sun streams through the open window. In an hour I go to 11 Place des Etats-Unis, for lunch at Marie Laure's.

"Madame la Vicomtesse is a bit behind schedule. But Monsieur Rorem has only to make himself at home."

Is this the house I lived in seven years? Like the streets last night, each corner and every odor here are so familiar, so utterly the photography of conscious recall rather than from the maze of dreams, that I feel no transport: neither admiration at the luxury nor nostalgia at a home regained. I cannot *see* the place, since I live here yet.

Alone, awaiting the hostess, I nevertheless reinspect the hexagonal parlor of the ground floor, the most perfectly proportioned and exquisitely appointed single place on this planet, combing my hair as once I combed it for two thousand days, in the huge mirror above the grate where now a small fire burns although the floor-to-ceiling casements are opened onto the garden whose late summer breeze hardly stirs the still-green bushes along the gravel paths, and from over the high granite walls come the cries of *pétanque* players spending their lunch hour in the Place des Etats-Unis as they have every noon for decades. There is the pale wood Gaveau neatly groaning beneath a fortune of marble eggs and satin art-books as before; here stand the same vast vases heavy with azure chrysanthemums flown in this morning from Charles de Noailles' estate in Grasse; in that angle the walnut liquor cabinet still stocked with gold tongs and Perrier water in silver containers; everywhere taste (so much more than *good* taste) gleams: from amber pillboxes, from the vermeil chinoiseries, the million-dollar rug like a rose window on the floor, the smaller masterpieces from the great Noailles collection smiling from the walls of this room which for the French bourgeoisie has been as often described (though for opposite reasons) as Mae West's white Hollywood apartment. The three Goyas have been removed to the upper stairwell, I noticed on entering, while passing through with André, the grayer but always inscrutable *maître d'hôtel*. Otherwise, except for my face in the mirror, nothing has changed.

Marie Laure will come in, take a wide silent look. —*Eh bien, il n'en reste rien,* she finally will declare. "You kept it longer than any of us. Now it's gone, there's nothing left." And we will go into lunch.

Marie Laure comes in, takes a wide silent look. —*Eh bien, je te trouve très bien,* she declares, settling that question, so we kiss and are pleased. She herself now seems benign, looking the same only more so. The heat's still there, but the fire's out. I am in love with her. She scares me a little when accepting the disk of my *Water Music* and the Tiffany trinket with those raptures of childlike gratitude indigenous to (though not always demonstrated by) the very rich. The tension is dissolved by the simultaneous entry of the Vicomte [Charles de Noailles] from his mother-of-pearl quarters elsewhere in the fifty-room mansion, and of Marcel Schneider from the outside world, accompanied by a bearded Turk who says nary a word for the next two hours. We five adjourn to lunch, not as formerly in the blue dining room, but in the foyer, I to be seated at Marie Laure's right, across from Marcel, behind whom hangs

Géricault's painting of twenty horses' asses to grace my constant
view.

The overrich meal is semistylishly served by the suave but edgy
André with an unaccustomed apprentice, and as usual the midday
sight of red meat repels. Like the salad, in seven shades of pale
green, the buttered potatoes are paradisiacal; not so the dessert, a
clafouti of apples with powdered sugar and a leather crust. During
the ingestion of these I grow easy, find myself the appraiser.

Charles has undergone a *coup de vieux*, must be seventy-seven
now, skin powdery, shoulders stooped, verbal intonations pinched
(but still so upper-class). One of the world's wealthiest inhabitants,
he remarks, when I ask if he ever visits New York (he owns half of
Wall Street): "I'd love to, but the trip's so horribly expensive, you
know." This, plus the word *nigger* launched in an English-spoken
phrase floating dismally present but unacknowledged like a fart,
raises my eyebrows. Nevertheless I tell him, in full earshot of the
servant André who knows family history: "On the plane yesterday I
read Francis Steegmuller's portrait of Barbette who claims you
are—*en toute simplicité*—the one real gentleman left on earth."
Applause from Marcel. Charles feigns interest, but denies knowledge of either Steegmuller or Barbette. Marie Laure interjects that
Steegmuller (whom she's surely mistaken for Frederick Brown)
must be that historian who last year asked everyone about
Cocteau's genitalia, which she herself now surmises to have been
pinkish, crinkly and capable of ejaculation without friction. From
which she proceeds in non sequitur to doubtful (if brief) epigrams.
Example: "I no longer believe in justice, only in injustice," pointing
one finger skyward, as Cocteau used to, signifying bravo. Another
example (to make me welcome): "All Americans are children." Has
time stopped? Were they, to whom I owe so much, always like this?
Was I? Am I? . . . Coffee is announced.

This beverage as usual is provided in the large upstairs parlor
to which we now repair (via a new elevator), and there find André
preparing a fire. "That's no way to make it burn," barks Marie
Laure. *"Mais si, madame la vicomtesse,"* he answers back, which he
never used to. "No, it isn't." The exchange occasions my sinking
into this protective enclosure I so loved, to constitute what has and
hasn't budged. The huge portraits, by Balthus and Bérard and

Berman, of Marie Laure, have been stored out of sight because, I
suppose, she avoids reminders of youth. Unchanged, however,
among the Reubens and Dalis, is the upholstery which everywhere
needs repair, and the white ceiling, thirty feet up there, still brown
with water stains.

An examination of Marie Laure's own recent painting reveals
her personal celestial domain intact, with feathery fingers beckoning
us to jump right into the canvas and join her there among her edible
colors. I make a date for next Tuesday with Marcel (he being one of
the critics I want to interview), make a date for tonight with Marie
Laure (she wanting me to meet Pietro Clementi) and, somewhat
dazed, come back here where at five o'clock I'm expecting Jacques
Bourgeois.

Jacques looked marvelous in a new toupee, subtly gray and
seemingly expensive. When I told him I'd just seen Marie Laure, he
answered, "I decided to accept lunch at Marie Laure's again about
three years ago: same guests, same conversation as three years
previous." He doesn't remember that in 1964 I asked him if he still
saw Marie Laure, and he replied, "Well I went to lunch again a few
years back: same conversation, same guests as always."

He continues: "If I look well, it's because, as Maurice Béjart
says—and it's Béjart above all (along with Maria—Maria Callas)
whom I promote these days, now that I'm a free-lance broadcaster
—he says 'There are two kinds of people, the young and the old,
and it has nothing to do with age.' You and I, Ned, are young. And
most certainly so is Béjart, it stems from his originality, despite your
feeling he's the poor man's Robbins. . . . How can I realize if things
have changed in Paris? Except, naturally, that most of the people
are dead, or act like it. Music-wise it's become a sort of avant-garde
capital: Varèse is the classical master, and the most popular
American is John Cage. There's a whole new public of Enthusiasts
who worship the trinity, Xenakis, Stockhausen, Berio, while utterly
ignoring Mozart symphonies. . . . Jolivet? No place left for him. No
room for 'La Jeune France,' for those intermediaries like Dutilleaux
and Daniel Lesur. Messiaen *is* grudgingly acknowledged as a
tiresome grandfather."

He adjusts his beige leather trousers, sips at his nonalcoholic drink, finishes the pear tart, and brings forth a Polaroid color snapshot of "the young friend," a painter posed before an easel which supports a portrait of Jacques himself. "This is our *jeunesse*. France now has a public, a great big knowledgeable young public for ultramodern art."

"Like America's for rock?"

Jacques is unsure. But he is anxious to impress the fact that the Events of May 1968—*les événements*—were a liberation for more than just civil rights. "And Karajan, *mon cher*, is *the* big *moment musicale* here: his three concerts next week have been sold out for over six months."

"But what about Xenakis?" I asked, confused by the sudden catholicity.

"It was I who first brought him to the radio, who first understood, intellectually, his music, rather than just bathing in it. I swear it makes a difference to know where he's aiming, to study assiduously, as I have, his stochastic method. And what more can I say than that with this method he creates an environment, a land, that doesn't bore me to visit?" With which he stood up, having a date with the young friend, and I one with Marie Laure. At my request he revealed the French name for mineral oil (*huile de paraffine*), since traveling gives me problems. Then he left.

Jacques Bourgeois, fifty, music critic, knows that to age is not to flow gently, but to jerk from plateau to plateau, mostly downward; hence the jitters of reunions, the need to show his up-to-dateness despite (have I noticed them?) those crow's-feet 'round his twin- kling eyes. What with Béjart and Callas he is well rounded, I suppose, like music critics ought to be. But to hop on the artistic bandwagon of the young is to lose your identity, Nazi style. Youth as mass may be correct politically, never artistically: how to write music is not a mass decision.

Confronted by the cold fact that I'm no longer a potential, but an accomplishment—that I *have become*—means both terror and strength. Jacques' role is to be open-minded. Mine isn't.

At 8:30 I fetched Marie Laure who meanwhile had been to the hairdresser, and was now impatiently waiting in her lobby, befurred and with bangs cute as Betty Boop's, leaning against César's ten-ton sculpture of a smashed automobile. She took me uninvited to Dino di Meyo's. Clementi never showed up, so we dined *à trois* on poached eggs and fish and a kind of chocolate paste at a minuscule table overhung with palms. Strictly gossip, mostly about Raffaello de Banfield's premiere this Friday and about Louise de Vilmorin who is (as everyone but me knows) Malraux's mistress, but losing interest rapidly now that Malraux no longer, etc. Then to my stupefaction Dino turned on the television and Marie Laure, enthralled, consumed a 1942 war movie from start to end. French TV does have the saving grace of clarity compared to ours, with sixty rather than forty lines per inch, or something like that. . . . We all drive back to the Place des Etats-Unis where, until midnight, we examine Marie Laure's scrapbooks containing mostly details on the 1968 *événements*. But I am too weary to concentrate on the dizzy talk accompanying each image. The fragrance of fire and fresh fruit become almost painful, so I excuse myself, thereby concluding my first full day back in Paris.

2 October (Thursday)

Cold and sunny. Fitful night.

Jacques Bourgeois' magnanimous points of view kept me awake. A composer can't afford to be magnanimous except about himself. Audiences may be dumb; but from a theatrical (if not a musical) standpoint, so is the avant-garde. The public will rather quickly grasp a theatrical (if not a musical) point, while composers just plod on. As to stochasticism, only secondarily do I care how a piece is made. First I must care about the piece. Seams show in any masterpiece, of course, for beauty limps—that's *Blood of a Poet*. Babbitt's total order and Cage's dice are fine, but their results are all seams, seams in space, as it were, minus the whole cloth. Art is a retention of childhood, not a return to childhood. Cage's "environmental" *Tunnel of Love* is a return, an expensive return, while Babbitt has no childhood at all. He's quite grown up.

At 16 *heures*, a visit to Didier Duclos, new director of Boosey & Hawkes' continental office. As contrasted to his predecessor, the suavely handsome Mario Bois, Duclos is bespectacled (like me) and eager, with that eagerness of agony: enthusiasm for lost causes. Presumably my visit is promotional, but like yesterday there now comes the praises of Xenakis who is not only the current French hero, but Boosey & Hawkes' chief product—after Stravinsky—of export. (As an American, I'm a product of import, without importance.) Again, like yesterday, I ask if the local lust for this composer corresponds to our own young freaks' for rock. Again, no clear answer. Or don't the French know that rock is meant to be a Way of Life? Can it be that their avant-garde is "appreciated" by such gigantic numbers on strictly musical terms? The young, the blacks, can, after all, be stupid like most people; still, to direct mass ignorance toward something essentially intelligent (and abstractly intelligent at that, which our rock isn't), seems both bizarre and old-fashioned, the avant-garde being in France a 1920s impulse, theoretically repugnant to revolutionaries.

Thoroughly cordial, with token encouragement about getting performances, Didier Duclos promises to phone next week, hands me some pamphlets on Xenakis, and says goodbye.

From Boosey & Hawkes' office in the Rue Drouot, I walk to Boulevard de Clichy where I am to drink tea with the Milhauds. The intervening labyrinth of gradually mounting streets and seething grocery stores which reopen at sunset when everyone's going home, of the Communist headquarters at Châteaudun, of Notre Dame de Lorette, and especially the Rue Pigalle, revives another promenade, that one nocturnal, in these byways eighteen years ago with George Chavchavadze who, like everyone else musical then, was selling me to the city and the city to me. We were ensconced, George every inch the Russian prince with his gold toothpick, I with bleached hair and nine-foot scarf a-trailing, at a bar in the Place Blanche, when a black-haired Legionnaire offered us five thousand francs if I would, for the next half-hour, croon Kentucky lullabies to him in a room at the nearby Hôtel des Martyrs. Did I? I remember only the following summer in their Venetian palazzo, Princess Elizabeth Chavchavadze in her eye-glasses, still very fat, working at petit point while George gave a lesson to Philippe Entremont on the nuances of Liszt. Soon after

came Elizabeth's Swiss sleeping cure from which she emerged
slender and self-assured with new conversation, but with the same
pair of glasses. Then their death together, gratuitous and sharp,
when their car skidded over a cliff, sadly relieving earth—as does all
death, I suppose—of the last representatives of a certain life-style.
The style was promoted less by money (there's still plenty of that
around) than by conjoining of art with high society at the expense of
political involvement, a conjoining exemplified at its height by
Diaghilev (to whom war was an inconvenience, as indeed, in its
realist sense, war always is for artists, because when war imposes
itself as subject matter it turns more urgent than the art it impels,
which in turn turns to propaganda); at its decline by Edith and
Etienne de Beaumont (whom I, perhaps luckily, certainly historically, visited with Marie Laure in 1951, shortly before their
respective deaths from natural causes, and was properly subdued by
their urban castle, still standing behind its white wall at 2 Rue du
Roc, decorated with maquettes of *Tricorne* and *Parade*, ballets
originally financed by Etienne, a lovable Charlus); and at its corrupt
collapse, confiscated in America by the Sculls, the Hornicks and
their likes.

I am the only guest at the Milhauds'. They appear weary, having
arrived this morning from England, though Darius in particular
looks healthier than when we last met two years ago in Oakland.
(But doesn't Darius always look healthier than we had remembered
him as looking?) Having been summoned for tea, tea is indeed
served, plus a heap of absolutely juicy cookies baked expressly by
Madeleine for the occasion. They are unleavened, oatmealy and
brushed before cooking with a faint film of peach. I eat fourteen.

Tactfully and without insistence Madeleine incessantly talks,
speaking for two, filling the lacunae of Darius who nods sometimes
painfully. Like her voice, her fingers constantly move, around the
knitting in her lap, while she weaves the mutual verbs of our gossip
forever to where her husband can easily interject his intelligence.
Last night in London they sat through Colin Davis' uncut version of
Les Troyens, found it sublime. Such an admission seems more
foreign to me than the Milhauds themselves seemed twenty years

ago. This late afternoon we all felt like Americans in Paris, momentarily immune to native darts.

The rush hour of Paris being every bit the joke it's reputed to be, my taxi needs seventy minutes from Place Clichy to the Eiffel Tower. During the trip my traveling companion, touch-and-go colitis, reappears with renewed vigor. At my destination on the Elysée-Reclus, resides Adrien Perquel, once jealously described by Marie Laure (who has never met him) as my one *mauvaise fréquentation* but who is really a luxuriantly successful Jewish banker of seventy-three, met on the *Ile-de-France* in 1952, a ladies' man and a faithful acquaintance with whom it is thrilling to realize I have no friends in common.

For years I languish about a given corner of this city, find it again and die. Then once the fact of being here is established—a question of an hour—the geography of memory falls into place. Thus there's no reason to rush back to first homes, here, in the Rue de la Harpe, and shed tears. I know they're there, urban proportions being safely reinstated, and like vital shots of whisky they can wait, isolated on altars, maybe even improving with age.

And so it is tonight tête-à-tête with Adrien. I have consumed this identical meal a hundred times, admired these too-marvelous manners before, attended each vicarious question ("Why is America so pornography-minded? so much more so than France?"), examined every so-so Kisling and telescoped the costly fibers that hold my host's *toupet* in place (do all the French wear them now?).

After supper the colitis has not eased. Which isn't why I decline Perquel's liqueurs: for eighteen months I've scarcely touched alcohol or tobacco, reasons of health and work and domesticity.

That voice, always interrogative, obliges me to reorder the conversation, since I'm still unrecovered from Monday's flight. "You all keep talking about *les événements*, those May Events, as though they combined the French Revolution with the Second Coming. Define them." The May Events: a fatal juggling of authority, a never-to-be-gone-back-on reassessment of who's boss in any relationship, parent and child, student and teacher, employer and employee, subject and state, even artist and critic.

The present tone of Paris—at least as I've heard it up to now—sounds removed from our Vietnam, which the French compare to their Algeria. No one talks of Nixon, and fantastically I feel safe, as though tomorrow the horrors would sail from China, high over France, and land with a terminal crash in faraway New York.

Bored by the same tune, yesterday from Marie Laure and tonight from Perquel, describing Americans as children. The French clutch at this faded notion which excites them the way Southern white housewives are said to be excited by Negro janitors. In fact, our degeneration into adolescence resulted precisely in 1957 from the simultaneous shock of Sputnik and Little Rock; our ensuing decay into adulthood appeared with this year's reaction to our new president; we seem headed as fast as Europe toward senility. In answering my own questions I learn little new about the country where I'm now a guest, unless it's that I push things to my own conclusion.

Preparing to leave Perquel I reexamine carefully his entire house, its boatlike structure, the downstairs kitchen, immense ceilings and long rooms, garden, gymnasium, Chinese relics everywhere, the best painters' worst paintings, and a carpet you really do sink into. Because I'll probably never be there again.

2 A.M. I've been reading *Le Figaro Littéraire* and the Xenakis literature. The former contains an amusing (to an American) poll organized by Claude Rostand, which asks various notables how they feel about a *stranger*, Herbert von Karajan, coming to be the conductor of the newly organized Orchestre de Paris. This inversion of American viewpoint follows an article, "in depth," on the movie *More*; a report of the near-obligatory suicide of the Marseilles schoolmistress of thirty who was sleeping with one of her students, then Pompidou's summation of *cette tragédie* in a quote of Eluard; the wise and boring Bloc Notes of the unkillable Mauriac.

As for the Xenakis, should go to bed, stomachache, tomorrow will be huge, but just a word, before stale ideas grow staler:

". . . *le jeu facile,* the nondifficult manner belongs to an esthetic and to a musical conception which are no longer timely. Because we've changed our perception, our way of thinking and of doing."

No. We have grown not more but less difficult. Look around, at what makes a difference, and at what doesn't.

". . . *de nos jours,* it takes a lot to be shocking, because we expect everything and we believe everything."

And we believe nothing.

". . . *Dans ma musique* there is all the anguish of my youth, of the resistance. . . . The traditional expressions of sensibility change as fast as dress design. . . . What's important in today's music is its abstract nature."

Importance is not the qualifier of "abstract nature" in today's music, since the nature of all music of all times has been abstract. The preceding remark is worthy of Casals, a remark which contains its own destruction, and accordingly that of composer Xenakis himself. Regarding the anguish of his youth, that is hardly abstract, yet forms the basis of his creativity.

". . . *Enfin,* the interest is to create a form of composition which is no longer the object in itself but an idea in itself."

Well, that is one interest. His premise is arbitrary: that inspiration is a thing of the past; nor can he prove that his own work is not inspired exactly as inspiration was defined in the good old days.

5 October
(Sunday afternoon)

Such perfect weather more than any person breaks the heart since beauty always wounds. I've bought a large plum pie, some scotch and eight plump ruby roses, for at sundown Maxine Groffsky's coming over, and also: Robert Veyron-Lacroix, Jean-Michel Damase, Jean Chalon, Jean de Rigault, Henri [José] Hell and maybe Raffaello de Banfield. The flowers: because here I don't seem yet to have hay fever.

The evening of last Friday was to signify my trial by fire. That morning as usual I ingested hot croissants with icy butter and foamy *café au lait,* seated at the kitchen window, watching the frenzy of the street. Friday being market day in the *quartier,* the block is blocked off, double lines of provisional canvas kiosks are erected, manned by women (. . . *des femmes à grosses poitrines/Et bêtes comme des choux . . .*) hawking their pure gold squash and healthy yellow tomatoes compared to which ours look like garbage.

I made a note about feeling lost and sad, though today, feeling well (such perfect weather more than any person, etc.), how stretch that out beyond declaring I felt lost and sad? Phone call from PQ in Marseilles inviting me down, a voice unheard in years yet familiar as this coffee giving rise to dreams until another call, from Marie Laure, explicated: "Some say you mistreated me. But tonight, we will protect you." The mistreatment referred to the diary; she had nonetheless granted written permission to quote letters, and to say anything except about her family, and about . . . Bargain kept. Her "we" referred to herself and Dino. "Tonight" meant the triple bill of little operas, by Henri Sauguet, Raffaello and Manuel Rosenthal, scheduled for observation, Opéra-Comique, before a "gala" audience consisting largely of those who used to be my friends.

A third phone call, from me to Gavoty, revealed that *"Monsieur est dans sa salle de bain,"* which cheered me up, "Would you call back in a quarter-hour?"

N'est pas antitraditionel qui veut—it's not that easy to slough off the past. Complete in Indian regalia, in front of Sacré-Coeur, two French hippie friends meet. And shake hands.

The élite tone of Paris is hardly pseudo-hip or post-mod like Manhattan's. French Youth, now more appetizing (while French cooking has become less appetizing) than ours, still wears neckties. To be daring is to sport a turtleneck at the theater, as did my evening companion, Jean de Rigault, although I, forewarned by Sauguet of the evening's sobriety, felt compelled to buy, Friday on the awful Avenue Saint-Ouen, black clothes which are now an encumbrance.

No one in that ugly lobby had aged any more than lodgers age in the Grévin Museum. There, instantly, was Claude, naturally with Charlotte Aillaud, leaving me thoroughly indifferent and mildly amused, my *De Profundis* suddenly acquiring a retrospect no more grave than *Lady Windermere's Fan*. Physical pain, unlike moral pleasure, is impossible to reconstruct *en souvenir*. As recommended, I did not say hello.

But I nevertheless tripped over that pair of beauties, Oh! Jeanne Ritcher, looking so tall and well postured beside Nora Auric, the latter still with stars in her clipped white hair, prettier than Joan of Arc in a snowstorm. I kissed Jeanne as Nora said *Bonjour monsieur*, then, double-taking, clasped me. *Mais je ne t'avais pas reconnu!* She melted, and I succumbed to the prodigal son's relief, and the *entr'acte* turned enjoyable. The surface cruelty of Parisians is gymnastic, rhetorical push-ups veiling a magnanimity we could well envy. The bickering feud, the witty censure, justified or not, are resolved with a "Come home, all is forgiven." Or so was the implication from greetings of Jacques Février (who had resented the impudence of my "the French don't know how to play their own music"), of the Rostands, of Nora's sister the anesthetist Nadia Dubonnet who quickly collared me about drugs in the United States, while Marie Laure, in black, stood over there with a dark young painter among the pillars, looking curiously absent, but no more curiously than nineteen years ago.

If socially the evening thrived, musically it brought catastrophe. To the social-minded, a definition for Concert is: that which surrounds an intermission. Friday was an unflawed example. The operas were particularly appalling in that I had been so recently brainwashed about the French avant-garde. Sauguet's 1930s bonbon, *La Gageure imprévue*, mounted (without sets) rather more charmingly two years ago by the Met Opera Studio, here came off as old-hat oom-pa-pa and overlong, although with a marvelously simple décor of a slightly lopsided sea-green eighteenth-century interior which Jacques Dupont always manages with skill. Rosenthal's revival, also from the 1930s, came off as plain uncomfortable with its wornout Javas and American pratfalls. Dear Raffaello's premiere, a pastiche of the 1930s and a solo vehicle for Denise Scharley, came off as a tango trying for macabre camp, but missing the boat, as an Italian in this area must. Was the hall blushing? It was not. *Le tout Paris*, no more discriminatory than ever in matters aural, nevertheless murmured later: "If only you had been here last summer when we presented Ives at . . . If only you could be here next month when we're having Berio at . . ."

But I am here now.

Supper at midnight with José Hell, Richard Négroux, Jean de R and his young friend, my first cigarette in two months, first vin rouge in two years despite the colitis (which diminished), a round of gay bars and a dryly proud dissertation from Jean de R on how Youth—capitalized in the Gallic psyche as in the Yankee—doesn't attend such operas, considers Marie Laure, even de Gaulle, as a dinosaur, says *merde* to every form of the past, is not oriented to rock but to the "integrity" of Xenakis, politics and to . . . Then he described—and he thinks of himself as Young—how his very old mother (surely a "form of the past") last year died in his arms, leaving him bereft, shattered.

Last night, Saturday, a long duck dinner chez José [Henri Hell] with Richard, and gallons of Evian water to assuage a dehydrating hangover. The apartment is directly above Robert Kanters', though it might as well be another world for the resemblance, Robert's being clean disorder, José's the reverse. Richard Négroux, still handsome at fifty and speaking better French than the French but with that rippled accent Rumanian refugees never shed, is José's friend, Dubuffet's secretary, a reader for Fayard, cultured and unpretentious, dapper and without a cent, and without an American equivalent, being descended from the wit of Kafka, a wit as different from ours as two blood types, despite how hard we try to interpret our disparate bureaucracy as central European.

After gruyère and pears, a long long long and languid stroll, covering that multitude of acres which once had been so personal to us three. Boulevard Saint-Germain now filled with dress shops like Saint-Tropez, Rue Dauphine seething with apple-cheeked students very conscious of being apple-cheeked students, whose parents, my colleagues, were pale and shorter and under the surveillance of Hitler Youth. Our Rue de la Harpe has become a casbah, albeit a lavishly fake one, there being a visible lack of Algerians in the city since the war's end. Number 53, the scene of my virginity with Xénia, is a movie house showing Bergman's *Le Silence*. At the pastry shop next door we purchase, at one franc each, some rosy orange Turkish delights, which the French call *loukoums*, speckling ourselves with powdered sugar. By way of Saint-Julien-le-Pauvre we arrive to inspect Notre-Dame, hosed clean, itself resembling a *loukoum*, mouse-bitten and filled with Day-Glo. Health improved, less depressed, incredibly gentle clean Indian summer. At 1 A.M., as a brief warm rain began, my friends put me into a taxi, after accepting an invitation to come by for tea and crumpets this afternoon.

6 October
(Monday morning)

Since Maxine Groffsky has the best figure in Paris, and means to keep it, she starves herself faint, works out at dance classes, takes sweat baths and (it's rumored) milk baths. Thus she was understandably anguished at the four varieties of salted nuts, not to mention the plum tart with clotted cream, on view at my tea party yesterday. She arrived early and departed eighty minutes later, again understandably, when the *garçons* began to arrive. She accepted two scotches, consumed a quarter-kilo of almonds with angry despair, tossed back her very long mulberry silk hair every three minutes (it's arranged, like Veronica Lake's, to fall in her eyes), and occasionally walked wonderfully across Guy's narrow Moroccan parlor in the manner a man would like to be turned into a woman in order to imitate. She has just moved from an apartment in the Rue du Dragon (ironically, the address of Charlotte Aillaud whom she resembles like a twin), to an apartment in the Rue de Tournon. Why does she stay on in Paris? Because she needs the higher intelligence ratio, appreciates the responsibility of representing *The Paris Review*, likes her social life, especially Harry Matthews, and feels safer than in America. Next question? Close your eyes and hear the voice, through hers, of Frank O'Hara and all his friends. She had parked her car during a bewilderingly blinding sunset in the nearby but equally bewildering Cité des Fleurs, but as it was dark when she left she got lost, perhaps forever.

The boys, minus Raffaello, chatted for two hours, then we went to dine *en bande* near the Odéon at a bistro sympathetically renovated in *fin de siècle* blood-colored plush.

J'ai dit que tout était en ordre—was the Cocteau curtain line. Intimation: When I soon leave France, everyone will continue in orderly fashion as though I'd wound the clock. Then some urge (for perfection?) will force me to throw away the key. The country will run down. I will never come back. It's excruciating.

After midnight

The good-looking—if less so than five years ago—Mario Bois, married to ballerina Clare Motte and formerly with Boosey & Hawkes, now runs a business for himself. For two hours this afternoon, he, so very *gentil*, all but beguiled me into a respect for his complex scheme of renting unpublished music by living composers, while retaining a huge percentage of the gross income. He is the third person in three days to announce himself the personal inventor of the great Xenakis. As though I cared—more than for the dry chestnut leaves strewing the Tuileries where I strayed, killing time, before fetching Michel Girard, Rue de Varenne.

Bookstores, errands, *flâneries*, no thought of cruising, only of the gentle city which now that I'm here, what's the difference, neither of us cares, so be passive utterly to the beauty, see all, not with new but with old eyes, finally unburdened with ambition.

At nineteen o'clock, October nightfall, streets jammed with hurriers-home, you look into windows of expensive restaurants, Rue de Grenelle or on the quais, and see a single table crowded with the cuisine personnel eating before the first customers appear, and standing around in the emptiness the white waiters wait.

The *rez-de-chaussée* of Michel Girard and Jean Pétain is no less sumptuous if somewhat more charged with rarities, than a hundred and twenty months ago. Young skinny whippets replace the old Wagnerian dachshunds on the divans of iodine-green velvet. The heads of the house, taller than ever, gray and nervous, look handsomely haunted and aristocratic after the simulated American-style immediacy of Mario Bois.

In a hired cab Michel escorts me to the excellent restaurant of my old Hôtel Bisson where, over a turbot and coffee, and under the sad stare of my host, I answer his barrage of questions, and he mine. With the deaths of the terribly alive Denise Bourdet, and of Julius Katchen who first introduced us, Michel and I sink into those commiserative bromides that soothe the soul and excite the past. The past when I, a Fulbright Fellow, used to come daily to work at his Pleyel.

The dead. Young Marion Jeanson (but was she young?) with whom one sunny noon I walked the five kilometers from the Rue Foyatier, where Monsieur Vadot the copyist lived, to this very Hôtel Bisson where I then lived, without either of us shutting up except for sips of pernod en route. And Valentine Hugo. And Hervé Dugardin, who yesterday in 1951 spoke of Kay Francis as though it were yesterday, but will plainly never speak of her again. Nor will Guy de Lesseps whose dying decapitates a third of the tripartite Medusa which was Auric, for if Georges was Nora's brain, Guy was her brawn, and now she's smarter, but walks, they say, with a limp. Most precious of all, Julius, and our Denise to whom I can't apologize for what she found as *mauvais goût* in the journal. Maybe we'll feel better when we're dead, but that will be the day!

But I explain that I've come to Paris less to open coffins than to ease birth pangs, notably those of our mutual acquaintance Gérard Souzay who next month in Philharmonic Hall will introduce my cycle *War Scenes*. He had written last March asking me to provide something new for his November recital and ensuing American tour. He wanted "dramatic" songs, his voice having grown more "interesting" than before. I fulfilled the commission in ten days, composing to five fevered extracts torn pell-mell from Walt Whitman's war journal. Since, *en principe*, I never want to set the French language to music again (it sabotages my inner nature), the choice of Whitman's depressing text served two functions: the words, being a century old, automatically contain archaisms which won't sound strange on Souzay's tongue, as would the poetry of, say, John Ashbery; and those words are otherwise timely, being vital descriptions of battle: the gore and poignance, ferocious anxiety and placid passion, are as close to Vietnam as to the Civil War. Dalton Baldwin, Gérard's impeccable pianist, had in fact phoned this morning to confirm our Sunday rehearsal date, and to say how much he enjoyed working on the accompaniment, adding, with a shocking naïveté which somehow only an American could pull off, "Thank God the war is still on!"

Michel asks after Marie Laure, not with the snide reference of yore—*et ta logeuse!*—but kindly, with an implication I'm convinced is valid: we grow old without inner change: if we are "good" at twenty we will be good at ninety, but whoever is graceless at ninety was always graceless.

While paying the bill he remarks on my ever-fluent French; and as we emerge into the green night on the Quai des Grands-Augustins, he mentions having seen my recent squib *On Nudity* translated in *Carrefour* by Claude Roy. The weather being propitious, we amble to the Louvre to examine the new moats, then to the sand-colored *Institut* by way of the Bridge of the Arts, and next door *La Monnaie*, an edifice whose perfection I (nor anyone else) had never noticed before the purges. We said good-night at the corner of the Rue des Saints-Pères, since I had a date to see the film about Rubinstein.

François Reichenbach's movie on Rubinstein, appropriately called *L'Amour de la vie*, is a most satisfying one-man show, similar to the documentary Reichenbach showed us ten years ago about a Black boxer. His not unknown experiments with pornography have benefited him here, detail and obsession no longer being the telescope of sex but of musical sound. To hear—I mean, to see—Rubinstein play Chopin and Schumann, the French line up for blocks at five cinémas where the film, in crushing color, is distributed. It's almost worth it.

7 October (Tuesday)

The French: talk.

They talk and talk. But not of politics nor of the world's end. At least not to me. Which is fine, since I'm less at home in politics than in art, being less concerned with a country's well-being than with my own well-being within that country.

Since 1944 I have composed an hour's worth of music every twelve months. The average was higher during the early years when impulse gushed without censorship, lower in later years when discipline presumably played a part, plus the interminable chore of orchestration which does not add hours to one's total *oeuvre*, but simply subtracts them from one's life.

The most fruitful single period—though much of the crop was underripe—came in Morocco between 1949 and 1951 when I wrote my first of everything in the big forms: quartet, sonata, symphony, opera, song cycle, concerto. All these are dated in Fez or Marrakech, and are directly due to the hospitality of Guy Ferrand.

The next most prolific period—though some of the fruit now seems rotten—came in France between 1951 and 1957 when I composed my second of everything. All are dated in Paris or Hyères, and are due directly to the hospitality of Marie Laure de Noailles.

These productive seasons were of protected isolation. Since then, too, I've worked best in the rural hothouse confines of self-exile, as at Yaddo or the MacDowell Colony. The quality result is something else. Some of my best pieces were simultaneous with (if not the issue of) a quite hysterical urban renewal. Of the total twenty-six hours I now qualifiedly claim ten, am not ashamed of five and am proud of less than one.

Over the phone the famous voice of Lise Deharme huskily declares: *Tu es une âme pure, mon chéri, et dans Paris il n'y a que deux âmes pures, la tienne et la mienne.* Amusing, because Lise surely strikes few people as a "pure soul"; indeed, her most telling trait is a compulsive knack for donning the threadbare cloak of worldliness with an actress' feline grace. Her very books show that she conspires with the devil, not with saints. So I invite her to the little welcome-home party Roro plans for me tomorrow.

This afternoon, lunch at Nora Auric's. (*Merlans frits*, new potatoes, green salad, *yaourt aux mirabelles*, Spanish coffee.) Within four minutes the comfortable rapport was reestablished: despite absence or misunderstanding we will be close forever. The Tiffany trinket, accepted with relish, did bring forth *"C'est le sentiment qui compte,"* though I'd thought it rather generous.

Surrounded by chrysanthemums in the spacious new apartment, Avenue Matignon, Nora remains pretty beyond belief, but still protesting her lack of concern about Marie Laure. We talked until five, mostly of Guy de Lesseps whose agony she recounted (for the first time, apparently) in pungent detail. Since his death she has not spent a night without dreaming of his face, a ruined face, on the hospital pillow. Her too few recent paintings depart radically from the children's portraits and submarine landscapes of the fifties; these are dazzling yellow, a yellow not of optimism but of jaundice.

Georges, due back Friday from New York, also leads an enforced new life, having just turned seventy and become disengaged as director of the Opéra. But he still struggles with the same "creative block," it would seem, since I asked Nora whatever became of the project of a libretto from Simenon. (At curtain rise a girl, standing on the bridge of the Canal Saint-Martin, sings an aria, then jumps in the water and drowns.) She shook her head. Then, out of the blue, revived an idea I had proposed ages ago: of making a suite from Georges' scores for *Sang d'un Poète*, *Le Million* and *Les Jeux sont faits*. But she added sadly, "Oh, it probably wouldn't have worked."

5:30, tea with Marcel Schneider, Rue de Turenne, in that ghostly section of the Right Bank called Le Marais. Mounting the four flights to Marcel's apartment, I am reminded of Denise Bourdet's aromatic paragraph about mounting the same four winding flights— a three-sentence evocation of the neighborhood's medieval history, the history of the becloved orange she was carrying as gift to her host, and of the host himself, Marcel, in pristine style, overlooking the Place des Vosges and the Carnavalet. My own gift is a record of Beverly Wolff singing *Poems of Love and the Rain*. Thereupon Marcel immediately inscribes a copy of his new *Guerrier de pierre*.

The purpose for this visit, other than friendliness, is to settle the local state of music. However, by now so many people have told me the same things (their proud avant-garde is firmly and expensively ensconced, they love it, or hate it, while defining it as America did around seven years ago: electronic-serial-chance, quite isolated from our current Vulgar-as-Deep, suspicious-of-excellence syndrome), that my interest lies more in his definition of *Les Evénements*. When I praise the rose-colored sugar-biscuits served with the jasmine infusion, Marcel chortles: *Ça n'a aucun rapport avec des événements*, which he then classifies as Sartre being out, Lévi-Strauss in, or one aristocracy replacing another.

A faintly acrid fragrance issued from somewhere, perhaps from, I might suspect (were he not so fastidious), my host's besandaled feet, or from the early bonfires that are beginning to glow in this most sanitary of cities. Regina Sarfaty phoned to cancel our evening's engagement, leaving me at loose ends, for I was of no mind to accompany Marcel to André Watts' recital.

I therefore dined alone on fried eggs at the Flore (reassured by the presence of the unchanged waiters, like the cashier at Loew's Sheridan who, decade after decade, shoots out tickets with flint-faced fidelity), walked to the Etoile, saw (part of) a terrible movie, *L'Américain*, with both Trintignant and Signoret walking through their turgid roles, picked up some magazines at Le Drugstore (France's giddy imitation of nothing ever seen before) and came home.

                              8 October (Wednesday)
                              Very late at night

Paris cab drivers. Their masculinity still seems more natural, i.e., earthy (dirty), than ours. Tough. Tough too's their femininity. One of them at four this afternoon deposited me at the Alliance Française where Jean Marais is directing Cocteau's *Oedipe Roi*, which he's also doing sets for and starring in. He didn't halt the rehearsal at my arrival; he simply introduced me to everyone, including two puzzled actors on stage. We proceeded to reminisce while he simultaneously yelled polite suggestions to the lighting expert (everyone's old pal, Fred Kiriloff) and to the Polish choreographer, maintaining that Cocteau-type generous-octopus tact that made us each feel like the Only One. But there was not much to reminisce about, beyond what had become of his friend, George Reich, who had danced in our lamentable 1952 collaboration, the ballet *Dorian Gray*.

Because I regress with everyone to my age when first knowing them (with my parents, still acting the infant, with Paul Bowles the brash adolescent, with Lenny Bernstein the insecure goyische aspirer), now, before Jean Marais, I reverted to the intimidated starstruck expatriate.

A chain-smoking body-builder, at fifty-six he's still beautiful in an old-fashioned Greek god manner, salt-&-pepper-colored hair with a forty-dollar haircut. If not the official widow, he is at least the (unspoken) official heir to the Cocteau flair which now, at least in his custody, seems dry as a yellowing snapshot serving as the whole décor. For instance, our conversation was accompanied by the persistent replaying of Maurice Thiriet's score for a former production, music with no point of view toward either the present or the past, being a pastiche of the Honegger-Hollywood machines, yet which Marais feels disposed toward since Cocteau had once approved it. "Did Cocteau originally mean for the play to have music?" I asked. Marais answered, "Did Maeterlinck intend music for *Pelléas?*"

Thiriet then arrived and Jean Marais introduced me as *"mon premier compositeur."* Together we followed the score filled with notes unrelated to those we were hearing, though no one including the composer appeared bothered. Suddenly Marais said—and I was very touched—"You're better now than you were then, maybe because, since I loved George, you were less visible."

Having time before my date with Pierre Bernac, I walked the length of Boulevard Montparnasse, pausing disturbed to let certain streets pass over me like perfume at an intermission, reactivating their molecules into the shape of vanished bookstores on the Rue Littré, or restaurants on the Rue de Vaugirard where every night of 1952 I dined with Henri Fourtine, or shadows near the Eglise Saint Roch where eighteen months earlier I was unfaithful to the future. Just as my return to Chicago ten years ago revolved around an involuntary search of façades behind which I had fallen in love as a child, so this afternoon, after leaving Jean Marais, the city echoed thunderously of my carnal twenties. For every bistro which excited the recall of a quarrel with Marie Laure or Julius Katchen, ten alleyways revived the swoon of fürtive unions with sibling strangers whose white energy has now surely turned to gray decrepitude. A detour into the silent Rue Barbet de Jouy where, at number 16, very very high over the wall, some sycamore branches fluttered with vitality, but no other sign of life, in the street or house, nor any sound of music as when Marie-Blanche de Polignac was still alive.

All this, totally disengaged from my body now, had been

nevertheless stamped irrevocably on Paris' heated streets through which I now was running, for night had fallen and I was *en retard*.

The sole thing in common between Pierre Bernac and Jean Marais is that both keep a great man's flame. Like our Frank O'Hara whose death gave birth to a flock of widows, Francis Poulenc is mourned by a proprietary clan of which Pierre Bernac is dean. Not that Pierre's interests are restricted—he teaches widely here and in America, the latter being a good deal more productive, he says—but to talk of his thirty years of concerts with Poulenc is to make his eyes shine like nothing else. We've spoken identically of this in other years, sipping the same tea in the same twilit room on the Motte-Piquet, sighing with pleasure at mutually favorite songs, with pain at mutually unfavorite singers. But now our leave-taking is sadder, because Pierre, about to be seventy, next month goes into the hospital.

At Robert Veyron-Lacroix', my little party is in full swing, champagne, orange juice and Georgette Rostand. Nora takes me aside to announce that our lunch yesterday had proved exorcistic: last night she dreamed normally of Guy for the first time since he died. Lise Deharme, black empress from the insect kingdom on the arm of Jean Chalon, like everyone, remarked on my dark hair, I having been blond during the fifties. Nobody wears maxicoats, and they all compare Boulez to Markevitch of forty years ago: creative genius turning to conducting sterility. At nine we watch the televised welcome of the astronauts.

To be dismayed by the astronauts' personal banality (are these the supermen we've spent millennia developing!) is to mistake their robot role, their specialization as servants of separate higher minds. They deserve ticker tape as trained seals deserve dried fish.

A formal address from the Academy's Marcel Drouon to these Americans was an eloquent, aphoristic, moving, well-built model of intelligence. The astronauts too, with earphones and grins, were a model of mannerly patience with their (to the French) childlike charm.

Long late *dîner en masse* with Nora, the Rostands and Jacques

Février plus his protégé, high in Montmartre at a new restaurant—recommended—called l'Assommoir. Although I first met Claude Rostand when he lectured in Fez with the Jeunesses Musicales in 1949 or 1950, we've talked only sporadically since. I was glad, therefore, to cement our acquaintance tonight, for I've always liked his mind which is that of a critic both cultured and articulate who owes these qualities, unlike most American critics, to steady and long-lived personal intercourse with creative musicians of all persuasions. Attending warnings, he no longer smokes or drinks.

9 October (Thursday)

If there is one regrettable page in *The Paris Diary* it is about Nadia Boulanger. Not a word conforms with my true and gentle attitude toward that unusual woman. If possible, I would retract all. Still, apologies are somehow more undignified than insults. With Mademoiselle Boulanger silence is a wise tactic in matters extramusical—if there are such matters: for her everything stems from or returns to music. To ignore that is to be the insolent falsifier who composed the diary pages.

With relief, therefore, I learned that Nadia Boulanger had invited me yesterday to visit, an invitation which, for geographical reasons, I was forced to decline. Today at noon, en route to Sauguet's, I left a gift with her concierge, and an envelope containing a few atoms of the respectful warmth of my feelings.

Despite the still heavenly weather, influenza's in the air, which dampened my appetite for Henri Sauguet's lunch of white melon, veal and mushrooms, salad, camembert and red and blue grapes, served by his new and expert Tunisian cook. (Everyone—at least everyone I know—has lunch at home, prepared by a male servant from either Spain or Northwest Africa.) New also is the blue-eyed cat, Parsifal, the replacement of the forty-pound Angora that five years ago lunched with us, elegantly sitting among the dishware licking his haughty jaws, since perished in the jaws of a Bordelais fox.

Henri, forever the royalist, found Nixon's speech to the

astronauts more moving than Drouon's. Our conversation otherwise turned around the state of music, which we all know, except for our place in it. Henri at sixty-eight feels left behind; the wittiest man in France grows sad. The irony is reinforced when after lunch we visit his offices. These are in the nearby Rue Ballu, at the Société des Auteurs et Compositeurs Dramatiques, founded by Beaumarchais in 1777 and now under the absolute monarchy of Henri himself, whom all call Monsieur le Président. Placed in a sunny garden, the edifice is so stylish, like Drouon's speech last night, so unrough, red-leathered and unofficial with a hothouse and birdcages, with Sauguet so kowtowed to, his sadness wears a halo.

Where now's the best pastry shop in our neighborhood? Chez Vaudron, à la Fourche, corner of the Avenues Clichy and Saint-Ouen, used to sell us warm flaky orange-custard tarts with real orange slices baked into them. Last week on discovering Vaudron's replaced by a hardware store, I was ready to take the first plane out of France. I would have, too, if a month ago I hadn't already made a date to dine tonight with Janet Flanner.

The idea of the meal was a strenuous expression of pleasure from Janet for my having turned nine portions of her "Letters from Paris," as they appeared in *The New Yorker*, into a piece for chorus and orchestra, at the Koussevitzky Foundation's behest in 1966. The published score has just appeared in a handsome edition, and I brought extra copies for Janet. "Nobody's ever done that to me before," she said, examining the musical notes printed above her dismantled text, as the taxi transported us from her hotel in Place Vendôme to a restaurant in Place des Victoires.

Three hours were passed over shrimp bisque, soles meunières and a kilo of raspberries in thick cream, a long time considering we took no wine. Tonight as always Janet Flanner churned midwestern reticence into continental clarity. Circumspect in writing, she is outspoken in talk. As always she asked after my "dear Quaker parents," not failing to add, "what on earth did they feel about that pornographic diary?" And she examined me reproachfully through her monocle, resembling a hip and handsome Amazon disguised as George Washington playing Greek tragedy.

No one—certainly no one reviewing the Paris peace talks—reveals the French political scene to the United States more lucidly than Janet Flanner; she is at home, articulate and organized within this subject as she is within the visual arts. About current American writing she seems less informed, while her report on matters musical has dwindled to nothing. "My active musical knowledge ceased with a recognition of Debussy's whole-tone scale back in the teens of this century when I permanently quit the ugliness of Indiana for the beauty of this geography. I'd *like* to write about music, because God knows I have trouble sometimes finding material for the Paris letter. But I don't feel secure about it any more, now that Doda Conrad and Noel Murphy aren't around to go to concerts with. Am I missing much? It seems to me that France lacks all distinction since de Gaulle."

If she ignores the names of music critics here, she appears equally unconcerned with local society as Society, but adores gossip about the artistic rich. Her personal milieu, I gather, revolves more around the American expatriates of then and of now, like Natalie Barney or Bettina Bergery or James Jones.

She hailed the waiter. I protested. "You can't pay, dear Janet. I'm a gentleman." "So am I," she answered.

As she had promised me a catalogue on Napoleon, I accompanied her to the Ritz where, since the demise of the Continentale last spring, she now inhabits a single room on the fifth floor overhanging the garden of the famous bar, with a treetop view of the obelisk on the left, and on the right the Eglise de l'Assomption's dome. It is a late October midnight, but a hyacinthine breeze enters the balcony window and ruffles for an instant the aquamarine nightgown which, earlier in the evening, a chambermaid had laid out on the narrow Spartan bed. "I'll probably die here," said Janet without passion, but with the straightforward poignance of one born in 1892.

The Ritz lobby contains a passageway one block long and two yards wide, bordered by mirrors and by several hundred display cases filled with luxury products representing the world's best stores. Empty and haunted now, at 1 A.M., I passed through it and onto the Rue Cambon where, in 1936, I spent a fortnight with my parents and sister Rosemary at the Hôtel de Castille which still stands there, unchanged.

10 October (Friday)

—*A bas Sartre, à bas Boulez, à bas Couperin,* one hears the French kids cry. One doesn't hear American kids cry "Down with Goodman, down with Cage, down with Gottschalk," because they've never heard of these men, much less of Sartre, Boulez or Couperin. Which is not to boast the superiority of French culture. The humblest French concierge knows the names, if not the works, of his country's cultural heroes for two thousand years, and is proud, while we, in a pinch, may know the names of Hemingway or Mailer (though not their works), but strictly as folk heroes.

They eat more sensibly than we, yet die young anyway.

They're all reading *Papillon,* the adventuresome memories of an escaped convict, or *Piaf,* the lubricious (and factually misinforming) memories of Edith's half sister, or *Un peu de soleil dans l'eau froide* by Françoise Sagan who, second only to Doris Day, remains my "inavowable" female passion.

Lesser fixtures go, like the Vaudron pastry shop. And there's no more Madame Alice enthroned and immobile behind the zinc of the Reine Blanche. In fact, no more Reine Blanche. No more Arabs. Bigger numbers remain, but are washed clean of character. You now can buy wine in snap-open cans.

The biggest aspect of all—point of view—remains intact. Rightly or wrongly the French have always condescended to cultures beyond their frontiers. Before the New Wave of 1960 they admitted to no American influence, since what, after all, beyond our "barbarism," did we have to offer? Surely not so-called Serious Music. Except for Gershwin's, names like Copland or Harris or Sessions were merely names when I first arrived here, and are merely names still. The "barbarism" of jazz, which they respected (or rather were dazzled by) they quickly mistranslated into Ravel or Josephine Baker. Today they eagerly await *Easy Rider,* thrilled by America's freedom to do her own thing, ignoring that the freedom of the easy riders is no more self-questioning, no less assembly-line than the conformism of the fifty annual Miss America contestants.

5 P.M. This morning, spoke with Georges Auric who three hours earlier debarked from New York, of which his chief impression is that all the actors in *Oh! Calcutta!* are circumcised.

Shopping, Rue de Rivoli. Mostly Lanvin and Rochas colognes. In Galliniani's the British edition of *The Paris Diary*, still at this late date, is prominently displayed. A clerk kept looking anxiously from me to my face on the book cover to me, but I didn't help him—how could I? Massive purchase chez Durand, the same as the purchases we used to make there: Chabrier, Messaien, Satie and, bizarrely, Schumann's *Pièces Fantaisistes*. A final visit to Didier Duclos, so that he could copy some tapes of *Lions* and *Sun*, in the heavy oaken offices of Boosey & Hawkes. Speaking with him of his predecessor, Mario Bois, proved only the Rashomonesque inutility of discussing the man with those who loved or loathed, or loved and loathed, him.

Back now for a nap before this evening's *sortie*.

12 October
Sunday midnight

Less than two days remain. (. . . *Allons plus vit nom de Dieu/Allons plus vit'* . . .) Friday, then, I picked up Jean-Michel Damase where—right next door to my Alma Mater, the Ecole Normale—he lives with his mother, harpist Micheline Kahn to whom Ravel granted the premiere of his *Introduction et Allegro* in 1907. Since we would be supping after the ballet (that gnawing hideous habit—the midnight supper), Jean-Michel now offered me merely some thin cheese sandwiches while he downed three fat whiskies, talking meantime (very man to conservative man) about how "we" will survive *malgré tout*, how his new opera, on a libretto excised by Louise de Vilmorin from her *Madame de*, although only half completed, is scheduled for Bordeaux next spring, and how Pierre Capedevieille is dead. This talk transpired in a parlor indistinguishable from thousands of other ceiling-lit bourgeois French parlors, except that it contained five harps. At 8:50 Jean-Michel introduced me to his beautiful mother, reading alone in her bedroom. Then he drove us in his Citroën, like the still youthful spirit that he is, to the Odéon in time for the 9 o'clock curtain just rising on the execrable Lazzini ballets.

Joseph Lazzini, a second-rate Béjart (himself a second-rate Petit, who is the poor man's Robbins), is terribly up to date with his mixed media, and music by none other than Mossolov—the *Iron*

Foundry, at that! The infinite relief of intermission brought rounds of muscatel at the Méditéranée with Félix Labisse. Saw Nouréev (as the French spell him) in the flesh, and embraced dear Boris Kochno who seemed calm and sober and more Old Russian than ever, and who has just finished a deluxe book on Diaghilev, who, like Cocteau for Marais and Poulenc for Bernac, is the joyful cross he'll bear till death.

Supper: in the now unrecognizable region of Les Halles at an unattractively lit actors' hangout with rubbery food and good wine, where Jean-Michel had a date who turned out to be an acrobat from the Folies-Bergères, of weak intellect, strong beauty and no little self-assurance. Bars until dawn.

Saturday very tired, still a queasy stomach and vaguely *enrhumé*. Party for me at the home of Noël Lee, the favorite of us all, with guests comparatively young. When they all went home, Noël fixed an omelette. I got chills, and went home too.

Still exhausted this afternoon for the rehearsal with Gérard Souzay and Dalton Baldwin. Dalton, cheerful, served tea with cookies swiped from the Hungarian airplane that brought them yesterday from Budapest. Gérard, haunted, no longer just a dapper genius concerned with cultured swooners one recalls at Hélène Jourdan-Morhange's years ago, sounds marvelous, if insecure in English. My cycle, meant for him, indeed sounds meant for him. If they practice hard, and they will, the piece will work.

Went straight to Jeanne Ritcher's where Jacques Février and someone else sat around quibbling for two hours before we went, the four of us, to La Coupole—again those endless late meals. Their company, after the sober dedication of Souzay, seemed glib. Not that I am not superficial too, nor that the presumable courage of admitting the superficiality in any way eliminates it.

La Coupole was swarming and I was bored with being pushed around, the slow service and with my friends' undignified ogling of the indeed hypnotically handsome and enviable *jeunesse dorée*, so I quit them midmeal and taxied across the city to bed.

At the hour of executions an italianate voice said, "*Ne quittez pas, Mademoiselle tient à vous parler,* we've been trying to reach you for days." Indeed, I am seldom home. But Mademoiselle who? Then Nadia Boulanger came onto the phone. "I wanted," she explained, "at least to hear your voice before you left Europe, and to say adieu." Her own tremulous voice, at once vivacious and ancient, belied her semiblindness at eighty-five, and her peculiar generosity which can be defined only through itself, as in these final words: "*Je veux quand même vous dire à bientôt. Evidemment ça ne veut rien dire, mais vous comprenez, pour moi ça doit tout dire.*"

Lunch at Marie Laure's, just the two of us. If, between 1951 and 1957, we lunched in each other's company about 300 times a year, and dined about 175 times a year, mostly in Paris and in Hyères; and if, during the long summers of 1961 and 1964, we again shared, in Hyères, only, an additional 300 meals; then today marks roughly the 3,220th time we've sat down to eat together, of which not more than 100 occasions were tête-à-tête, and fewer still in public and at my expense.

She was entranced with Boulanger's remark, a reaction proving once again—if proof were needed—that she, like Michel Girard, is "good" (there being no love lost between her and Nadia). On the other hand, mention of Julius and Denise gives rise to a screen of ennui merging with her Gauloise smoke, for she still kills three packs daily. Marie Laure hates death. Unlike Perquel, who constantly moons around the subject, she is intolerant even of her friends' sicknesses, and speaks of her own with sarcasm. Or used to. Despite pride in the horoscopic category of Scorpio, her sting is gone. (Born on Halloween, 1902, she claims an astrological link with me, and the link's a mutual pact with the devil of eternal youth.)

As she is almost 100 percent self-involved, a childlike focus blurs her every borrowed opinion now, although her painting is more personal, clear, professional and outgoing than ever. After lunch we spend an hour again inspecting her newest oils, certain of which I praise wholeheartedly, whereupon André is summoned to wrap one as a gift "for America." Another hour is passed thumbing through old scrapbooks: when finding a sudden photo of my former body, I'm stunned less by how the flesh decays (one learns early to blind oneself to that), than by alterations in men's fashion. There we stood, Wilder Burnap, Boris Kochno and me, on the Saint-Tropez jetty in April of 1951, trousers waving like granny skirts at our ankles, in contrast to crew cuts stoically braving the mistral.

Marie Laure escorts me to the great entrance hall where, beside the César sculpture, we say goodbye in the casual manner of our hello twelve days ago. This is the last time we will meet, since tomorrow I leave for London, then New York, and surely she will never return to America where her 1921 honeymoon provided "mixed impressions." Thus our casual kiss embodies an invisible farewell. Though I don't worry about her. As I leave (the wrapped picture neatly under my arm) a wild-haired young painter strewing autumn leaves passes me in the lobby, and goes immediately to embrace the Vicomtesse.

Henry-Louis de La Grange now lives three blocks from Place des Etats-Unis, a four-minute walk in the 5 o'clock sunshine. We passed a strained half-hour in his super-modern sky-high duplex. Strained, because twenty years ago Henry-Louis was a Fauré-playing Boulanger protégé who in turn protected the likes of Barber and Menotti while researching for a "definitive" biography of Mahler. After a series of transmutations, this honest and consecrated young man of means became, three years ago, a first-rank promoter, financially as well as morally, of what the French call avant-garde (while remaining faithful to the still unfinished Mahler book). His current protégé is conductor-impresario Maurice Fleuret with whom he shares this luxury apartment as well as the woolen-eyed eagerness of sound and fury. Our common interests faded, Henry-Louis is nothing if not a gentleman while attempting to explain the "fact" of me to Fleuret who examined, briefly and without interest, my two burnt offerings—*Sun* and *Music and People*. (My cold grew worse, I began getting hives, phoned the Aurics to cancel our goodbye drink.) As we shook hands Henry-Louis thanked me for the information I'd mailed him thirteen years ago: about Mahler, who, during an American visit in the early 1900s, met Charles Ives and planned to program Ives' scores on forthcoming European tours. But Mahler's death annulled the project which might otherwise have changed the international face of music.

Tonight as prearranged, Robert Kanters will take me to Moravia's comedy, symmetrically rounding out my visit with a little sleep.

Hotel Stafford
London
15 October

At Moravia's play I suffered investigatory stares from Christian Mégret, himself hardly the paragon he once was in Venice; later, chez Wepler in the Place Clichy where I invited Robert for a final supper, my once so valuable Jean Leuvrais joined us and cast the same cold eye. My French friends distressed me. The distress became translated into boredom: seeing myself in their eyes, their differentiation dissolved, which hurt, since it lay my infant ego bare. "When next I return," thought I, self-protectively, "you'll all be really old." That's unfair, if unimportant—they don't reason this way.

Still, you *can* go home again, and be welcomed warmly. If the experience proves sad, it's not that home has changed but that you have. To realize that seeing all these old acquaintances, one by one, or tightening professional contacts, or phoning critics and feeling the scene (as though musically it weren't the same everywhere, business, business, the business of pleasure)—to realize that it all equaled not one fresh tomato from the high heaps of tomatoes at the open market there, or the early evening lights on the Rue de la Jonquière, or the troubling midnight *pissotière* where anxiety-ridden heads float disembodied. Paris too floats disembodied, self-contained like a soap bubble, moving directionless, which I loved as a child and no longer need.

Still, my Paris is mine: firsthand reports of facts automatically diminish thirdhand fictions like, say, Frederick Brown's bio-abortion on Cocteau. Impersonally observed, the French capital appears in agony. Her present loveliness is of an autumn maple wearing the heavenly red of death, or of an old whore forced to the reality that cleanliness is next to godliness, yet who has not forgotten the art of applying eye shadow.

London's National Gallery. Very moved, moving from room to room seeing mostly other viewers growing more familiar as our paths crisscross, but seeing old friends too, like Velásquez' Philip IV who, if crossbred with Joan Sutherland, would spawn a shoe. So beautiful, but never, nothing, beautiful enough. The satisfaction emanates not from the pictures but from us.

The Young Lord. No satisfactory emanations whatsoever. At once too skillful and too loose, it cheats. Henze's ideas are less first-rate than their main source, Britten. Britten, whether one likes him or not, is England's first great composer since Purcell. But Britten is an eclectic, not an original, therefore a dangerous model. Henze, in borrowing refinements rather than raw material, debases himself. The set numbers, arias and trios, etc., seem graciously standard, but are not. Once finished they leave no recollection of arch or direction, no tuneful residue. The trouble lies in Henze's focus, or lack of focus, on (to use a metaphor from this afternoon's experience) his basic canvas. A composer like Terry Riley keeps his canvas bare. Ligeti prepares his canvas with blurred mixtures, then abandons it (the listener becomes the foreground). Ives prepares his canvas with blurred mixtures on which he draws a clean melody. But Henze prepares his canvas with blurred mixtures on which he superimposes a final blurred mixture posing as clean melody. In being able to identify and detach this "posed melody" the audience applauds itself, with pride but mirthlessly, since the whole show has been unnourished. The pride is that of a child who extracts a hair from a glass of sour milk.

Tea yesterday with Wilfrid Mellers whose up-to-dateness seems most pedantic. Dined with Basil Horsefield at the White Elephant which served a dessert of huge raspberries in tiny chocolate baskets.

This afternoon, with John Mordler and the forever faithful Jack Henderson, a grand warm family kitchen lunch with Ethel Reiner in the country. Although she can scarcely walk now, stoical Ethel from the neck up remains the very picture of the glamorous American, coiffed and *maquillée* to a T and overflowing with theater talk, while her midriff (she asked us to feel it) is stiffened to marble by an undiagnosable malady.

People born in the same country at other times and places speak separate languages. But although over-forty is very different from over-thirty, we all remain pretty much forever as we were at four. A painter's style may change beyond recognition, but not his signature. To be young is no accomplishment. To be young in heart is abject. Young and New aren't synonymous. The only people as dumb as the young are the old (not forgetting the middle-aged). To be aware in heart is an accomplishment.

New York
23 October

Today is my birthday, bringing me exhausted across the homeland frontier where the customs inspector politely asks:

"You were abroad how long?"

"Twenty-one days."

"Value of your imported purchases?"

"Around fifteen dollars—of Rochas' Rose cologne for my mother."

"Was your trip for pleasure?"

"For pain."

25 October

Souzay premiered *War Scenes* six nights ago in Washington. The reviews, which arrived today, are the best I've ever had.

1 November

A friendly Halloween with Lenny Bernstein, who phoned *à l'improviste*. JH and I invited him to Virgil's where we were going for supper. Virgil also wanted a chocolate cake "from that nice store on Columbus Avenue," since the rest of his menu (ordered from Casserole Kitchen) would be "essentially white."

At seven Lenny came by, casually handsome in a tan turtle-neck, and over a slow drink we relived the death of Bill. At eight we arrived at the Chelsea where the one other guest was Virgil's secretary, a callow swinging playwright who bogged down the conversation by insisting that none of us knew where it's at. (This, apropos of my article in the *Times* "Against Rock," to which Lenny was sympathetic, Virgil indifferent and the playwright hostile.) The meal turned out to be creamed lobster and watercress salad. During its ingestion a massive hijacking occurred in the sky outside.

By eleven Virgil was nodding, so we withdrew into the unseasonable night, walking up Seventh Avenue from 23rd to 57th where we decided to grab a cab, pick up some music, go to Lenny's. At midnight, I performed *Bertha*, playing and singing each role, wishing I had the felicity of my host in being able to put over a bare score. We also played a tape of *Sun*, which Hanson conducted last May, and of Berio's *Sinfonia*. Lenny's working on a large-scale religious piece about which he didn't talk much. At two his daughter returned from a date, thus ending the evening for us all.

Visit this afternoon from Andreas Brown, anxious to procure manuscripts of musical settings of Cummings' poetry. I feel uncertain about this.

6 December

My mother, Gladys Rorem, seventy-two today, donates many hours weekly to the Greenwich Peace Center, to soliciting funds for North Vietnam, to standing on cold corners in favor of abortion, to civil rights, to meetings of the Society of Friends. I do none of this, and am proud of her, as I am Father, for other things.

In Kate Millett's sometimes original book there are sentences which quite miss the point. For instance, on Genet: "Older, distinguished by fame, wealthy and secure, he became a male. . . ." Did he? The highest castes are female, the rich are queens who lust for the lower classes (e.g., Charlus). Nor are the "males" in Genet's work (as described here) wealthy, famous, secure or, previously as youths, "passive." . . .

None of the girls I used to know sees me any more. If one could refer to unique individuals as a breed—Libby Holman, Jean Stein, Gloria Vanderbilt—that breed has dropped me flat. They have their special reasons. And certain women, once married, understandably give up those men they used to court.

Memory is benevolent. It becomes dangerous to renew acquaintance when intermediary years have been fertile. Rubies are strict, inviolable, like art, but one's reaction to rubies can change, even into no reaction at all.

Leo Sowerby has died, and with him recedes farther and farther into the past my own musical beginnings. He was the first professional I ever knew, and his encouragement during my adolescence was the springboard of my career. My first performances (those by Bill Strickland and by Paul Callaway when the War was on) are traceable to contacts made through Leo during those schoolboy harmony lessons. Since he was one of the "older" people I was most anxious to make proud, his dying now makes my own seem more terribly imminent.

New Year's Eve

"And now, to end on an optimistic note!" Why do lecturers all say that, thereby deflating the impact of their presumably pessimistic speech?

So impending are deadlines (like New Year's Eve) that I grow hysterical. Reasoned essays to complete, piano practice for three recitals, music to be composed—all waited for, all expected to be of my "usual caliber." Toward what does such panic impel me, beyond writing this useless paragraph? Passed the morning moronically studding an orange with a thousand cloves.

"There is always one moment in childhood when the door opens and lets the future in," says Graham Greene. Was my door opened in the Chicago of 1930 by those lamé forearms of Mary Wigman? By Garbo, Debussy, Hugh Walpole or The Bobbsey Twins? By study of zoology through breeding birds or by preadolescent mooning over the pages of *Nature Magazine* and *The Well of Loneliness*? None, by definition, of these—these *effects*. Causes, so far as this subject goes, we cannot know, ever. If we could they wouldn't be causes.

If I should die this evening, what could, well, could . . .

The musical road I have long trod—a road whose landmarks and pitfalls are better described by the music itself than by any prose—has narrowed to a thread and reached a dead end on my doorstep. Indeed, only I can get away with the language I sing.

Beware all travellers who ride with me.

I invented you all.

I repent all, retract, abstain forthwith. Can I now assume silence before warning everyone? Did that need for warning flaw the works of my entire life?

Marie Laure used to say these pages reflected a state of mind far less than they reflected a state of body. Do you suppose it's possible to pare narcissism from one's soul? Surely a novelist, *Times* reporter, movie critic is "expressing" himself as much as is a diarist, and the pronoun "I" appears with ever greater frequency in music reviews. And botanists, geometricians, by the nature of things, are more self-absorbed than any of these.

Still, with the New Year, why not attempt less personal tones, or at least less lavish laments on the density of my own sweat, beating others to the draw? Old saws are always wrong: After a certain age any leopard can change his spots.

1970

. . . how few of life's days and hours (and they not by relative value or proportion, but by chance) are ever noted.

—Walt Whitman

New Year's Day

And what have all these words to do with me? Or with anyone, for that matter. That anxious need to express and to document is gone; nor can the need be realized: expression, no sooner emitted, changes shape and sense, and thus will not be fact or document. There are no documents, no facts. There is no immortality. Of that which we were, nothing remains. A Bach fugue is itself, it is not Bach. An equation of Einstein is itself, not Einstein. Chartres is itself, not generations of builders, nor love of the Lord, nor even that thrill of eternity small poets feel. Perfection is mute.

Yet on I plod. For if a song of mine is no longer me, it still could not have been without my help.

24 January

This afternoon at Rutgers Church, during a space of four hours, Eugene Istomin and Donald Gramm recorded *War Scenes* and five other songs on Whitman texts for Desto label. The result is satisfying to a point of tears: I've heard no better performance of any of my music by anyone ever, nor can it—need it—be surpassed.

To celebrate, took Eugene with Shirley and JH to Casey's.

26 January

This noon at Florence Kimball's, young soprano Joyce Mathis rehearsed a dozen of my songs which she will "interpret visually" on a Ford-sponsored TV show in Michigan next month. Very pretty, as was her pianist.

At 1:30, taped a broadcast about Bill Flanagan, with Howard Moss on Virgil's weekly show. Hearing the playback this evening

315

over WNCN was odious. That arrogant testy tone I took with Virgil whose guest I after all was!

29 January

Marie Laure is dead.
    The fact alone seems all that can be registered.

30 January

Such things don't happen.
    At 6:30 in the afternoon, about to go out, I found a cablegram slipped under the door, *Marie Laure died this morning very sad love James,* from James Lord. First reaction: God planned the brief return to Paris last October so that after so long an absence I could say goodbye to friends condemned, and so that others who will survive could say goodbye to me.
    But I went on by inertia to Arnold Weissberger's flamboyant party. JH was waiting when I got home, and I cried for the first time in years. We drafted an appropriate cable, which like all such messages was inappropriate. (Listened to Igor Kipnis broadcast my *Spiders* on WBAI. Hard to concentrate.)
    This morning the *Times* carried a reasonably large obituary considering how little known she was here. Emphasis on the 1930s. Her activities as a painter after 1945 were ignored.
    Phone calls from Jerry Lowenthal, John Gruen and Lenny Bernstein, to me as bereaved widow.
    Just a week ago today Janet Flanner came to talk about Marie Laure regarding an introduction for Horst's book on the thirties. My every remark now seems impertinent, as though there were a moral difference (there isn't) between what we say of the quick and of the newly dead.

4 February

Purple.
    "I don't believe you really have those dreams, you make them up," she purred in lovely iambs over tea.

Do thought waves function in time-space terms? Throughout the universe Now is stable, invariable, is now. Hypothesis: if your lover spends the weekend in a galaxy a million light years away, will your ESP communication be instantaneous, or will it have to "travel"?

Seeing the earth as photographed from the moon, the two moving together, seeing the little earth which housed our close cousins Hannibal, Shakespeare, Eleonora Duse, seeing that blue, blue world, gave rise to fraternal sweat.

Discouraged.

12 February

Yesterday, rehearsal at noon, John Stewart. At 4:30, taping at WKCR of me interviewing Bob Abramson (I'm now the elder, posing unctious questions to the young). Today, rehearsal at noon with Anita Darian.

Not an hour goes by that I'm not struck by the force of Marie Laure. As though a parent had vanished. Or a child. . . .

She was the sound and soul of France, and my only teacher. What need to go back?

14 February

Recordings keep any listener abreast of the times by keeping him at home. Not having been to a piano recital in years, I found myself at two within a week, standard fare by friends: Jerry Lowenthal playing Liszt and Bartók, Zaidee Parkinson playing Schumann and Debussy. Zaidee's audience was amateur in the real sense (creative and well off but not very musical), while Jerry's was professional (or, as they say in Rent Control, semiprofessional—students with scores in their laps). The performers' performances resembled their audiences.

A performance can also resemble its title, as was the case last night with "Music by Women Composers"—though this may not be the historic moment to say it with tact. The music, presided over by a blue-haired dowager, turned out to be placid sonatinas and settings of haiku. If the Whitney's current show of Women painters asks to be judged on merit regardless of sex, the same could not be done for this concert: a blind man would hear this as Ladies' Music, an epithet understandably disgusting to serious composers who happen to be female.

Valentine's Day, Love continues tranquil (comparatively) and productive.

Washington's Birthday

Yesterday, long melting letter from Henri Hell detailing the funeral of Marie Laure. According to him, the past, like a slap in the face, became the present again for all of Paris, if briefly, at her death which occurred exactly one week after that of old Tony Gandarillas whom she herself had escorted to the hospital. She hated death, or rather, *avoided* it. Only sixty-seven, she was "taken" before the horrors of old age overcame her. Had she survived, it would have meant total paralysis. Displayed on her death bed, dewrinkled and placid with an inscrutable smile, she resembled the photographs from 1925, the Picasso portrait, the studies of Beaton, Balthus, Berman. Funeral on a rainy day at Saint-Pierre-de-Chaillot, vast assembly of great names, of unknowns, of servants dissolving in whimpers around a catafalque of red velvet, the Noailles coat of arms, thousands and thousands of white bouquets and mysterious young men.

In her last hours Marie Laure—the renegade surrealist, the *non-croyante*, the Jew, the artist—called for a priest.

Both her houses, Saint Bernard in Hyères and the Hôtel de la Place des Etats-Unis, are already up for sale. *Quelle tristesse.*

28 February

In Morgantown, West Virginia, for a Rorem Festival organized by the indefatigable Carolyn Reyer, with the Seneca Glass Factory, the extraordinary house of the (Frances Yeend) Benners, the golden youth, the sparrow-drab wives, a bad cold, master classes and TV interviews promoting me as sinner.

Forty years' delay, and *Mahagonny* gets mounted in America by Capalbo. This utterly original opera was shown privately in Marie Laure's ballroom in 1932, but on this side of the Atlantic we've had our appetite whetted only through the printed score, Lenya's wheezy old disk and the translations by Auden and by Blitzstein.

So wrong! Lacking the courage of his publicized convictions, Capalbo (reportedly waiting a decade to "come back" through Weill) updated the piece with dirty hip lyrics, television, a rock band. Charmless actors emanated nothing but hate over which was imposed an aura of Masterpiece, alien and smug. Left intact, *Mahagonny* might have proved to "date well" (as Stravinsky said of Varèse), but this version precludes all others for a generation.

Afterward, cherry blintzes at Ratner's with Shirley, JH and George Perle.

This afternoon: total eclipse.

If the aleatory by definition cannot be calculated, why does John Cage so often succeed? Answer: through personal charm.

Finished my translation of *Mateo Falcone* for Robert Phelps' Mérimée series. Far harder than I'd imagined. I admire Richard Howard more than ever.

With JH, gave a well thought-through dinner party last night (stroganoff, Miss Grimble's cheesecake with my own apricot glaze) for these six: Jane Wilson and John Gruen, Sylvia Marlowe and Leonid Berman, Francis Steegmuller and Shirley Hazzard. No reason, beyond admiration for them all. But it fell flat. I'm not a grand hostess, don't know how to keep the ball rolling and (grave flaw) lose interest when conversation flies off on its own, away from my center. Washed dishes until four in the morning.

17 March

Today, Saint Patrick's Day. Bread-and-butter notes from Shirley
Hazzard, and from her husband who adds: "I don't usually send
obituaries in return for good company, but perhaps you haven't
seen these"—clippings from *Le Monde* and *France Soir* detailing the
deaths of Marie Laure, Louise de Vilmorin and the quasi-grotesque
demise of Charles de Bestigui, whose ball in the Palazzo Labbia I
attended nineteen years ago with Marie Laure. Louise I encountered no more than three or four times, but to meet her once was to
know her: like Cocteau she *gave* completely, never stopped talking.
Those clover bows in her straight hair, her famous limp, her famous
brothers and lovers (Jean Hugo, Malraux), her famous verse through
which, as set in the songs of Poulenc, I mastered the French
language, though that was no help with cab drivers when I first
arrived in Paris.

20 March

Shyness: I'm not indulgent of it in others because I'm still so shy
myself (which no one believes because of my diaries, but doesn't the
fact of them prove it?). Horror of entering a room. To go onstage is
easy: there's no personal contact.

Shyness is never rewarded, and unfeigned shyness uncontrolled
and constant I've no pity for. Only the stupid are not shy, but that's
no justification for the sensitive. I vanquished it, why can't they?

A diary may be trivial in format, but is actually more selective than
a journalist's column. Mine, in favoring the seemingly urgent—personalities, heartbreak, alcohol, premieres of my music—omits the
truly urgent: daily labor. I seldom write of childhood, of current
geography.

The only diary besides Daisy Ashford's, which makes of the
quotidian a literary virtue, is the eighteenth-century "old maid"
who noted her long untarnished life with another woman in the hills
of Wales, an optimist's version of Beckett's *Happy Days*. Yet if this
were not all quoted within the context of a larger journal—the

infallible Colette's *Ces Plaisirs* (pp. 155–86)—how far could its literary virtue be pushed?

Letter from Natalie Perrone, Marie Laure's younger daughter in Rome, replying to my condolence, and saying she's off to Hyères with her father and her sister Laure for Easter to see about closing the house. Can I imagine how she's dreading it? Those rooms . . .

April Fool's Day

This diary no longer even reflects emergencies. But if they were there to reflect, I would not be in a position to write. Since 19 December 1967 my domestic life has changed so radically that the frenzied highs and lows which characterized the earlier years are gone. I do not smoke or drink or fuck or use foul language. I work and proselytize, and am content and bitter.

6 April

In Tully Hall last night Thomas Scherman began conducting *Eleven Studies for Eleven Players*. After five minutes it became clear that the players were sabotaging the conductor with my music as weapon. After thirteen minutes, or roughly halfway through the piece, I got up and walked out. (The *Post* today reports a beautiful performance of a beautiful work!)

I've rarely enjoyed hearing my music in public unless I'm performing, and hence tangibly responsible for the catastrophe. To sit impotent during a massacre is to be blamed for the massacre in place of the massacrers. Even during a glorious rendition I am uneasy, embarrassed by those sounds thought up too long ago to cover my present nakedness.

26 April

Alone to *The Rake's Progress* at the new Juilliard theater. At the Venetian premiere in 1951 I had found it stale but was afraid to admit it. Everyone was saying, "Why do people call it a pastiche when it's pure Stravinsky?" It *is* pastiche, and quite impure. A few very inspired tunes, but the libretto's overrefined with In-jokes and the prosody's burlesque. I left before the last act. (The babble of that international Venetian cast! Schwarzkopf's German accent, Tourel's Jewish accent, Roundsville's Broadway accent, Cuénod's nonaccent from Switzerland, and the Englisheries of dear Nell Tangeman's two or three hardworked lines.)

Today, visit from Madeleine Renaud and Michel de Ré, shepherded by Jean de Rigault. It is Sunday, spring has settled in, and the vast environs of Bethesda Fountain resplendently resemble the Place Jemâa-el-Fnâa minus cobras and flame-swallowers but with the addition of forsythia and four simultaneous bands. I wished, as I walked there at noon, that our French friends could enjoy it, but darkness fell when they arrived at six, so instead I gave them whisky, chocolate cheesecake and the adoration of Shirley and Eugene.

Renaud, here in Beckett's *Oh les beaux jours*, is so excruciatingly a fine actress that our American theater turns all to farce beside her. She knows her own language, which can be said for no one in American plays, and for very few in American songs.

Alternating in two plays of Pinget, Michel de Ré looks cuter and thinner than in the days when his then wife Heddy, mother to his daughters, was my valued daily companion.

In 1953 or 1954 I last saw Madeleine Renaud with Barrault at Marie Laure's in Hyères, and later Michel de Ré that same summer. Michel seems uncertain about the whereabouts of Heddy who remains apparently pretty and a bit drunk. Madeleine meanwhile reports that Denise Bourdet's sister has committed suicide in Bordeaux. They both add that Paris *n'est plus gai en ce moment*, indeed nothing's the same since the Events of May '68 which were in part abetted by the Living Theater.

American stars are aloof and grand. French stars are artificially warm. Madeleine tutoies me, and wonders why we couldn't have long known each other better, which makes me want to marry her when I grow up.

Columbia, South Carolina
30 April

Many months ago James Dickey invited me to join a two-day symposium at his university in South Carolina. The other guests will be Richard Lippold, John Simon and John Barth. We will give separate talks, and the final morning conjointly participate in a round table. It makes me nervous to go south.

In the waiting room at Kennedy Airport John Simon, whom I've met exactly once (with Maggie Paley during an intermission) but whom I admire, approaches and says in French that he'd wanted to phone me last night, figuring we'd be on the same plane, but couldn't find the number, and did I know where the toilets were? he has to pee. When he comes back he continues in English. It turns out he's in second-class and I'm in first (whenever a contract states that expenses are included, I get a first-class ticket, don't you?), but since the plane's half empty I sit in his section and we talk all the way, on our best behavior. Seems he was friendly, years ago, with Janet Lauren, a singer from Curtis days who told him then to send his poems to me. His *poems*!

Upon landing in the hot South we are each assigned a serf, and separated into our various chambers where I take a bath and collect my faults (I meant to write thoughts), since I'm the first of the four events and my speech is set for tonight.

Dine tête-à-tête with one Ashley Brown, friend of Elizabeth Bishop, who then delivers me to the auditorium where Dickey introduces me ("Now I don't know about his music, but if you ain't read his *Paris Diary*, you ain't read anything"), and I read *The Poetry of Music*, followed by a well-amplified playing of Eugene and Donald's taped performance of *War Scenes*, and a question period. Questions below par, as happens with non-musical specialists. (Simon surprisingly belabors a fact: Didn't Duparc write fourteen songs, rather than thirteen?)

Party. Talk at length with Morse Peckham, and am nervous by the impression I'm making in this foreign land. Very hot with the smell of magnolia, or so it seems.

1 May

10 A.M., Richard Lippold's speech, more casual and charming than mine, about creative method.

Noon, lunch with music department in a revolving penthouse restaurant. Free-for-all confab with music students in a rather sad building.

John Barth reading, at 2:30, which I couldn't understand, from a book in progress, about the Greek wars.

Dined with Lippold in his woolly sweater, and at eight we go to John Simon's lecture, dapper and brittle, about movies.

Huge party at the Dickeys' on Lake Katherine.

2 May

The round table this morning was not good. Without rehearsal, strong egos can't carry off ensemble numbers. But I made new friends and a thousand dollars.

The Settlement
Music School
Cleveland
4 May

When he met the plane this afternoon, Burton Garlinghouse's first words were, "It's a bad time for a concert." Apparently some protesting students at nearby Kent University had been hurt, maybe killed. . . . By evening we learn that four of them are dead.

Rehearsed several hours with young Penelope Jensen and Steven Szaraz who give a program of my songs here tomorrow. Both first-rate.

Alone then in a strange city I took a walk, and got lost in the confines of Western Reserve campus where a midnight peace march was taking place. Hundreds upon hundreds of silent students, each with a lighted candle, walked single file or in pairs curving endlessly through the dark around dormitories and tennis courts veering toward the lake and Severance Hall, like the monks at the end of *Lost Horizon*. I feel impotent, an outmoded Quaker.

A sense of danger, the air's grown cold, Cleveland is ugly and Lake Erie stinks.

5 May

Interview this morning with Martin Perlich on WCLV in the Terminal Tower (terrible name, like Cancer Ward), then lunch with him and Robert Conrad in a dark hotel on this bright day.

The city is clearly tense, with everywhere a feeling not of lament but belligerence. Practiced piano three hours.

At tonight's performance *War Scenes* made more sense than when I composed it, with texts on needless murder and the pain of the very young. Yet I am the last person to admit the possibility of political music.

Afterward, a big friendly non-New Yorkish reception with Protestant cookies.

6 May

Four-hour seminar on my songs this morning. Lunch with Louis Lane at the museum. Another two-hour class in the afternoon. An 8:55 plane back to the East Coast where now I am, I guess.

9 May

Finished orchestration of the *Piano Concerto*.

16 May

Philadelphia this afternoon for wedding of my oldest nephew, Christopher Marshall. The reception for him and Anita during the evening, in a suburban outpost, was the most *gemütlich* I've ever attended, because there was no *reason* for it—no *professional* reason—beyond the cause of marriage. Chatted about Fauré with Linda Van Steenwyk who's writing her doctorate on him, and ate four kinds of homemade spice cake.

28 May

We gave a dinner party last night for: Sondra Lee and Harlan Klieman, Ellen Adler and David Oppenheim, and Virgil Thomson. After-dinner guests: John Simon and Sharon Mitchell, and later still, Edward Albee with friend. Boring, fractious, drunken, rude. Everyone lit into poor John Simon, now that he was palpable, like sharks into bloody meat, centering on the wound he'd dealt Zoe Caldwell last week. Not that he hadn't asked for it: no sooner arrived than he drew forth and read aloud proudly a letter from Sheldon Harnick, addressed to the editors of *New York* magazine, canceling a subscription because of their ignoble drama critic. Virgil (unclear about JS's identity) sang a solo on how critics, although it's their duty to expose the mediocre, should do so with regret, not with relish. Edward meanwhile, too tight to stand, pointed a shaking finger and declared that when he became president of the something or other he would see that John Simon was the first to fall, while the friend sat on the floor babbling dirty words.

John phoned this morning to ask if I had staged it.

29 May

On rereading the epitaph confected for the Flanagan Memorial program some weeks ago, I find it not bad, especially as complement to the pedagogical appraisal written for the ACA Bulletin ten years earlier. Yet how is another's humor captured, retained, then transmitted in words from me to you?

I avoided unprofessional essentials—like his descent counterbalanced by Edward's rise, obvious to all but always skirted as an artistic *donnée;* like his jealousy of, or at least his competition with, me (he once confessed that, knowing himself to be no less talented than me but without the strokes of fortune, he had emulated for a time my every gesture, my every seeming motive, my every presumably opportunistic move, even to learning how I wrote business letters and then writing similar letters to the same people); like his victory of mind over matter under the aegis of Doctor Protetch who shed him of eighty pounds in three months so that at forty-four he might dance nightly with the twenty-two-year-olds of the Stonewall.

But the humor? Bill's parents attended the memorial. His mother has since written me a few heartbreaking notes, posing those "simple" questions that stump the masters: "Why did he do it? *Did* he do it? Was it an accident? Where was my mistake?" She has also kindly returned a mass of letters I wrote to Bill between 1948 and 1969. Now these, intertwined with the forty-odd letters from Bill to me, contain precisely that vitality which the essays lack, even considering that a whole segment seems lost or deleted by the Flanagan estate. (Bill and I had the habit of corresponding in the style of eighteenth-century pornography, using archaic euphemisms for Manhattanesque perversions, and picturing ourselves as well-heeled but miserably unhappy sisters in a Laclos novel.) The exchange is snide, frisky, musical only in a professional way (we never discuss theory) and intelligent in that we don't discuss intelligent things, we assume them. Is anything more classically *déchirant* than rereading youth?

15 June

Ten days ago, coinciding with the death of E. M. Forster, my two plays, *The Pastry Shop* and *The Young Among Themselves*, thanks to the enterprise of Robert Haddad, finally opened for a three-week run at The Extension Theater, with attractive players (Sue Lawless, Cecily Floyd, Mary Boylan, Bennett Yahya), attractive sets and costumes (Jim Hardy, Roseanna Richardson), and a press that has been unanimously if compassionately negative (consensus: I should stick to my songs).

Presumably an artist wants his work judged on merit, although his promoters (and often he himself) hasten to cite extenuating circumstances. Not as an excuse, then, but as a touristic curiosity do I situate these plays as period pieces, from 1959 and 1960. They remain intact, unchanged, though both are overstuffed with symbolism which today makes me cringe. They placed a shroud on the 1950s, which ended with the burgeoning of off-Broadway. Both works are about words, and both most headily about the heart. If both draw liberally and literally from diaries of that already distant decade, they are not, for that, autobiographical: out of context the passages quoted are as different as fish in a lake and on a skillet.

These plays are my only fiction. As such, ten years ago, I

showed them to everyone, and received fifty reactions. Here, for instance, is a telegram from Ruth Ford in October 1960: *I just think* The Pastry Shop *the most marvelous divine beautiful thing I've ever read it has to be mine for me no one else.* And this, a week later, from Carl Van Vechten: *Dear Old Ned, I have never thought of you writing prose, but you have turned out a brilliant bit of bravura. Of course it should be played by a male whore in drag. . . .*

To less eager reactions I rationalized: "I've nothing to lose, having no ambitions in the theater; I'm just a composer diverting himself." That *is* an excuse—one that will hardly rescue me now as I watch the composer-playwright I used to be, fade, gradually, into a domain more distant than his infancy. Nevertheless it was precisely that combination of incentives which led to these plays.

Imitation is the cruelest form of flattery. The most lasting reaction came from a youngish playwright who read these plays, then adapted each trick of mine as a trick of his own, most notably in *America Hurrah!*: the spoken fugue, the vicarious landlady, the young couple who write on the wall, the final gratuitous demolition of the set. Of course, we were "saying" different things, and anyway ideas are not only cheap, they're free. Artists have borrowed from each other since the beginning, and only our century puts a premium on what's called Originality. Why not admit where I myself found the devices (though not their results) for this double bill of rooms. The suicidal young couple are Annabella and Jean-Pierre Aumont in *Hôtel du Nord.* And if smashing the décor has come to be the obligatory finish for many a Now drama—most recently in *Coming Apart*—I arrived at the notion in reverse. As a child I was taken to see Nazimova in *The Cherry Orchard.* That actress, during the long ending minutes, in silence sadly moved through her room from object to object, caressing each for the last time ever, then left, while the curtain fell to the faraway sound of axes.

21 June

In search of librettos I visited Paul Goodman for the first time in years where he lives with Sally across from the gardens of General

Theological Seminary. He complains of The Young, how they don't understand him, neither his ideas nor, indeed, his grammar.

Do you understand their not understanding you?

Yes.

Is it possible they understand your concern that they don't understand?

No. But then, they don't fall in love any more.

Still, they did five years ago, and will five years hence. Love goes in quick generations. Does love help or hinder work, especially your work, so much of which stems from—smells of—love? Oh, if only I weren't in love I'd find time to compose a love poem.

They're embarrassed when he reads his poetry aloud, so he counteracts by reading them Milton's "personal" sonnet on blindness.

Yes, but Milton himself didn't read that sonnet to them. If someone else read your poems to them they'd be less embarrassed. How can they chat man-to-man with you about, say, fucking, when you've just read them a poem about fucking, and your own formal poem to boot (and your own fucking)? Granted, they weren't reared for active participation in Christmas carols, but for reactive participation in folk-rock. It's you they don't understand, not your ideas. For if, as you claim, they do hang around and seem to want something though they aren't sure what, we both know that they want your patronage, your advice, your approval, which they'll take and use up and throw away, as youth must.

(Until recently I never understood Paul's poem *The Dead Cichlid* because I didn't know a cichlid was a fish. I thought he had, in choked emotion, mistyped the word child, and saw that it was good.)

22 June

What is more tiresome than another's sorrow? It dehumanizes, renders dull, especially after forty. Like precocity, unhappiness is unseemly to the middle-aged. Breast-beating, however, is no property of today's young, that being an individual gesture and the young now being outraged collectively. They don't write Miltonian sonnets but act conjointly in peace marches. Misery in youth was once beguiling, a charming act that sometimes led to suicide. In the old it's not an act. But the reality could be prevented if the old learned not to fall in love with the young. Tears flowing down saggy cheeks are more embarrassing than tender.

An author, inasmuch as he writes about tragedy that befalls him, uses that tragedy to his advantage. A composer has no such definite raw material.

Tonight, last performance of my double bill at The Extension. Afterward, with JH, prepared a succulent buffet for thirty people we hardly know.

Tomorrow, leave for Peterborough.

Peterborough
28 June

The MacDowell Colony again.

Pretty weather, malcontent, *Anne of a Thousand Days*, Margaret Croyden and Marvin Brown, sunsets on Monadnock, *The Longest Journey*, spiders in fog, Rust Hills, rain, rain, strawberries and chameleons, Noel Sokoloff turned holy father, Paul Earls and George Costinescu, *The Seagull* by the British being badly Russian on TV, Maeve Brennan in the flesh.

2 July

There has been a Gay-In. The last oppressed group has had its first say. (Group, not Minority. Women, after all, are a majority, and so on a world scale are Blacks. Nor is it demonstrable that homosexuals are a minority.) So, despite brave frivolity, homosexuality gets an official seal.

Yet it remains the last group (along with policemen!) subject to derision, spoken or unspoken, from all classes, including presumably tolerant intellectuals. (A beaming reference by Norman Mailer, on the Dick Cavett show, to Sade as a faggot, gets a nervous laugh—nervous only because people wonder who Sade is.) The biggest bigot has less contempt for the negritude of Negroes or the womanhood of Women than for the queerness of Queers. For women or Negroes he feels fear or maybe pity. Contempt he reserves for those who have made a wrong choice. Homosexuals, as opposed to women or Blacks, are felt to have chosen freely. It may one day be shown that they *have*. What then needs to be shown is that the choice wasn't wrong. A woman, a Negro, whatever status they finally gain, will remain visibly woman and Negro. A homosexual, in principle, may choose to be invisibly so.

On the same page of *The Village Voice* we read Jonathan Black's compassionate report of the Gay-In and Barbara Long's caustic reference to fags. Bernard Berenson, in his last journals which I was perusing today, comments with refined distaste on Gide's "buggery." (For the record, those who would know maintain that Gide was not at all impelled to the act of buggery. His sexuality, when not simply vicarious, was no more "responsible" or "sophisticated" than anonymous masturbation of little boys in darkened movie theaters. Mauriac, from his reformed Catholic heights, publicly lamented his colleague's wicked ways. During the war an anecdote circulated about Gide's making love with an Algerian youth. Gide tells the boy, "You've just slept with France's greatest author." "Yeah? What's your name?" "François Mauriac.")

Less than ten days in this honeyed clime where despite the mosquitoes I have proudly completed a *Gloria* (nine songs in Latin for two voices and piano, so singers will no longer complain about a dearth of duets), and four mini-operas on Marianne Moore's succulent translations of La Fontaine. Although I've made seven new friends, read all the plays of Hofmannsthal, Molière, Pirandello and James Merrill, and seen four movies, I miss JH and want to go home.

New York
19 July

With disbelief we witnessed a movie called *Joe*—which could have been called *Laurel and Hardy Meet the Hippies* for all its "unpalatable truths about us all," to quote Judith Crist in *New York* magazine.

Crist stated she'll never again take seriously the critical writings of Rex Reed, having seen him in *Myra Breckinridge*.

Understandable (he's terrible) if unfair (you don't censor a critic for being an actor). But it is not unfair to say that Crist's own performance, as critic on home ground, can never again be trusted.

Dennis Patrick's Compton, a one-dimensional jellyfish, could never hold down a $60,000-a-year job. Audrey Claire, though prettier than Marguerite Dumont, emulates the latter's contempt of the Lower Classes who eat with their hands, the youths are uniformly ill-bred cruelly criminal junkies unselective as call girls but with less reason.

The two principals, both evil, are "sympathetic," not finally with the naturalism which begins the film, but as hams milking laughs. ("Offices are all made of paper." Miss Crist's office too?)

One imagines conferences: We'll have a scene where the hard-hat and the rich guy smoke pot, a series of gag scenes contrived to make a Situation Tragedy. Etc.

Alitalia Flight #619
New York–Rome
21 July (Tuesday)

Less than one week ago an American representative of RAI invited me to participate on a TV round table in Rome next Monday, and I who virtually never act on impulse (this for me is impulse) accepted. A free return to the holy city of thrilling misery where, in the cold season of 1954–55 (Italy, thinking herself tropical, was never then equipped with central heating) I languished for P and composed *The Poets' Requiem*. As an omen, probably good, who should be now sitting here on the plane but Harold Stevenson, last seen in the Paris of 1964 when his 88x90-foot portrait of El Cordoba was exhibited from the Eiffel Tower and rained upon, now en route to an empty villa in the Neapolitan environs which he plans to furnish next fall.

Our suppers consumed with Valium, our gossip concluded, we now attempt to sleep, but cannot.

> *Hotel Forum*
> *Via Tor de' Conti 25–30*
> *23 July*

Chaotic arrival, serious hotel mix-up (RAI had booked me into the hideous Hilton which was fortunately overflowing), but, thanks to the patience of Harold Stevenson, I've ended up here near the Foro Imperiali where in this late afternoon we breakfast, unslept and alfresco, on greasy shrimp. (Somewhere Auden begins a stanza about arriving in a country whose dignitaries whisk him off to his duties—*Unshaved and unshat.*)

Walk to American Express. This being the first visit since the 1957 honeymoon with PQ, it's quickly clear that contrary to the standard trick of recall, distances seem far longer than shorter, so in the fair blue I arrive just before closing time. No air-conditioning, Amexco smells like a girls' locker room, and during long long minutes I become a tourist and not a guest.

Messages from Guglielmo Biraghi, Frazier Rippy, Alexei Haieff, Gian-Franco Zaffrani.

Frazier and I make a date for nine. Meanwhile (while I shower and sleep) he will phone the Hassler, the Excelsior, anywhere, to spring me from this *albergo*. (No dice. He called nine hotels, all full of visiting firemen, and despite his plea on behalf of "an illustrious American Maestro," he was marvelously told there were no rooms—*nemméno per Beethoven.*)

His plus-twenty Roman years have brought Frazier far out of the Bobby Breen plumpness we first knew in Chicago's grammar school and deep into an ultra-leanness of the papal secretary he embodied in Fellini's *8½*. Yet no change in his manner which was already European, or at least Whartonian, when he was ten. Through his eyes I retrieve a town of which he is no less proprietary than Romulus himself. We dine in the Jewish ghetto, stroll mile upon unfatigued logical mile to collapse over midnight *gelati* in Piazza Navone where a febrile stranger approaches with a friendly "Hello, Ned." Who the hell? Someone from high school? I introduce Frazier, and the stranger says, "You don't recognize me? It's Gore."

Gore Vidal on the phone this morning seems not so much depressed as apologetic that I'd not recognized him. "I've aged terribly," he explains, inviting me to dine tonight. "There'll be Camilla Pecci too, but we can still talk tail."

Meanwhile a taxi to Parioli for lunch with Guglielmo. How sensible, this unplanned village. The thousand autos crisscross yet rapidly advance, no odor of gas, and a sky, unlike New York's, more benevolent than indigo crystal. (Is indigo crystal benevolent?) The hundred-degree light does not oppress, the million tourists do not offend and, suddenly lighthearted, I feel at home here where fifteen years ago I felt foreign.

Guglielmo receives me alone, surrounded by gold-framed portraits of his beautiful wife. An orange-carpeted twining staircase leads to the dining room where a not-young maid serves us creamed veal.

Guglielmo too has aged, with handsome gray temples, no longer aspiring, arrived—upon the nonglorious settled plateau of film critic who writes acceptable plays. We talk of old times for as long as we can, then he drives me back through the paradisaical sun to Via Veneto whence I return *in piedi* to this cool room, order tea and petits fours, bathe in a circular pool of Balenciaga cologne, read until six, then take a two-hour nap in anticipation of another of the thorough visits Gore Vidal and I have been having quadriannually since 1949.

24 July

Arriving hungry at exactly 8:30 I knocked on the dark wood door (hung with a poster for the movie *Myra Breckinridge*), and Gore ushered me immediately onto a shabbily lavish roof garden, saying, "Some day all this will be yours." He inhabits what Americans would rightly call a penthouse (slumping edifice), though it's only four flights up, calmly overlooking the frantic Piazza Argentina and, in the other direction, San Pietro wearing a lavender halo in the sunset.

Howard Austen is there, and a handsome frail English girl. Gore and Howard have the top floor, a circular sequence of high-ceilinged chambers, a bit crumbling and expensive like palaces in Paris, with ten-ton antique beds and old velvet bed-tables on which are *Partisan Review* and *The Atlantic Monthly* (the latter containing an article on critics by our host), and, unostentatiously, a copy of Howard's *The Myra Breckinridge Cookbook* on the cover of which actress Joan Collins is eating a banana. The kitchen is spacious, and there seems to be a lot of orange juice around, but no sign of a meal in progress, nor of a maid. ("We dismiss the maid at five because the bunnies come at five-thirty, and then we take naps until the real guests show up at eight.")

Camilla arrives, we are served champagne in jelly glasses (I have orange juice), Gore looks more rested and collegiate than last night, and it is clear we are meant to converse until ten-thirty.

"Sartre's in town. He was at the bank this afternoon. I *observed* him. For an hour he waited in line patiently, neither carped nor demanded priority. He was, so to speak, controlling his meditations. People his age, you know, are less hurried than we are, less concerned by time passing." (His age? But he's only sixty-four and you're already forty-six. We're closing in on him each day. Surely the old are *more* concerned than we about time passing; and we—are no longer We Young.)

I didn't ask if *he* had demanded priority by speaking to Sartre or if, indeed, they had ever met. Possibly Sartre does not know that much about Gore Vidal, and obviously Gore admires Sartre. We are silenced only by those we admire, and a body is no less intimidating than a mind.

Gore is American in seeing greatness as an aspiration rather than as a *fait accompli* (and in the way he wears his hair), but he's French in that small talk becomes big, nothing's unimportant, there's little letup, guests must all be alert. We finally repaired to the Campo di Fiori and dined outdoors in the shadow of the Palazzo Farnese.

He says: that he heard this morning from Paul Bowles ("What did he write? Oh, you know, he tells you what he had for breakfast"); that he doesn't have hangovers, and works out daily at a gym—a Roman gym; that my diaries are the last statement on romantic love which he's been able to read without laughing; that freedom (apropos of bondage in Bulgaria where some friends are shooting a movie) is perhaps not the natural state of man; that sheer avarice led him to approve the filming of *Myra Breckinridge* (which he pretends not to have seen); that he shall next year buy property in Ireland where art is tax-deductible; that he prefers the mental company of women ("I'd rather dine with, say, Claire Bloom, than with any man I know"); that the lawsuits between him and Buckley are not a joke and may well be resolved in his disfavor; that the reason he's effective on talk shows is that he spends only two or three minutes plugging his new book or whatever, then uses the remaining precious time on "important things," like ecology or Vietnam; and that America is slated for quick demolition. He doesn't waste words, is always onstage.

I'm sympathetic to virtually everything *chez lui* except the cynical stance. Those steely epigrams summing up all subjects resemble the bars of a cage through which he peers defensively. "It's not that love's a farce—it doesn't exist." Defensible. Yet it's just one definition, of something without definition. Rather than risk being called a softy, he affects a pose of weariness, adapted in part from Paul Bowles (who in 1950 wrote: "I myself should think it would be quite impossible to *fall in love* with an Arab, as I had always thought it went without saying that no one ever did such a thing. It would surely be a sad waste of time. One might as well fall in love with a shark"). Still, Paul remains in Morocco and Gore in Italy. These are romantic decisions as well as practical. Vulnerability is a major factor in any artist's makeup. To disguise the fact is merely another way of making art.

Again I felt: with all that virtuosic intelligence (not to mention raw charm and a certain talent) he eludes the big scope. That's masochistic, because it is not the big scope which eludes him. Greatness, or whatever you want, cannot come to one who chooses to stand above his material, indifferent to hate.

The night had turned cool. At 2 a.m. I walked Camilla through the Vecchia Roma to her mother's house in Piazza Aracoeli, where years ago the solitude was cut by hospitality, and then fled over the haunted expanse separating this site from my warm rented room.

25 July

Lunch yesterday on the roof of this hotel with Frazier; then a stroll with him on the Palatine beneath hot, dry, clear, lean, orchid skies.

Frazier pointed: "Way over there is the pensione where your sister stayed in 1965 on the way to Uganda. The concierge told me, when I stopped by, that she was out on the hill with her children. And so over there"—he grandly turned and pointed another way—"is where I first saw Rosemary again, after a quarter century, sitting in the grass surrounded by her brood like a *fin de siècle* Sargent study in pale yellows and greens, with the rosy cheeks of the young. John's dead now, and everything's changed."

We descended into the city, made purchases in Via Frattina of soft wool scarves for Rosemary and Mother, went for cappuccino to Café Greco, promised to meet Sunday.

Dined with Alexei Haieff who resides oh quite comfortably in Palazzo Doria. Mark Schubart there too, with Claire Rosenstein, everyone clean, scholastic, old-maidish. The usual midnight sherbets, Piazza Navona. (Coincidence: the first time I ever saw Gore Vidal was, I'm certain, during a Pyramid Club klatch at Claire Rosenstein's around 1947.)

Long walk this morning along the Tiber alone. Lunch with my good old Zaffrani, retired now and living mostly in Sicily, royalist, francophile, still reeking marvelously of Lanvin cologne, generous, gourmand to a fault.

Eight o'clock at *Tre Scalini* met John Corigliano (also here for the RAI thing which I was forgetting) and John Atkins, traveling with a Kitty Krupat of *Esquire*. We dine at Santa Maria in Trastevere amidst a jolly fair.

26 July

Swimming today with John and John and Kitty, but we didn't swim, too much mob at Foro Italico. Lunch, Piazza del Popolo where in 1957 I'd dined with PQ and Guglielmo and was jealous.

6:30 Frazier. Went to see *Una Dramma della Gelosia*. Mastroianni and the infinitely attractive Monica Vitti. Walked in the Borghese gardens until dark. Dined near the Pantheon.

Solitary sight-seeing (San Pietro in Vincoli, Santa Maria Maggiore) until 2:30, then to RAI for an appalling rehearsal of our television show tomorrow.

Having been summoned to a "round table on contemporary music," I was looking forward to this exchange (with what RAI termed "other international notables") on a subject I felt informed about. But early in the long inexpert taping session I realized I'd been had. The subject turned out not to be Contemporary Music as I understood the phrase, but rock. Nor was I there as American composer, but as author, years ago, of an essay probing the subject. Hasn't the novelty of Minds illuminating this mindless matter worn thin? Yet here, under the serious scrutiny of a Roman TV staff (which one somehow can't take seriously), sat a collection of intellectuals, half of them over fifty, ready for another go.

The participants, besides me, numbered eleven, all apparently distinguished in their way, though we were never properly introduced. Three Italians: a conservative musicologist from *Messaggero*, a radical movie director who admittedly knew little about music, and the conductor of the Turin Symphony. Six Englishmen: novelists Anthony Burgess and Colin MacInnes, *Times* critic William Mann, pop authorities Geoffrey Cannon and Tony Palmer and the percussionist (with his agent) of a rock band whose name I've forgotten. And two Americans: composers John Corigliano and Frank Zappa, the second of whom, by prearrangement, was to enliven the occasion by performing on his drums.

Program in two parts. The first, an hour's worth of prefilmed scenes—some random, some rehearsed—about pop. The second, our verbal reaction. The film contained clips of mini-skirted groupies going wild, interspersed (really) with shots of Buchenwald prisoners, followed by interviews with "serious composer" Richard Rodney Bennett who stated that his kind of music and that of the pop scene are now happily merging, and with Paul McCartney who told us that "pop is tomorrow's classical."

Bennett's remark sounds dated already, and is also untrue: instances of such mergers, from Milhaud to Gunther Schuller, have never been happy (and why the need to homogenize everything?).

The remark goes against McCartney's concept which, in turn, forbids continued coexistence of the two kinds of art which for millennia trod parallel paths.

I was embarrassed by the apologetic mood: Let's not get left behind! America has already left behind the fear of being left behind, while Europe (with the pomposity of ourselves in this very studio seeking youth's approval by approving of youth) is indeed lagging, not that it makes much difference.

(Popular once equated unrespectable, and now defines the acceptable—to avoid the word *relevant*. The acceptable is easy. What is not easy is not popular. What is not popular is disqualified by tastemakers, i.e., distributors, and distributors with the strength of the witless have persuaded almost everyone including intellectuals—never a musical class anyway—that pop is where it's at, because pop speaks to our time. What speaks, of course, is the accessible lyrics. If the same held true in the '30s—that thoughtful though not basically musical minds granted musical value to what was said extramusically, meaning politically—folk song then was the exception while now it's the rule, and music is still judged for being what it is not.)

Well, it was just a rehearsal. Tomorrow might be a cut above.

Left a note for Balthus, Villa Medici. Tea at 6:30 with Ginny Becker at her absolutely swell roof garden, Via della Vetrina. Then Frazier, *da lui*, Via Vascello. Taxi ride to Via Masina where the ants and birds added to the anxiety of 1955, and where now nothing, *nothing* is dredged up. To Margarita Rospigliosi's, and with her (another voice from the past turned from middle age to old) and Paul Wolfe we dine *en ville*. Frazier exemplary.

28 July

The final day. Not one to be proud of.

Tony Palmer and Angela Huth were my guests at noon, again on the hotel roof. Limousine to RAI. Filming, scheduled for two, began at four. Meanwhile we were paid in lire, which Frazier had prearranged to have changed into dollars, provided I contact the money changer by seven this evening. But the filming made slow headway.

Someone spoke about the imminence of a Beatles opera, implying that opera as a genre was the Ultimate Test, and that such a test, when passed by the Beatles, would dislodge standard repertory. . . . Now, the chief hurdle for an opera composer is drama, not music; the process of constructing and sustaining formal tension isn't among a rock group's needs, which are instant, lyric and fragmented. This is not to deny rock its theatricality, but t'ie theatricality is one of detail, not structure.

Then another (Mr. Burgess, actually) suggested that a composer be judged by his ability to make a piece last, i.e., by length, by classical development methods. Rock, having no organic sense of how to go on, is thus by him disqualified from immortality, a criterion which would also disqualify Scarlatti, Schubert, Satie, Webern. Meanwhile, the Beatles have officially disbanded, settling that problem.

We were asked, is rock music? Yes, but not the only music, nor is most of it good anymore. And it does contain three extramusical ingredients: its words serve as antiestablishmentarianism; it is socially activating, bringing together disparate groups; it's commercial. These ingredients aren't new. As politics, rock is no more nor less influential than the '20s songs of Weill. As incentive for mutual grooving it is no more nor less sentimental than the old senior prom. As money-maker it is no more nor less crass than art has ever been, just wider spread. Having your political heart in the right place does not insure original communication, much less a work of art; nor is rock validified as art by making people like each other, or by making lots of money. Still, these points get some people uneasy, so they have round tables in Rome.

At 6:30 an intermission was called. Cash in hand, I sneaked out, never to return. The most unscrupulous action of my career.

Changed money.

At hotel, no message from Balthus. Nor is Natalie Perrone in town.

Farewell dinner with Gore and his entourage: Howard Austen, the handsome frail English girl, Rossellini *frère*, and John Philip

Law. None was amused by my recital of this afternoon's unprofessional gesture. (Later I learn that the introductory portion of the film was redone, that I was cut.)

Gore, when the others had gone, walked me halfway home in the predawn fog, past the old bridges and gardens and Piazza Caitani which now contains nothing but the ghost of her who founded *Botteghe Oscure* and who never received me. (When in 1954 I forwarded letters of introduction from Mimi Pecci and Marie Laure, she told Bill Weaver who told me: "Of the ladies recommending him I've known one all my life and wish I hadn't, and have never met the other and hope I won't.")

He said: It's too bad I can't love anyone. But of course he doesn't mean it.

Fire Island Pines
10 August

Golden wedding anniversary of my parents. Purchased for them from Tiffany a solid-gold fruit bowl.

13 August

A body washed up on the beach early this morning near our house on Fishermans Walk. The young man who yesterday afternoon at the Pines entered the ocean with his *new friend* (italics those of the gossipmongers) was never, despite hundreds on the beach, seen alive again. Dredges like glowworms patrolled the shore until midnight. Now there, near the police truck, beneath a makeshift sheet, is the lump, the snow-white feet, the bloodless meaningless laughterless youth who yesterday loved.

Fog cleared, sand and sky lie like glass and silk, and the sun climbs over our coffee cups providing a temperature perfect as an unnoticeably vital caress. Howard Moss stops by, to invite us for a drink tonight (tonight still exists, doesn't it?), and to discuss the drowning with warnings about treacherous undertows known as Sea Pussies.

19 August

Golden weather continues. We're all corpses on parole.

They said: If arrogance could be canned and sold, NR would make a million. But it *can* be canned and sold, and he's not made a million. The false assumption is that there would be buyers.

NED ROREM = MODERNER. But I haven't an experimental bone in my body.

Nineteen summers ago Christian Mégret made this anagram: *Qu'il ERRE ou qu'il DORME il ORNE le MONDE.*

10 September

Tomorrow, return to the city.

In seven weeks here we've seen no one. Occasional cup of cider with Morris or the Towleses, occasional visit from the Rorems or Sylvia Goldstein, but no party-going, no new friendships. I've prepared one hundred forty-seven meals, and read almost that many books while enjoying the thunderstorms, but have composed not a note.

16 September

Immense reception last evening at Gotham Book Mart for publication of *Critical Affairs*. Milling like the finale of *Petrouchka* or the last page of *Inside Daisy Clover*. Today, noble letdown. Celebrations of art honor the past, that is, something already dead within the artist. I'm touched by, but not interested in, praise for my early songs.

Steegmuller's *Cocteau* is finally out, and (admittedly with little competition) is the finest essay on the subject. The last quarter sags the way Genet's novels do. A horse approaching the stable begins to run. One loses interest in a subject once the subject's *en tête*. (Why can't thoughts be photographed? Mozart's symphonies overlapped in his rapid mind. If he hadn't wasted time writing them down, he might have composed twice as many.)

Steegmuller's portrait is drawn from the confines of his personal cage, presenting the poet through his own perspective, and is no less limited than Sprigge's constant praise or Brown's constant slander. He sees what he sees (where does one stop? I knew Cocteau, but in a sense knew him less than Steegmuller who never knew him), and willfully misinterprets for his gigantic pigeonhole.

One verifiable example, page 142: ". . . does not hide what was ever to be one of his chief preoccupations. (*'Je ne crois guère aux hommes de petite verge,'* he wrote Ned Rorem in 1950.) Nevertheless . . ." That quotation is truncated from the full context which Steegmuller copied from my letters in 1966: *"Je crois que tout compte chez un homme, et je ne crois guère aux hommes de petite verge."* This wrote Jean Cocteau apropos of learning that Kinsey requested genital dimensions of all male interviewees. In direct opposition to Paul Goodman, Cocteau never spoke literally; his phrase meant: "I believe in people with self-assurance." Nothing of his life or writings could lead one to believe that "one of his chief preoccupations" was *la verge*. The rare unintelligent paragraphs in Steegmuller's work (viz., page 402) all echo *niaiseries* about homosexuality, referring to "tastes" of Gide or Diaghilev, or assuming that homosexuals attract (rather than repel) each other by wearing makeup. But if I count key omissions in the index (the Bourdets, the Vilmorins, Dietrich; Nathalie Paley, Marianne Oswald, Montherlant, Tony Gandarillas, Markevitch, René Crevel, Arletty, André Dubois), God forbid that I split further hairs. For I read my own history as I see fit, shredding my bones for others and keeping the marrow for my dreams. (This is called Poetic Prose.)

22 October

Completed the last of five versions and my worst book review, on *Great Songs of the Sixties*, though I've never worked harder. How to say No! Francis Brown, with that reasoning of the typical nonmusical intellectual (why typical? Intellectuals *are* nonmusical), assumes that I, being a musician, should know how to write up the book. (Insult to injury, *The Times* is actually the publisher of the lousy volume as well as of its review.) He's probably right, as things go these days. Once a country of specialists, America now lumps all arts together French-manner, encouraging general practice in everything but medicine and politics.

23 October

Birthday. Why are Manet's unpolluted floods of sunlight so sad? Because we die anyway. And there's nothing left to say of that that's not banality.

30 October

Annual meeting for the prolongation of New Music Edition at Virgil's with Frank Wigglesworth. Wistful and futile now that Henry Cowell's dead. Dine at the Gruens' (take pecan pie).

Unlike my partners in crime, i.e., my friends the musicians, I cannot fraternize with the lower classes. P? He was European, and I was younger. But life is shortening, and it's stupid to sit around saying nothing. Last night, with JH and Shirley, saw *Ice*. (That's lower-class, but I was with friends.)

5 November

Word from Paris is that Claude Rostand has died. Why am I stunned, the news is not unexpected? Because an entire critical fashion vanishes with Claude. Yes, he was like most French critics (in contrast to American ones who hold themselves socially aloof from the milieu they criticize) in that he believed knowledge of music came from musicians, and so musicians were his friends. But he was unlike French critics—was, in fact, unique—by being able to straddle without prejudice the gulf between the old avant-garde and the new avant-garde. His coverage over the years of *Les Six, Le Groupe d'Arcueil, La Jeune France,* remains the only fair and thorough portraits of those composers, while his appreciations of younger creators, dating from 1953 (year of the first *Domaine Musicale* manifestations), are as informed and uncrabbed as any by more one-sided reporters like Claude Samuel.

Rostand did not make, as Tovey did, particularly memorable literature; he will be remembered more for the results of his work than for the work itself.

A critic writes about everyone, but no one writes about him. Who talks about the person, as opposed to his professional notions? If he bestows homage or spleen on dead or living artists, who will grant him even such a paragraph as this? Yet precisely his invisibility (we don't even know what he looks like) becomes the reviewer's armor; he destroys with impunity. To his credit Claude Rostand never relished saying the bad things he had to say.

20 November

First hearing at two pianos of my Concerto with Jerry in Steinway's basement for: Stuart Pope and the Markhams, Ronit, JH and Shirley, Herbert Breslin, the Gruens.

25 November

Mishima's suicide.

Boston
29 November

Dine with Sarah Caldwell and others in Knox Street restaurant. Little to say.

Accompany Donald in *War Scenes* on his poorly attended but always masterful recital in Symphony Hall.

Pittsburgh
4 December

Jerry Lowenthal has given the world premiere of my *Piano Concerto in Six Movements*. And so this huge piece, which I'd never dreamed of writing were it not for an unexpected commission, has passed through sixteen short months of labor pains—not really so painful—and copyist fees and publisher's patience, and come to be born on the stage of the Syria Mosque in full view of a paying audience, healthy and elegant, thanks to the accurate arms of Jerry, the curt baton of William Steinberg and the seeming goodwill of the Pittsburgh Symphony.

In his program note, Frederick Dorian calls this my Third

Piano Concerto, and so it is, if you count the unpublished and unplayed 1948 miscarriage for Eugene, and the jovial essay in 1950 for Julius Katchen. This is the fourth work of mine that Steinberg's conducted over the years, not only locally but on tours here and abroad, yet I've no idea how he feels about my music. I do scarcely know him, and, like all old-school European conductors, he's intimidating; during our few warm, if formal, meetings we seem to speak different tongues. (If he does generally champion my work, he has *not* scheduled this concerto for New York. And he was overheard remarking to a board member: "Incredible that Lowenthal should learn the Rorem piece by heart, just to play it here!")

Since atomic metronomes don't yet exist, and since therefore all conductors play all music either faster or slower than the ideal tempo (whatever that may be), Steinberg errs on the fast side, and I like that. Ormandy errs on the slow side. I like that too, though I wonder if my tunes can take it.

Jerry meanwhile is the ideal player of this piece, each note of which is his.

31 December

As much as any composer can cite a mannerism as derived from specific works, my use of the descending minor-third as the most "telling" moment of a melodic line comes from the aria "Te de Llevar" in *The Wind Remains* of Paul Bowles, which he first played for me in 1943 or '44 (it was a recording of Maria Kurenko and the CBS Orchestra conducted, probably, by Max Goberman). The same "dying fall" recurs in Messiaen's *Louange à l'Eternité de Jésus* which Maurice Gendron and I first played together in Hyères during April of 1951. These two works affected me deeply. Other uses of this dropping third (which is frequent, after all, throughout Mahler, and in Mompou's Catalonian songs, or Franck's *Psyché*, or Copland's *Organ Symphony*) strike me always as coming from Messiaen or Bowles.

I put on my glasses and am therefore hidden from you, though I now can see you. I remove my glasses and am therefore visible to you, though now I can't see you. A lesson for singers and actors.

Four years ago in Salt Lake City, a few seconds after the trial fitting for contact lenses, I shrieked: Please God, remove these spiders from my eyeballs and I'll be good forevermore. And I've been good forevermore.

1971

See that long lonesome road
Don't you know it's got to end
But I'm a young woman
And I can get plenty men.

—Bessie Smith

New Year's Day

Out of the blue of Cambridge comes a letter from Philip Rahv inviting me to contribute to *Modern Occasions*. He assures me I need not restrict myself to "the theme of music."

Except for my notes in *Commentary*, of all places, five years ago, no cultured periodical other than *Kenyon Review* has for ages carried even an occasional piece on serious music (not *The New Republic*, nor *Partisan Review*, nor . . .). The fact that intellectuals are not musical, and that they aren't *embarrassed* about it, is a theme to develop sometime. Meanwhile, I'll present to Mr. Rahv a sequence of mini-essays from this very diary, tightened and degossipified, on matters musical (though sometimes indirectly), all from a composer's standpoint.

3 February

Huge party here last night for Roro. Cost circa $500. Another sad quarrel with David Diamond.

Dined tonight at Sondra Lee and Harlan Kleiman's where Ruth Ford, wearing the same striking outfit (simple black with silver chain and boots) as at our party yesterday is embarrassed but doesn't mention it, nor do we. Sondra does imitations, cruel and funny.

4 February

Buy long winter underwear for Yaddo.
Gold Diggers of 1933.

5 February

Leave for Saratoga, Trailways bus, 1 P.M.
I once searched through Gide's journal to learn what he did the

351

day I was born. But that date was left blank. In forty years some no-longer-young poet, born on February 4, 1971, may be gratified to see what I was up to that day.

Yaddo
7 February

Ethel Reiner died today in Barbados.

10 February

Heavy snow, Ping-Pong, Elizabeth Ames.

I am, so to speak, living with Jules Feiffer and Philip Roth since we share two meals a day, inhabit the same storm-borne mansion, and even (at least at the Spa) take baths together. Technically my juniors, they are nevertheless my mother and father, though I won't say which is which. Tonight they are taking me to hear Bernadette Devlin speak at Skidmore College.

Polly: "Why should I go to dirty cities when I meet the cream of America here at Yaddo?" She is in a way right, especially about the dirt. Yet she meets only a *part* of America's cream, and not a representative cross section. A certain kind of artist (Larry Rivers, say) wouldn't think of coming here. Those who do, present only their working (their suspended animation) side to Polly, not their ambitious, or mean or social side.

13 February

Working almost solely on prose, a short story, and my piece for *Modern Occasions* which Philip Roth says is the best new magazine going, but which in fact is too politically backbiting too late in the day. . . . To avoid the word *Jew* in conversation I refer to "those of the Jewish persuasion." Well, Philip's narcissism is that of the ultimate Semitic nonliterary sober straight. Mine, that of the ultimate Gentile literary drunk queer. Both add up to the identical *Ouch!*

16 February

Malaise pour malaise, I'm more at home with heterosexual Jews than with heterosexual Goyim.

And with homosexual Jews?

There aren't any. Homosexual's a Wasp thing. When a Jew turns queer he turns goy.

Les bien-portants sont les malades qui s'ignorant, said Doctor Knock.

How I love American cooking! Cranberries, corn on the cob, baked sweet potatoes, angel food cake. Thus are evening meals here, classily bland, with Granville Hicks presiding every night. But every morning conversation is not (as in Europe) about nutriments at hand, but about—for God's sake—philosophical concepts.

17 February

> I am reminded of the reviews of *Five Years.* Of that book, by actual (generous) count, less than one-seventh had any relation to sexual matters at all, yet every review concentrated almost entirely on some monstrous sexual revelations which occupied even less space in the book. The book was primarily on Method.
>
> —Paul Goodman (from a letter in *Commentary*)

How comprehend Paul's seemingly genuine puzzlement about these reviews? As with *The Paris Diary,* which preceded *Five Years* five years ago, the suavest American readers weren't yet accustomed to first-person disclosures. Both books did contain bizarre juxtapositions: laments on our political state, followed by detailings of the creative process, followed by an account of the joys and perils of cruising. Does Paul truly feel that readers will react "fairly"—will keep an even temperature—while scanning this drastic variety of subjects. Philip said yesterday that his own book was not "about masturbation," but my God, we do recall it. Red's brighter than gray. We may not remember *Genesis* for those endless begats, but they are there, and important, why not? In diaries, as opposed to novels, entries can be added or substracted without harming structure, since diaries have no structure, that's why they're diaries. Paul knows that homosexual matters, discussed personally rather than "objectively," are more taboo and repugnant and annoying and fascinating than are matters of Method; indeed, this knotty predicament is one he's spent a lifetime unraveling. Still, it's not his talk of, but his *placement* of, "monstrous sexual revelations," that raises the eyebrows. Surprise at public reaction (I have feigned the same "surprise") is to be either self-protective, gee-whiz innocent or plain humorless.

The book's both seductive and repugnant, like pie for diabetics or gin for alcoholics. Alas, the ingredients (indeed, like pie and gin) don't mix well, even for deformed appetites.

Attempting *Under the Volcano* for the twentieth time. It represents all I detest in literature: the curse of Hemingway's rhapsodic virility, the un-French looseness, the ballsy self-indulgence that declares in twenty pages what could be declared in one. I choose friends between those who do or don't like Malcolm Lowry, Albert Schweitzer, Joan Sutherland, William Faulkner, Helen Keller, Bob Dylan, Dylan Thomas, Thomas Stewart, Stuart Preston, Preston Sturges.

Yet my carnality centers on masculinity, even on exaggerated masculinity. I love men but loathe manly prose. (What has hitherto been known as "womanly" prose was actually just undisciplined— too many bracelets! Today, of course, the tersest authors are female. Philip's good too, though he's no Colette. And John Updike is also a first-rate woman writer.)

Reading Flannery O'Connor for the first time, painful, enviable. Also Borges, and, as every year here, the little mags. Jules meanwhile's been reading my diary. Unsolicited he commiserates with the drama I surely endure today considering, as he says, "how beautiful you once were." *Once were!* Does he not see how luscious I remain?

Tomorrow I leave. So that all may bid me goodbye this afternoon I've purchased Chivas Regal and lots of salted almonds.

I've worked well. That's always a risky statement.

New York
20 February

In Saratoga we forget priorities. On rounding the Hackensack bend, the first glimpse of Manhattan is a shocker. The clouds of pollution seem so neat, so localized, fitting like great gaseous dunce caps on the eager skyscrapers.

23 February

Maison Française, concert of music by Henri Sauguet. Then yesterday, with Guy Ferrand, Sauguet comes to lunch. Insatiable spirit for his seventy years (he eyes JH like the golden apple), and so French (absolutely naughty and absolutely proper) that his presence changes the red dining room on Seventieth Street into his Clichy-esque parlor three thousand wet miles away. He talks at length of Marie Laure (had she survived she'd have been mute in a wheelchair), and of his own slackening due to lack of audience more than to lack of ideas. I play him a tape of my Concerto which he finds more muscular than my "Paris period" music, more considé-rable. (Though not necessarily more significant. Why, finally, must a long work be more important than a short one? If history retains me, however briefly, it will probably be for scatterings of single pages—for tiny poems musicked, for an unaccompanied hymn.)

3 March

Screening of Panic in Needle Park, rough cut, for which I'm being "felt out" as composer by producer Dominick Dunne. (I do not understand this film. What is the viewpoint? Those tired close-ups of shooting-up! The young actors are appealing, but somehow sapped. A very heterosexual script, and I've not one musical notion. How music?)

21 March

New York premiere in Tully Hall of my Letters from Paris, nine settings of prose extracts from Janet Flanner's prose, for chorus and small orchestra, conducted sensitively by Louis Hooker. Nice review in *Times*.

24 March

The Nephew, play based on the motionless Purdy novel, opens in Buffalo with my music, composed (for flute, viola, cello) in three days, mailed upstate, recorded there and superimposed onto the production without further ado. Exactly, I've always felt, as these things should be done. (Virgil's contention, that a composer must supervise each split second, is pure literature, and makes no final difference, even in opera.)

7 April

Stravinsky died last night. Today is Shirley's birthday.

With Shirley's first husband Seymour Barab, old friend and fine cellist, acting as contractor, we assembled twenty solid performers who, for four hours this morning and four more this afternoon, recorded the score for *Panic in Needle Park*. In less than a month I've composed a half-hour's worth of original music for this film, orchestrated it, copied the parts myself, assembled and arranged another half-hour's worth of "source" music and dealt with a thousand nonmusical details, wrangling with 20th Century-Fox through Dunne, who's really quite decent. Although I'm no conductor I conducted the sessions, as I always do with my stage music (good union musicians just need someone to beat time), under the jaundiced eye in the control booth of the film's director, Jerry Schatzberg, who knows what he wants, and now I'm exhausted, but with honor, and relieved. Tomorrow we edit.

16 April

Special delivery from Dunne stating with distress that they have decided not to use a score, any score, in the film. Only sound effects, as in a documentary. Beyond shredding my ego, this news brings no compensation. My fee was too small to admit without shame, and the music can't be easily incorporated into a suite, since technically it's the property of the studio according to the terms of the contract which I gluttonously signed, like a fool. Wasted month.

People are either visual or aural. One suffers where the other benefits. An experimental artist nourishes at least one conventional taste; within himself revolve mixtures as unbalanced as the stylish media outside him. If improvisatory poets compose homages to Prokofiev, I on the other hand turn out words like these. My music, pristine and orderly, contradicts a hysterical and sloppy prose. Yet the poets and I know where if not who we are. Meanwhile those whose business is to mix media are in a quandary when selecting specialists for their hash.

The film-maker must explain what his film means, then say where he wants the film illuminated by music. The composer will find the means for the meaning. The film-maker distrusts him, because composers won't use words like tender (or sinister, or romantic, or breathless) to explain musical intent. Music in itself is not tender, only in association. Tender scores may be made tenderer by kinds of music we have come to identify with tender. On the other hand, a scene might be heightened in tenderness (changed for the better) by another kind of music not (yet) identified with tender.

All that can be said about the music in advance is that it will be slow, loud, fast, long, short. And the practicalities of instrumentation can be discussed.

Then producers discard finished scores with the excuse that they "change the mood of the movie." Weren't they meant to?

If paintings seen in the movies exist, like music, in time, music continues to possess more activating forces than painting. A dancer will not be impelled to move by the fact of a picture: décor is not accompaniment but background.

Yet a choreographer is most creative when he goes against his music, not taking it literally.

Music does have literal sense since it makes us move. It has no symbolic sense. Music means only what it says.

Somewhat unexpected, a second solicitation from Philip Rahv for *Modern Occasions*, this time explicitly requesting a review of Charles Rosen's *The Classical Style: Haydn, Mozart, Beethoven.*

What do I know of such things? Composers "know" less than musicologists, or even enterprising laymen, about music, at least repertorially speaking. For a week I've been buried in the book, baffled with admiration at discussion of what takes place on the simple five-lined staff.

Thrice Rosen examines the cause of poignancy as expressed in a "long-range linear sense, overriding the immediate voice-leading. . . ." On page 35, for instance, apropos of a section in the *Hammerklavier* wherein a note, G, is left "hanging in air," he wonderfully states that "two measures later the melody curves upward with a movement of exquisite grace, resolving the note to an F-sharp and, in so doing, connects and resolves audibly, even at first hearing, a part of its own past." On page 244, regarding the slow movement from Mozart's *Concerto K. 488*: "Most remarkable, perhaps, is the withholding of the resolution of the D in the third measure of the melody until the sixth measure. . . ." Again, on page 349, in an elision of a Mozart Symphony, Rosen hears "the violin move to take up the line left suspended by the flute" four measures earlier.

For each of these examples one could prove, by witness of both eye and ear, that resolution occurs instantly: Beethoven's "lost" G resolves on the very next note in the right hand (alto voice), and the resolution is confirmed on the second beat of the same measure in the left hand (bass voice); Mozart's D resolves from top to bottom voice on the following beat; in the Symphony the flute connects directly to the violin a ninth below.

Rosen is right and so am I. He makes a case for coitus interruptus. I make one for quick take-overs from one body to another.

I counted fifty uses of the word *wit* (or *witty*) before Rosen on page 159 defined it somewhat: "True civilized wit, the sudden fusion of heterogeneous ideas with an air paradoxically both ingenious and amiably shrewd. . . ." He will continue to overuse the word throughout the large book, mostly in reference to Haydn: ". . . the highest form of wit, the musical pun. . . ." (page 96); ". . . the listener who can hear the last movement without laughing aloud knows nothing of Haydn" (page 140); ". . . the result in Symphony no. 88 is incomparably funny . . . while the same witty effect is raised to the point of comic magnificence in Symphony no. 93" (page 338).

Was Haydn so aware of his own wit? Did he indeed think himself witty? Much of what Rosen names Haydn's wit depends on Rosen's own funny bone. His description on page 98 of the device of holding back applies as easily to Ravel, but whereas with Haydn the device is sly, with Ravel we call it excruciation.

Charles Rosen has plenty of wit himself, albeit less humoristic than aphoristic. His book will endure, not because the contents—or even their expression—are new, but because they are comprehensively stated. So elegant is *The Classical Style*'s style that itself seems almost a classic. (Shall I begin or end with that sentence?)

There are as many definitions for sonata as there are sonatas. Etc. (That will never do.)

There is really no Classic style but only a style of the classicists, Haydn and Mozart. They wrote in the fashion of the times, and were distinguishable from others by virtue of being better rather than different. Etc.

(List his aphorisms, pedantries, his too personal readings, his etc.)

What do classical and baroque mean in the *visual* arts? Classical sculpture is 2,500 years old, classical music 150 years old. And a classic is a classic. Classical is so frequent a term that we take it for granted as referring to a delimitation of the frozen past. But classicism was not aware of itself, being, of course, a modern term. (I think.) The word's meaning changes daily as we advance into the future, has changed since Rosen wrote his book. As many definitions as there are (admittedly few) worthy scholars to define it. Rosen is one such scholar; his book is thoroughly modern. Etc.

Classic means standard, accepted, long familiar, in the repertory. To me it used to mean: as opposed to Romantic: form before meaning as opposed to meaning before form. It grows from inside out, while Romantic grows from outside in.

Was Greece classical? The Renaissance? Is there Classical French music?

The word is bandied by the ignorant who use it as differentiation from Popular. Maybe they're right.

But.

1 May

> An artist is half man, half woman,
> and the woman is insufferable.
> —Picasso

Because I am evidently a token something, the Theater for Ideas invited me (late in the day) to sit among the elect in the first six rows of Town Hall last night for their Women's Liberation Forum.

Who would escort me? Robin Morgan refused on the grounds that she wouldn't be seen beneath the same roof as Norman Mailer. Ann Birstein refused because she *had* a date, but volunteered her protection once I arrived. Finally Shirley agreed to take me.

Everyone and her brother was there.

Germaine Greer can cross the stage with a marvelous slouch, has poise, panache, posture, studied clothes and high beauty. Her keening on woman-as-object thus carries more credence than if heard from, say, Betty Friedan. *N'est pas objet qui veut.* It seems disingenuous for a good-looking woman to complain of being "used" as sex-object when the situation cannot apply to her plainer sisters, a vast majority. To be desired is rarer and stronger than to desire: it implies far more. The beloved wields the whip, the rapist cowers. To be ignored is the final humiliation.

Woman is half drudge, half goddess, says Greer. Would the uglies give that percentage? Now a woman who makes herself plain (Robin) is costumed like any model, male or female. Cunt is no more insulting for a woman than Prick for a man. What about man-as-object? To homosexuals rough-trade is an object though his role is hardly passive: he does the work, ramming the twitching lips, and is paid off without a word (what could he possibly *say*? verbal intercourse personalizes). But who's to prove he's a "thing" without knowing what goes on behind the scenes of all concerned?

That "passive" homosexual deals the cards, purchases the merchandise (I command you to dominate me!), writes the sonnet, ends up literarily if not literally on top. Yet the trade, when he murders his client, does so for having been sucked off or sucked into, verbs indicating passivity. Meanwhile, everyone knows that some snatches have snapping teeth while others, like blotters or quicksand, are capable of absorbing whole human bodies. That aggressive cramp a twat inflicts might kill a man, and Wagner's not the only one to have died in flagrante. (What's the Latin name for vaginal constriction?)

Greer evoked Mozart's sister as not having been given a chance. Was Mozart, flung to a pauper's grave that rainy day, given a chance? Were chances then what they are now? Is there room for that much genius in one world, let alone in one family? Who remained home to tend house and nurse a traumatized psyche while Clara Schumann was the toast of all Europe?

Mailer arranges to give the impression of being a repressed homosexual—it's good publicity for so obviously "masculine" a type—whereas in fact he's a settled heterosexual. (The inverted "pose," as the Divine Marquis would say, was once standard fare for theatrical European females—Juliette Greco, Marlene Dietrich—but not for literary American males.) These days, of course, nobody cares, so Mailer does seem to protest too much, as though to make clear that in his role of sublimated homosexual he is active, not passive. Anyway, Shirley and I found him quite cute.

(Mailer: speaks before he thinks and writes it down afterward.)

Diana Trilling was reasoned and serious, too much so for this vaudeville. Even Diana, war goddess and interferer, didn't deserve the upstaging she got from that Village Voice columnist who simulated sapphic rapture all over the stage with two very bull dykes.

Questions from the crowd, and general free-for-all.

Lean Susan Sontag rose from her front-row seat to ask why the female panelists had not objected to Norman's calling them Lady

Writers. "One doesn't introduce Jimmy Baldwin as a Black writer," she explained (thereby introducing him as a Black writer), "much less as a Man writer," an inadvertent irony which brought smiles from those who *knew*, including Susan. Homosexuality's good for a smile; and poor Jimmy—forever singled out as the Black author whom one doesn't single out as such.

Lady is an antiquated word, Mailer knows it, used it affectionately, not to insult but to tease his fellow panelists. Since none of those was, in fact, a Lady, why be offended? (Ladies give teas, talk clothes. To use the word for, say, the Sontag, is to ironicize endearingly.) Despite their insistence that the whole mess is verbal, that we need redefinitions, the trouble lies not in the word but in the word's placement, in who uses it in what geography. Queer is four syllables shorter than homosexual (*five* syllables shorter than Gore Vidal's homosexualist) and—it all depends—is no more objectionable to me than, presumably, Nigger by a Black to a Negro.

Perhaps we should not identify an author by her (his) subject matter. When we call Genet a homosexual author we are supposedly defining his topic. Which he himself would call merely sexual if he called it anything. Is Lady Author worse than Woman Author? Surely Greer's a Woman Author, given her subject, while Jane Austen's an author *tout court*. In English words like Negress, even actress, were a generation ago considered by the emancipated to be animalistic as well as plain incorrect. Is the feminine suffix in or out tonight?

Susan's confusion is like objecting to notions about pornography that don't include Vietnam. False syllogism: pornography is obscene, the war is obscene, the war is pornography—so how dare one resent literary pornography in the face of the war, etc.

The audience was all intellectual and well off (no musicians, there never are) who had the answers before they came.

To deflower virgins is the ultimate for certain pushy types, male and female. We all take a wrongheaded interest in collapse: sawing into a perfect soufflé, a bank vault, an anesthetized pet. Some prefer the quite kosher role of soufflé. To win in the parlor, to lose in bed, ah charity.

Greer, saying "men treat us as goddesses" means "us" as beauties. Beauty is never unaware of itself. Only the mad ignore reactions they provoke, and the mad are not beautiful. Much beauty is reaction to reaction. Intelligence isn't required for beauty, but stupidity precludes it, although dumb people can be sexy.

I talk of people (women) famous for their physical beauty, not those whose faces, like, say, Margaret Mead's or Eleanor Roosevelt's, supposedly express "beauty of soul."

Beauty is learned young. Beauty which refuses to acknowledge itself, which turns to "more important things," forsakes itself and becomes plain. But beauty also forsakes the possessor who desires to retain it, usually through growing older, although some rare chosen ones with good cheekbones actually improve with age.

Buildings break our hearts more than old lovers years later, because they remain comparatively unchanged, when not destroyed utterly. Ultimately they too must go.

If these Erinyes do not choose to behave like ladies, might they not behave like gentlemen? Would they howl at Black males, if any were present, as they do at white? Certainly not, although Black males are chauvinist pigs too, they are not revolutionary sisters.

(At the Frick, Veronese's "Wisdom and Strength" are portrayed respectively by a woman and a man.)

The homosexual thinks of himself in terms of homosexuality virtually always. The heterosexual thinks of himself in terms of heterosexuality only during discussion of that subject which is virtually never. Black thinks of itself as black always, whereas white thinks of itself as white only in Harlem, which is never. The non-artist does not consider himself as non-artist, nor does an artist think of himself as one except when he's not being one, that is, when he's away from his work and playing the part at a party of non-artists who hold him in awe, which is virtually never. None of this is either good or bad.

364

All blacks look alike to me. That phrase is not bigotry but blindness—inexperience—and is never pronounced by a (white) person raised among blacks. Introduced unprepared to a new milieu anyone will detect big differences between himself and the milieu rather than small differences between individuals of the milieu. All Latvian sounds alike to me, and will continue to sound alike until I study it. (All young people, all modern art, all rednecks, etc. . . .)

28 May

Bach was the greatest composer who ever walked the earth. Thus committed, let me admit that *The Goldberg Variations*—said to have been written as balm to the commissioner's insomnia—always puts me to sleep. Yes, the theme is marvelous, but why are the variations so sacredly great? All that G major! can't hold a candle, in beauty or invention, to *The Well-Tempered Clavier.*

Jerry Robbins' ballet last night was an improvement on Bach. Which isn't to say Jerry comes before Bach (he lives in the twentieth century, and so comes after Bach). It's to say a better piece would have made a worse dance.

2 June

Tonight Maurice Abravanel conducted my *Third Symphony* with the Utah Orchestra in Carnegie Hall where, more than twelve years ago, its premiere was given by Bernstein. I wore a dark blue suit (bought in Paris in 1953), an old sky-blue shirt with royal-blue tie. The piece hasn't weathered the years as well as the clothes.

Later who should be at Shirley's but Lenny himself, only mildly interested in the news of the symphony, but full of the Berrigan brothers and his own ambitious *Mass.*

7 June

In the dream I awakened and perceived you standing among the shadows by the door. You were twelve feet tall, and though your face was in darkness I knew your eyes were wet. You said, "Ned, I must leave, and can never come back." The voice seemed faint and sad beyond description, and became inaudible as you dissolved. The room grew suddenly white and empty. I awoke into reality, disconsolate.

Yaddo
22 June

Libby Holman has killed herself. Somehow this doesn't come as a surprise. For if Libby was the richest woman in the world (becoming richer as the men in her life died off), also celebrated and honored with special friendships, the specter of violence tracked her from the start. (She once said: You want to know the truth? The night Smith Reynolds died I was so drunk I can't remember *what* happened!)

There are a very few people of talent you can thoroughly know within an hour, and who yet continue to nourish you for years. Their capacity comes not so much from their genius as from their generosity. Cocteau was like that. So certainly was John Latouche. Marc Blitzstein somewhat, and Libby too. She was reticent with money, but lavish with warmth, and owned the most original of baritone voices which she gave to us all. I remember dining with her and Marc (1959? 1960?), just the three of us, in a bistro near Marc's one evening, before a lecture by Alan Watts. A few years later Marc would be painfully slain on the island of Martinique and last night in the garage of her Connecticut home Libby died.

My intuition was that Libby, like other famous female talents with a penchant for beautiful cripples, in deciding at fifty to reverse the coin and espouse a stolid middle-aged painter, would have found a certain peace through Louis Shanker, as Marie Laure found through Oscar Dominquez. Intuition's discouragingly false.

25 June

A hailstorm as I write, expecting in a few minutes twenty guests (including JB) for the usual going-away drink in this recurrent roseate room. Before returning to 70th Street tomorrow I shall stop by the doctor's for a shot: JH has hepatitis. . . . Three weeks of good work, new friends (Filipa Rolf, Josephine Rhyder, the Susans

Elias and Crile, Robert Lucid, Tom Filer, Marya Zaturenska, and as ever, Hortense and Curt), swimming and heat and reading (*L'Etranger* again, with astonishment, Borges, De Quincey, Moravia's *L'Attenzione*, Thomas Pynchon with displeasure, Ellen Glasgow), and the always so easily renewed acquaintance with Elizabeth the Beloved.

New York
1 July

"What's *Carnal Knowledge* about?" asks Shirley.

"Sex."

"It's not about sex at all," protests David Oppenheim. "It's about anxiety."

He's only half right. Art generically is always about anxiety, so why mention it? Insofar as this movie depicts anxiety solely through carnal attitudes of two men who presumably have other interests, it is about sex. That fact's so clear, why mention it either? except to tell Shirley what the movie's about.

Then another said: "Like I wrote in my letter, your evocations, especially that section, that one short paragraph on Le Square Lamartine, were so . . . so *evocative* that, well, I had to meet you. Why, I even sat a whole afternoon in that square, seeing it as you must have, each detail, the elm with its steaming trunk, the shadow of the new apartment building from which X emerged with his cigarette, so very long ago, and the entire pale smell of that fall day, your fall day, then became present through myself now so . . ."

So I answered: "Here is now. Write about this hospital room, this white hand on the whiter sheet, the bedpan there, the streaked window, the sound of nurses down the hall. Because nothing's now, nothing lives except in retrospect. What matter to you, here, that I, breathing, am here too now, except as something to think about later? You're young without concern of the present as past, and I am able therefore to stifle instantaneously. You aren't getting the point."

Reading Muriel Spark's *The Driver's Seat*, suave; Mary McCarthy's *Birds of America*, engrossing (I love recipe books) if a trifle deenergized. Rereading *Les Caves du Vatican* with great glee. Do you remember Gide as having humor? slapstick ha-ha humor?

18 July

Spent the past week on Kent State's campus, dancing the usual dance. Arrived Sunday starving and was deposited in the abandoned dormitory of a closed-up town. Lonely walk through the campus, thinking of the slaughters a year ago last May. Monday, rehearsed *Lovers* with a young quartet, administered a Master Class (meaning: a couple dozen singers, each with his own pianist, sing my songs to me, after which I give them compliments and then tell them why they're going about it wrong), dined with John Browning. Tuesday morning, rehearsal of my choral works, afternoon another Master Class (I'm no master, I'm a slave to the insufficiencies of musical notation, and to the ironically legitimate mutations of vocal interpretation), dined again with John Browning, then a concert of Messiaen songs. Wednesday, still another Master Class, conference on tempos with old friend Louis Lane, more chamber music rehearsals (*Lovers* and *Eleven Studies*), dined with Burton Garlinghouse and Eric Dalheim, cut lip severely on split toothbrush, attended concert of Browning protégés, and went for a drink after with him and the Marcelluses. Thursday, arrival Jerry Lowenthal, rehearsal of thirty-odd songs with singers good and bad, evening concert of these, then nocturnal ice cream (peach) with Jerry, Louis and Herbert Schultz. Friday, lunch at the Twin Lakes duplex of Alex Gildzen and Charles Walker (*croque monsieurs* and *sangria*), attended Boulez rehearsal and later chatted briefly (and pointlessly) with him, rehearsal of my Concerto at Blossom where of all people Arthur Berger showed up, dined on the Blossom grounds with Jerry plus Gildzen and Walker, and then Jerry with Louis Lane gave an opulent performance of Concerto to hysterical crowd, after which, backstage, Arthur Berger with strident *politesse* declared, "I liked it better at rehearsal," then more nocturnal ice cream (fudge ripple) with Jerry at a Howard Johnson's as guests of Ruth and Jaime Laredo. Yesterday returned to New York with insulting reviews in my pocket.

Nobody, even God, comprehends his own bad press.

If the best writing today lies in critical penetration, nothing cuts duller than meanness as a conceit devoid of humor. Critics like Kael and Simon are mean with wit. Critics like Schonberg or Henahan are just mean. Not that they aren't correct, they're just no fun, and thus not instructive. Cleveland's reviewer, Wilma Salisbury (locally known as Vicious Vilma), wrote up the Concerto meanly, but lacked style. Now, for her to be right doesn't make me wrong; she criticized my genre rather than discussing whether I succeeded within that genre. If my genre lies in subconsciously evoking soundtracks from thirties movies (although it doesn't) is that genre less kosher than the Gentile evocations of, say, a Douglas Moore and his hymn-tune infancy? Thirties movies are the folklore of my generation.

Miss Salisbury doesn't teach me anything, whereas John Simon always reveals some unsuspected angle. Admittedly, John's not writing about my music. Still, even when he's wrong he's right. I agree with most of his theories but with few of his supporting examples. (I seldom go to the theater, and then always with disappointment because of the bum steers of John's bright reviews, e.g. the dreary *Sleuth*, the endless *House of Blue Leaves*.) How he loves to be hated! When I told him Tourel despised him, he beamed.

Is it unfair for professionals, who are also friends, to resent what they say about each other in the press? X no longer speaks to Y, yet the only nasty things he's said he's said behind Y's back. Or: Why does Z resent those awful words I wrote about her? I never said them to her face.

(. . . Even in the holy pages of *Time*. *Time* magazine does resemble the King James translation in that both hire a mass of individuals who keep to one voice.)

Fire Island Pines
8 August

Depression during the rain is assumed. But depression during good weather? This evening another sunset is staging itself on the beach even as these words are being noted. Every ten seconds removes another screen to reveal a more astounding superimposition of nectarine on widow-gray. The whole sky reeks of menstrual blood. Sun, enlarging as she sinks, grows huge now, and very low. The horizon becomes a hunching snake gulping the red-hot egg. A digestive moment, suspension of motion. . . . Now all grows rapidly dark. With Sun swallowed, every ray of hope disappears.

What do you do? do you like blackberries? do you like Tiepolo? when were you born?

> You ask a lot of questions. Mind your own business.
> Stopped in our tracks, what else is there to talk about?
> But those questions are so dumb.
> There are no dumb questions, just dumb answers.
> Passing the buck.
> Well I just wanted, as they say, a little contact. To let

information unfold in its own sweet time is to take a big risk, to anesthetize art, to push discipline to ridiculous limits. People die from hour to hour.

Thursday is my parents' fifty-first wedding anniversary.

Year after dumb year as taxes rise higher I pay not only in full but on time, although everything I was taught and still believe forbids the act. Like a lazy lamb to the slaughter, like an orderly Jew reporting to catch the coach to Dachau.

15 August

August fifteenth, Assumption of the Blessed Virgin, the one day of the year Marie Laure used to dread, the day when the end begins, and we ease back—die back—into autumn. Here since the first, this time subletting the Slade cottage and bayside garden. Despite a table carefully spread with inks and pens, huge sheets of orchestration paper and a hundred sharpened pencils, I've done little work: the absence of a piano should be a challenging virtue, a change of tune, so to sing, but in fact it's an excuse to read, or to cook according to old Fannie Farmer who when Lady Fingers are required (as in a Charlotte Russe), gives you recipe for same, and assumes you have a Lady Finger Machine, or homemade mayonnaise, or an ice house, or bushels of homegrown peppers. Books thus far: *The Groves of Academe* which I'd never read back when, and like for its vitality; Simenon's newest, *Il y a encore des Noisetiers*, about, for a change, rich people with a happy ending; Patrick O'Higgins' *Madame*; (try Fannie Farmer's frantic Apple Cream, page 566); *Salammbô* with bored amusement; *Killer Dolphin* by Ngaio Marsh.

Aunt Agnes died yesterday, father's oldest sister and Ohio hostess to childhood summers filled with kohlrabi and zinnias.

Like the Person from Porlock a mosquito's persistence at 3 A.M. can alter destinies.

24 August

Finally laboring a bit, at copy of what might be called *Chamber Music for Large Orchestra* (vignettes for unlikely combinations: three violas and tuba; piano and string septet with four English horns; double bass and timpani with eleven alto flutes). Today in an hour, composed a *Confitebor tibi*, for single voice, to fit with the other canticles.

27 August

Visit Wednesday from Morris with John Ashbery, rising out of the bay like Botticelli visions. John friendly: our first real conversation since my setting of *Some Trees*, three years ago, which he didn't like my attitude about, or so they say.

Reading Bruce Cook's *The Beat Generation*, mainly because my name's in the index. Nice, but adulatory, treating The Beat Generation as though it had existed.

Friday, rain, JH in New York, alone, ominous crickets, night falling, too quiet. Deaths of Michael Davis (father's colleague from the 1930s), Ted Lewis (idol of my infancy), Margaret Bourke-White, Bennett Cerf. Thunderous silence. A hurricane—Hurricane Doria —scheduled for the early morning. Island may be evacuated.

28 August

The hurricane arrived at 5 A.M., slowly, purposefully, from a great distance with the final force of Bengal whipping this bedroom window like Hitchcock's *Birds*. A three-hour siege, then it passed utterly. This morning, bay and ocean churn still from shock, but the sky is a proud clean baby-blue, relieved as though it had puked.

Visit to Gerald Cook in Cherry Grove. Tomorrow my essay on opera in the *Times*. Daily cooking, daily cooking and the insects. Plagues of butterfly and horsefly.

13 September

Parents for two weekends. French toast. Reading *Le Père Goriot*, Rousseau's *Confessions* and Simenon again with relish, *La Grande Perche* and *Les Fantômes du Chapelier*.

Heavy rain. Last day. Swept out cottage. As I write, the radio brings quarter-hour reports of the sad revolt in Attica prison. Back to civilization.

New York
21 September

Morris and Virgil came to dine last night. Rosh Hashanah.

Tonight, saw Terrence McNalley's new play. Half of it. Tomorrow Robert Phelps to dine, with Rorems. *Boeuf Carbonnade. Bavaroise aux raisins noirs.*

30 September

I never, never go to restaurants anymore. The noise and grease are insupportable, the expense farcical, the company strained when one is sober, and one can do better at home. Yet Monday I lunched at Pavillon with Arnold Weissberger, and Tuesday dined at La Grenouille. Pavillon wins: more elbow room. (As we left Arnold paused to chat with Hurok and Gentele who, on learning I was a composer, said: "Why not write an opera?" Why not indeed! Eternal gulf: impresario and composer.) To think! between 1944 and 1946 I dined every night at Drossie's, whose mere name, more than Romany Marie's, evokes an époque of Zadkine, Allan Ross McDougall, stroganoff, rye and ginger ale, and that wry little gingery lady herself.

This afternoon, Anaïs Nin at Gotham Book Mart. I extend her new diary for a signature, dropping my own name. She feigns affectionate surprise, and from her purply heights she, priestess of such matters, declares approval of my books. Inscription: *For Ned a witty diary with sudden depths and moving spirits, Anaïs.* Whose diary does she mean? Tonight I dip into her's, appalled at the femininity.

Working well and regularly on *Day Music.*

Have you read Eudora's latest?
    Eudora who?

3 October

Cuite, first time in months . . .

Titles: *Dictated but Not Signed*
            Old Dogs, New Tricks

    Rehearse *Ariel* at Phyllis'.
    Evening: Masselos concert, Town Hall. (I never use epigraphs anymore.)

8 October

Vernissage Léonid.
Dine at Gruens', with cloudy Penelope Gilliatt and others.
    The whole theatrical scene is a crock of shit. Actors, perfectly serious like a bunch of children, play grown-up. Or rather, like a bunch of grown-ups, act childish.

13 October

Visit to Sylvia Marlowe and Léonid Berman and purchase of a spacious sad painting of mussel-breeders on the Isle of Oléron in early evening. Evening, John Myers here for supper (chicken paprika) pretends not to notice Léonid's picture.

14 October

Visit to Alvin Ross and purchase of two small oils, one of dead hydrangeas, the other of eggs on a napkin.

19 October

Picasso exhibit at Marlborough. Cocktail at Baldwin Piano Company for Whittemore and Lowe. Reading *Betrayed by Rita Hayworth* with disappointment. (Mini-reports do not detail details: composition, correction of composition, correction of proofs, business dates, repairmen.)

   (End whole diary with a postscript à la *Sad Café* describing in great detail a Salt Lake City movie palace—the ceiling of stars [twinkling like crab lice in a massive black vagina] that carry me forward to perhaps a bourgeois universe of peace or of terror, and that carry me back to movie theaters in Chicago, and finally to the obvious uterus.)

24 October

Until last night I'd met Beverly Sills exactly twice. First, at Carl Van Vechten's in 1956, when she still sang in English. (All I recall is asking, "What's the highest you've gone?" and her answering, "To the A above Queen of the Night's F, but I was aiming for another note.") Second, backstage last year at Hunter College when we all acted silly to raise money for the vandalized International Piano Library. On that occasion she referred to a letter I'd mailed in the interim, thanking her for the "gift" of *Julius Caesar* which I'd heard on my birthday.

   So I was pleasantly puzzled to receive, two months ago, an invitation to dine last night ("I'm cooking, so bring Alka Seltzer"), but figured she'd remembered October 23 as my birthday.

   Also present were the Richard Clurmans, Tom Prideaux of *Life*, husband Peter Greenough, Alan Rich, all more or less musical.

But when the question arose of musical settings in English—a question about which I am by definition knowledgeable—heads turned toward Beverly who was postscripted by Alan in the stance of critic-as-star. The talk was otherwise of business and bel canto. Informed that Sills gets $10,500 per recital, I mentioned that the sum surpassed what many a composer gets to write a whole opera. (Stares of compassion. Quick shift of subject.) At 11:30 I took leave. "Why so early?" "It's my birthday and I have a date." "Your *birthday!*" No shock of recognition. But she grabbed a brass sculpture from the mantel—a fat viking midget playing a lyre—thrust it into my hands, struck up "Happy Birthday" ("saving" her voice, however) which the others joined, and I was sent into the night—actually to Julius' Bar where I met Morris and talked about myself.

Beverly Sills is valiant, rare and gifted, filling a need of the same society that once invented the golden calf which gallops ever farther from the intricacies of creative art. Fine. But that's a route more foreign to me than the one to Arcturus. She and I are both "in" music, and are consecrated, even pure, with our self-realization. Yet we now have nothing in common. She at least still *talks* in English.

25 October

Death of Carl Ruggles.

29 October

Rehearse in morning with Phyllis. James Purdy for supper, and recitation by him of forthcoming novel based on Paul Swann. Ever since Chicago, circa 1938 when his roommate corrupted me at my request after seeing Zorina in *Goldwyn Follies*, we've gone to different schools together.

Halloween. With Shirley to the Christa Ludwig recital of Brahms in Carnegie. Madame Ludwig less dowdy than pictures, almost Rita Hayworth, and she can *walk*—which American women can't. (In same box are Felicia and Shirley Bernstein, and Helen Coates, all coolly affable.)

4 November

Party for Virgil's seventy-fifth birthday at Arnold Weissberger's. Black tie. As in high school, I'm required to "escort" Rita Gam, and so I do, though we have nothing to talk about, but being older than in high school, know how to fake it. Among the guests: Anne Baxter, Carol Channing, Alexis Smith, Ethel Merman, the Bernsteins, Alexei Haieff and Sheila Bridport (who didn't like anyone, but I was dazzled), and Maureen Stapleton whom I offered to bring home, and did, since she was high and lives across the street. No one, not Einstein nor Cleopatra nor Margaret Mead nor Mae West, not even Maureen Stapleton, nor Ned Rorem, is clever when drunk.

5 November

Alexei's new piece, *Caligula*, on words of Robert Lowell, at the Manhattan School. One trouble: Lowell's not poetic.

9 November

Visit to Ben Weber at Lenox Hill Hospital. Came away depressed. All that indicates he'll live's the determined twinkle in the distant red eye. Exhibits of Anne Thorne, Harold Stevenson.

25 November

WABC television interview for Brazil, because *Music and People*, the sole book of mine to be translated, now exists in Portuguese.

Thanksgiving. All the Rorems and all the Marshalls here for turkey, entirely prepared and cleaned up by JH. Tomorrow, with Sylvia Goldstein and the Popes, to Washington for premiere of *Ariel* at Library of Congress. Very sore back.

1 December

Dine at Maggy Magerstadt's with JH and Joe Rosner. For dessert a persimmon pudding, surprisingly chocolatish and crusty.

To Sigi Weissenberg's icy Chopin recital with Arnold Weissberger. En route we stop at Arlene Dahl's where I know nobody, and vice versa, and her piano is graced with a photo of Nixon. Fact: Arnold's and Sigi's names are side by side in *Who's Who*. Opinion: to observe repeats in a piece should bring an altered viewpoint. The repeats in Weissenberg's version of Chopin's *Sonata in B-minor* were not even photo duplications—which would, after all, show another dimension—they were instant replays. Defend instant replay by stating that since it comes later we are older and so hear differently.

Alan Kaprow makes one set of symbols (words) explicate another set of symbols (nonartists' art) and they collide ponderously like a pair of drunk dinosaurs on the barren pages of *Art News*.

With Rosemary to Perry O'Neil's last night. Later, party at the Gruens', on whom I bestow the new record of my *Third Symphony*. Gordon Davidson is there, and Jean-Pierre Aumont.

    With Pia Gilbert tonight to see *Murderous Angels* for which she's composed the score, Conor Cruise O'Brien the text, and Davidson directing mostly Aumont. Liked it rather. JH in Kansas. Alone, lonely.

My head is empty. Opinions come from those I admire. Still, I choose whom I admire.

One unfortunate benefit of keeping a publishable diary: you are applauded for thumbnail plots, whereas an amateur who recounts to you his never-to-be-written novel is disdained. Such is the power of print.

    I'm impatient with potential, with unrealized talent, with conjectures about what Schubert would have bequeathed if he hadn't died young. Impatience turns to despair when directed inward toward an increasing procrastination in notating those genial notions which only I can notate. Works may be praised only after the fact. Potential is nil. An idea is worthless until given flesh, including the idea of this paragraph. (Has the idea of this paragraph been given flesh by virtue of having been notated?)

I'm not an exhibitionist. Paradoxically, the keeping of a diary, like getting drunk, is the shutting off of one's self, the private gesture of one who may not dare the physical parade.

   Nor am I a very interesting person. No diarist is, really. What he says may be, but when you finally meet him you discover you've already read his conversation. An interesting person is one versed in subjects beyond himself. A diarist is no more self-aware than an actor—though with a broader vocabulary.

   Rereading my journal (why journal? it was mostly written at night), I find it difficult to follow the thought, not because the thought is so removed, but because it is so full of what I still repeat that it goes in one eye and out the other. I cannot concentrate enough to know if I still believe those brash clichés.

   Jean-Pierre Aumont comes to tea. (Camembert, apple cake, fresh strawberries, rye whisky.) He wanted to visit because my books showed him "a fascinating man." But I am not fascinating, my books are. He asks me to explain "The way to raise children is to treat them like drunks." A bon mot must explain itself. I, meanwhile, have read *his* autobiography, *Souvenirs Provisoires* (1957). There now we sit in silence, already knowing each other too well, afraid to break further the illusion-preserving ice.

Twenty-six years ago I began this journal whose chief obsessions were about making out. How do you talk to strangers? make friends? what do you do in bed, and how do you get there? How do you persuade others of your talent, and become famous? How, for that matter, do you write diaries, and then, of all things, get them published? Today, with some of the riddles solved, the obsessions remain identical, for the solutions are already a thing of the past: how can I communicate, be appreciated, make friends, get laid? Accomplishment is significant only to outsiders. We cannot nourish ourselves by rereading our own books or hearing our own music, by, so to speak, performing ourselves. The Ned then made friends or thought he did; the Ned now wonders how; the future Ned, like Madame Du Barry to the Angel of Death, requests a minute's reprieve—I was just about to understand . . .

There is nothing to do. What can be done? Where can I go? There is nowhere to go. Nowhere to go, what can I do? Nothing more can be done. Aphorists cornered spew bromides.

What do I think of Anaïs Nin? But I never think of her. At least, I never think much about her. To read her diaries finally is to be chilled at the thought that she still believes all that bullshit about fulfillment and dreams and the rich life. Humor is hardly her strong point, and neither is depth, but while eschewing the one she misses the boat on the other. Of course, humor is by nature objective which diaries by nature are not. Nor need they be more than the contemplation of navels. But Nin overlooks the lint in favor of her own perfection, and perfection is boring.

One feels no shred of self-doubt *chez elle*, none of the vulnerable anxiety that besieges artists. Yet why am I surprised at her conceit, since the very fact of a diary is conceit? It is also a book about how hard it is to write a book. And it is on-the-spot gossip. But Nin reflects. Worse, her reflections are mushy (what used to be called feminine). Where is the book she writes about?

Her diary discourages me from my own, not from envy but from exasperation at the tiresome process. Still, like Aumont, she must come for tea, so that later we may write about each other in our diaries.

To expect the miracle, the radical sea-change! That Nixon will awaken and stop the war, that Franco will ask Auden's advice, that friends will turn against us, that the bourgeois couple next door will play Debussy's *Trio* on their phonograph instead of hard rock, that the world will see the dawn as we see it. There are no revelations. What we become, however startling to strangers, derives from what we are. We have a single flow, undivided into sudden intervals. We remain, more or less, stagnantly wise or stagnantly stupid.

She passes her time, her days and years, reading and in good health, in the sunniest library nook, in the palest of dotted swiss, in the hottest of whole-wheat toast, the smell of coffee, of peonies and well-tuned cellos. Out there, the planet Mars is invaded by steel. No blood blackens her gown before she dies. She never dies.

Why soft-pedal your homosexuality?

Because anyone can be homosexual whereas only you can be you. Sexual identity, like beauty, is partly an effect of will. Talent is given, not willed. What we make of our talent, as of our beauty, is a responsibility. Talent, however, cannot be lazy: it only exists by proving itself. The thrill of Mozart lies not in his genius but in what he did with his genius. But mere homosexuals and beauties can fritter their lives away, for they need prove nothing.

Rechy, Rader, Krim, and all, write of themselves as rough trade. Those with whom they "trade it" are treated, at best, with a cold affection, like gifts. Has the fellator, the *enculé*, ever drawn his side of the picture? Not yet, not as a serious writer, at least not in the first person singular, not even Genet. Yet it is precisely from among the accomplished that we find the homosexual who is attracted to the nonaccomplished, the everyday, the workman. Now Rechy, Rader, Krim, and all, necessarily align themselves with the nonaccomplished, at least in fantasy. The smaller classes (intellectuals, artists) seem always attracted by the larger classes (students, sailors). How many delicate poets incognito are down at the docks blowing butch poets incognito? Despite the Harold Actons of this world, aristocrats do not recoil before their servants.

In a misfired epigram James Dickey writes: "Marilyn Monroe was a masturbation fantasy of bellboys, Grace Kelly of bank executives." He is exactly wrong. Men tend to masturbate out of their class, women within it (if they use images at all).

In his song from the 1930s, *Down in the Depths on the Ninetieth Floor*, Cole Porter incorporated his most aristocratic couplet, about the perfectly good love life of his janitor's wife. Aristocratic—or as they said back then, capitalist. The implications were horrendous.

Why *shouldn't* your janitor's wife have a good love life? Do you feel that, in the order of things, your love life should be "better" than your janitor's wife, though under the present temporary circumstances . . . ? Do you feel that the lower orders have better sex than the higher? If they don't, do you resent the possibility that they might? Does the janitor's wife not deserve her good love life? and how do you even know about her love life?

As facts stand, Cole Porter would surely have preferred being the janitor's wife than the singer of his song. Nor is it just homosexual aristocrats who prefer the working classes, viz., Lady Chatterley and Miss Julie. Can we write about tears in our eyes with tears in our eyes? Of course. But to disclose what we "know best" doesn't guarantee the clearest pronouncement, precisely because, since we *live* it, we can't *know* it. *Maurice*, Forster's "frankest" novel, is also his weakest.

How measure time? Seven minutes looking at the clock is not comparable to seven minutes of a Mozart quintet. Seven minutes of private rehearsal is not seven minutes of public performance. Seven minutes waiting for your lover is not the length of seven minutes from a three-hour stroll on the beach, or from a three-day working stint on your tax report. The first seven minutes screwing are shorter than the last seven dying.

Growing older, the hide can't feel the gradual advance, temperament remains childlike. Nor does it feel it through the eyes of friends, nor in mirrors which always lie. But in the vacant stares of strangers, and in photographs old and new, we confirm that that which can happen to others but not to us, can happen to us.

Struck with disfiguring eczema—God's punishment for the years that showered favors upon me. Or have I for those years had eczema and only now awakened from God's generous drugged stupor?

Sooner or later you've heard everything your best friends have to say. True love is tolerance for endless repetition. This holds for self-love too. Friends are growing fatter and grayer but not much brighter. They offer ever less surprise. To myself too I offer no surprise. This should be awful, yet I'm complacent, still behaving in terms of tomorrow-when-I-grow-up, when it's clear there are no more revelations in store.

Twenty-one years ago I was twenty-six and had been living in France and Africa for two years. Twenty-one years before my birth the premiere of *Pelléas* took place, and Stravinsky had composed nothing we know, the century had just turned. In twenty-one years we will be in 1992. Brahms would have been ninety in the year of my birth (1923), and if I survive his span (1833–97), I'll be dead in 1987. Vainly searching the encyclopedia for musicians born in 1823; everyone was born in the teens or the thirties of the nineteenth-century, and also of our century.

My unadmirable corroding capacity for grudge, for unremembered slights. I forget, but I never forgive.

Innocent civilians. And . . . guilty soldiers?

Les gens ne lisent pas, ils se lisent, wrote Cocteau. He spoke the marvelous sentence in despair. But who can find in a masterpiece more than what he brings to it?

Morris finds my recent tone dogmatic, less (as he calls it) vulnerable than *The Paris Diary*. Still, I no longer write about my love affairs but about other people's opportunism. The phrase "In my opinion" is, in my opinion, abject and prolix. One assumes an opinion belongs to its author. Apology is redundant.

Use black metaphors gingerly now. Yet how insolent to consider all black reference as racial! Black humor, black magic. The night *is* black, and thus for human eyes mysterious, but not necessarily wicked. And is wicked wrong? In China, white means mourning. Our funerals are heavily justly black, containing all. Before learning to spell we learned that white was absence of color, while black contained the whole rainbow at once. Black is the *presence* of color, so Negroes are correctly called colored. (Alvin Ross, reading this paragraph, contradicts me: Black is the *absence* of color. Well then, Negroes should correctly be called white.)

The new permissiveness is chilling. God knows, from 1938 to 1967 I led a gaudy life, promiscuous, self-indulgent, guilty as hell by

382

standards then. But without guilt where are we? And precocity is
unbecoming to the middle-aged.

Jean Genet in the early fifties was a conquest among the *dames
du monde* vying with each other about stolen objects. "So he swiped
a gold salt cellar from you, did he, dear? From me he took an
alabaster vase." Today they purchase life-size replicas of people
fucking, but don't permit people to fuck beneath their Chippendale
chairs. I am not queer, I am a composer. I am not a composer, I am
my parents' offspring. The divine specific, creator as creation. Even
Beethoven was not Beethoven but a product of the elders. Anyone,
in principle, can be Beethoven, but only he can be his parents'
child.

Times haven't changed so much when at this late date, in the face
of black and female freedom, homosexuality is, in the eyes of
intellectual pedants, still good for a "how come" or a laugh or a
sneer. When a Stanley Kauffmann, with untypical fuzziness, asks in
a review of *Sunday Bloody Sunday* how two such comparatively
cultivated types could fall for a cipher like Murray Head—*that*, the
very week Forster's *Maurice* comes out. When, in the current issue
of *Sewanee Review*, a Peter Taylor will disclose his hero as
homosexual by declaring—what else?—that "his gestures and his
walk have become effeminate—but not exaggerated." When, in the
same issue, one James Blish, in an essay on Poe, concludes with this
gratuitous paragraph:

> Such arguments as those between Edmund Wilson and Vladimir
> Nabokov over the latter's translation of Pushkin, or indeed almost any
> of the tempests which rage in the letter columns of *The New York
> Review of Books*, more closely resemble the domestic spats of
> homosexuals than they do any kind of literary controversy. Such
> people seem to thrive, or think that they thrive, in a climate of
> insult. . . .

But since Wilson and Nabokov are not homosexual, nor are the
policy makers of *The New York Review*, why doesn't the author say
"spats of heterosexuals"? Such a person seems to thrive in a climate
of insult.

Having composed my settings from *Ariel* I no longer need Sylvia
Plath. People bring me essays about, or newly recovered verses by,

Plath; I am no longer interested. Not that having once lived "within" her I now find her less good; it's simply that the urge is exhausted—something I'd never say of Whitman or Hopkins or Frank O'Hara, or Roethke or Byron or Kenneth Koch.

The Markhams give a late evening party (a huge Brie with winter pears, a huge chocolate cheesecake, champagne and Turkish coffee), so that Phyllis Curtin, David Glazer and Ryan Edwards can perform two run-throughs of *Ariel* before the premiere at the Library of Congress. The piece is in five sections, for soprano and clarinet and voice.

Virgil Thomson, who has come with Claude Alphand looking very very cool in her white boots and lavender leather jacket, later declares: Either the words are a put-on or the music is, I'm not sure which. Well yes, Virgil, maybe they're both a put-on, but you're not supposed to be sure: that's art!

Words about music can't have suicidal settings. Why should the composer do what the poet's already done? Virgil prefers French to German, classic to romantic. He prefers comments on self-expression (like Racine who makes Phaedra speak of her anxiety) to self-expression (like Sylvia Plath speaking of her own anxiety). Virgil keeps himself one step removed from the fatal crime.

They all want to rewrite your music for you. I had, for example, invited my favorite critic, John Simon (a critic for the pun of it: he called the piece Plathitudes), who brings a Ms. Beck along. Ms. Beck seems hazy, young but unsteady, as though drugged by the very rightness of it all, or, who knows? by the music's beauty. She approaches to say: You've missed the point, you can't write music like that to poems like that, they scan differently, you haven't hit it, and besides, you have to be a woman to understand Plath.

But I *am* a woman.

1972

Diary-keeping, a mental metabolizing activity at one time, now appears to me like a bad habit. To the addict it could become an end in itself, and one for which he might not only exploit experience but force it as well. For myself, then, and touching wood, this will be *nunc dimittis*.

—Robert Craft, in *Themes and Episodes*

Local premiere of my Marianne Moore *Fables* at Thomas Martin's Opera Workshop at the National Arts Club in Gramercy Park.

Visit to Shirley Verrett's to hear my *Resurrection*, which is the St. Matthew Passion condensed into fourteen minutes. Shirley sings the piece better than it deserves, but brings back the heady heat wave of 1952 when it was composed on the Rue de Vaugirard.

Conjunctivitis. Milky medication, I wear dark glasses as Shirley and I drop by Gombergs' nice party for their daughter, and thence to an unthinkable dinner given by PEN for Yevtushenko, a pompous ass turned into a lion by our leading minds. For an hour he bored his betters by chanting the praises of Hemingway. Whimsy is not his strong point. Has no one thought to question his credentials, which resemble those of Rod McKuen?

Because we are all different we speak a subdivision of our native language. A poet's subdivision, at least on paper, is identifiably unique among millions. A peasant also differs from his closest friend (because he is not his closest friend) by avoiding certain adverbs, favoring various verbs, swaying to his own metronome with hastenings and pauses that are his alone and alter with his time of day, his age and pulse, indeed his whole horoscope.

When I went to live in France I wished to master French sufficiently to transfer the character of my personal English—the Nedisms of my mother tongue—into the other tongue.

"They" always claim that unlimited possibilities of synthesizers and computers are inherently advantageous to composers. On the contrary, limited possibilities have always made for tighter techniques, less self-indulgence, more stringent exploration. The French have half our number of words, and how they overshadow us. They have a word for it, and it isn't Moog.

Scientific discoveries herald eras. Works of art conclude eras.

28 January

In his recent *Conversations* Elliott Carter maintains (and he says it thrice if he says it once) that composers "aren't doing the one thing music can do, which is to 'go,' to move." That's a contradiction; all music, by definition, *goes*. And when he states that what he's "talking about here does not . . . seem to be the concern of most composers today" (who are most?) "who generally have the most primitive and obvious way of dealing with time," he is suggesting that his methods and preoccupations are *a priori* superior to others.

And he does oversimplify things when he justifies his own music at the expense of other people's, including *The Rite of Spring*, by defining "repetitiveness, in itself [as] the basic avant-garde ploy. . . . In *The Rite*, there are patterns that just repeat over and over again. Well, obviously it's a scandal if you repeat *anything* sixty times in front of an audience. . . . My music has consistently avoided [the] notion of repetition. . . . I [am] concerned with progression and change. . . . My music is related to the historical past—to Bach, Beethoven. . . ."

But repetitiveness has been a basic "ploy" of all music of all periods. Bach in the *Crucifixus* repeats the ground thirteen times without alteration or interlude. Beethoven in the *Thirty-two Variations* repeats the same chord progression thirty-two times without alteration or interlude. But where in *The Rite* does Stravinsky repeat anything sixty times? And was scandal all he was after?

4 February

Last night, dinner party for Pauline Kael, Virgil, Ruth Ford and Ellen, for whom JH and I prepared pot roast and Maggy's persimmon pudding. Afterward two friends of Ruth's dropped by uninvited, Dotson Rader and screenwriter Larry Kramer, and later still, Jack Larson and Jim Bridges, fresh from premiere of Robbins' *Watermill*. But again, let me swear off such excitements which provoke headaches and hemorrhoids. Too conscious of the salad dressing, I missed the repartee and felt that these good minds are acting silly. If Pauline and Virgil are the greatest critics in our world, what finally can they speak to each other that they can't speak better in print? Dotson, a born flirt, baited Pauline, not a born flirt, with inanities like "Ballet isn't where it's at," so that what in Saint Simon seems epic here seems trivial. Tonight, with a bad cold and with Shirley, went to Lou Harrison's chamingly businesslike concert at Loeb Student Center where we sat coincidentally next to Virgil who stayed awake.

5 February

Death of Marianne Moore.

14 February

As I watch with disbelief Pasatieri's televised *Trial of Mary Lincoln* (redeemed somewhat by stately Elaine Bonazzi), the phone rings, JH answers, then tells me: Someone who says he's Tennessee Williams wants to speak with you. Since it's been eight years and he's unpredictable, I agree to come immediately over to Dotson's and visit him and Ruth. When I arrive neither Dotson nor Ruth is there (they're in Florida), and Jack Weiser acts as host. With Tom Seligson, we are four then, and Tennessee, bearded, trim and fairly lucid, talks with me, mostly about my books (which I'm not sure he's read), as the others listen warmly for two hours, and I come home feeling not bad.

22 February

Simultaneous visit from Martin Greif and from Marian Castleman Skedgell, both of whom bring burnt offerings from their respective publishing houses. Snow. Marian laughs savagely which provokes a hearty nosebleed. We deposit her at Grand Central en route to our dinner date chez Tom Prentiss and Nan Stibane who are now legally married.

2 March

With a mild sense of guilt I went alone last night to *Clockwork Orange* at precisely the moment when Leopold Stokowski, in Town Hall, was conducting my *Pilgrims for Strings*. Now Stokowski is a great man, an idol of my childhood, and more than once he's played my music. But I don't like *Pilgrims* any more. My contention: the worse a piece is the worse it will sound the better it's played, like a wart in a well-focused photo. Apparently the maestro gestured for me to rise, but I was invisible, so he shrugged and went on to the next work. (I know about this from the newspaper. No one invited me either to a rehearsal or to the program.)

5 March

Carnegie Hall this afternoon for Leontyne Price's recital. She sang *Psalm 148* from *Cycle of Holy Songs*, the first piece of mine I've ever heard her do, and again, like last Wednesday, I squirmed at the selection. If Leontyne is the leading soprano on earth today, couldn't she perform, by that token, something more "representative" from among my 130 published songs? I feel right about only fifteen; the rest are to be had for the asking. What I love, nobody sings, what they sing, nobody loves.

17 March

The Tokyo Story. Tedious masterpiece.

18 March

Exhibit of Susan Crile, the good-natured girl with long clean hair who charmed us at Yaddo last year. The pictures—all four of them—are gigantic Oriental rugs, poised, already halfway to heaven as though we the watchers were actually fakirs on a ride. A magician is nothing if not an individual, and Susan has a big touch of the poet: of the faker. . . . Down the street, Joan Mitchell's paintings seem heavier with the sound and fury of a school than of a person. If they now seem dated, I realize I never directly cared, only through contagion via Frank O'Hara with whose death died my interest in Abstract Expressionism.

19 March

Sunday brunch at Irene Diamond's for Janet Flanner. Evening, premiere of Lee Hoiby's opera, *Summer and Smoke*, which I'll review for *The New Republic*.

23 March

Sam Barber, who has no identifiable style, has identifiably styled Lee Hoiby, though that bon mot is not for publication. The proof is *Summer and Smoke*.

Corsaro directed with occasional touches of contempt. For example, he rendered the minor role of a young poet named Vernon—the only character with "creative tendencies"—as a sappy fruit, to provide comic diversion before returning us to the serious business of heterosexual frustration. Now, given the tendencies of so many concerned, this device ought to appear dishonest. It merely seems exhausted.

The Northern cast performed dutifully with Southern accents. In the South singers work hard to rid themselves of accent, and do spirituals straight as a dye.

Years ago Lee Hoiby and I were more frequent friends than now. Opening night, attended in my capacity of critic, who should be sitting beside me!

Tennessee Williams, untrained in music and unreactive to all but the most visceral tunes, instinctively resisted for three decades the petitions of very distinguished composers. Indeed, Hoiby is advertised as the first ever granted the rights to one of his plays, although for the record this honor goes to Raffaello de Banfield, circa 1954. (In the Paris days I used to say: whoever writes that music for Raffaello back home in Trieste isn't very talented.

N'empêche que—I've never heard *Lord Byron's Love Letter* without shivering wonderfully, and I've heard it many times.)

A "conservative" composer's talent for opera is usually delusory. Guided as he is by that sense of the past which is most characteristically translated through song, his earliest efforts are, recognized as showing "a gift for melody." But such a gift, with opera, is less helpful than a gift for drama.

Our best-known American opera composer is not American, nor has he ever employed an American theme in the plots of his own devising. Yet for a quarter century he has been the widest influence in the field. Merotti's unprecedented glory during the '40s led dozens of friends and enemies to try their hand at the genre. Some, like Barber and Hollingsworth with first attempts, *Vanessa* and *The Mother*, achieved a transient renown, but none hit the jackpot as Menotti had, nor has anyone since. No other American's full-evening operas have become repertory fare. But if Menotti's pseudo-Puccini jargon paradoxically sounded "real," he was, after all, reared where such language was the lingua franca. His followers imitated his imitation of Italian verismo, filtered this through Americanistic plots and provided novelties that for a while seemed nourishing. Yet the predigested matter garnished with their minor talent faded into such a thin flow of perfumed urine that by the mid-'60s it reached a sticky dénouement, and has today quite evaporated.

25 March

Apropos of the plays or home movies or concerts or public readings of various acquaintances, JH says: "The most we should expect of our friends is that they not embarrass us."

No piano teacher is more sensitive than Virgil, although accuracy is not his forte. He can, paradoxically, sabotage his own music without misinterpreting it. He raises his hands, then lets them descend, with crashing authority, on all the wrong notes.

The final criterion that X is an artist lies in my saying so, for I am an artist. No one has crowned me, because I have crowned myself.

Music: all logic, no reason. Interpret music logically and reveal the impasse: The themes are people, the notes are people's actions. When all is dead and sung . . .

It isn't evil that's ruining our earth, but mediocrity. The crime is not that Nero played while Rome burned, but that he played badly.

Who has not prayed, "Grant me, God, the illness of Proust, that I may complete work without the mad distraction"? The mad distraction is, of course, the carnal drive, ever more unseemly yet no less intense as the groin decays. But who, including God and Proust, will prove that without the mad distraction work can grow and retain heat? The work is madness made marble. The spirit, not the flesh, grows weak and unwilling with time. Denial comes through choice—choice to deny the body. Still the body screeches. To ignore the screech is to atrophy. Proust's book exists despite, not because of, his illness.

28 March

Reading by Reed Whittemore at New Manhattan Theater Club. Rather witty, but a mirthless setting. Coffee. Bump into Ann Birstein and her daughter who drink ginger ale at our table. Stayed up till three with income tax.

30 March

Preview of Tennessee's new play, *Small Craft Warnings*. With stupefaction we stay on, as banalities flow like Cilea arias orchestrated by Saroyan and sung in slow motion.

3 April

Saturday, Joe Brainard's charming vernissage. Visit from Richard Dufallo to select, maybe, scores for his various enterprises. Dined chez parents. Then, exceptionally, got drunk at Kenward's party for Joe, and recall only the dubious ministrations of Ruth Kligman looking as she looked in our "drinking days." Deathly ill yesterday, indeed too ill to do much for JH's birthday, or to enjoy the wonderful *Transfiguration* of Messiaen.

4 April

Another visit from Dufallo, to go through score of *Bertha*. Evening, with JH, to two-piano recital of Yvonne Loriod and Messiaen at Hunter College. An almost empty house. (How well Messiaen holds up, yet how unfashionable he's become, with his honest bigger-than-life schmaltz and first-rate tunes!) Backstage to kiss Yvonne, no longer the slim genius I remember from Morocco in 1950, but the husbandly mate of the Great Man (greater but no more extraordinary than Yvonne herself) to whom she introduces us, and I'm intimidated for the first time in years.

5 April

Dined at Braziller's in honor of Nathalie Sarraute, who pretends to remember the one time we met. (In February 1952 at the Catalan Restaurant. She was sitting with Dora Maar, and I—very blond then, she says—with Marie Laure. A week later I received an inscribed copy of Sarraute's *Portrait d'un inconnu* which I couldn't, and still can't, make much of.) I talked mostly with the spouse of a West Point officer, Josiah Bunting, whose first book Braziller publishes next month. Very good buffet.

6 April

JH and I give a nice tea party for Janet Flanner. Natalia Murray, Jack Larson, John Gruen, Jane Wilson, Stella Adler, Mitchell Wilson, Helen and Tom Bishop eat the apple cake.

9 April

Evening visit from Jack Larson, weary from rehearsals of his and Virgil's opera, to watch the Academy Awards.

16 April

Dinner party here for the Gruens and the Harnacks. For dessert, creamed pears in port, one of those failed recipes from the *Times*. Virgil says they always jealously omit a key ingredient, like any good chef guarding his secrets.

18 April

Dress rehearsal of *Lord Byron*. Cocktail at Stella's for Mitchell's new book, *A Passion to Know*.

23 April

Visit from Billy Masselos and Ben Weber looking like a new man. We have tea, play my tapes and those of Ben's *Violin Rhapsody*. Later my parents come to dine with Eliza Critchlow, a Pittsburgh Quaker.

24 April

Practice with Phyllis.

26 April

O'Hara memorial concert at the Whitney. Party later at the Fosses'.

It is important to be alive. For every Sylvia Plath who made a living out of dying, twenty good poets' credit is canceled by death. Death does not reduce a painter's cachet, since his work is an investment; but an original manuscript by a Plath isn't "worth" anything. As for composers, Hindemith was forgotten the day after his funeral, while Bartók became rich the day after his. No sooner does any artist die than his work locates itself, becomes less urgent, asks to be balanced and judged.

We have just given a memorial concert: recent settings by seven composers of poems by Frank O'Hara who died six years ago. The settings were all unsuccessful though not because they were commissioned for the occasion (despite the obvious conclusion that if these composers were not moved to use O'Hara living, then why O'Hara dead?). They were unsuccessful because of the uncertain distance between the poetry's composition and the music's. O'Hara's poems are far enough away to be experienced as the past, yet too close to be convincingly embellished by the present. The poems are 1960s, their music is 1970s. Debussy set Baudelaire a half century after the poet's death, and both are now remote enough for us to see (hear) them as one. O'Hara was nothing if not a poet of the present. But we are his future, unfocusing his quiet grave. The tone of the immediate past juxtaposed upon the tone of the present produces a unison just slightly out of tune. To a trained ear this is more discombobulating than a juxtaposition of centuries. The legend of Othello, adapted by Shakespeare, prosified by Boïto, musicalized by Verdi, recorded by Tebaldi, reaches us with no sense of anachronism. But if we can caricature the '50s now, the '60s are still too close for comfort.

30 April

A year ago tonight Shirley and I went to that Women's Lib thing in Town Hall. How already dated all that reads now.

Turning back through these pages makes me wish there'd been more entries on ordinary events. Today's commonplace becomes tomorrow's singularity, and the history of ancient Rome might (might!) be less dry, more thorough, if we knew the biographies of slaves. Still, I am not my Boswell, nor finally should I pretend that the commonplace intrigues me. The convenient excuse is that I'm not a writer but a composer. Words mean only other things, music means only itself.

Notably present, beyond myself, are cameo walk-ons by celebrities. Notably absent are invisible stars shedding daily manna. Blood friends. Yet what does one write of the regular? Besides Colette, and she only in retrospect, who can report quotidian bliss? Without my parents I would breathe uneasily, as I would without Shirley. Without the ones I've known forever, old friends, Morris, Eugene, Maggy, would I function as well or better? Without JH I would disappear. Beyond this I can write nothing. Tomorrow I leave for Yaddo for three weeks.

Margaret Bonds is dead. So closes the miniature dynasty of female piano teachers who taught me all I knew by the time I was fifteen. Nuta Rothschild, Belle Tannenbaum, Margaret Bonds, two Jews and a Negro, all dead. In this or any day it's scarcely revolutionary for a child to have a female tutor. But for a white pupil to have a black piano teacher was not standard practice in Chicago during the 1930s, and is there a reason not to be proud of it? (Margaret was only ten years older than I.)

Yaddo
24 May

The three weeks here have drawn to a close. During this time I:

Reviewed three books (particularly Robert Craft's marvelous diary) for *The New Republic*.

Compiled three biographies (on Paul Bowles, Bill Flanagan, Lou Harrison) for *Grove's Dictionary*.

Completed the suite *Night Music* for fiddle and keyboard (which makes sixteen pieces, or fifty minutes' worth, of violin music composed in the past year).

Read: *Les Innocents* of Simenon, *Ni Marx ni Jésus* of Jean-François Revel, Forster's *A Room with a View*, and all the little mags.

Saw the Louis Falco Dance Company with pleasure, and with less pleasure: *Cabaret, The Godfather*.

Witnessed on the TV an infected speech by Nixon (May 8, Rosemary's birthday), and the nonassassination of Governor Wallace (May 15).

Endured the endless rain and odor of new lilacs.

Enjoyed the company of: Polly, Hortense and Curtis, Pamela McCorduck and Nicolas Sapieha, Richard Bunting who came from Fredonia to discuss an opera commission, Lore Segal. Mark Strand, Daniel Lang, Miriam Waddington, Donald Justice (who each get silver stars), David Del Tredici, Rosemarie Beck, Larry Josephs (who each get gold stars) and my precious Elizabeth Ames who gets a star sapphire.

Went swimming with David at the Y and broke a toe, but learned to like his music.

Gave a party for all of this.

Reflected plenty.

New York
26 May

Back in the city and struck by the agreeability of being again among possessions. Thirty years a gypsy, I'm thrilled now by ownership. Others, they say, shed facts in favor of ideas as they age, while I grow increasingly superficial—though why superficial?—and life is a list. *Je tiens aux objets,* especially the paintings by Joe Brainard, the Janes Frielicher and Wilson, Léonid, Cocteau, Alvin Ross, Tom Prentiss, Marie Laure, Rosemarie Beck and Norris Embry. But there's a high value to the letters and manuscripts and books and deep blue kitchenware too.

28 May

Death of the Duke of Windsor.

Ride in Central Park on JH's new bike. Arthur Laurents' *Invitation to a March* on TV.

31 May

Evening at the Gruens', where Lenny Bernstein, filled with his *Mass,* disapproves a screening of John's début, with Clarisse Rivers, as movie star. Heat.

Informed that I'd just completed a long work for violin and piano, Lenny exclaims, "Are people still writing that sort of thing!" The only subject that now sparks Bernstein being Bernstein's *Mass,* one is forever grasping for new things to say about this mildly attractive but not ingenious entertainment. Lenny disingenuously states that he will conduct no other music unless it's taped and televised. A far cry from the pioneer and servant of even five years ago.

5 June

Recording of my *Day Music* for Desto. Jaime and Ruth Laredo play like angels. Like devils.

8 June

The Sorrow and the Pity with Ellen. We came to pray and remained to scoff.

14 June

Elliott Stein comes to dine, and to renew acquaintance after so long. Baked fillets of sole. Dessert: fresh raspberries, blueberries, straw-berries, blackberries, black raspberries, gooseberries, yellow plums, white grapes, melon balls and black cherries in two quarts of heavy chantilly. Elliott is as committed to movies as a saint to good works.

17 June

Reading by Kenneth Pitchford of his "militant" verse last evening in the Church of the Holy Apostles. Some of it worked. Exceptionally this poetry must be heard aloud, and Kenneth, while dressed for the part, can't act, although as a poet he is the real thing. Unfortunately when one is the real thing one's evasions ring louder than a liar's lies. To propagandize, he concedes—with that same hayseed style of seventeen years ago when he appeared on my doorstep with the gift of his person.

Afterward, a small and curiously *comme il faut* gathering at Kenneth's and Robin Morgan's. Also there: Adrienne Rich, who has a mind that functions resonantly and who, without conceding, draws you to her poems. Robin, on learning I'd set Plath to music, turned on me with (was it ironic?) wrath: "How dare you touch her, she's for our sisters to make songs out of, she belongs to us." As though poetry, once written, belonged to anyone, including the poet.

Kenneth, in his guise as gay militant, now uses his poetry to promote the cause of the Flaming Faggot. The term originates from the *auto da fé* which could produce flames foul enough to consume a witch only by tying homosexuals into bundles of kindling. Now when Kenneth reproaches the Warhol-Morissey syndrome for picturing homosexuals as drag queens who confirm bourgeois prejudices, he censors not only an artist's materials but the use of those materials. Would Kenneth pander to the Establishment by whitening artists' obsessions? by making Bosch blander? Am I losing my humor, who in *The New York Diary* spoke of Miss Average Man?

This evening, tête-à-tête with John Gruen over scrambled eggs, grape jam and espresso, after which, summoning courage, we went to *Left Handed*, a so-called breakthrough in pornographic film. It's the first animated undercover erotica I've ever seen, and it's very very exciting for ten minutes. Snapshots passed around in childhood were of middle-aged potbellies with winter underwear and handlebar moustaches self-consciously caressing the distended pudenda of sad circus queens, while here the couplings are between Adonis and Apollo. But when there is no theme, only variations, lassitude rapidly overcomes you. We found ourselves concentrating on the impassive faces of the entirely male and mostly over-forty spectators.

19 June

Reception at Rizzoli's for Vera Stravinsky, Robert Craft, and Paul Horgan. Mrs. S has a tone no American female could think up, much less bring off: too much *maquillage*, which is not too much. Like Marilyn Monroe in her potato sack, Vera remains an empress. She thanked me for the review of Craft's chronicle, but when I said we'd met once before—during a show of her paintings at the Obelisco in 1954—she didn't remember, and now I'm not sure either. Did Robert remember when last we met? Yes—on the Lido beach in September 1951. Correct. What more do we say, now that the crowd's so massive, and the books are written? Still, I found time to offend Mr. Horgan by stating I was offended by his too easy put-down of Cocteau in his otherwise gentle memoir. Since I don't drink I'm miserable at these gatherings, and returned with JH to the (comparative) calm of home.

29 June

Visit from Warren Wilson, to borrow the Mompou songs. (Useful vignettes, by the way, which old Mompou himself gave me in Barcelona in 1952. Someday I should write that up—except that I just have.) Rereading Paul Goodman's *Grand Piano*. Endless rain. Every once in a while a few mean sun rays like little brass hatchets chop through the clouds, but are quickly extinguished.

6 July

Last night with JH, Hitchcock's *Frenzy*. Nothing in it works, but it all works.

Tonight Wallace Fowlie came to dine, and, with JH, we spent the evening *à trois*. A good listener. Of all my vicarious friends (like Robert Phelps, whose *raison d'écrire* is the glory of others), Wallace is the least generalized (he has France by the tail, from the *Chanson de Roland* to Roland Barthes, but has never heard of, say, John Cheever, whose vacated rooms he nonetheless occupied at Yaddo), and the most self-involved (despite hero-worship he autobiographies: his brief souvenirs called *Pantomime* are no less *troublants* than Julien Green's). Warmth itself, yet every inch a gentleman (without being straitlaced or wishy-washy), Wallace has, all the same, composed a book—sandwiched between his Mallarmé and a history of French criticism—detailing each lubricious encounter of his life.

8 July

Pose again for Rosemarie Beck. Later, *Joan* by Al Carmines. I rather like the man himself, have fairly heard him through three productions, and am not amiss to basking in good tunes (how I've loved those of Alex Wilder! of Vernon Duke!). But I don't find what others find in him. Admittedly, drama critics and not musicians surround him, swelling his molehill of banal tune into a mountain of inventive melody.

9 July

Semieclipse. Watercolors at Morgan Library. Japanese movie, *Princess Kwei Fei*, with Shirley.

19 July

Victorious return from disastrous sojourn to Nantucket. Victorious because embarkment is daily touch-and-go from that fog-bound isle. Disastrous because twenty-eight years ago, with Morris, the population explosion had not commenced. One still sees mile on mile on mile of impenetrable woodlands, two feet high. There still are vendors of maple sugar and peanut-butter fudge. And still the cute scrubbed churches, cranberry bogs, corn muffins, cheap bicycles and no insects. But the island's overrun with right-wing hippies, bourgeois unappealing Nixonite young Wasp perspirers from Boston crowding into the cruel museums that exhibit rusty harpoons and old prints of bleeding whales, crowding into the pseudo-quaint inns where they overeat with empty eyes while shouting college songs in sour unison, crowding roachlike through the cheap wharf galleries disgorging expensive driftwood artifacts. In addition, the Harbor House had an all-night piano manned by a cheerleader, mirthless tough beds, barking dogs, overcast weather.

Already Monday, after an outing in Siasconset, as JH and I were finishing our chowder at The Tavern, toying with the notion of leaving next day, stopping our ears against an aggressive accordion and trying to compare notes on our mutual loathing of the local Catholic dishwater-blond fauna, and exclaiming, My God, there's not one Jew in this town, much less anyone we'd ever want to know! who should enter in all his swarthy glory but Philip Roth, and Barbara. So they sat and chatted a while, cheered us up some (we'd seen no humans hitherto), and we made a date for Wednesday but didn't keep it because we fled instead. Tuesday we did enjoy a comfortable meal in the Jared Coffin House, and went to an expert violin recital by Masako Yanagita at the Presbyterian Church enmeshed in bougainvillaea. But that's not what we'd come for. On the plane back, we jovially encountered Claire Reis.

22 July

Heat continues. Witnessed a mugging in lobby at noon. Pose for Becki. Dine chez Rorem.

28 July

Edward Albee on Dick Cavett's show, disappointingly at home with the cliché banter.

Visit, on the recommendation of David Garvey, of Peter Matthews, a youngish composer from Ann Arbor, and his friend Betti McDonald, an impressive soprano. Later Parker Tyler and Charles Boultenhouse for tea. I give them fresh cherries, a savory Brie, and Miss Grimble's apple cake. We discuss Florine Stettheimer, a reproduction of whose painting, if an appropriate one exists, would be perfect for the cover of *Three Sisters Who Are Not Sisters*.

31 July

Pose for Becki. Heat. Homemade gazpacho. Lime mousse.

4 August

Shirley phoned, very early, to say Paul Goodman died last night in New Hampshire. We meet for lunch at Eugene's. Then convene to hear the edited tape of *Day Music* at Grenell's office. We're all pleased. But a pall hangs over the street. Shirley, bicycling home, is hit and injured by a taxicab.

(By sad irony, the last time Eugene and I had a meal together in his home rather than in one of those eternal restaurants he so thrives on, was August 31, 1969, the evening we learned of Bill Flanagan's death.)

5 August

Dine at Rorems' with cousin Jan.

Am writing a memorial on Paul for *The Village Voice*, and calling it "Remembering a Poet."

9 August

Pose for Becki, whose ketchup-colored version of my person grows ever wilder.

Tomorrow, parents' fifty-second anniversary. Buy champagne, make a salmon mousse and a nectarine-cucumber salad. Chocolate chiffon pie. Cousin Jan and her friend Irene Nelson are coming too.

Whatever the impression of disparity to the outside, to me I'm not spread thin, since everything said is the same thing, the same (so to speak) poet speaking, whether he speaks in prose or in notes, in haphazard diaries or compact essays. Essays are a mere development, if not an advance, of the self, and indicate that with the New Permissiveness whereby any diarist may admit to all, I have become more circumspect, more decorous, am no longer on the open market. Nor am I any longer the person who writes this book.

(As dressing for the cucumber-nectarine: sour cream?)

10 August

The piece on Paul Goodman appeared in this week's *Voice*, yet so much of what was unsaid persists in the foreground.

My falling away from Paul (beyond the fact that he grew less interested as I grew more independent and lost my baby fat), stemmed from an incident. *A Meeting in the Lobby* is the title of a skit he devised in 1947 for me to set for a now-vanished soprano called Nancy Reed. I scoffed to someone about Paul's marginal notes on how the music should be composed, saying that he erred as poets often will by "helping out" their musician, and that anyway he seemed here to have thrown the words together. He (maybe rightly) felt it was not for me to broadcast how he worked, that the skit emerged from special experience and that I was ungrateful to the very person who had put me on the map. Actually Paul was no more "known" than I in those days, and if *The Lordly Hudson* is now the famous title of his collected poems, it was then strictly a

song by me, not us. But I *was* ungrateful. I learned far more from
him than he from me.

In *Seven Little Prayers*, my first cycle on texts of PG (and indeed my
first songs of any quality), I was still confounding prosody with
"gracious" sounds. For example, knowing that long open vowels are
easier to sing high than tight *e*'s and *u*'s, I took the word *son* as an
arbitrary climax to one of the prayers. Paul said:

"Why did you put *son* on that long loud B? Because you knew
the song was really about my daughter? Or, because it's the same as
sun shining high? Or from love or resentment of my poem? Why?"

"Because it's a good word to sing high."

"That's no answer."

Paul actually had a pretty fair ear, but he was somehow
too—well—too *intelligent* to let his ear lead, rather than follow, his
idea. Thus in his novels when a character speaks colloquially, any
given phrase rings true, but the sequence of phrases degenerates
into philosophy. When we realize he's actually *named* a character
(with a pseudo-ordinary name at that, like Minetta Tyler) we grin
uncomfortably. Proper names are for individuals, not for symbols.
Paul's folks are Everyman: not a businessman but Business Man, not
a poet but Poet, not a suffering cultured housewife but *the* s.c.h.
(For plot and speech imitation, an author like, say, James Herlihy,
writes rings around Goodman. Yet Herlihy says less. Or does he?)
Still, consider the flawless third section of Chapter Four in *The
Dead of Spring*: the conversation is silent there, and the respect for
manual labor is depicted with such gentle contagion that it's
difficult to imagine such writing outside a novel. Like a master, Paul
did not follow rules, he made them, and made them only after the
fact of finding them in his own pieces.

His theater does not work. He knew all about it except how to
make it.

Who of his old friends does not recall Paul Goodman, nearsighted as
a bat but refusing to wear glasses, the smartest man on our planet,
continually crashing into the furniture?

(In 1966 he gave a blurb for *The Paris Diary*. "A touching story of
how a young fellow, protected alive by music and sex, outgrows his

normal bedazzlement with Names and comes gradually to an inkling that there might be some real things and perhaps even other people.")

The difference, as guru, between Ginsberg and Goodman is that one catered to the feelings of the young while the other catered to their minds. Obviously Ginsberg won out.

11 August

Great events do not impel great works, but they do alter method and certainly attitude. When his son died George Rochberg is said to have reassessed and found wanting the principles by which he composed.

In the light of Paul's death, an article by Boulez in Sunday's *Times* falls like a shadow of lead. The dead parent, humid with inspiration, puts into relief the dustiness of the surviving parent. Then too, now that Boulez is no longer handsome, his ideas are no longer blinding; it is clear where his followers faulted by taking him *au pied de la lettre.* If this reads like a superficial appraisal, influences of art *are* superficial, a dime a dozen, though they can sometimes be put to profound use. Socrates' carnality was more than just intelligence.

12 August

Letters from geniuses scribbled or maltyped *n'importe comment,* I value as *things,* as microscopes focused on my being, like those ten or twelve from Cocteau (now, alas, irremediably glued in yellowing scrapbooks rather than singly breathing between cool museum folders) or the one from Gide, Gide who knew Wilde who knew Victoria who could have known Schubert, and my! how old I'm getting.

"Beautiful as you—as you once were, life must now seem a constant letdown." The speculation insults by its assumption that beauty is a virtue rather than a gift, that beauty is not otherwise industrious.

But it pains too, since beauty does not see itself in the past tense, does not see itself (any more than anyone) getting on. I myself am relieved to be relieved of corporal responsibilities. We can all arrange forever to get laid, but only I can carry my tunes.

If I were not a musician daily involved with the vicissitudes and occasional rewards of the current competitive scene (and lone wolves with all their disdain are *engagés*; to be aloof is to admit the presence and hence the force, however slight or transient, of that to which one is aloof)—not a musician but a layman, cultured but disinterested, would I find this rat race funny? or magic? or boring? or would I see it as a rat race? Or even see it?

Statistic. On page 12 of his new book Philip Roth writes: "A phenomenon . . . took place within my body between midnight and four A.M. on February 18, 1971, and converted me into a mammary gland disconnected from any human form." On the afternoon of February 18, 1971, I gave a party at Yaddo for five guests, including Philip R. I remember clearly how he looked.

16 August

Another long clear delightful week at Morris' on the Island. Death of Edna Lewis. Death of Oscar Levant.

31 August

Rehearse *Poèmes pour la paix* with Sandra Walker, JH's plangent discovery. . . . Sent a page to Milhaud whose eightieth birthday is next week. Sketched a huge 8 and a huge 0 around these words: "*Si le huit est le temps qui se recourbe sur lui-même / le zéro c'est l'absence du temps et c'est vous. . . .*"

5 September

In *Des Bleus à l'âme* Sagan comes to her own defense by anticipating her critics, then by telling them how they're wrong. It is not, as she believes, the idle milieu they reproach her for, but what she does within it—which is zero after eighteen years. Those nine novels blur into one.

Rereading my diaries, I'm embarrassed by nine-tenths. Would the tenth that pleases me please me out of context? I'll not take my own defense. (Except that's what I'm doing. . . .)

Labor Day weekend a bit marred by pollinated breezes at Tommy Thompson's in Rhinebeck. Yesterday, touristic visit to the Roosevelt mansion in Hyde Park. There, on pushing a button, you may hear the voice of Franklin D, declaiming over a Thanksgiving dinner. How facile now to bring back the dead (listen to the tapes of Marc Blitzstein, of Francis Poulenc, still talking to us across the room), yet how, by inflection, they situate the past. With her first words Gloria Swanson in *Sunset Boulevard* froze forever the pseudo-chic '20s, the rich American posing *à l'anglaise*. Roosevelt's voice today contains those same dated nuances of upper-crust East Coasters, intelligent, a bit embarrassing, uptight, still available in the speech of William Buckley or Gore Vidal. Yet three and a half decades ago our high school class was halted to hear that President address our nation (I hear it still, chillingly, across the years): "These are ominous days."

Returned to the city (always brand-new after even one day away) in convulsions of hay fever. It takes quite a spell to recuperate from the shock of fresh air.

Sunday my article on New Opera appears in the *Times* directly beneath an interview with John Cage on the occasion of his sixtieth birthday (how old I'm getting). With all his persuasive pixeries, John has never expressed an argument not easily punctured. Now he talks about people who maintain he's more philosopher than musician, and states that if they were told his work was philosophical they'd say, no it's music. This is a straw horse; they have *not* been told the work is philosophical, nor can we know what they'd say *if*. John just isn't a musical philosopher, but a philosophical musician, which he remains, and he knows it.

Have I become merely contemptible: someone who settles crabby scores in *The New Republic*, spouts cheap aphorisms in the Sunday

Times, and who at forty-eight onanizes in literary mags? I watch him impotent, when I should be composing. Pretense of meaning.

12 September

Crippling hay fever continues, in spite of which we dined last night at Arnold Weissberger's, with Lehman Engel and Gian-Carlo Menotti. The latter recalled how, in his Dramatic Forms class at Curtis, in 1943, I presented the musical setting of a dialogue from Flaubert's *Temptation of St. Anthony*, with student singers Ken Remo and Ellen Faull. That he should remember what I'd nearly forgotten of my pre-opus I is flattering. (Actually the composition— is it somewhere in a trunk?—was an English translation of a conversation from Huysmans' *A Rebours*, wherein Des Esseintes arranges for a woman ventriloquist to quote the Flaubert.)

26 September

Dreams, indelible and regular as ever, are seldom the color of nightmare as in my drinking days, though usually the color of sadness. Someone who is me seems to have a body racked from sobs. Last night I wandered lost through ancient Rome, searching for the grand piano in those fields where, at 5 P.M., I was to accompany a clarinet recital. Moments later, in the midnight of Paris, I murdered an old woman whose remains, the size of a walnut, I hid among my bedclothes. This occurred again, the murder and the hiding, and again, the murder and the hiding, and again, when Shirley and I were imprisoned within a rocket ship. Our fate was clear and unclear: we were to navigate a collision with a great machine, but we did not know the outcome. The machine and our rocket approached in space, full speed and motionless, gradual and white hot, frenzied, trembling, until we "entered" the machine. Outcome: Shirley and I had our eyes torn from their sockets by the impact, and both of us were withered into mummies. She preferred to commit suicide, and threw herself from the hill. I preferred to return.

Reading Lillian Libman's book on Stravinsky's last years with emotion. During that publicized feud of last spring, when I had admired Robert Craft's *Diary*, I too quickly asserted that I preferred his lies to Libman's truth. There is no truth, and nothing is more cruel than circumstantial evidence. We all whistle a different tune comes the dawn.

My professional schedule for the next three months is hardly backbreaking. Yet it involves a great deal of piano practice, air travel and the effort of decent public manners. Dissemination of music seriously interrupts its composition. For me this is bad: I lose interest in performance, and society tires me mortally.

1 October

Last night in precisely three hours they recorded *Ariel*. The trio of performers worked as one, or rather, their separate tentacles curled from a single psychotic jellyfish, if that makes sense. Phyllis Curtin sang Plath's words with the urgency of the poet making them up; Joseph Rabbai's clarinet was disturbingly right, like a jester skirting the already devious meaning of a mad ruler's statement; and Ryan Edwards' pianism bound firmly the strands of these solo voices. I monitored with Horace Grenell, having little to say (players get the point without our saying anything, or don't get the point even after hours of talk; a composer should verbalize on all music except his own). Meanwhile Gene Cook took seven hundred photographs, and Phyllis' mother, Mrs. Smith, acted as audience.

Mrs. Smith, who had never attended a recording session, was overwhelmed by the fact of it, as well as by the music which she'd heard her daughter so often rehearsing alone. She asks, "Doesn't it drain you to compose a piece like that?" On the contrary, it fills me. In taking anxiety's notation for anxiety itself, Mrs. Smith reacts according to the artist's plot.

Have I ever felt drained by my work? Relieved, perhaps. I feel good when I work, bad when I don't. Total concentration—immunity to the outside—was mine before twenty, but never exhausted me as it is said to have exhausted Beethoven and others. Mrs. Smith undoubtedly confused music with text (I hope she did), for if anyone was drained it would have been Plath. To work with Plath's poems was not draining; it was exercise in propriety, like all vocal settings. Besides (and this is something the public refuses to learn), inspiration is the least important fraction of the compositional process. Nor could inspiration be kept at fever pitch for the period it takes to notate a piece or a poem. A mad poet is not mad during the moments of writing about his madness.

Jack Larson and Jim Bridges stop by this radiant noon for coffee and tangerines. With them is young Timothy Bottoms who, when permitted a word, declares that *The Last Picture Show* is the best '50s film ever made. We say it's not a '50s film, but a '70s film about the '50s. He says No it's a '50s film, he's the star. But he wasn't born then. Otherwise he seems open to suggestion.

2 October

X is to have an abortion tomorrow. Why does this shock me? Because the word, like cancer, has come to seem dirty while my own youth was cleaner than snow? Because X is so close a relative? Yet abortion and intelligence are closely related too, and such operations cast a healthy if fragile light upon an otherwise so dark moment.

No one who does not speak against the war has a right to speak out against abortion. JH's question to Catholics: If abortion is murder, why does the church not celebrate requiem masses for miscarried fetuses?

My country is sick, I am a part of the country.

Phyllis tells of her discouragement when a student asks without embarrassment: "But why learn such-and-such, since you're only going to sing it once?"

Afternoon sunlight flowering throughout the Chinese-red dining room, plant tendrils crawling through the windowpanes, and the cool weather bringing the first nonpollinated winds in a month. All my life I have read an average of three hours daily. Now it is two New York papers, four weekly magazines, and an average of seven books monthly (novels occasionally, and poetry from duty). Plus an hour a day shopping, two cooking.

Sans date

Dined with J and K and R, none of whom I'd seen in ages. They hadn't changed much, except for the cobweb masks worn by everyone over forty.Their build and physiognomy seemed the same as fifteen or twenty years ago. The same, with the urgent difference that although they spoke of sexuality they no longer exuded any. How locate this invisible switch? Like trees in late afternoon, identical to their morning selves but without the direct sunlight. Shadows flutter in the evening, waving at their real selves so recently lost. I am embarrassed. But not until later do I direct the embarrassment at myself, for I feel so physically good.

Ames, Iowa
14 October

Because they are going to sing his songs for the composer, they all get nervous. Wouldn't anyone, in their infrequent position? What they don't (need to) know is that the composer, when composing, had no finalized notion of interpretation, especially where his songs are concerned. His "preconceived idea" alters with each perform-ance, and there are as many versions of a song as there are singers to sing it. In theory, each version could be authentic. (This principle does not hold for nonvocal music when the sex of the performer is not a consideration.)

A successful performing career—no matter whose—consists of a sequence of disappointments punctuated by an occasional tri-umph. The reverse never obtains. An unsuccessful career consists only of the sequence of disappointments.

15 October

If an artist does not know who he is (and who does?), he knows *what* he is. Yet it is precisely who he is that gets him invited to campuses. Campuses won't object to what he is if he keeps quiet. He may retain naughty habits, even indulge them openly, but he must not talk about them.

Isn't talk education? An artist not permitted to advocate

himself becomes a mere symbol, accepting fees with contempt or refusing with tears. On campuses, although his work may be worshiped, the flesh of him is neither Who nor What.

An artist's flesh is stigmatized; what he speaks is peripheral to what he does. What the critic speaks *is* what he does, his business being to tolerate trends. The artist's business is to protect himself. The critic is always fair, the artist never—not even to himself. In theory his work is his armor, but in practice he is wholly vulnerable, and so, alas, he talks.

When I come out on jaunts like this I always think I'll either fall in love, or that I'll die before I get back home. But the tow-headed undergraduates keep a respectful distance, and there's never time, never time for the complex hemming and hawing of sex, nor time to die.

What I refrain from saying aloud I say in print. By that token once removed am I a composer: silent by nature, I make noise by proxy. A case could be made for The Artist as Timid Soul were it not for the horde of shy mediocrities. A case might also be made for The Rambunctious Genius as Timidity in Reverse, or Shyness Repressed. For no sensitive person need ever be loud.

Five nights in Iowa and now the stint's complete. *Day Music*, for which I was summoned hither, was presented earlier this evening by its commissioner, Miss Ilza Niemack, who retires this year from the faculty. How appropriate that a farewell concert should feature a world premiere—that this violinist should say goodbye to the recital stage through allowing a new work to say hello from that same stage.

Despite a continuing allergy (and despite debilitating anti-dotes, cupfuls of mucus issued from my nostrils) it was considered correct to seat me with the University's president, an agricultural economist by training, and possibly apprehensive that our conversation would flow less freely than my nose. We both wore red ties. At intermission I went backstage. During that time one of my father's cousins (Iowa seethes with Rorems), having been told I was in the fourth row with a red tie, approached the president and exclaimed, "Ned, you were one year old in Radcliffe when last we met."

New York
18 October

Rain. Continental Baths. Dream: Edward Albee and his friend yell: Ned will compose the background score for the movie on Stravinsky, ha ha! At the speed of a glass helicopter, not rapid, but purposeful, I skirt the waves, am overwhelmed, hear the simple tune more contagious than a siren's coming from a wagon on the waves. It is Dominique Sanda, forced by her parents to play this organ. "Here comes Ned," they tell her, "to grant his approval." She relinquishes her seat. So I begin playing, only to realize that the music is Death. That frightful gasp of dreams: to stop is to die, to continue is to die, and all that can maintain us is the constantly reiterated, the affirmative No.

22 October

Memorial for Paul Goodman at the Community Church on East 35th, half filled, with faces from the distant past, called together by Isadore From and Paul's brother Percival, to be with Sally for a few hours. Eugene opened the subdued afternoon by playing the slow movement of Schubert's *A-Major Sonata*. I accompanied Betti McDonald in nine songs on texts of Paul's. Then came statements, sober and nostalgic, by, among others, George Dennison, Neil Heims, Barbara Deming.

As often happens the day went too long and at the end I fled, unsure of myself, not wishing for compliments (which, what's more, might not be forthcoming), and tried to remember the name of the poet at whose funeral Cocteau remarked: *Allons-nous-en, il n'est pas venu!*

Paul is gone, and tomorrow's my birthday.

What is the temperature in the shade of fifty? Forgetting the ugly irony of having always been a spoiled child (as I still believe myself to be), it feels warmer than thirty. Although I no longer believe in afterlife—or even in life (that life has *meaning*)—I'm less morbid. Days are no longer darkened by hangovers, possibly because I no longer feel carnally competitive. That saves time which can be spent on what once were called simple pleasures: the cat gliding through the parlor, that cluster of grapes catching the gold of the early sun, or getting more careful work done (not *more* work, more *careful* work).

I'm happier. Forgive the expression, for to be too happy is to be immune. Unhappiness, barring bad health, can be willed away after a certain age. Unhappiness, already unbecoming to the young, is fatal to the middle-aged.

Fifty's shade is JH's shadow, whole months are recluded. I'll no longer go out to experiences, they will come to me. Must I accept them as they dance outside this glass case? The point is: I have made them come, they come because of me, thus I accept without joining. My work propels experience, it no longer derives from experience. Suppose the glass case later becomes surrounded by just an unmoving horizon? Horizon is the sole experience.

The hopeless blank page that confronts me each morning still cannot impel experiment—at least not experiment with the manners of today. For me to try, as Lukas Foss does (same old Lukas, forever up to his new tricks!), would not ring true. I am too lazy to betray myself.

And with each passing minute my past grows far more complicated than my future. *Tant bien que mal,* that past is all I find useful.

What American composers are there? Without hesitation I'll reply. Of the youngish crop, Barbara Kolb (if she'd shake that dreary practice of quoting the classics), because her arrows, though jagged with extraneous feathers and dipped in unnecessary poisons, go straight to their mark, singing all the way, and injure pleasantly with real tunes. David del Tredici, because he's our only musician with wit; his jokes are new and they all have punch lines; if you miss the point, his instruments from their extreme registers will guffaw for you. Lou Harrison, as always, and Bill Flanagan who, if he'd not gone and died, could have strengthened our fragile repository of song. Crumb? Well, I don't grasp what others hold to be his . . . his message. *His* practice of quoting classics, unlike Kolb's, is his sole trump card. Is his language otherwise so different from Henry Cowell's in 1919? (That I myself am dismissed while Crumb is praised for sound effects makes me feel like Virginia Woolf banned from the men's reading room.)

I'm not one for revision once a piece has left my desk and been replaced by newer problems. The piece shifts for itself, bedecked with warts or beauty marks. When I do reexamine an old work and consider alterations, these are always in the guise of simplification. Still, I do nothing. After the forgetful years it would be risky to de-gild the lily. Youth, precisely because it does not need ornaments, wears them with charm.

Charm. That word today is accusation. Charm is a fault. How dare you! in the light (or dark) of Vietnam, etc. (Max Ernst's painting called *Menacé par le rossignol* could stand as frontispiece to my autobiography.)

Yet with only a bit of perspective don't many works take on the dreaded charm? Is the *Sacre* without it? And Stockhausen's nothing but. Even Boulez, whose power is his sobriety, made music which now strikes us like a rainbow of shrapnel mixed with the impressionist grain. Life is short and so is art, at least the life of art's "meaning" at any given time.

Art is fantasy made fact. Not that I was beautiful, but that I thought so. Not that I was gifted, but that I thought so. Not that I was in demand (for how long, O Lord), but that I imagined myself to be. Private letters and public essays attest to the beauty, talent, and social acceptability, so imagination becomes reality. Not that these facts are facts, but that I care whether they are. The concern is fantastic.

These few lines seem levelheaded. Is the levelheadedness folly?

26 October

Monday I became forty-nine. At four the phone rang: the entire staff of Boosey & Hawkes sang Happy Birthday.

At eight, John Gruen's public interview with Schuyler Chapin (they both have a newly solidified self-assurance, John's that of one who is at ease with The Great because of his publicist potential, Schuyler's that of Met Opera chief whose underlying preoccupations are now diametrically opposed to his past), after which, with the Gruens, we went back to Shirley's where JH and Eugene and Zaidee joined us for a homemade cake and some *blanc de blancs* and another rendition of Happy Birthday.

John insisted I read aloud a few paragraphs from this diary, just published in *Shenandoah*. I did, blushing and regretful, mostly because of Eugene who has always, I think, felt I lacked a *sens de la mesure*. The error lies not in writing but in reading aloud: one writes precisely that which cannot, for one reason or another, be spoken.

Just now, reading Pauline Kael, I was struck anew at how she can do what cannot be done: see an extraordinary movie, then transmit that extraordinariness through her medium of the written word. She is very very dedicated and finally gentle. Am I not? No. What I hear and see inevitably disappoints and then disgruntles me, and it's ever harder to discover the good side of things.

27 October

But oh what a bore is Brando! Because he's all we've got we overpraise him to the skies. Because of his "charisma" we permit him to bog down every film with artless monologue. We assume the charisma is what carries him through, since he offers neither mind nor sense of pace. The assumption is in the American grain (Europeans do not, for long, allow mindlessness in a star), and preconditioned: could anyone hitherto unaware of Brando buy that facile vocalism of *The Godfather*, and now the plodding machismo of *Last Tango in Paris*? Might not Pauline's essay have been a decoy, a replica, more exquisitely fashioned than the actual thing?

Brando aside, *Last Tango* does make a major point which nobody's mentioned: about affirmation—the need to continue in the face of death, to prove aliveness by sex on the tombstone—and about how this very affirmation is doomed to failure. It must fail not only because the Brando character is a mediocrity but because even great men's lives (if not their works) are nothing much.

The ending, cribbed from *Breathless*, is more logical than in *Breathless*, because here the crime is not gratuitous—it is a crime of agism. A nasty stab deflates all romances, of course, but never more conspicuously than May-December ones. One partner goes too far, thus closing a situation as illogically as it opened. (Isn't there a resemblance, surely unintentional, to Colette's *Le Képi?* When Marlon cockily dons her father's hat Maria can no longer face him without embarrassment. When Colette's aging heroine coyly dons her young lover's képi he loses sexual interest.)

In *Last Tango* this situation contains an interesting complication. If to invest another human with olympian virtues and then to expect that monster to reciprocate is the fantasy defining the huge chutzpah of falling in love, then all lovers' fantasies are impractical. (Although the politician who invests *himself* with virtues sometimes succeeds: Napoleon thought he was Napoleon.) Now, the guiding fantasy of *Last Tango* is a male-homosexual one. The obligatorily anonymous encounter is far less germane to heterosexuality, even in brothels, than to men among themselves who mutely endow their partner—who just may be a ribbon clerk—with the attributes of a gladiator. Anonymity, imposed upon a healthy young French woman, explains her getting fed up with her American freak (especially when he is unmasked as a banal freak), and lends the movie its special eccentricity.

One scene lingers, through briefly illuminating two of the players' previous identities. Massimo Girotto and Marlon Brando, cramped in that hotel bedroom, recall their earlier roles as defeated pederasts, quite separately, in *Teorema* and in *Reflections in a Golden Eye.*

28 October

Except for their apparently bottomless store of sinusitis-producing substances, these long fall weeks have brought sheer light. From day to day, almost from hour to hour, Central Park—the world's eighth wonder—merges from mercury to magenta to slate with no less flamboyance than the Iroquois foliage of Pennsylvania. Whatever the weather I walk there each afternoon now that we live so close. No Paris garden surpasses Central Park in surreal luxury. We used to say that the spired skyscrapers on Fifth Avenue were male, those split ones on the west side were female, and that when no one was looking they flew into the sky and clashed by night.

Twenty autumns ago I returned from France for the first time
to spend three months in the Chelsea Hotel. My 1952 agenda shows
me visiting vigorous Frances McCollin during a weekend in
Philadelphia, and Gertrude Ely in Bryn Mawr; seeing Nell Tangeman every day; then, with Nell chez Alma Morgenthau, performing
a concert of my songs for, among others, Eva Gauthier, John
Latouche and Marc Blitzstein, and afterward drinking beer with
Marc and Touche on Lexington Avenue—where one drank in those
days; being introduced to Frank O'Hara at Touche's a few days
later; arranging with dear Frances Osato still another recital at the
home of Olga and H. V. Kaltenborn, with Julius Katchen (unmar-
ried then) telling me how well-behaved I was. I see that I saw
George Freedley five times, that Eisenhower was elected President,
that Paul Goodman handed over thirteen new poems (which I made
into songs the next summer), and that I spent just one evening with
Bill Flanagan (compared with our daily meetings during the 1960s).
I dined with Paul Bechert on November 17, Carmel Snow the 18th,
Hortense Monath the 20th and Libby Holman the 24th. On
December 3rd I lunched with Douglas Moore, on the 7th had a date
with young Tom McCullers, on the 8th saw Judy Holliday in *The
Marrying Kind*, and on the 20th attended a rehearsal of Stravinsky's
new *Canticles*. George Copeland invited me to lunch on the 23rd,
after which I had an interview at the Carl Fischer offices. Christmas
we passed with Van Steenwyk in Ambler, and two days later I
boarded the SS *United States* and returned to France. Everyone
mentioned in this paragraph is dead.

Very much alive is James Lord, here briefly now from Paris, as I was
then. We've been on cool terms since that Cocteau review in 1967;
indeed, we last met around 1965. But, my God, our lives were
parallel if not synonymous during the years in France, and there's
been a hecatomb there too, time to bury the hatchet.
So last night we dined together execrably on Cornish hen at
New Jimmy's (I go out maybe thrice a year now), talked almost
solely of Marie Laure and of Paris today so changed now that she's
no longer in it, and conjured up old friends still living for whom he's
writing his treatise on Giacometti, because, unlike in America, in
Paris if you're not a success you're not automatically a failure, and
James is pushing fifty.

He paid the check. Twelve minutes in a gay bar, which, now that I don't smoke or drink, seemed merely a loud tomb. Long walk down Third Avenue, commiserations on how well we're holding up. Then at eleven, a warm farewell, despite the first chilly breezes of autumn sneaking through Central Park.

29 October

Fracas in this morning's *Times* about America's 70 Top Intellectuals. But the word is not defined. Isn't an intellectual someone for whom learning is an end rather than a means? Thus Aristotle is an intellectual while Aeschylus is an artist. Thus Saul Bellow and James Baldwin—despite whose essays, which, though reasoned, aren't learned, much less philosophical—should not be listed, nor Philip Roth, nor—heavens!—Robert Lowell. Susan Sontag is rightly included, but Paul Goodman and Mary McCarthy are only half intellectual—a half which seldom coincides with their artistic half. John Simon's strictly an intellectual whose trump card is culture, while Pauline Kael's strictly an artist whose card is reacting. Certain intellectuals, like certain great artists, can be lousy family men, mean reactionaries, illiterate, politically retarded or strictly theoretic and divorced from the world as functioning aquarium: Freud, Kristol, McLuhan, Pound, and all the buzzing hive around McKeon when I was a child in Chicago.

30 October

JH's hour-long program yesterday of Thomson's sacred works for organ and chorus was a miracle. Without drawing attention to performance but focusing on what was being performed, he managed to lend variety and drama to music not containing these qualities. Such contradictions are resolved by only a special breed of interpreter: not, for example, by a Bernhardt or Billie Holiday who often performed mediocre art marvelously by drawing attention to themselves; nor by a Schnabel or Lotte Lehmann who performed great art marvelously by drawing attention away from themselves; nor by a Gielgud or Glenn Gould who perform great art marvelously by drawing attention to themselves. No, those who perform

mediocre art marvelously by drawing attention away from themselves are as paradoxical as the black holes of outer space. Like Piaf
and Duse, JH can turn the trick. At least he turned it yesterday in
the Chapel of the Intercession. (In fairness, JH professes to be
deeply touched by the music he performed.) Afterward in the choir
sacristy, Virgil, very manic, bestowed enthusiasm on all but me.

It has been six months since I wrote up Virgil Thomson's *Lord
Byron*. *Les petits amis* were quick to tell me then that Virgil was
less than thrilled by my words. I've not seen him since.

Six months is long to hold a grudge, especially for one who
retained his cool during fifteen years of dishing out put-downs for all
the world to read. Meanwhile, in *The New York Review of Books* his
review of old friend Paul Bowles' autobiography (appearing simultaneously with my review of it in *The New Republic*) is so
nonconstructively mean that mine seems indulgent by comparison.

I miss Virgil's camaraderie of three decades' standing, during
which I nursed no rancor for his cold criticism (worse, absence of
criticism) of my work. But this is the trial of a judge. Like most
smart people Virgil can be uncannily trenchant about everyone but
himself.

The fact is, Thomson's talent's not a musical one. The fact is
also that *Four Saints in Three Acts* is the best, indeed the only,
American opera. But *Four Saints* is a fluke, the right formula at the
right moment. The success has not to do with music but with
words-&-music, with theatricality. Now, an opera survives on its
music, sometimes on its gimmickery (bel canto) which is international. But *Four Saints* is meaningless to European publics. It is a
feat for English-speaking audiences.

I'm not commenting casually, but as one who knows as
thoroughly as the composer himself a good portion of his output. As
his copyist in the 1940s I learned *how* Thomson put together his
pieces, but not *why*. I never comprehended, even philosophically,
what pushed this man to inscribe for posterity these arbitrary
charmless sequences.

I owe you a lot, Virgil. But I owe you for what I took, not for
what you gave. You deserve your glory, but your music does not.

31 October

Halloween. Marie Laure would have been seventy today.
Ezra Pound died tonight in Venice.

7 November

Finished Judith Malina's journal, *The Enormous Despair*, and am impressed by how unimpressive it is, as though composed by an actress playing radical rather than by a radical who happens to be an actress. Judith brims with conviction, but her book does not. She will overcome, so long as each hardship's publicized. Perhaps I misread her as I inject into the bland writing a red serum, taking her on faith since she's not blessed with all the talents. One shouldn't suspect the Becks of insincerity, should one?

Because John Gruen last night publicly interviewed Miss Bette Davis and afterward gave a party for that woman, it seems historically indicated to write a word. Now, what word can we say that Bette can't say better? She's disappointing as copy, mainly because, unlike Talullah whose life was her work, Bette's work is her life and we already know the work by heart. Still, her disciplined energy is enviable, and I like her old-time way of calling everyone Miss or Mrs. or Mr. The packed-to-the-rafters mob, preconditioned by TV, applauded her every preposition, her every cigarette, less distracting than appropriate to her show biz cool.
  Between the interview and the party, I stopped by Arnold Weissberger's to greet Alexis Weissenberg—Sigi, to those who knew him when. Gielgud was there (he talks nonstop about nothing much) and Rex Reed, and two others I didn't know. Conversation was around "music"—the heaven of bel canto and the hell of modern opera (meaning *Wozzeck*)—just as though I weren't present. I grew glum and left.

Today I voted for President (McGovern) for the second time ever.

10 November

Wednesday, yearly sortie with Ellen Adler. In the hurricane's deluge the cab took an hour from Columbus Circle to Boosey &

Hawkes. At five, 57th Street was an ocean of escaping flesh upon which chunks of concrete tumbled from Bonwit Teller, jet-black and sodden (sodden concrete?). Made it to Robert Dash's show and purchased a small optimistic oil. Talked for an hour in the back room with Judy Feiffer (who resembles Anouk Aimée) about men and women, returned with Ellen into the deluge, refuged then in a Greek bistro on Madison Avenue (spinach pies), reemerged to 57th now at seven deserted as after an air raid, strewn with shattered glass and the cadavers of umbrellas like bats turned inside out, or mutilated mushrooms. Stéphane Audran and Delphine Seyrig may be the most stylish stars of our planet, but even they do not rescue the great Buñuel's new film from cuteness.

Last night at the Thornes', with Newell Jenkins and Jack Hurley. Persistent allergies so stifled my respiratory tracts—which feel like sewers—that I returned home midway through the veal.

Tonight at William Warfield's, private hearing of *Last Poems of Wallace Stevens* which Monday receives a world premiere in Town Hall.

The winds have died, a yellow-blue Della Robbia sky's washed cleaner than before the Industrial Revolution. For all practical purposes, it has been nearly five years since I have touched either alcohol or tobacco. Do I feel better?

11 November

Saturday morning, sneezing at the typewriter while Jeanne *la bonne*, minuscule Haitian, sprays the adjoining rooms with fumes of lemon wax, as she has for fifty weeks. This diary will end forever on New Year's Eve. I'm endlessly repeating myself. The *leitmotiv* is far more legitimate as a musical device than as a literary. Even were this not so, my social life and working problems fatigue me; I'm more interested in what people do than in what they say about what they do (even that phrase is a *leitmotiv*). Conversation becomes undifferentiated, being only purposeful when discussing action with the maid rather than reaction with John Gielgud. Among close friends all has been said long ago, and speech now merely confirms we're still alive; we'd rather hear each other at work. (Exception: I've never had conversation with JH that didn't lead somewhere. Of course, our talk is mostly in the shape of recipes, concert planning or tax returns.)

                                                          16 November

First frost. Blessed end to hay fever. Rudolf Friml dead at 92.

Monday the David Ensemble movingly premiered my *Last Poems* for soprano, cello and piano (Sheila Schonbrun, Jonathan Abramowitz, Warren Wilson). Peter Davis in the *Times* wrote two things I agree with. "While a suggestion of blank note-spinning pervades the cycle . . ." Yes, *more* than a suggestion. All music is the spinning of notes into a fabric whose seams mustn't show. "Stevens already seems detached from earthly considerations—one wonders, in fact, if another man's music isn't an unnecessary intrusion. . . ." Yes, again. All music is an intrusion on the poetry it illustrates. When is that intrusion necessary? When Schumann intrudes on Heine? Music does not intensify the sense of words, it changes their sense. (Music does not heighten, it broadens a text.)

Earlier that day, because David Diamond's *Piano Quintet* was to be premiered elsewhere the same evening, I attended a rehearsal with him. The piece is sturdy, businesslike, adroit, expertly "telling" for the instruments, not too poetic, but healthy, like David himself whom I hadn't seen since his last return from Italy.

In the twenty-nine years of our up-and-down friendship I've received twice that number of letters from David; rereading them this morning made my very body reexperience the flux of temperature he continually underwent; but he was nothing if not committed. If he's difficult, am I less so?

Yesterday afternoon in New Jersey with the youth of Montclair State College. Lecture, three sessions of my music, master class of songs, long ride. It flows naturally, yet I've not a Socratic bone in my body. Return depressed.

(Rehearsal of *A Sermon on Miracles*, the cantata written in 1947 with Paul. A chorus of about fifty undergraduates plus a small string orchestra did a run-through for my benefit. Invited to comment, I began by asking, "How many of you know of Paul Goodman?" Not one hand was raised.)

Performed by an orchestra of inexperienced volunteers simple music sounds even worse than complex music. Haydn and Satie, sloppy and out of tune, are less tenable than Berlioz and Schoenberg sloppy and out of tune. It's hard to be easy.

17 November

Me voici tout seul. Father is seventy-eight today.

Giving as little notice as an epileptic seizure, a wave of melancholy can invade the most unexpected places—not dark theaters or cemeteries, but laughing gardens or grocery stores. (That's what *The Pastry Shop*'s "about.") Quick take over of soul is by a leadenness as concentrated as a meteor, concentration on death and the past. It is not unpleasant—a sort of voluptuous futility. I sit here now, at ten in the morning, limber and rested, watching the thrilled November sunlight speckle the dining room, and want to cry. Another might write a poem. I feel merely pointless. The sadness of sadness is to make nothing of it.

21 November

Clear and cold.

With Eugene and Shirley last night to John Gruen's interview of Balanchine. Disappointing. Mr. B seemed incapable of answering a question. His every retort was facetious or poetistic, and we came away with the uncomfortable feeling of having gained nothing, indeed of having lost. Unfairly, I'm now less interested in his ballets. Interviews are treacherous.

One would expect that over the years Balanchine would invent stock replies to stock queries. (How *does* one choreograph? There *is* an answer.) The creative specialness of dance, of course, defines itself; if that self could be expressed in words, dance would not exist. However, the craft that goes into the specialness can be expressed in words. We may not know how pregnancy develops, but most of us know how it starts. Does Balanchine teach a class, or demonstrate a step, with more than feet of clay?

22 November

In the study JH rehearses the vocal quartet for our concert Sunday. Now they are singing, with starts and stops, my *Canticle of the Lamb.* I have never heard it before, and am pleased by the blend, the spirit, the faintly wry harmonies and by the fact that it works. The premiere is, in a way, taking place this moment as these words take shape in my lap. I could be in the grave, while they could still be rehearsing that music in the next room.

Intelligent Barbara Rose unintelligently likens the suicide of photographer Diane Arbus to that of Marilyn Monroe, declaring both to be martyrs to the "feminine mystique"—symbols for a whole generation of unfulfilled women.

Now all artists are so monstrously prey to society's insensitivity, that the fact of their sex is comparatively insignificant. Yet an artist is not a martyr, but one who has chosen, who thus is the most fulfilled of humans, and who does ask for appreciation, but not for understanding (how can he be "understood" if he is real?). To be a man or a woman is a rule. To be an artist is an exception to the rule, whatever your sex. To be an exception is to suffer and be sanctified. Marilyn couldn't have it both ways, nor could women claim her suffering for their own: too many great males who may have wished to be housewives perished on their own scaffolds: Valentino, Forster, Pollock, Mishima. . . . To erect straw rivalries between sexes as artists is aimless.

23 November

Thanksgiving, broiled chicken, cranberries, a homemade (failed) walnut cheesecake, alone with JH.

Channel 13 performance of *L'Enfant et les sortilèges,* choreographed by Babilée. How well that work holds up! And oh how my theory that the French can't play their own music falls down! The performers, vocally and orchestrally, were extraordinary: they knew what the piece was about, and conveyed the knowledge accurately through beautiful sound. I never cry, but cried, as I thought back on fifty previous performances beginning in 1946 when Howard Moss played Ernst Bour's 78 rpm record, a turning point for us all. Staged performances, from Kirstein's Ballet Society version to the Opéra-Comique's, have seemed superfluous, but a concert version in Rome, circa 1954, sticks in the memory. People have always suggested that Disney—or at least animated cartoon—would be the best sieve through which to strain this fantasy, if it *had* to be visual, which I'm not sure of. Anyway, filmed close-ups are the only solution if Colette's words are to be grasped (and they *must* be grapsed: no poet—not Boïto or Wagner or Maeterlinck or Büchner or Cocteau—has ever concocted a more intimate libretto than Colette; even her stage directions could be sung) and the child (those so-very-French eyes) in this film, dubbed though he clearly was, will be forever memorable as a contribution to, not a sabotaging of, one of the great scores of history.

When I was the age of *l'Enfant* my literature, for which I saved a weekly allowance, was within the pink-and-silver "sheet music" sold at that little store next to the Frolic Theater on Chicago's 55th Street. To this day I can repeat a thousand stanzas from *Hot Voodoo, Doin' the Uptown Lowdown, Let Yourself Go, After Sundown, You Are My Lucky Star. . . .*

25 November

Sore throat, vomiting, diarrhea, anxiety. No amount of experience controls nerves before concerts. On the contrary, successive performances teach us that they can't teach us.

And yet: the ecstasy of torture. The final pages of Georges Bataille's *Les larmes d'Eros* (my *livre de chevet* for a decade) features photographs taken in 1905 of a Mongolian regicide being cut, living, into a hundred pieces. On his face, beatific peace.

Tomorrow at the Chapel of the Intercession, JH's presentation of my music, the first time we will have performed on the same program.

It belongs to the past. The program, plotted for months (particularly by JH, rising daily at dawn to phone singers, rehearse the unprepared, order pianos and tune organs, cajole the temperamental and memorize new notes), has played itself out in the space of an hour to a packed Chapel which today again stands empty as it stood before, shading the Trinity cemetery which houses Audubon.

The program was of my "sacred" music: Phyllis Curtin and Helen Vanni (blonde in black, brunette in white) premiered, with a reverberatingly noble stridance, *Gloria* for two voices and piano; JH conducted the premiere, with the musicality of a choreographer, of seven unaccompanied *Canticles*; young Sandra Walker in brown and cream revived, with a mature mezzo's assurance, *Poèmes pour la paix*; and the concert opened with the entire chorus in unison, JH at the organ, performing *Proper for the Votive Mass of the Holy Spirit*. This morning, influenza still rampant, that feeling of what difference does it make. (Hardly a day passes that I wonder about my survival should JH die. Yet I'm more than fifteen years older and will surely die first.) But at Shirley's party Rosemary appeared from Philadelphia, and Father summed up all converse with bons mots, while Mother preached pacifism to Stella Adler (as preface to Norman Vincent Peale's statement today that Nixon is a Prince of Peace), and that makes a difference.

1 December

What is a Quaker like me to make of a Jew like Irving Howe as he argues against Ezra Pound with a reasoned passion (is there such a thing?), passing out grades for—even judging degrees of—hate. "In its magnitude of accumulation anti-Semitism has shown itself to be an evil somehow worse than all other evils," declares Howe. "For this persuasion I could offer six million reasons. . . . To murder two people is twice as bad as to murder one. . . . In our century we deal with large numbers. . . . Since only an accident of geography has kept me from becoming a lampshade, I regard it as a sacred moral obligation to remember those murdered by Hitler."

By extension then, if to hate two people is twice as intense as to hate one, the intensity chez Irving Howe is magnified by six million. Is he relieved not to be a gypsy, a homosexual, a Hungarian or member of some other degenerate classification massacred by Hitler, which would magnify the intensity of his hate by yet another eight million? To admit, as he does, that the effects of time are something he does not know ("contemporaries of Dante were aroused by political struggles of his moment in a way I cannot be. I am a creature of my time. . . .") leaves him all the more responsible to this century. Does he then hate the Turks for slaughtering four million Armenians in 1915 (but no, he's not Armenian)? Does he hate Americans for killing Vietnamese? (How many, and which ones?) Or the Russians? Or the Jews themselves for their righteous pleasure in destroying Arabs? Or blacks for killing whites?

Where do I stand regarding Pound? Who throws stones with impunity? How measure? Where begin? when stop? Is there no redemption? Can hate breed understanding? Can a young man remember before he was born? Have Jews the right to publicize their suffering above that of others? Am I betraying my own questions by reacting so righteously to Irving Howe?

2 December

Dined at Stella and Mitchell's with ten good friends.

A *quiche Lorraine* like Chrysis' golden veil; roast lamb in two sauces, mint and raisin, with *haricots verts à la française* exquisitely underdone; and a homemade apple tart obscene in its combined perfection: the pie proper was reminiscent of your Aunt Martha's flakiest, while the hard sauce brought back the better kitchens of France. All this escorted by appropriate wines, as usual not for me, and later by liqueurs with Turkish coffee in the overstuffed salon, and stuffed dates and rosy bonbons because I like sweets and was guest of honor. Yet I injected a sour note, they said, by bringing up the Jewish concerns still much on my mind, while my hostess in her mint-green kimono implied that I couldn't *know* about these things being a Quaker and a musician and how would I feel if a Nazi were raping my sister? There I sat on her rosy sofa munching her stuffed dates, being shushed by certain others and brushing crumbs from my new hundred-dollar velvet jacket. Yet must we always sit around gossiping, and saying about art things we've heard each other say a million times, wishing we could go home and work more in the short years left to us? I'm no more anti-Semitic than I am antihomosexual. Groups don't have rights or vices, though they do have traits, and this she won't admit.

4 December

Father showed me a family tree which his niece, Helen Roberts, has been constructing for a decade. I'd no idea that even Mormons could trace so far. Yet there flow our Rorem arteries, fanning out over farms in the valley of Rørheim on the island Ombe in the Fjörds of Stavanger, and back absolutely to the twelfth century.

If by miracle we found ourselves in a rural Norwegian pantry in the year 1481, and then in a rural Norwegian pantry in the year 1581, would we feel a difference? Would we detect that difference through furnishings? through an advance in language? or through a mere assurance that those molecules inhaled are less exhausted?

Surprise birthday party last night for Phyllis Curtin. The one nonmusical guest was Ed Lee, Betty Allen's husband, social worker, handsome and quite black, who told how good it felt to walk through the Norwegian hamlets which they visited a few years ago, because, he explains, "we were not demons but curiosities, the way *you* might be to some Congolese tribe." Yes, but suppose we were ugly?

Tonight in the rain with JH to Fellini's *Roma*. So disappointing.
We're all coming down with colds.

6 December

Mother's seventy-fifth birthday.

When Leighton Kerner writes, as he does in today's *Voice*, that *La Voix humaine* is "typical of Cocteau's soap-opera 'realism' made notorious if not famous, by such works as *Les Parents terribles* and

Les Enfants terribles . . ." it makes me wonder where I missed the boat.

Soap opera is any realistic drama without a hero. *Death of a Salesman* and *Streetcar Named Desire* are soap operas, Fairy Tales and *Oedipus Rex* are not. Verdi never composed a soap opera, Menotti writes nothing but. *Who's Afraid of Virginia Woolf?* is soap, but *Tiny Alice* isn't. . . . So sure, *Les Parents terribles* is a soap opera (a boulevard tragedy without heroes), though *Les Enfants terribles* is not (being "unreal," with heroes large as Orestes and Elektra). Soap opera's a generic term not inherently contemptible. *La Voix humaine* meanwhile's the first soap opera cum comic-strip, and as such foreshadows by two decades the pop art without which the present, including Kerner, would be quite other.

Do people so snidely dismiss Cocteau for being frothy and glib because our new generation is so much deeper and disciplined? Am I too an outmoded fop still blindly glazing surfaces of yore?

Practicing Chopin *Etudes* again. Funny how a measure here and there can transport me to the practice rooms of Northwestern where in 1940 I spent my first autumn away from home. The chewed-up Breitkopf & Härtel edition is filled with fingerings penciled by Harold Van Horne. Oh those mornings when I appeared, hung over, for a trembling lesson! When I learned of Van Horne's suicide a few years ago, my reaction was: But *I* had the hangovers, not he, and I'm alive; how am I responsible for his death?

12 December

Sad visit from one Robert Merideth, an earnest California scholar compiling the first posthumous book on Paul Goodman. Interviewing people he does not know about a man he did not know will result in the Rashomonian hearsay that becomes even more variegated in the wake of death than in more distant years. Yet in more distant years, when we draw back the telescope farther and farther, receding into the future, Merideth's book will have become but one of many, none definitive, until in the unfocus of biographical slant and literary "interpretation," Paul's own voice just fades into outer space. What, one wonders, can old friends say about Paul's work that he couldn't have said? Yet the enterprise is worthy, for if we can't speak better we *can* speak differently, and in the last analysis Paul Goodman no longer belongs to himself.

Our discussion was mostly on the musician. Probably I was too quick to pooh-pooh Paul's "readings," his brotherly dissections of, say, Beethoven—his *knowing* Beethoven would "know," when in fact Beethoven might not.

The musical Paul could ingenuously state, as other professionals couldn't, that anyone who did not feel as he felt about "the deathless *Cavatina*" could not understand his work. ("Music looses the soul so flow the tears; soon breathing is formal with song.") Of course he's wrong, nor would he want his work understood on so simplistic a premise. I, for one, feel no response to "the deathless *Cavatina*," yet I understand Paul's writing as I can (while the music of other composers looses my soul to flow with tears).

Merideth wanted to dredge up the late 1930s in Chicago, but that was a time for Paul to recall me more clearly than I him. Still, I did revive, as with a whiff of ambergris, those adolescent snowy Thursday evenings when David Sachs introduced me into the Poetry Sessions at Monroe Library. More than Paul or David, or Bill Earls or Edouard Roditi, I remember how difficult the Joycean rhetoric sounded, yet how easily my long knit scarves flowed behind me, and I ached, for it was then they said: We'll screw Ned, but never ask his opinion.

That's the core around which diaries revolve, though somehow now it just seems useless, lacking color for others. Robert Merideth went off, and I felt like crying as anyone must when great men begin to be woven into peripheral necrophilia.

Betti McDonald came to dine, after which we rehearsed *King Midas*. She asked: "Can you be honest when you write a diary other people are going to read?"

I'm not sure what honest means, nor indeed if it's quite the word she means. How, for instance, would she locate *dis*honest? Through truths left out? through lies put in? An author is not concerned with verity but with emphasis. If I paint my portrait in reverse, the reversal is of my devising. I choose my falsehoods, they belong to me, so they are "honest." My dreams are lies? By whose decree? I invented and offer them. Facts don't exist. The sole truth lies in a tone of voice. Is my nonfiction narrative more true or less true than Portnoy's. (As it here stands this paragraph is the fourth of seven versions, each essentially on the same matter, each aiming for clarity. Which version is, or was, the most honest?)

> See how they love me,
> Green leaf, gold grass,
> Swearing my blue wrists
> Tick and are timeless . . .

Thus does Howard Moss beautifully open the seventh poem of *King Midas*. During the long years since I set the poem to music I've pondered that word timeless. If our life span is ticked off in the pulse, then surely our wrists are not timeless but time itself. Obviously I've missed the point . . .

1914 Rittenhouse Square
17 December (Sunday)

Philadelphia was home for a while, during that year at Curtis in 1943. But in 1944 I moved to New York. Mother and Father lived there through the '50s. Now they too are in New York, and only Rosemary remains with her semidispersed flock. I feel like the well-connected Frenchman who, on returning to Rome, knew only the ambassador and the Pope. In Philadelphia today I know only Eugene Ormandy and Henry McIlleny. I've just passed the weekend as guest of the latter on the occasion of a performance by the former.

Burdened as always by bodily breakdowns in advance of public appearances (particularly, like the present case, those in which I function passively, not as a player), I arrived Thursday night in the sleet, doubled over with a rectal fissure, and was shown by the Irish manservant into apartments which, for comfort and taste, rival only those of Marie Laure from another time and place. Henry not being home, I took a solitary walk through the freezing air up Locust to Broad where signboards featured my name in large letters in this city that contains only my past.

Friday morning: final rehearsal with Ormandy. We've not seen each other since ten years ago when he conducted *Eagles* in Carnegie Hall.

"You haven't changed a bit, Maestro."

"So haven't you."

Gaffe to concertmaster Norman Carol:

"Didn't we last meet when you played the Sibelius with Wallenstein at Ravinia in 1959?"

"I've never played the Sibelius, or with Wallenstein." (I'd confused him with young David Abel who performed Lalo's *Symphonie Espagnole*. So much for my total recall!)

Big lunch at Henry's. (Cauliflower au gratin, steak and kidney pie, baked apples.) My entourage: Shirley, JH, Morris, John & Jane Gruen, and Rosemary. Henry's entourage: Max de Schauensee, Nancy Grace, Emlen and Gloria Etting, Mrs. Norris Darrell (daughter of Judge Learned Hand) and a Mrs. Matthews with a Greek composer named Zottos.

John Gruen to Gloria Etting:

"Do you mind if I smoke?"

"Yes, I do."

"How original of you."

Abandoning Cézanne's apples which glowed from the walls more realistically than those real ones on the table there, we punctually piled into cars that proceeded through a thick rain to the Academy where Jerome Lowenthal gave the first local performance of my *Piano Concerto in Six Movements*.

It sounds like a repertory piece. In the two years that he's been playing the work it's become second nature to Jerry who now takes visual chances (as Rubinstein once did to delight those who *look at* sound), raising hands unnecessarily high, then letting them fall with laser accuracy that shatters the ivory into splinters, blinding the public. For twenty-six minutes piano never stops (this wasn't planned, it just turned out that way); and while Jerry is nothing if not dependable, he manages at the end to counterfeit such appropriate insanity that he turns into Hedda Gabler before our eyes.

As for the orchestra men, they're more than amply prepared, every effect makes almost sense. At worst their sound is too beautiful, a bit neutral, like beige on tan (oh, the *best* beige, the best tan), but one longs for lows of hot black or highs of ugly blood which will never be forthcoming so long as the Friday afternoon ladies (who are no fiction but an insolent reality) remain so crassly insistent on the lackluster. (Backstage, to autograph people's programs makes me feel guilty. I should be home writing music which gives me the right to autograph programs.)

After the concert Shirley takes our friends into the lobby of Curtis. I may have been a star an hour earlier, but in that spongy hall which intimidated our teens, the sole whispered sensation was, My God! I haven't finished my homework.

Tea at Henry's. Supper with Fred and Sylvia Mann. Everyone goes back to New York except me and Morris who accompany Rosemary to her house in Powellton Village and visit until midnight.

Saturday morning. Am reminded of Gide's single mention, in his journal, of the Noailles. Circa 1930, during a brief stopover in Hyères he notes that his breakfast tray does not contain a spoon, so he stirred his coffee with a knife. Yesterday when my freshly squeezed grapefruit juice and toast with orange marmalade were delivered promptly at 8:30 by the McIlleny butler, there was no knife. The mechanics of the household being what they are, and the sunlight, after a week of showers, so ineffably right as it streamed over the perfect pewter tray and onto the million-dollar carpet, it seemed indecent to signal the oversight. So I buttered the toast with a spoon handle.

To the Barnes collection with Morris and the Davises. Never having been there in the old days, it's maybe naïve to be enthusiastic now. But can anyone *know* Renoir who has not paid Barnes a visit? I, for whom museums are a chore, was moved as I haven't been in years. No small part of this excitement was due to the bright weather—the absolutely correct lighting upon these cheerful paintings.

Gaffe to Mrs. Darrell whom I pass in the corridors:

"I've changed my viewpoint toward Impressionism. Suddenly I love Cézanne to whom I was indifferent, but I no longer like those Soutine carcasses."

"You mean you once did like them? Life's too short for ugliness."

Immediately I came to the defense of an artist I'd just rejected. "You don't like Soutine? Then you don't like the Bible? or Dostoevsky, or Bach's *Crucifixus*, or Britten's *War Requiem*? One can't disqualify a work by subject matter; that's too much of a truism to need further discussion. . . . Well, goodbye." She stiffened, and waved her hand.

Why must I be preemptive, dogmatic, cold? Mrs. Darrell is warm, stylish, intelligent.

Nap. An affectionate supper, with Rosemary and Charity, of stew and yogurt and gingerbread. Rosemary had purchased fourteen gallery tickets for the Saturday night performance. In sub-zero temperatures we returned to the Academy, sat through the concert again during which Jerry outplayed himself, while the audience, packed to the rafters, hardly reacted.

Exhausted from being guest and host.

22 December

Exhausted maybe, and evermore the sworn recluse, but no sooner off the Metroliner Sunday than I went to Natalia's annual party for Janet Flanner, the first of such red-and-green festivities, warm refuge from slush, the start of the finish of this book. In the elevator I learn of the death of Eugene Berman. So the year ends.

Monday night, the Weisgalls' well-done party for Lord Harewood in their ample Great Neck cottage. No highs or lows, though I continue to admire Hugo for both his music and his Sartrian features, and for the largesse he displays before fellow composers.

Tuesday, lunch at Ca' d'Oro with Lillian Libman, to discuss the possibility of a series next autumn of two or three concerts, 1973 being the thirtieth anniversary of my first public hearing (Bill Strickland's conducting of *The Seventieth Psalm* in Washington's National Gallery during the war). Lillian remains bitter and hurt about the Craft debacle. Later that evening, Boulez concert featuring Stravinsky's *A Sermon, a Narrative, and a Prayer* (one of the composer's few total duds, that screams from dislocated Hip), and *Le Fils des Etoiles* (which, with your eyes closed, becomes watered Messiaen).

Yesterday noon at Trinity Church, Larry King routinely directed the premiere of my *Praises for the Nativity* for double chorus and organ, composed two years ago for—but never performed by—St. Patrick's Cathedral. The work doesn't work, is extrinsically miscalculated. Failure instructs, but success does not. (Because failure is a common rule, while success is unique and inimitable.) I based the piece on what had previously proved viable, rather than on avoidance of what had previously proved unviable. Therefore this piece will instruct me, though itself flopped. Discouraging to realize that I can continue, with all my technique, to compose what falls flat technically. The tunes are inspired, but their working out's too fussy.

Christmas party today in the offices of Boosey & Hawkes where Doris Pope presented me with a homemade plum pudding. Talked for an hour with Leon Kirchner (whom I've seen only casually since our joint forum concert in May 1949!) about Noam Chomsky, who strikes me—whatever else he is—as not a poet. I do feel the need of a new first-rate mind, but is there one in America? (Most artists, even great ones, have rather second-rate minds. Paul Goodman was a rare exception, while Virgil Thomson's good mind is not that of an artist. And if John Latouche suddenly reappeared, how first-rate would he seem any more?)

Finished Simenon's *Lettre à mon juge*, the first of some thirty novels by him that seems mediocre, even tedious. Reading now Simone de Beauvoir's *La force des choses*, which holds the interest if only because it deals precisely with the years I was in France. Yet her famous strength escapes me, nor (like Chomsky) is she remotely a poet, nor even a stylist. If her ideas center on political episodes, they seem for that the more remote in the light of current horrors. She's likable, if a touch thick, and easy to skip through being literal-minded. She takes poor Nathalie Sarraute to task for admitting that the world of events does not touch her as an author. *Quand je m'assieds à mon bureau*, declares Sarraute, *je laisse à la porte la politique, les événements, le monde: je deviens une autre personne.* How (wonders Simone) can a writer, during the most important action of his existence, not include his entire self? She

accepts Sarraute's statement at face value. As though any artist
were free to choose! An artist, in fact, is the least free of persons,
the least democratically ruled. His presumed "choice" to ignore
politics becomes itself a political remark; his planned absence
becomes presence; his economy is extravagance, for all he is is
contained in all he does. Or what makes him an artist? This
Beauvoir does not see, not because she herself is not an artist
(although maybe she's not), but because, thinking herself an artist,
she can no longer function as an audience. Thus, too, her remarks
on music, occupying as they do one page in this thousand-page
tome, become, despite their highminded intent, the remarks of a
very serious dabbler.

23 December

The Final Diary is merely a title, like *Journal of the Plague Year* or
The Great American Novel. Which does not mean it's fiction.
(Fiction freezes my pen. The discipline of invention—that which is
not fact, as I comprehend fact—eludes me.) For a fortnight JH and
I have been trimming the fat from this volume, fat being the truth
that endangers. The book still seems bloated, for I'm as fond of my
fat as an analysand is of his fears: with each slice I scream. Yet
here's a hundred deleted wounds to others and to myself, lascivious
narratives, family daguerreotypes, puerile anecdotes and dirty linen.
Precisely because they are "interesting" they will remain posthumous. Well, one must, at least in appearance, grow up sometime.
For only children are punished. Thus only children are frightened.
Alas, only children are worthwhile.

Christmas Eve

Nobody *is* anything, yet everyone passes his life trying to prove he's
not nothing. If I hadn't for years imagined myself to be ornamental,
talented, charming, I'd not have become too different in personality,
though my music would have been another story. Today I imagine
myself as unornamental, uncharming, while talent is no issue
(certainly no concept) for the talented. Anyone who calls himself a
composer, or who allows himself to be called a composer, practices

a mere trick of speech. This paragraph's a trick too, and self-protective, like all paragraphs.

Less morbid than years ago, I'm still shadowed by the perpetual reality—*reality*, not nightmare—that logically I'll die in twenty years, and that my sweetest memories are far behind. The period of exploration, even of experience, is over; no more expiring with new love in green spring, nor travels to strange lands. What remains is organization.

I *have* changed since the revolution. Reared both wisely and too well, told that "Negroes are just like you," I never realized the Negro's daily hurdles, nor those of females or of the elderly, while hurdles of the "imaginative" I crazily thought were also yours and his and hers. Liberal backgrounds are limiting for the unimaginative. As are any backgrounds.

Looking over my shoulder this evening, there is Sodom in flames. I myself struck the match, and do not turn into a statue of salt, that is, as the master put it, a statue of tears. On the contrary, having burned the bridges I feel free, not deprived.

Busily seeking texts appropriate for two sizable commissions, both choral, with imminent deadlines.

The sky for a month's been an unalleviated Siberian gray. The radio predicts partial clearing for tomorrow.